LIVING AND WORKING
IN
NEW ZEALAND

A SURVIVAL HANDBOOK
by
Mark Hempshell

SURVIVAL BOOKS • LONDON • ENGLAND

First published 1999
Reprinted 2000
Second Edition 2002
Reprinted 2003 (with changes)

Survival Books Limited, 1st Floor, 60 St James's Street
London SW1A 1ZN, United Kingdom
☎ +44 (0)20-7493 4244, ▤ +44 (0)20-7491 0605
✉ info@survivalbooks.net
▣ www.survivalbooks.net

British Library Cataloguing in Publication Data.
A CIP record for this book is available from the British Library.
ISBN 1 901130 76 2

Printed and bound in Finland by WS Bookwell Ltd.

ACKNOWLEDGEMENTS

My sincere thanks to all those who contributed to the successful publication of this edition, in particular Joanna Styles (updating and rewriting), Shona Gow (research), Joe and Kerry Laredo (proof-reading and layout), David Hampshire (for chapters 19 and 20 and Appendices), *New Zealand Outlook*, *New Zealand News UK* and everyone else who contributed in any way and whom I have omitted to mention. Also a special thank-you to Jim Watson for the superb cover, cartoons and map.

What Readers and Reviewers

When you buy a model plane for your child, a video recorder, or some new computer gizmo, you get with it a leaflet or booklet pleading 'Read Me First', or bearing large friendly letters or bold type saying 'IMPORTANT – follow the instructions carefully'. This book should be similarly supplied to all those entering France with anything more durable than a 5-day return ticket. It is worth reading even if you are just visiting briefly, or if you have lived here for years and feel totally knowledgeable and secure. But if you need to find out how France works then it is indispensable. Native French people probably have a less thorough understanding of how their country functions. – Where it is most essential, the book is most up to the minute.

Living France

We would like to congratulate you on this work: it is really super! We hand it out to our expatriates and they read it with great interest and pleasure.

ICI (Switzerland) AG

Rarely has a 'survival guide' contained such useful advice This book dispels doubts for first-time travellers, yet is also useful for seasoned globetrotters – In a word, if you're planning to move to the USA or go there for a long-term stay, then buy this book both for general reading and as a ready-reference.

American Citizens Abroad

It is everything you always wanted to ask but didn't for fear of the contemptuous put down – The best English-language guide – Its pages are stuffed with practical information on everyday subjects and are designed to complement the traditional guidebook.

Swiss News

A complete revelation to me – I found it both enlightening and interesting, not to mention amusing.

Carole Clark

Let's say it at once. David Hampshire's *Living and Working in France* is the best handbook ever produced for visitors and foreign residents in this country; indeed, my discussion with locals showed that it has much to teach even those born and bred in *l'Hexagone*. – It is Hampshire's meticulous detail which lifts his work way beyond the range of other books with similar titles. Often you think of a supplementary question and search for the answer in vain. With Hampshire this is rarely the case. – He writes with great clarity (and gives French equivalents of all key terms), a touch of humour and a ready eye for the odd (and often illuminating) fact. – This book is absolutely indispensable.

The Riviera Reporter

The ultimate reference book – Every conceivable subject imaginable is exhaustively explained in simple terms – An excellent introduction to fully enjoy all that this fine country has to offer and save time and money in the process.

American Club of Zurich

Have Said About Survival Books

What a great work, wealth of useful information, well-balanced wording and accuracy in details. My compliments!

Thomas Müller

This handbook has all the practical information one needs to set up home in the UK – The sheer volume of information is almost daunting – Highly recommended for anyone moving to the UK.

American Citizens Abroad

A very good book which has answered so many questions and even some I hadn't thought of – I would certainly recommend it.

Brian Fairman

A mine of information – I may have avoided some embarrassments and frights if I had read it prior to my first Swiss encounters – Deserves an honoured place on any newcomer's bookshelf.

English Teachers Association, Switzerland

Covers just about all the things you want to know on the subject – In answer to the desert island question about the one how-to book on France, this book would be it – Almost 500 pages of solid accurate reading – This book is about enjoyment as much as survival.

The Recorder

It's so funny – I love it and definitely need a copy of my own – Thanks very much for having written such a humorous and helpful book.

Heidi Guiliani

A must for all foreigners coming to Switzerland.

Antoinette O'Donoghue

A comprehensive guide to all things French, written in a highly readable and amusing style, for anyone planning to live, work or retire in France.

The Times

A concise, thorough account of the DOs and DON'Ts for a foreigner in Switzerland – Crammed with useful information and lightened with humorous quips which make the facts more readable.

American Citizens Abroad

Covers every conceivable question that may be asked concerning everyday life – I know of no other book that could take the place of this one.

France in Print

Hats off to Living and Working in Switzerland!

Ronnie Almeida

IMPORTANT NOTE

New Zealand is a diverse country with many faces, a number of ethnic groups, religions and customs, and continuously changing rules, prices and regulations (particularly regarding social security, education and taxes). Note that a change of government in New Zealand, which can occur every three years, can have far-reaching repercussions for many important aspects of daily life.

I cannot recommend too strongly that you check with an official and reliable source (not always the same) before making any major decisions or taking an irreversible course of action. **However, don't believe everything you're told or read (even, dare I say it, in this book).** Many useful addresses and references to other sources of information are included to help you obtain further information and verify details with official sources. Important points have been emphasised, in **bold** print, some of which it would be expensive, or even dangerous, to disregard. **Ignore them at your peril or cost!** Unless specifically stated, the reference to any company, organisation or product in this book doesn't constitute an endorsement or recommendation. Any reference to any place or person (living or dead) is purely coincidental.

CONTENTS

9. EDUCATION 131

10. PUBLIC TRANSPORT 149

11. MOTORING 161

12. HEALTH 187

13. INSURANCE 201

14. FINANCE 219

15. LEISURE   241

16. SPORTS   261

17. SHOPPING 279

18. ODDS & ENDS 293

19. THE KIWIS 311

20. MOVING HOUSE OR LEAVING NEW ZEALAND 319

APPENDICES 325

SUGGESTIONS 340

INDEX 341

ORDER FORMS 349

AUTHOR'S NOTES

- All times are shown using am (ante meridiem) for before noon and pm (post meridiem) for after noon. Most New Zealanders don't use the 24-hour clock. All times are local, so check the time difference when making international telephone calls (see **Time Difference** on page 307).

- All prices shown are in New Zealand dollars unless otherwise noted (e.g. £ = GB £ sterling). Prices should be taken as estimates only, although they were mostly correct at the time of publication.

- His/he/him also means her/she/her (please forgive me ladies). This is done to make life easier for both the reader and (in particular) the author, and *isn't* intended to be sexist.

- Most spelling is (or should be) British English and not American English.

- Warnings and important points are shown in bold type.

- The following symbols are used in this book: ☎ (telephone), 🖷 (fax), 🖳 (Internet) and ✉ (e-mail).

- Lists of **Useful Addresses, Further Reading** and **Useful Websites** are contained in **Appendices A**, **B** and **C** respectively.

- For those unfamiliar with the metric system of weights and measures, Imperial conversion tables are shown in **Appendix D**.

- A map of New Zealand is contained in **Appendix E**.

INTRODUCTION

Whether you're already living or working in New Zealand or just thinking about it – this is **THE BOOK** for you. Forget about those glossy guide books, excellent though they are for tourists, this amazing book was written especially with you in mind and is worth its weight in kiwi fruit. *Living and Working in New Zealand* is designed to meet the needs of anyone wishing to know the essentials of New Zealand life, including immigrants, temporary workers, businessmen, students, retirees, long-stay tourists, holiday home owners and even extra-terrestrials. However long your intended stay in New Zealand, you will find the information contained in this book invaluable.

General information isn't difficult to find in New Zealand; however, reliable and up-to-date information specifically intended for foreigners living and working in New Zealand isn't so easy to find, least of all in one volume. Our aim in publishing *Living and Working in New Zealand* is to help fill this void and provide the comprehensive *practical* information necessary for a relatively trouble-free life. You may have visited New Zealand as a tourist, but living and working there is a different matter altogether. Adjusting to a different environment and culture and making a home in any foreign country can be a traumatic and stressful experience, and New Zealand is no exception.

You need to adapt to new customs and traditions and discover the New Zealand way of doing things, for example, finding a home, paying bills and obtaining insurance. For most foreigners in New Zealand, finding out how to overcome the everyday obstacles of life has previously been a case of pot luck. But no more! With a copy of *Living and Working in New Zealand* to hand, you will have a wealth of information at your fingertips. Information derived from a variety of sources, both official and unofficial, not least the hard won personal experiences of the author, his family, friends, colleagues and acquaintances. *Living and Working in New Zealand* is a comprehensive handbook on a wide range of everyday subjects and represents the most up-to-date source of general information available to foreigners in New Zealand. It isn't, however, simply a monologue of dry facts and figures, but a practical and entertaining look at life in New Zealand.

Adapting to life in a new country is a continuous process, and although this book will help reduce your learner's phase and minimise the frustrations, it doesn't contain all the answers (most of us don't even know the right questions). What it *will* do is help you make informed decisions and calculated judgements, instead of uneducated guesses and costly mistakes. Most importantly, it will help you save time, trouble and money, and repay your investment many times over!

Although you may find some of the information a bit daunting, don't be discouraged. Most problems occur only once and fade into insignificance after a short time (as you face the next half a dozen). Most foreigners in New Zealand would agree that, all things considered, they love living there. A period spent in New Zealand is a wonderful way to enrich your life, broaden your horizons, and with luck please your bank manager. I trust this book will help you avoid the pitfalls of life in New Zealand and smooth your way to a happy and rewarding future in your new home.

Good luck!

David Hampshire (Editor)
February 2002

1.

FINDING A JOB

The main problem facing people wishing to work in New Zealand isn't usually finding a job but meeting the stringent immigration requirements, particularly concerning qualifications and English language proficiency (see **Chapter 3**). Although New Zealand is one of the few countries in the world that is keen to attract new workers from abroad – most countries positively discourage them – this doesn't mean that it's necessarily easy to find a job there. New Zealand has a relatively small labour market and there's strong competition for the best paid jobs, although in certain industries where skilled staff are in short supply it's possible to pick and choose from an abundance of vacancies (this is, however, very much the exception). In common with most other developed countries, New Zealand has suffered the ravages of unemployment in recent years and its economy went into a deep recession during the early '90s, which resulted in the wholesale closure of businesses throughout the country. In 1992, unemployment reached a peak of around 11 per cent, virtually the worst on record. In the late '90s, however, the economy picked up, and in late 2001 unemployment was around 5 per cent, although it's only 3.8 per cent among those of European descent compared with 12.3 per cent among the Maori population.

Anyone arriving in New Zealand looking for a job should expect to find stiff competition from the locals. The New Zealand workforce is well educated and trained and highly motivated (the unemployment benefit system helps; you don't get the dole if you don't seek work). You shouldn't expect employers to favour you simply because you've uprooted yourself and your family and travelled half way round the world (in fact the opposite may be the case). Even well qualified local graduates can no longer expect to walk into a job (as used to be the case), and a recent survey found that as many as 60 per cent of graduates still didn't have a job commensurate with their qualifications a year after graduation. It's also important to note that many young (and not so young) people leave the country each year in search of better employment opportunities overseas, mainly in the UK, the USA and Australia. If many New Zealanders cannot find a job in their place of birth, it's bound to be more difficult for a foreigner.

However, although some people don't find it easy to find employment, there are relatively few stories of failure and only a small number of new migrants with good job skills fail to find a job (the unemployment rate among skilled migrants is much lower than the national average). Most people who are prepared to work hard and adapt to the New Zealand way of doing things find that they do better in their job or career there than they would have at home. Nevertheless, it's essential to have a plan of action, do your homework before arrival and (if necessary) be prepared to change your plans as you go along.

During the last decade there has been a major shift in the New Zealand economy towards services industries and away from manufacturing. Many manufacturing industries have disappeared altogether and others (such as car assembly) don't have a bright future. On the other hand, the service sector is expanding fast, and some estimates claim that up to 75 per cent of the workforce is involved directly or indirectly in service industries. Job vacancies in the business and financial services industries have increased considerably in recent years, making it the fastest growing employment sector in the country. Although many workers have been retrained, not all have been able to make the move from manufacturing to service jobs. The result is that there's often a surplus of manufacturing skills but a shortage of service industry skills.

Accountancy and IT jobs are two areas where it's relatively easy to find work in New Zealand, as there's a major shortage of skilled professionals. Health workers are also in demand, including doctors, nurses, specialists such as radiologists and (in particular) health workers prepared to work outside the main cities.

Many employers have something of a haphazard approach to recruitment and are often reluctant to plan ahead, with the result that they're slow to lay off surplus staff during periods of recession and are equally slow to recruit new employees (and pay sufficient attention to improving skills and training) when business picks up. They do, however, appreciate 'old-fashioned' values such as hard work (particularly yours) and a willingness to 'muck in' and get things done. Therefore, anyone who arrives in New Zealand with a strong work ethic will have something of a head start in the job market.

QUALIFICATIONS

The most important qualification for a job in New Zealand is a good level of spoken and written English. All employers expect their staff to have adequate English, which varies with the type of job you're after – the more skilled the position, the better your English must be. When you apply in the business investor or general skills categories (see **Chapter 3**) you will need to prove that you have a high standard of English. **You will also need to show that you come from an English-speaking background and/or pass a test set by the International English Language Testing System (see page 62).**

With regard to more formal qualifications, it's a condition of employment for most jobs in New Zealand that overseas qualifications must compare with New Zealand's standards and be accepted by local employers. An organisation named The New Zealand Qualifications Authority (NZQA) assesses foreign qualifications to determine whether they meet New Zealand standards. Information and forms are available from the New Zealand Immigration Service or direct from NZQA, PO Box 160, Wellington (🖳 www.nzqa.govt.nz).

Registration

For certain jobs you must be registered with the appropriate New Zealand professional organisation. The registration process includes an assessment of your professional or trade qualifications and leads to membership of the appropriate body, thus allowing you to work in New Zealand. If your trade or profession is one where registration is required, you should contact the relevant body well in advance, as you may need to take an examination or undergo a period of retraining, for which you must pay. In some cases examinations can be taken in other countries, although they may be held on one or two days a year only. Since January 1996, it has been necessary to obtain registration (where applicable) before applying for permanent residence.

Occupations where registration is required and the relevant bodies with which registrations must be made are listed below. (Note that occupations are continually being added to the list, so you should check before applying for residence):

Architects: Architects Education and Registration Board, PO Box 11-106, Wellington (☎ 04-801 8972, 🖳 www.aerb.org.nz).

Barristers and Solicitors: New Zealand Law Society, PO Box 5041, Wellington (☎ 04-472 7837, 💻 www.nz-lawsoc.org.nz).

Dentists: Dental Council of New Zealand, PO Box 10-448, Wellington (☎ 04-499 4820, 💻 www.dentalcouncil.org.nz).

Dental Technicians: Dental Technicians Board, PO Box 11-053, Ellerslie, Auckland (☎ 09-579 7096, ✉ results@jdw.co.nz).

Electricians and Line Mechanics: Electrical Workers Registration Board, PO Box 10-156, Wellington (☎ 04-472 3636, ✉ licensinggroup@med.govt.nz).

Engineers: Institution of Professional Engineers (IPENZ), PO Box 10-156, Wellington (☎ 04-472 3636, 💻 www.ipenz.org.nz).

Estate Agents: Real Estate Agents Licensing Board, PO Box 1247, Wellington (☎ 04-520 6949).

Medical Practitioners: Medical Council of New Zealand, PO Box 11-649, Wellington (☎ 04-384 7635, 💻 www.mcnz.org.nz).

Midwives and Nurses: Nursing Council of New Zealand, PO Box 9644, Wellington (☎ 04-385 9589, 💻 www.nursingcouncil.org.nz).

Pharmacists: Pharmaceutical Society of New Zealand, PO Box 11-640, Wellington (☎ 04-802 0038, 💻 www.psnz.org.nz).

Physiotherapists: Physiotherapists Board, PO Box 3287, Wellington (☎ 04-471 2610, ✉ physioboard@physioboard.org.nz).

Plumbers, Gasfitters and Drainlayers: Plumbers, Gasfitters and Drainlayers Board, PO Box 30-229, Lower Hutt, Wellington (☎ 04-589 5310, 💻 www.pgdb.co.nz).

Surveyors: The Survey Board of New Zealand, PO Box 5501, Wellington (☎ 04-460 010, ✉ ifargher@linz.govt.nz).

Teachers (in primary and secondary schools and free kindergartens)**:** Teachers Registration Board, PO Box 5326, Wellington (☎ 04-471 0852, 💻 www.trb.govt.nz).

Veterinarians: Veterinary Council of New Zealand, PO Box 10 563, Wellington (☎ 04-473 9600, ✉ vet@vetcouncil.org.nz).

Chiropractors, Dieticians, Dispensing Opticians, Medical Laboratory Technologists, Medical Radiation Technologists, Occupational Therapists, Optometrists, Podiatrists and Psychologists (if employed in state services or a licensed institution)**:** Registration Boards Secretariat, PO Box 10-140, Wellington (☎ 04-499 7979).

Degrees attained from universities in most western countries are considered equivalent to degrees from New Zealand universities and most school qualifications are recognised by employers and university admissions staff.

GOVERNMENT EMPLOYMENT SERVICE

The New Zealand government employment service is run by an agency called Work and Income New Zealand (WINZ) operated by the Department of Labour, which provides a job-finding (or 'vacancy-filling') service to employees and employers. WINZ was formed in late 1998 by the merger of the New Zealand Employment

Service (NZES), the Community Employment Group, Income Support and Local Employment Co-ordinators, and combines employment services with income support. WINZ runs a JobBank service that's updated daily, where employers can advertise vacancies and job seekers can post their CVs. You can check vacancies via their website (🖥 www.winz.govt.nz). Vacancies are for unskilled, semi-skilled and skilled jobs, including casual and temporary vacancies; and those posted on the Internet are country-wide, while those handled in regional offices tend to be in the local area. The aim of WINZ is to ensure that everyone who's unemployed has access to free help with finding a job or training – or, as the more cynical might say, that everyone claiming benefit is found a job as soon as possible!

There are WINZ offices in every medium-size and large town and several in each of the major cities. It's usually necessary to visit a WINZ office in person – they cannot help you find a job from abroad, although you can visit the website. The service is free, but you must be a citizen, a permanent migrant, hold a valid work permit or have applied for refugee status. The only exception is Australians, who aren't required to fulfil the above criteria in order to use the WINZ services. Officially, WINZ provides a service to the unemployed and not to those looking to change jobs.

Unemployed people registering with WINZ and claiming unemployment benefit (previously known as the Community Wage) must make a 'Job Seeker Agreement' under which you're obliged to look for full-time work or training and take a suitable job if offered one. If you fail to meet your obligations without good reason, your unemployment benefit is suspended. If you fail to do so three times, your benefit may be stopped for 13 weeks. There are exceptions for those with children under 14 and those caring for a disabled or dependant relative.

WINZ also offers help with job applications, writing CVs and training, and provides many helpful brochures such as *Getting Work Skills and Experience* and *Need Help to Find Work?*, which can be downloaded from the website. The head office of WINZ is Level 8, Bowen State Building, Bowen Street, PO Box 12-136, Wellington (☎ freephone 0800-559 009 or 09-913 0300, ✉ info@winz.govt.nz, 🖥 www.winz.govt.nz). The main regional WINZ offices are:

Auckland Central: Private Bag 68 911, Newton

Auckland North: Private Bag 93 106, Henderson

Auckland South: PO Box 76 095, Manuaku City

Bay of Plenty: Private Bag 3016, Rotorua

Canterbury: PO Box 5292, Christchurch

Central: Private Bag 11 400, Palmerston North

East Coast: Private Bag 6015, Napier

Nelson: Private Bag 24, Nelson

Northland: PO Box 947, Whangarei

Southern: PO Box 297, Dunedin

Taranaki: Private Bag 2005, New Plymouth

Waikato: PO Box 19 199, Hamilton

WINZ operates a Career Guidance and Counselling programme giving job-seekers access to professional careers advisors. There are two levels of assistance: Career Guidance, where job-seekers' skills, interests and aptitudes are assessed and help given to find suitable jobs or provide relevant training, and Career Counselling, which is those who have been unsuccessful at the first level and involves a thorough investigation of why a job hasn't been found. The programme's (ambitious) objective is for participants to be in full-time employment or in training/work experience within eight weeks of starting the programme.

RECRUITMENT AGENCIES

There are many organisations in New Zealand which can find you a job (or at least try). They can be broadly divided into recruitment consultants and employment agencies. Recruitment consultants tend to specialise in skilled, professional and executive jobs, while employment agencies handle all kinds of jobs, including unskilled and temporary jobs. You can find local recruitment consultants and employment agencies by looking in the yellow pages, available at major libraries and in the reading rooms of some New Zealand Consulates and High Commissions overseas, or on the yellow pages website (🖳 www.yellowpages.co.nz). Employment agencies are also listed on the New Zealand Immigration Services website (🖳 www.immigration.govt.nz). Some immigration consultants can arrange an introduction to recruitment agencies.

Usually an employment agency cannot help you unless you're in New Zealand, although they're normally willing to provide general information about local job prospects over the phone or you can consult their websites. Once you arrive in New Zealand, agencies will ask to see your visa or migration papers before they will help you. In the past, agencies were lax about enforcing this requirement (some may still be), but severe penalties for employing illegal immigrants have prompted them to obey the law. If you're working for a temporary employment agency, you may find that you are in fact employed by the agency.

Both recruitment consultants and employment agencies are engaged by employers to fill vacancies and therefore don't charge you for finding you a job (they're finding an employee for the employer, not vice versa). Other services such as compiling CVs and counselling may be offered, for which you may be charged, so check in advance. Some recruitment consultancies have offices abroad, and if you plan to use them it pays to make a few simple checks before doing so. For example, the law of your home country may permit them to make a charge for finding you a job or even for simply registering your details. Also check exactly what they will do for you. A recruitment consultant who merely sends your CV to prospective employers is unlikely to find you a job, whereas a consultant with employers on his books in the industry in which you want to work (ask for proof) could prove to be a useful contact. Among the largest recruitment agencies are:

● Debbie Graham & Associates (🖳 www.dgal.co.nz)

● Manpower (🖳 www.manpower.co.nz)

● Momentum Consulting Group (🖳 www.momentum.co.nz)

● Resource Edge (🖳 www.people.co.nz)

● Robert Walters (🖳 www.robertwalters.com)

TEMPORARY, CASUAL & SEASONAL JOBS

Temporary, casual and seasonal jobs which last for a few days, weeks or months are available throughout the year in New Zealand, particularly during the summer and early autumn when the largest employers, the tourist and farming industries, are at their busiest. If you aren't a New Zealand citizen or migrant, **it's important to make sure that you're eligible to work in New Zealand on a casual basis before you arrive**. Most nationalities (with the exception of Australians who may work in New Zealand under the 'Closer Economic Relations' agreement), aren't permitted to work in New Zealand, at least not without wading through a mountain of red tape. There are special working holiday schemes available for young people from Canada, Chile, France, Germany, Hong Kong, Ireland, Italy, Japan, Korea, Malaysia, the Netherlands, Singapore, Sweden and the United Kingdom, through which you're entitled to look for seasonal, temporary and casual employment. Students from the USA can spend up to six months working in New Zealand under the 'Work in New Zealand Program' operated by the Council On International Educational Exchange (CIEE, 205 East 42nd Street, New York, NY 10017-5706, (☎ 1-800-2COUNCIL or 212-822-2600, 🖳 www.ciee.org). Other nationalities can obtain visas for temporary jobs only if there's no New Zealander or permanent migrant available to do a job (see **Chapter 3**).

In common with other countries, pay and conditions for casual and temporary jobs are usually poor. You may be paid less than the minimum wage (see page 31) or charges for food and accommodation may effectively reduce your wages below this level, and you may not be entitled to benefits such as holiday pay. Jobs obtained through reputable agencies are likely to be better in this regard than jobs obtained through small ads or by word-of-mouth. Tax regulations also make casual work less financially attractive to temporary visitors, as casual workers have a flat rate deduction of 22.1 per cent taken from their wages by employers to cover income tax and ACC contributions (see page 202). Any extra tax charges or refunds are made after you've filed an income tax return at the end of the tax year, which is easy in theory but difficult if you're no longer in New Zealand. Some casual workers have doubts about whether less scrupulous employers pay the tax they deduct to the Inland Revenue Department at all!

If you're seeking a casual or seasonal job, you should be prepared to be persistent and compete with the local casual labour force. Many jobs of this kind are the preserve of Pacific Islanders, particularly Samoans and Pitcairn Islanders, whom the New Zealand authorities allow to look for work in recognition of the fact that there are precious few job opportunities in the Pacific Islands (most countries have a source of cheap labour and New Zealand is no exception). These migrants tend to be at the bottom of the jobs heap and are willing to do almost anything for almost any wage. Opportunities for temporary, casual and seasonal jobs include:

Tourism: New Zealand attracts tourists all year round, particularly during the summer (November to March), with a tourist boom over the Christmas and New Year period. Jobs are available in shops, at tourist attractions and on boats and beaches throughout the country during these periods. For the rest of the year, the tourist industry centres mainly around skiing, when Queenstown in the South Island is the busiest resort.

Hotels and Catering: Hotels, motels, lodges, restaurants and bars normally require waiters and waitresses, barmen and barmaids, chambermaids, receptionists and handymen throughout the year. Employment agencies such as Kelly Recruitment (which specialises in this kind of work) usually have vacancies. If you want to go it alone, there's nothing to stop you approaching hotels and restaurants directly, although it's wise to telephone and ask about vacancies before travelling to the back of beyond looking for work.

Farming: There are thousands of farms, small and large, in New Zealand which usually need help, particularly **during** busy periods such as harvest times or sheep-shearing. Available work ranges from skilled jobs such as cattle herding and sheep shearing to unskilled tasks such as apple and grape picking. The work is likely to be hard and the hours long, but in addition to wages (around $350 per week, unless you're paid a 'piece' rate according to how much produce you pick) you may receive free accommodation and food (all the lamb and kiwi fruit you can eat!). Good places for fruit picking include Nelson, Motueka, Blenheim, Kerikeri, the Wairu Valley, Gisborne, Tauranga, Te Puke, Otago and the Christchurch area. The soft fruit picking season (apples, strawberries, grapes, peaches and – need we say – kiwi fruit) starts in December and lasts until April or May.

You don't need to go far to find a sheep farm (sheep station) in New Zealand, but the far north-east and south of the North Island, and the Otago and Canterbury regions of the South Island are the main centres for this industry. Vacancies for farm work are sometimes advertised on notice boards in local hostels. If you think you would enjoy the experience of working on an organic farm (low or no pay, but free accommodation and plenty of organic food), an organisation called Willing Workers On Organic Farms (WWOOF, PO Box 1172, Nelson, ☎ 03-544 9890, 🖥 www.wwoof.co.nz) can arrange placements on almost 600 farms throughout New Zealand (a fee is charged for the list of members). The main farming concern is Fonterra Co-operative Group (🖥 www.fonterra.com), New Zealand's largest company and one of the world's top ten dairy companies. A useful publication for job-seekers is the *NZ Dairy Exporter Magazine*, which advertises farming vacancies.

Business: Employment agencies specialise in temporary and casual job vacancies in offices and shops in most parts of the country, though principally in Auckland and Wellington. It's obviously an advantage if you have some experience; if you have a qualification in a profession such as banking, finance, insurance, accountancy or law, you could walk into a well-paid job, as these industries frequently have short-term staff shortages. Hundreds of New Zealand professionals leave the country each year to spend 6 or 12 months working in London on making the traditional overseas 'tour', and qualified staff are needed from abroad to fill the vacancies.

Industry: As in most countries, there are often casual jobs available in factories and warehouses such as cleaning, labouring, portering, driving and security work. Particularly numerous are casual, temporary and seasonal jobs in some of the massive plants which process and pack meat, fish, fruit, vegetables and dairy products. This kind of work is notoriously unreliable, and plants that may be working flat out one week stand idle the next, e.g. when there's a slump in the market or the season is over. Jobs of this kind can be found through employment agencies, in local newspapers or simply by turning up at the factory gate (very early!).

There are many books for those seeking holiday jobs, including *Summer Jobs Abroad* by David Woodworth and *Work Your Way Around The World* by Susan Griffith (both published by Vacation Work).

JOB HUNTING

When looking for a job in New Zealand it's best to use every route available – the more applications you make the better your chance of finding something suitable. Contact as many prospective employers as possible, by writing, telephoning or calling on them in person. Positions are often obtained as a result of networking (i.e. through contacts – see page 30). Naturally it's easier to find a job after you've arrived in New Zealand, although you should start preparing the ground before you arrive by doing research into potential employers and contacts.

The way you market yourself is also important and depends on the kind of job you're seeking. For example, the recruitment of executives and senior managers is handled almost exclusively by recruitment consultants. At the other end of the scale, manual jobs requiring no previous experience may be advertised at WINZ offices (see page 22), in local newspapers and on notice boards, or may simply be passed around by word of mouth (a less posh name for networking). When job hunting you may find the following resources useful:

Internet: The Internet is a useful option, particularly if you aren't in New Zealand – not only can you get a good idea of the jobs available but you can also apply for jobs online. Useful New Zealand websites include the following:

General Sites

- www.jobs.govt.nz (jobs in the public sector)
- www.kiwicareers.govt.nz (a comprehensive site with job vacancies as well as job finding tips and detailed information about New Zealand industries)
- www.monster.co.nz
- www.workingin.com (also has vacancies for Australia)

Accountancy

- www.kpmg.co.nz

Engineering

- www.ipenz.org.nz

Farming

- www.maf.govt.nz (Ministry of Agriculture)
- www.farmnews.co.nz
- www.fencepost.co.nz

Hospitality

- www.artisan-recruitment.com
- www.traveljobs.co.nz
- www.mall.co.nz/hospjobs

Information Technology (IT)

- www.itfutures.co.nz
- www.qube.co.nz
- www.sabrenz.co.nz

Medical (doctors and nurses)

- www.moh.govt.nz (Ministry of Health)
- www.nursingcouncil.org.nz
- www.nursingnz.co.nz

Police

- www.police.govt.nz

Skiing Industry

- www.goski.com
- www.nzski.com

Teaching

- www.edgazette.govt.nz/vacancies
- www.learningmedia.co.nz
- www.teachersonthemove.com
- www.teachnz.govt.nz

New Zealand Newspapers: Obtain copies of as many New Zealand newspapers as possible, all of which contain job sections. Vacancies are advertised most days, the most popular days being Wednesdays and Saturdays. New Zealand's main newspapers are regional rather than national and include *The Dominion* (Wellington, employment sections in the Wednesday and Saturday editions: www.dominion.co.nz), *The Evening Post* (Wellington, includes employment vacancies on Wednesdays and Saturdays: www.evpost.co.nz), *The New Zealand Herald* (mainly Auckland news and vacancies with some national coverage www.nzherald.com), *The Otago Daily Times* (Dunedin) and *The Press* (Christchurch: www.press.co.nz). It's worth checking city libraries abroad, as they sometimes have New Zealand newspapers. If you live near a New Zealand Consulate or High Commission or a New Zealand Immigration Service information office, you may find that they have a reading room containing recent copies of New Zealand newspapers. Most New Zealand newspapers are available online (see website addresses above) and will also post you a copy on subscription, although it will take at least a week for it to reach you in Europe or the USA, by which time the vacancy may have been filled.

Most newspapers also carry a 'Situations Wanted' column, although unless you're exceptionally well qualified or have a skill that's in short supply, you cannot expect much of a response when placing an advertisement of this kind.

Foreign Newspapers: If you're seeking an executive or professional position, you will find that vacancies are sometimes advertised in the national newspapers of other countries. For example, the UK *Times Higher Education Supplement* and the *Sydney Morning Herald* occasionally carry vacancies for jobs in New Zealand. The fact that employers have gone to the trouble of advertising jobs abroad means that the vacancies are proving hard to fill locally and that they require unusual or exceptional skills and qualifications.

Trade Journals: There aren't many trade journals in New Zealand, although those that exist carry a range of job advertisements for qualified and experienced people. The main journals include *NZ Business* magazine (☎ 09-630 8940, 🖳 www.nzbusinessmag.co.nz), *Education Gazette* (PO Box 249, Wellington, ☎ 04-917 3990, 🖳 www.edgazette.govt.nz), *e.nz Magazine* (Engineering – PO Box 12241, Wellington, ☎ 0800-103 903, 🖳 www.ipenz.org.nz), *Management Magazine* (☎ 09-630 8940, 🖳 www.management.co.nz) and *Farmnews* (Mokotua RD5, Invercargill, Southland, ☎ 03-239 5444, 🖳 www.farmnews.co.nz).

Opportunities in New Zealand, usually at the executive and professional level, are also advertised in trade journals in other English-speaking countries, mainly Australia, the UK and the USA.

Employment Offices: Visit WINZ offices in New Zealand (see page 22). Jobs on offer are mainly non-professional, skilled, semi-skilled and unskilled.

Recruitment Consultancies and Employment Agencies: If you're looking for an executive or professional position, you can apply to recruitment consultancies in New Zealand and abroad specialising in the kind of position you're seeking (see page 45). They will usually be pleased to help and advise you, whether or not you have applied for permission to live in New Zealand. On the other hand, employment agencies can usually help you only if you're already in New Zealand and have been granted permanent residence (or, exceptionally, a working holiday visa).

Professional Organisations: If you're a professional, it may be worthwhile contacting professional organisations in New Zealand. Although they cannot find you a job, they can often help with advice and provide the names of prospective employers. For addresses see **Qualifications** on page 21.

Government Departments: If you're considering a position or career with a government department or another public body, it's worth contacting the relevant organisation directly. It isn't necessary to be a New Zealand citizen to apply for many official positions, particularly in areas where there's a shortage of skills. The government periodically holds exhibitions abroad, particularly in London, mainly to attract young New Zealand professionals back to their country but also to attract professionals of other nationalities.

For many years the New Zealand Ministry of Education has welcomed (in fact, lured and enticed) teachers to fill vacancies in schools in order to combat a serious shortage. Vacancies are advertised through its own recruitment agency, NZ Teach, which operates in English-speaking countries world-wide.

The New Zealand police is also suffering a shortage of experienced officers, as several Australian forces (particularly Queensland) have a habit of poaching experienced New Zealand officers with the lure of a 20 to 30 per cent pay rise. Your local New Zealand Consulate or High Commission will put you in touch with the relevant government department.

Unsolicited Job Applications: Apply to companies directly in New Zealand, whether or not they're advertising vacancies. Needless to say, it's a hit and miss affair, but the advantage is that you aren't competing directly with dozens of other applicants as with an advertised job vacancy. This approach can be particularly successful if you have skills, experience and qualifications that are in short supply in New Zealand. When writing from abroad, enclosing an international reply coupon may help elicit a response. Useful addresses can be obtained from trade directories (such as *Kompass New Zealand*), which are available at major libraries and New Zealand Chambers of Commerce abroad or from the New Zealand Chamber of Commerce, PO Box 11043, Wellington (☎ 04-472 3376, 🖳 www.chamber.co.nz).

Networking: Networking (the term originated in the USA, although the practice is universal) is making and using business and professional contacts. You should make use of contacts both in New Zealand and with any New Zealanders you come into contact with abroad, including friends, relatives, colleagues and business contacts. If you're already in New Zealand, seek out expatriate links such as clubs, pubs and churches. Generally people who have moved to another country are interested to get to know others in a similar position and are happy to pass on job tips or leads.

WORKING WOMEN

New Zealand has a long history of women doing traditionally male jobs which dates from the pioneering days when women had to run the house, prepare the food, look after the children *and* work on the farm (in some cases they still do!). Consequently, it isn't unusual to find women doing such jobs as truck driving, factory work and 'politicking'. At least a quarter of New Zealand politicians are female and the country has now had two female Prime Ministers. Over 45 per cent of women are employed in New Zealand, a relatively high figure that's made possible in part by the country's excellent system of early childhood education (see page 138). There's no reason why women shouldn't take jobs in almost any industry, although, as in other countries, women tend towards the caring professions and education. The growth in service industries, always a popular career choice with women, has created additional opportunities. Women have also made good progress in professions such as law and medicine, although few reach the top levels. For more information, contact the National Advisory Council on Employment of Women (NACEW, 🖳 www.nacew. govt.nz) or the Ministry for Women's Affairs (☎ 04-473 4112, 🖳 www.mwa. govt.nz).

All members of the workforce are entitled to equal pay for equal work under the Equal Pay Act 1972. In practice the average wage tends to be marginally lower for both female and ethnic minority workers. A recent survey by Statistics New Zealand revealed that women's wages were, on average, much lower than men's, but this is partly because women and ethnic minorities are more likely to do unskilled or semi-skilled work, and, in the case of women, because they often work part-time. Discrimination in the workplace is illegal in New Zealand under the Human Rights Act 1972, which protects employees against discrimination on all grounds that are irrelevant to the performance of the job. However, this doesn't extend as far as the home, where male chauvinism is alive and well and the country's reputation as a land of 'rugby, racing and beer' is still largely deserved (although it isn't generally not quite as marked as in Australia).

A non-profit organisation, the Equal Employment Opportunities (EEO) Trust, promotes equal opportunities in the workplace and has around 300 member organisations from a wide range of employment sectors. Members are committed to EEO policies and ideas, and employees generally enjoy greater equality at work. The EEO Trust will provide a list of members and can be contacted at PO Box 12-929, Penrose, Auckland (☎ 09-525 3023, 💻 www.eeotrust.org.nz).

SALARY

It's usually quite easy to determine the salary you should command in New Zealand, as wages and salaries are normally quoted in job advertisements. There's a marked difference between salaries in the major cities of Auckland and Wellington and in the rest of the country, where they're often up to 20 per cent lower. This reflects not only the fact that living costs are higher in these cities but the tendency for jobs there to carry more responsibility (i.e. stress). New Zealand employers can be rather coy when quoting salary figures, using terms such as 'salary to'. For example, 'salary to $55,000' usually means you're highly unlikely to receive $55,000 – the employer is probably thinking in terms of paying $40,000 (he just wants to attract as much interest as possible). The term 'negotiable' is frequently used in job advertisements, e.g. 'salary $55,000 negotiable', which means that you will need to work hard to convince the employer that you're worth $55,000! If you have qualifications or skills that are in short supply, you may be able to negotiate a higher salary. For example, the wool industry was thrown into turmoil when shearers began flocking to Australia in their hundreds in search of higher pay, and the Shearing Contractors' Organisation was forced to raise pay rates by 20 per cent.

A national minimum wage applies in New Zealand, which is currently $7.70 per hour. This doesn't, however, apply to those under 18, to whom the 'youth minimum wage' of $5.40 per hour applies. (In 2001, unions were campaigning to have the youth rates of the minimum wage abolished.) A recent survey carried out by Statistics New Zealand revealed that some 40,000 adult employees received less than the legal minimum wage but that most (over 1 million) earned at least 30 per cent more than the legal minimum wage. The average hourly wage in October 2001 was just over $18. In late 2001, the lowest average wages were earned by hotel and restaurant staff at around $450 per week; weekly wages in the retail sector were around $470; the construction industry paid an average of $700 per week; not surprisingly, the highest wages were in the financial and insurance sectors, at around $925. However, as few wages in New Zealand are negotiated on a collective basis, there's often a huge variation in pay in different industries and areas.

Executive and professional salaries are typically lower than other developed countries such as Australia, France, Germany, Japan, the UK and the USA, although a lower cost of living, particularly housing costs, compensates. The average salary for top company bosses is around $200,000. Executive salaries are often subject to much greater rises (e.g. 10 to 12 per cent) than average rises in wages, which are usually around just 2 per cent annually. New Zealand employers don't traditionally shower executives with fringe benefits on top of their basic salary package, but may offer certain benefits to lure an outstanding applicant. Nevertheless, company cars are widespread at executive level, as are health insurance benefits (55 per cent – see page 211) and superannuation or pension schemes (60 per cent – see page 210).

Productivity bonuses and profit sharing may also be offered. Relocation costs and contributions towards housing expenses are usually offered only to employees with particularly desirable skills (but it's worth asking).

SELF-EMPLOYMENT & STARTING A BUSINESS

The idea of becoming self-employed or starting a business in New Zealand is appealing and often considered by those planning to live there. New Zealanders don't traditionally have a 'wheeler-dealer' personality and there isn't an ingrained enterprise culture. Most people work from nine-to-five for a large company – going it alone, which often involves working up to 18 hours a day, isn't seen as an attractive proposition. However, since the mid-'80s a more adventurous attitude has spread throughout the country with people opening a wide range of small businesses and in 2001 some 95 per cent of New Zealand businesses employed fewer than 20 people.

Generally speaking, it isn't wise to start or buy a business in New Zealand in which you don't have some expertise, particularly if your only experience of New Zealand is a holiday. Setting up a smallholding or a bungee jumping business may seem like a good idea, but it's rarely as simple as it appears. That said, many experts consider New Zealand to be something of a 'virgin' market for business ideas that are commonplace in the USA or Europe. Many business ideas imported from Australia have successfully taken root in New Zealand.

Professional Advice: Before embarking on a business project in New Zealand, ensure that you take advice regarding the legal and financial aspects from a good lawyer and accountant. Useful guides for anyone going into business in New Zealand are *Start Your Own Business*, available from WINZ offices or from their website (🖳 www.winz.govt.nz) and *Planning for Success* published by BIZ Info (see below). There are also numerous organisations offering information and advice to the self-employed:

- BIZ Info: a business information service with comprehensive and useful advice including some *Quick Facts* factsheets and useful publications (☎ 0800-424 946, 🖳 www.bizinfo.co.nz);

- Business Migrants: a website linked to the business migrant visa category with plenty of general information about setting up a business in New Zealand (🖳 www.business-migrants.govt.nz);

- Bzone: plenty of useful tips for starting up a business as well as expert advice (☎ 09-355 5200, 🖳 www.bzone.co.nz);

- Home Business: a comprehensive guide to those running a business from home (🖳 www.homebizbuzz.co.nz);

- Kiwi Careers: although essentially a site for job-seekers, there's also useful information and a good links page for the self-employed (🖳 www.kiwicareers.govt.nz);

- New Zealand Industry: a website linked to the Ministry of Industry with a wide range of information and advice on each industrial sector in the country (🖳 www.industrynz.govt.nz);

- Trade New Zealand: an excellent website for investors (🖳 www.tradenz.govt.nz).

It's also essential to check your visa status (see **Chapter 3**). It's possible to migrate to New Zealand under the business investor category where your investment funds, business experience, qualifications and age are assessed under the points system. If you haven't any business experience or substantial investment funds, you may not be eligible under this category. However, there's little to stop anyone migrating under the general skills category and initially taking employment and then buying or starting a business. This can, in fact, be a good course of action, as it allows you to test the water before taking the plunge with a new venture.

Government Help: The Ministry of Economic Development operates several schemes, the purpose of which is to help and advise those wishing to run their own business (whether by starting or by buying a business) and also to help small businesses grow. They can help with planning and preparation, the law regarding business names, taxation and other financial regulations, locating premises, marketing, finding staff and management. As with free government services in any country, the help provided is limited, but they can direct you to other sources of help. For more information contact the Ministry of Economic Development, 33 Bowen Street, PO Box 1473, Wellington (☎ 04-472 0030, 🖳 www.med.govt.nz). The Ministry publishes *Connectionz*, a quarterly newsletter with business news and information. If you know the type of business you want to start, it's also wise to contact the relevant trade association (your local chamber of commerce can put you in touch).

Finance: You should usually reckon on having at least 50 per cent of the cost of a business purchase or start-up. New Zealand banks look more favourably upon an application for a loan if you have a substantial lump sum of your own to invest, not to mention good business experience and a well thought-out business plan. As with banks elsewhere, they will also expect security for your loan, preferably in the form of property in New Zealand.

Restrictions: There are few restrictions on the kinds of business that can be started or purchased by new migrants in New Zealand. Foreign involvement in telecommunications and transport used to be heavily restricted, but is no longer, and American investors raced to snap up New Zealand companies the minute ownership controls were relaxed. Restrictions have also been eased in broadcasting, which was the last area to be protected by law. Government approval via the Overseas Investment Commission (🖳 www.oic.govt.nz) is required in the case of foreign investments (at least 25 per cent of a business) when the business or property is worth over $50 million and when the land occupied is over 5 hectares (12 acres) and/or worth more than $10 million. The main point to bear in mind is that, if your business involves practising a trade or profession that must be registered in New Zealand, you must register before you can start trading (see **Qualifications** on page 21).

Buying An Existing Business

As anywhere, it's much easier to buy a going concern in New Zealand than to start a new business; the bureaucracy is considerably less, as is the risk. It isn't entirely risk-free, however, and every precaution must be taken to ensure that you don't buy a going-nowhere concern. You can find businesses for sale through local estate and commercial agents, and also through ads in local and regional newspapers. However, it's vital to inspect a business personally (never rely solely on the glowing description you're given by an agent) before agreeing to buy it, shop around and compare it with similar businesses, and obtain independent advice regarding its value and prospects.

One of the most important aspects to consider when buying a business in New Zealand is its location, particularly if what appears to be a thriving concern is offered for quick sale at a temptingly low price. One thing to look out for is a situation where a town centre has been left as a ghost town (or soon will be) by the opening of a new out-of-town shopping mall or the building of a new road which will take potential customers right past your new business – at 100kph! (See also **Location** below.)

Starting A New Business

Most people are far too optimistic about the prospects for a new business, whether in their home country or abroad. Be realistic or even pessimistic when estimating your income, overestimate the costs and underestimate the revenue (then reduce it by another 50 per cent!). While hoping for the best, plan for the worst and make sure that you have enough money not only to set up the business but to keep it going until it's established. Bear in mind that while New Zealand is a virgin market with many new business opportunities waiting to be exploited, it's also a small and relatively conservative market. In the good times fortunes have certainly been made by shrewd entrepreneurs, but when the economy takes a nose-dive (as it did in the early '90s) they have been lost just as easily. While there's always room for the entrepreneur in New Zealand, it makes sense to play it safe and hedge your bets by not choosing anything too risky. Newcomers in particular tend to have an idealistic view of starting a business in New Zealand, which is all very well, but try to be practical and also look at possible negative aspects of your proposed 'dream' business. For example, jet-boating, scuba diving and yacht charter businesses, café-bars and smallholdings are great business ideas, but hard work and often only seasonal.

Location: Choosing the location for a business is even more important than choosing the location for a home. Depending on the kind of business, you may need to be in a town or near a housing development, have good access to roads or be close to a tourist resort. Don't forget that future development plans can affect the desirability of the location. Plans for new roads or shopping developments are usually available from the local town authorities.

Employees: If you're starting a new kind of business or one which requires specialist skills, you should check that these skills are available in the local workforce. The New Zealand workforce is well educated and trained, but certain sectors have grown so fast in recent years that it's difficult to find skilled and qualified staff in some trades and professions. Even if staff are available, you may find that they demand sky-high salaries. Make enquiries with WINZ (see page 22) regarding the availability of labour, as well as with recruitment consultants if you're going to need executives and specialist staff. The Inland Revenue Department (IRD) publishes two useful booklets, the *First-time Employer's Guide* and the *Employer's Guide*, containing information about employers' obligations and how to make tax payments and deductions from employees' wages.

Business Entities: The simplest form of trading entity in New Zealand is an individual trading on his own, which involves unlimited liability. There are no accounting, auditing or reporting requirements other than the need to keep accounts for the IRD. You can also form a partnership, which is governed by the Partnership

Act 1908, where it's usual to have a formal written agreement between the parties. This doesn't need to be drafted by a lawyer and the rights and responsibilities of each partner are governed by the agreement rather than employment law. A partnership can be either special, in which some partners (who cannot be involved in the management of the business) may have limited liability, or general, in which all partners have unlimited liability.

A limited company or corporation can be established under the Companies Act 1993, which makes no distinction between a public and a private limited company. There's no requirement to appoint a secretary, and directors can be held personally liable for the debts of their company if they're found not to have carried out their duties properly. Registration of a company is a relatively simple procedure, which involves making an application to the Registrar of Companies giving details of the directors, the registered address and the company's constitution (☎ freephone 0508-266 726 or 03-962 2602, 🖳 www.companies.govt.nz). It isn't necessary, however, to have a constitution, as the Companies Act serves as a ready-made constitution for companies without their own. Postal registration takes one day and costs $100 plus $25 to register the name; if you register electronically, the prices are $70 and $15 respectively and registration is almost immediate.

Taxation: The usual financial year for companies in New Zealand runs from 1st April to 31st March. It's possible to adopt an accounting year which doesn't correspond to the financial year, but permission is required from the Commissioner of the IRD. Businesses must prepare and file an income tax return with the IRD by the following 7th July and are required to make interim 'provisional' tax payments on the seventh day of the fourth, eighth and twelfth months of their income tax year, based on an estimate of the tax due. The final balance (terminal tax) is payable on the 11th month following the balance date. Resident companies pay income tax at a rate of 33 per cent on their world-wide taxable income. Employers are also required to make contributions to the Accident Compensation Corporation (ACC) scheme (see page 202). You may also be required to pay Fringe Benefit Tax (FBT) of up to 64 per cent (see **Chapter 14** for details).

Goods & Services Tax (GST): If the turnover (or expected turnover) of your business exceeds $40,000, you must register for GST (see page 231). Note that this figure refers to turnover and not to profit. If your business is registered for GST, you must levy GST (at 12.5 per cent) on your goods and services, although you can reclaim GST paid on anything you buy for your business and certain other expenses. To register for GST, apply at your local IRD office. Once registered, you must file a GST return every two months, although businesses with a turnover of less than $250,000 are usually permitted to make a return every six months. There are substantial penalties for not registering for GST when you should and for filing late returns.

Customs: If you're moving to New Zealand with the intention of becoming self-employed, buying an existing business or starting a business, and you want to bring specialist tools, equipment, machinery or stock with you, you must prepare an inventory and obtain permission from the Collector of Customs. You may be permitted to bring some tools and business equipment with you free of customs duty; otherwise, you must pay GST at 12.5 per cent and customs duty on their value. Note that you can bring any household items (which can include those with a combined work and household use) to New Zealand free of GST and duty when you first settle there (see page 231). For further information contact the Collector of Customs Offices

(☎ freephone 0800-428 786, ✉ feedback@customs.govt.nz) or apply to one of the following offices: PO Box 29, Auckland (☎ 09-359 6655), PO Box 14 086, Christchurch (☎ 03-358 0600) or PO Box 2218, Wellington (☎ 04-473 6099).

TRAINEES & WORK EXPERIENCE

New Zealand is a participant in an international trainee programme designed to give young people the opportunity for further education and occupational training, and to enlarge their professional experience and knowledge of other countries. Participating countries include Austria, Belgium, Canada, Denmark, France, Finland, Germany, Ireland, Luxembourg, Netherlands, Norway, Spain, Sweden, Switzerland, the United Kingdom and the USA. If you're between 18 and 30 (21 to 30 for Americans) and have completed a minimum of two years' vocational training, you may be eligible for a trainee position in New Zealand. The trainee agreement covers many professions but your position must be in the occupation for which you were trained. Positions are usually granted for a year and can sometimes be extended for a further six months. Information about the trainee programme can be obtained from the department of employment (or similar) in the participating countries.

Technical and commercial students who wish to gain experience by working in industry and commerce in New Zealand during their holidays can apply to the International Association for the Exchange of Students for Technical Experience (IAESTE), which has over 60 member countries. A good knowledge of English is essential and applicants must be enrolled at a college or university and be studying engineering, science, agriculture, architecture or a related subject. Your wages should cover your living costs and your employer should insure you against accident and illness. Travel costs must be met by the trainee. Information is available from the IAESTE website (🖳 www.iaeste.org) and in New Zealand from UNITEC Institute of Technology, Private Bag 92 025, Auckland (☎ 09-849 4180).

Young people who are studying or working in agriculture, horticulture or home management can participate in an exchange programme operated by the International Agricultural Exchange Association (IAEA). This programme provides between 6 and 14 months' work experience on a farm in New Zealand. A fee is charged, although participants are given wages and free board and lodging. For information contact the IAEA office in your home country or IAEA, Park Lane Arcade, The Strand, PO Box 328, Whakatane (☎ 07-307 0086).

ILLEGAL WORKING

New Zealand developed a reputation as something of a 'soft touch' when it came to illegal working, particularly among immigrants who had been turned away by countries such as Australia, Canada and the USA, which have stricter immigration regulations. New Zealand's work regulations and enforcement were lax in comparison and a blind eye was often turned to those working without the necessary visa. Many people who work illegally have been refused a permit or didn't bother applying at all and simply settled in New Zealand as a permanent visitor. Asylum seekers have also become a serious problem. While New Zealand has always been a refuge for victims of oppressive regimes, the number of applicants during the early '90s put a huge strain on the social security budget, when officials struggled to process a never-ending stream of asylum claims and appeals against refusal which took many months or even years to come to court. Note that it's legal to arrive in New Zealand on a tourist visa, find a job and then apply for residence (most other countries don't permit this).

In the last few years, however, the New Zealand authorities have become increasingly concerned about the country becoming an immigration 'dustbin' for those refused by other countries, particularly the unskilled from poor Asian countries who have tended to regard the country (particularly its relatively generous social security system) as a promised land. It's estimated that illegal immigrants claim at least $8 million in social security payments annually. High unemployment in the early '90s meant that a blind eye could no longer be turned to illegal workers, even those doing unpleasant and poorly paid jobs, which in the past New Zealanders wouldn't entertain. As a result, new laws were introduced that provided stiffer penalties for illegal workers (including fast-track deportation) and also fines for employers who employed them. The police and immigration authorities have begun to enforce the regulations, mounting periodic 'dawn raids' on companies likely to employ illegal workers, such as fruit farms and large factories.

Despite tougher immigration regulations, many employers still won't ask to see your visa or immigration papers before taking you on. They will, however, usually expect to see your IRD number. This can be obtained from the nearest IRD office simply by producing your immigration papers and proof of your permanent address in New Zealand, such as a utility bill or driving licence.

LANGUAGE

A good knowledge of English is a pre-requisite for living and working (or even holidaying) in New Zealand. If you cannot speak and write English well, not only will you find it extremely difficult to find a job, but you probably won't qualify for a work visa in the first place. You will, however, be relieved to hear that you won't be required to speak Maori (which was made an official language in 1974) as well! Although New Zealand is officially bilingual and there have even been proposals to replace some English place names in favour of Maori names (hopefully shorter than Taumatawhatatangihangakoauauotamateapokaiwhenuakitanatahu – the place where Tamatea, the man with big knees who slid, climbed and swallowed mountains, known as 'landeater', played his flute to his loved one), English is still the major language of business and spoken by all. New Zealanders aren't generally adept at speaking foreign languages; when your nearest neighbours are hundreds of miles away and even they speak English (of a sort), there's little opportunity to practise French, German or Spanish. Some shrewd New Zealanders with an eye to the future have made great strides in Japanese and other Asian languages, but don't bank on it. If you don't speak English well in New Zealand, you will be sunk!

Don't be fooled into thinking that New Zealand English is more or less the same as Australian English, it's not. As any New Zealander will tell you, New Zildish is the proper Antipodean version of English and it's the Australians who have corrupted it. You will find that Australian words and phrases aren't used in New Zealand (the same applies to American, Canadian and other versions of English). The use of 'proper' English often comes across as rather snobbish or superior in New Zealand, where people at all levels of society use New Zealand's own dialect, even at work.

The main distinguishing characteristic of the New Zealand dialect is to shorten words so that they end in 'o', 'y' or 'ie'. For example, 'arvo' for 'afternoon' or 'kindy' for kindergarten. Like accents in any country, a New Zealand accent can vary from slightly difficult to understand to completely unintelligible. Nevertheless, whatever variety of English you speak, if you speak it well, you will be easily understood. (See also **Language Schools** on page 146.)

2.

WORKING CONDITIONS

Employees in New Zealand generally enjoy good working conditions and terms of employment. Working conditions in New Zealand are somewhere between those in the UK or the USA, where they're relatively lightly regulated, and those in France or Germany, where they're extensively regulated. New Zealand industry suffered a large number of trade union disputes and strikes during the '70s and early '80s, but the situation became more conciliatory in the '90s, with employers and employees more willing to discuss and even avoid problems. Between 1998 and 2001 the number of strikes remained around 30 annually. In 2000/01 some 4,000 employees went on strike at a cost of some $1.6 million in lost wages and salaries (the lowest figure for some years). Most work stoppages occur in the manufacturing industry followed by the health and community services.

The cornerstone of modern industrial relations in New Zealand is the Employment Contracts Act 1991, which gave employees the freedom to decide whether or not they wished to belong to a trade union and outlawed 'closed shops' (where all employees are required to belong to a union). Most importantly, it gave employees the right to negotiate their terms of employment and raise any problems directly with their employers, rather than comply with agreements negotiated by trades unions or other bodies. This has allowed both employers and employees to tailor their working terms and conditions to suit their particular circumstances and therefore avoid unnecessary disputes. As a result, working conditions have improved in many industries, although in others they've become less favourable. For example, many unskilled and part-time workers in service industries feel that their pay and working hours have suffered as a result of the decline in union 'muscle'. Many companies have taken advantage of the opportunity to negotiate individual agreements, with the result that working hours, holidays, pay and other benefits are no longer standard throughout the country for a particular industry. The Employment Relations Act passed in October 2000 further consolidated industrial relations and introduced the principle of 'good faith' in negotiations, to which both employers and employees are obliged to adhere.

Equal Rights: New Zealand has a relatively good record on equal rights and the participation rate of both women and ethnic minorities in the workplace is favourable when compared with countries at a similar level of economic development. It's also one of the few countries where a woman has been able to reach the highest office in the land (prime minister). As childcare provision is relatively good, substantial numbers of women are able to go out to work, although there are frequent calls for free childcare to be made more widely available to enable more women to work full-time. All members of the workforce are entitled to equal pay for equal work under the Equal Pay Act 1972. In practice, however, average wages tend to be marginally lower for both female and ethnic minority workers. This is often due to the fact that they're more likely to do unskilled or semi-skilled work, or, in the case of women, because they frequently work part-time. (See also **Working Women** on page 30.)

Discrimination in the workplace is illegal under the Human Rights Act 1972, which protects employees against discrimination on any grounds that are irrelevant to job performance, including sex, ethnic group, sexual orientation, age or disability.

TERMS OF EMPLOYMENT

When negotiating your terms of employment for a job in New Zealand, the checklists on the following pages will prove useful. The points listed under **General Positions** (below) apply to most jobs, while those listed under **Executive Positions** (see page 45) usually apply to executive and senior managerial appointments only.

General Positions

- Salary:
  - Is the salary adequate, taking into account the cost of living? Is it index-linked?
  - Is the total salary (including expenses) paid in New Zealand dollars or will the salary be paid in another country in a different currency, with expenses for living in New Zealand?
  - When and how often is the salary reviewed?
  - Does the salary include an annual or end-of-contract bonus?
  - Is overtime paid or time off given in lieu of extra hours worked?
- Relocation Expenses:
  - Are removal expenses or a relocation allowance paid?
  - Does the allowance include travelling expenses for all family members? Is there a limit and is it adequate?
  - Are you required to repay the relocation expenses (or a percentage) if you resign before a certain period has elapsed?
  - Are you required to pay for your relocation in advance? This can run into thousands of dollars for normal house contents.
  - If employment is for a short period only, will your relocation costs be paid by the employer when you leave New Zealand?
  - If you aren't shipping household goods and furniture to New Zealand, is there an allowance for buying furnishings locally?
  - Do relocation expenses include the legal and agent's fees incurred when moving home?
  - Does the employer use the services of a relocation consultant (see page 83)?
- Accommodation:
  - Will the employer pay for a hotel or pay a lodging allowance until you find permanent accommodation?
  - Is subsidised or free temporary or permanent accommodation provided? If so, is it furnished or unfurnished?
  - Must you pay for utilities such as electricity, gas and water?
  - If accommodation isn't provided by the employer, is assistance provided to find suitable accommodation? If so, what sort of assistance?
  - What will accommodation cost?
  - Are your expenses paid while looking for accommodation?
- Working Hours:
  - What are the weekly working hours?

- Does the employer operate a flexi-time system? If so, what are the fixed working hours? How early must you start? Can you carry forward extra hours worked and take time off at a later date or carry forward a deficit and make it up later?
- Are you required to clock in and out of work?
- Can you choose whether to take time off in lieu of overtime or be paid for it?
- Leave Entitlement:
  - What is the annual leave entitlement? Does it increase with length of service?
  - What are the paid public holidays? Must you take them on the due day or can they be 'moved' to another day either at your or the employer's request?
  - Is free air travel to your home country or elsewhere provided for you and your family; if so, how often?
- Insurance:
  - Is extra insurance cover provided besides obligatory insurance (see **Chapter 13**)?
  - Is free life assurance provided?
  - Is free health insurance provided for you and your family?
  - For how long will your salary be paid if you're sick or have an accident?
- Company Pension:
  - Is there a pension scheme and what percentage of your salary must you pay?
  - Are you required or able to pay a lump sum into the pension fund in order to receive a full or higher pension?
  - Is the pension transferable to another employer?
- Employer:
  - What are the employer's prospects?
  - Does he have a good reputation?
  - Does he have a high staff turnover?
- Is a travel allowance (or public transport) paid from your home to your place of work?
- Is free or subsidised parking provided at your place of work?
- Is a free or subsidised company restaurant provided? If not, is an allowance paid or are luncheon vouchers provided? Some companies provide excellent staff restaurants, which save employees both money and time.
- Will the employer provide or pay for professional training or education, either in New Zealand or abroad?
- Are free work clothes or overalls provided? Does the employer pay for the cleaning of work clothes?
- Does the employer provide any fringe benefits, such as subsidised banking services, low interest loans, inexpensive petrol, employees' shop or product discounts, sports and social facilities, and subsidised tickets to local events?

- Do you have a written list of your job responsibilities?
- Have your employment conditions been confirmed in writing? For a list of the possible contents of your employment conditions, see page 46.
- If a dispute arises over your salary or working conditions, under the law of which country will your employment contract be interpreted?

Executive & Managerial Positions

The following points generally apply to executive and top managerial positions only:

- Is private schooling for your children paid for or subsidised? Will your employer pay for a boarding school in New Zealand or abroad?
- Is your salary index-linked and protected against devaluation? This is particularly important if you're paid in a foreign currency that fluctuates wildly or could be devalued. Are you paid an overseas allowance for working in New Zealand?
- Is there a non-contributory pension fund? Is it transferable and, if so, what are the conditions?
- Are the costs incurred by a move to New Zealand reimbursed? For example, the cost of selling your home, employing an agent to let it for you or storing household effects.
- Will your employer pay for domestic help or towards the cost of it?
- Is a car provided? With a driver?
- Are you entitled to any miscellaneous benefits, such as membership of a social or sports club or company credit cards?
- Is there an entertainment allowance?
- Is there a clothing allowance? For example, if you arrive in New Zealand in the winter you could find it distinctly chilly, particularly in the south.
- Is extra compensation paid if you're laid off or fired? Standard redundancy or severance payments are usually quite small, but executives often receive a generous 'golden handshake' if they're made redundant, e.g. after a take-over.

EMPLOYMENT CONTRACT

All employers are entitled to an employment contract when their employment commences. Under new legislation introduced by the Employment Relations Act, employment contracts must be in writing and oral 'contracts' are illegal. The terms of the contract can be either collective or individual, i.e. they apply to all employees in the same company (or the same industry) or just to one employee. Collective contracts are less common than they used to be, particularly as trade union power and membership has decreased. If your employer has a collective contract with his employees, and both you and the employer agree, you can be issued with a collective contract of employment. Alternatively, it's up to you to negotiate an individual contract of employment with an employer. If you wish, you can appoint a trade union or another person as your agent to negotiate your contract for you. If you're a non-union member and join a company where there's a collective employment agreement in place, your employer must notify you of this and employ you on the terms and conditions of the agreement for the first 30 days of your employment. After 30 days you must decide whether to join the union and accept the collective agreement or negotiate an individual agreement.

A contract of employment must, by law, cover certain areas, e.g. wages and holiday provision. The provisions of the contract in this regard mustn't be less than the statutory minimum provisions. The contract must also specify the procedure to be followed in the case of disputes. All contracts must include effective personal grievance procedures, effective disputes procedures and, if the contract is part of a collective employment contract, a contract expiry date.

EMPLOYMENT CONDITIONS

Employment conditions are an employer's general rules and regulations regarding working conditions and benefits that are applicable to all (or most) employees, unless stated otherwise in your employment contract. Employment conditions are explained in this section, or a reference is given to the chapter where a particular subject is covered in more detail. Further information regarding all aspects of employment relations and conditions can be obtained from the Employment Relations Service at the Department of Labour (freephone 0800-800 863, ▣ www.ers.dol.govt.nz). The Employment Relations Service provides a number of useful factsheets, which can be downloaded from its website.

Validity & Applicability

Employment conditions usually contain a clause stating the date from which they take effect and to whom they apply.

Salary & Benefits

Your remuneration may be quoted either as a salary, payable monthly, or a wage, payable weekly or fortnightly. It's more usual to have your salary paid into a bank account by direct credit transfer. If you wish, you're entitled to ask for a cheque (e.g. a cashier's cheque or bank draft), although you aren't entitled to receive cash. New Zealand employees don't receive an automatic annual bonus (the so-called 13th month payment) as in some countries, although some industries operate productivity and performance-related bonus schemes.

Working Hours & Overtime

There aren't any standard working hours in New Zealand. Traditionally, the working week has been 40 hours, commencing at 8.30am and finishing at 5pm, Mondays to Fridays, with a half-hour break for lunch. However, since the Employment Contracts Act took effect, employers and employees have been free to set the length of their working week and their start and finish times. The majority of employees still work around 38 or 40 hours over five days a week, although some companies (mainly larger organisations and manufacturing companies) have introduced different working patterns in agreement with their employees. Some large factories, for example, work four ten-hour shifts spread over seven days. Generally, workers in New Zealand expect to have Saturdays and Sundays off, although this is changing as more organisations (particularly service industries) operate at weekends.

Overtime is traditionally paid at a rate of 'time and a half', although in many industries it has effectively been abolished, as employers have agreed with employees (or have insisted) that they take time off in lieu of overtime.

Flexi-Time Rules

Some New Zealand employers operate flexi-time working hours, the conditions and rules of which vary with the employer. They're most common in the public service sector and are more likely to apply to those in administrative, managerial and professional positions. However, many employees can work flexible hours if they need to, and working parents are usually permitted to leave work for a short period at any time for family reasons. A flexi-time system usually requires employees to be present between certain hours, known as the core or block time. For example, from 9 until 11.30am and from 1.30 to 4pm. Employees may make up their required working hours by starting earlier than the required core time, reducing their lunch break or by working later. Many business premises are open from around 7am until 6pm or later, and smaller companies may allow employees to work as late as they wish, provided they don't exceed the safe maximum permitted daily working hours.

Travel & Relocation Expenses

Travel and relocation expenses depend on what you've agreed with your employer and are usually included in your employment contract or conditions. Given the expense of moving people and goods to New Zealand, even from Australia let alone from Europe or the USA, employers usually pay expenses only for executives or key employees with specialist skills. It's worth asking, however, and even if the entire cost of travel and relocation isn't forthcoming, your prospective employer may be prepared to make a contribution. Currently, for example, New Zealand is so short of qualified teachers that the Ministry of Education makes a contribution towards the relocation of foreign teachers and New Zealander teachers wishing to return home.

If you're hired from outside New Zealand, your air ticket and other travel costs are usually booked and paid for by your employer or his representative. In addition, you can usually claim any extra travel costs, e.g. transport to and from airports and hotel expenses en route. Most employers pay your relocation costs to New Zealand up to a specified amount, although you may be required to sign a contract stipulating that if you leave the employer before a certain period (e.g. five years), you must repay a percentage of your removal costs.

An employer may pay a fixed relocation allowance based on your salary, position and size of family, or he may pay the total cost of removal. The allowance should be sufficient to move the contents of an average house, and you must usually pay any excess costs (such as insurance for valuable items) yourself. If you don't want to bring your furniture to New Zealand or have just a few belongings to ship, it may be possible to obtain a grant towards the purchase of furniture locally up to the limit of your allowance. Check with your employer. When your employer is liable for the total cost, you may be asked to obtain two or three removal estimates. You may be expected to settle the remover's bill and then claim reimbursement, or your employer may instruct a New Zealand remover with agents in your home country to handle the removal and bill him directly.

If you change jobs within New Zealand, your new employer may pay your relocation expenses when it's necessary for you to move house. If you're moving from a rural area to either Auckland or Wellington, you should also ask for a pay rise to cover the extra cost of buying or renting a home (and the higher cost of living)!

Social Security

Social security is largely non-contributory in New Zealand, and officially neither employees nor employers make contributions. In practice, however, employees and the self-employed must contribute to the Accident Compensation Corporation (ACC) scheme, which provides compensation in the event of an accident, either at work or elsewhere. ACC contributions are deducted from salaries usually via the pay-as-you-earn (PAYE) system at the rate of $1.30 per $100 of liable earnings up to an earnings limit $85,795. For further information see **Chapters 13 & 14**. It's important to note, however, that receiving any sort of government benefits, which are collectively known as 'government transfers', isn't conditional upon having contributed to the scheme. Unemployment and sickness benefits, for example, are available to all New Zealanders and permanent residents irrespective of their employment history, although there may be other eligibility criteria and means testing.

Health Insurance

Some companies and professional organisations have their own supplementary health insurance schemes that pay out for medical expenses, e.g. doctors' consultation fees, prescription charges, and hospital out-patient charges, that aren't covered under the national healthcare system. Some even provide for private medical treatment. These schemes may be either contributory or non-contributory. In cases where they're non-contributory, they should be considered as part of your salary rather than a 'freebie' from your employer, and the value of the benefits (on which you will be taxed) will depend on the employer's scheme. If the scheme is contributory, it isn't usually obligatory to contribute, although as schemes usually take advantage of bulk insurance rates it's unlikely that you would be able to purchase similar cover for less independently. For more information, see page 211.

Company Pension Fund

Many employers offer either a contributory or non-contributory pension scheme, which provides you with an additional private pension upon retirement. It isn't obligatory to join, although schemes usually offer a good deal that's difficult to match when buying the same pension independently. See page 210 for more information.

Annual Holidays

Holiday entitlement in New Zealand is governed by the Holidays Act and cannot be changed by a contract of employment. It is, however, the biggest area of dispute between employers and employees, and the Labour Department annually receives hundreds of complaints about breaches of annual holiday entitlement. Employees are entitled to three weeks' paid annual holiday after they've completed 12 months' employment – on average less than any developed country other than the USA. Any leave taken before they've completed 12 months can only be taken as unpaid leave. You're entitled to take two of these weeks as an unbroken period. Holidays must usually be booked and agreed with your employer at the start of a calendar year. As the peak summer holiday period in New Zealand includes Christmas, you need to plan well in advance to obtain your preferred holiday dates.

Employees who have completed six months' employment are also entitled to five days' special leave for the following year, which can be used for periods of sickness or for attending funerals, etc.

If your contract provides for more than three weeks' holiday per year, you can negotiate with your employer if you wish to receive pay instead of the additional holiday. This doesn't, however, apply to any part of the statutory three weeks carried over from previous years; if you have unused holiday, you must take it.

Public Holidays

New Zealand has 11 statutory annual public holidays on which employees cannot be required to work unless it's stipulated in their contract of employment. In practice, many employees in essential services are required to work on public holidays, for which they're offered additional pay or, more usually, time off in lieu. In some cases, you can take your public holidays on a different day from that on which they occur. There are, however, two public holidays, Waitangi Day and Anzac Day, which cannot (by law) be moved and on which employees cannot be compelled to work. New Zealand's statutory public holidays are as follows:

Date	Holiday
1st January	New Year's Day
2nd January	New Year Holiday
6th February	Waitangi Day
Late March/early April	Good Friday
Late March/early April	Easter Monday
25th April	Anzac Day
First Monday in June	Queen's Birthday
Fourth Monday in October	Labour Day
25th December	Christmas Day
26th December	Boxing Day

Each region also has an Anniversary Day, which has the status of an official public holiday in that region.

Parental Leave

New Zealand employment legislation provides for an extensive period of leave for mothers, both before and after the birth of a child. The leave entitlement begins once you've worked for an employer for 12 months, whether full or part-time (provided you normally work for more than ten hours per week), and you cannot be dismissed for applying for or taking parental leave. All periods of maternity and paternity leave used to be unpaid, but in mid-2001 legislation was introduced under which maternity leave will be paid as from 1st July 2002. A maximum of $325 per week before tax will be paid for up to 12 weeks, although some sectors, such as self-employed women, don't qualify. According to the Equal Employment Opportunities Trust some 35 per cent of New Zealand employees already have some form of paid maternity leave in their contracts, usually for six weeks, although this varies from company to company. However, under private maternity leave schemes the mother is obliged to return the payments if she decides not to return to work after the maternity leave. The new government scheme has no penalties for not returning to work after maternity leave. Note that parental leave isn't automatic and you must apply for it.

Expectant mothers are entitled to 14 weeks' maternity leave, which can begin up to six weeks before the birth, and are also entitled to ten days' leave during pregnancy for ante-natal care and pregnancy-related illnesses. Fathers can take up to two weeks' leave around the period of the birth (but aren't entitled to extra time off for pregnancy-related illnesses!). It's often possible for either or both parents to take up to 52 weeks' extended leave after a birth, although an employer isn't obliged to keep a job open for this period.

No Smoking Rules

Many New Zealand workplaces don't permit smoking on the premises. These can be identified by groups of furtive-looking people gathering around the entrance for the mid-afternoon or mid-morning 'smoko'. No-smoking rules are taken seriously and people *never* smoke in a no-smoking building. Although there's no legislation against smoking (yet) in health-conscious New Zealand, you may be asked whether you smoke when applying for a job and be discriminated against if you answer 'yes' (although not officially).

Drug & Alcohol Testing

An increasing number of employers in New Zealand require employees to undergo drug testing, both at the outset of employment and at other times on a random basis. This is legal and, if applicable, will usually be stated in your contract of employment. It's particularly found in occupations where you're required to drive or operate heavy machinery. Urine samples are tested for the use of cannabis, morphine, heroin, cocaine, amphetamines and benzodiazepine, and breath tests are also carried out for alcohol. Positive testing can lead to instant dismissal.

Health & Safety

New Zealand has an appalling health and safety record and on average, according to union statistics, some 700 workers are injured and two die at work every week in New Zealand – one of the highest rates in the developed world. Additionally it's calculated that eight people die each week from work-related ill health and disease. In 2001 there was a high-profile union campaign for a new health and safety law in the workplace.

Under the new law, each workplace would have an elected and trained health and safety representation whose job would be to notify employers of any unsafe machinery or work procedures. Unions want these representatives to have the right to prevent work from continuing if an unsafe situation cannot be made safe. It remains to be seen whether such a law is introduced.

Paid Expenses

Expenses paid by your employer are usually listed in your employment contract and may include travel costs from your home to your place of work. This is more likely for Auckland and Wellington commuters than residents of other towns, where employers may provide employees with a rail or bus pass or free car parking at or near their place of work. Large employers provide a subsidised employee restaurant or canteen, whereas smaller employers may provide employees with luncheon vouchers.

Part-Time Job Restrictions

There may be a clause in your contract of employment to the effect that you cannot work part-time or on a freelance basis for a company in the same line of business as your employer. However, there isn't usually a restriction on taking other kinds of part-time work.

Retirement

There's no fixed national retirement age in New Zealand, although the usual retirement age is 65 for both men and women. However, employees may retire earlier or later, and it's illegal to force an employee to retire because of their age. You should, therefore, check your employment contract to see at what age you will be expected to retire. It isn't unusual for people to go on working after they reach 65, particularly in family businesses or small companies.

Dismissal and Disputes

The situations under which you can be dismissed will be specified in your employment contract and include incompetence, embezzlement and absenteeism. Under the Employment Relations Act of 2000 a new Mediation Service was formed within the Department of Labour consisting of some 40 mediators, who can be contacted by employers and/or employees at any time and will travel to the workplace to mediate *in situ*. In the first six months of operation, mediators dealt with some 2,000 cases and resolved nearly 80 per cent of them successfully. Any problems unresolved by mediation are referred to the Employment Relations Authority, whose aim is to resolve disputes in a 'speedy, informal and non-adversarial' way. More serious issues, together with appeals against the decision of the Employment Relations Authority, are heard by the Employment Court.

Redundancy can occur when the position filled by the employee is no longer needed or when employment can no longer continue for commercial reasons. Employees generally have no right to redundancy compensation but this can be negotiated at any time, including after notification of impending redundancy.

In New Zealand you have no right to strike except in a few situations, including to support bargaining for a collective agreement and at least 40 days after bargaining has started. Employees who fail to work under the terms agreed with their employer (e.g. by initiating a go-slow or a work-to-rule) can be 'locked out' (i.e. prevented from working without formally being dismissed), which is what happens in many industrial disputes in New Zealand.

Union Membership

There are numerous trade unions in New Zealand, most of them members of the Council of Trade Unions, which presents (or at least attempts to) a united front to the government on employment issues. Union power and influence has declined considerably in recent decades, particularly since the Employment Contracts Act took away a union's right to negotiate terms and conditions of employment on behalf of its members. Membership of trade unions is currently around 320,000, compared with a peak of 700,000 in the early '80s, although in 2000 union membership rose for the first time since 1985. Unions remain strongest in the older industries, such as engineering and motor manufacturing, but have little influence in the newer service industries.

Under New Zealand law, trade unions are permitted to organise on any company's premises, although closed shops are banned and unions must be registered with the Department of Labour and must be democratic. Trade unions are permitted to negotiate employees' working conditions only if authorised by them to do so. Employers must recognise unions, but aren't obliged to negotiate or settle with them (although most do so where unions are active). They *are*, however, obliged to negotiate and settle with individual employees.

3.

PERMITS & VISAS

Before making any plans to live or work in New Zealand, you must ensure that you have a valid passport and the appropriate permit or visa. Nationals of Australia can live and work in New Zealand with no more official documentation than their passport. All other nationalities (with a few exceptions) must apply for permission to stay in New Zealand, either temporarily or permanently, *before* their arrival. New Zealand makes a distinction between those staying temporarily, who must apply for a visa or permit, and those wishing to stay permanently, who must apply for residence.

Although New Zealand is a land of immigrants (some 85 per cent of its population are descended from Europeans, most of whom came to New Zealand within the last 150 years) immigration is a contentious issue, some wishing to increase it (they claim that the South Island could continue to absorb immigrants almost indefinitely) and others wishing to cut it sharply (they obviously wish to keep New Zealand's many delights to themselves). This can result in confusing messages being sent to prospective migrants. However, immigrants of the 'right type' are welcomed; in the words of the official literature, 'people who will contribute to New Zealand by bringing valuable skills or qualifications, setting up a business or making a financial investment'. New Zealanders generally feel that there's a need to diversify the country's skills in order to maintain international competitiveness, and one of the ways of doing this is to attract skilled immigrants.

If you plan to migrate to New Zealand, you should 'intend to live there for a long time, be able to adapt to New Zealand's lifestyle, obey New Zealand's laws and have no previous criminal convictions'. In the past, New Zealand took a rather lax approach to immigration, but procedures have become more rigorous in recent years and illegal immigration and overstaying is taken much more seriously than previously. The country sets an annual immigration quota (45,000 in 2001) which will remain more or less the same until 2004, but may be increased or decreased annually by 10 per cent.

Immigration is a complex subject and the rules are constantly changing. You shouldn't base any decisions or actions on the information contained in this book without confirming it with an official and reliable source, such as the NZIS (see below) or The Emigration Group (see inside the front and back covers). Residence regulations are taken seriously by the New Zealand authorities and if your application isn't in order it can result in rejection. The authority responsible for controlling entry to New Zealand is the New Zealand Immigration Service (NZIS), or *Te Ratonga Manene* in Maori, a service of the Department of Labour (🖳 www.immigration. govt.nz). A list of NZIS offices, branches and agencies in New Zealand and world-wide can be found on the website. New Zealand embassies, consulates and high commissions (see **Appendix A** for a list) also provide information on immigration.

VISITOR'S VISAS

If you plan to visit New Zealand for a short period (e.g. for a holiday, business trip or to assess the country before applying for residence), you must apply for a visitor's visa, if applicable. Australian citizens don't need a visa to travel to New Zealand, and nationals of certain countries can use a 'visa waiver scheme', which allows you to travel to New Zealand without a visitor's visa and obtain a visitor permit on arrival. Currently, countries that operate the visa waiver scheme are: Andorra, Argentina, Austria, Bahrain, Belgium, Brazil, Brunei, Canada, Chile, Czech Republic, Denmark, Finland, France, Germany, Greece, Hong Kong, Hungary, Iceland, Ireland, Israel,

Italy, Japan, (South) Korea, Kiribati, Kuwait, Liechtenstein, Luxembourg, Malaysia, Malta, Mexico, Monaco, Nauru, the Netherlands, Norway, Oman, Portugal, Qatar, San Marino, Saudi Arabia, Singapore, Slovenia, South Africa, Spain, Sweden, Switzerland, Tuvalu, the United Arab Emirates (UAE), the United Kingdom, Uruguay and the USA (except for nationals from American Samoa and Swains Island). **Everyone else needs a visitor's visa to travel to New Zealand and you won't even be allowed to board a plane to New Zealand without one.**

A visitor's visa is an endorsement in your passport that allows you to travel to New Zealand. The visa may be for a single or multiple journeys, but does not necessarily allow you to remain in New Zealand. Those who travel to New Zealand with a visa or visa waiver must complete an arrival card on their outgoing journey, which serves as an application for a visitor permit that is processed on arrival. A visitor permit allows you to stay for a short period (usually three months, or six months if you're a UK citizen) as a tourist, to see friends or relatives, study, take part in sporting and cultural events, undertake a business trip or undergo private medical treatment. Visitors may stay a total of nine months in an 18-month period. It doesn't state on the permit that you may use it to look for a job or visit New Zealand with a view to living there, although many people use it for this purpose (and it's perfectly legitimate).

Travellers under the visa waiver scheme must have a valid return ticket, sufficient money to support themselves (usually around $1,000 per month or $400 if staying with friends or relatives) and a passport valid for three months beyond the date they intend to leave New Zealand, and they must intend to stay in New Zealand for not more than the period of the permit. If you comply with these requirements, you may travel to New Zealand and should be granted a visitor permit on arrival. Visitors may stay for a maximum of nine months (which can be made up of a number of shorter periods) in an 18-month period. Once you've reached the maximum, you're required to remain abroad for nine months before returning to New Zealand as a visitor. Visitor permits can be extended by a further three months on application to the NZIS, although this is at their discretion, and you may be required to be able to support yourself financially without working.

You can be refused a visitor permit (and also a visitor's visa) if you don't meet the above requirements or are someone to whom Section 7 of the Immigration Act 1987 applies. This includes those who:

● have been deported from any country;

● are the subject of a New Zealand 'removal order';

● have committed a criminal offence which resulted in imprisonment of 12 months or more;

● have been convicted or sentenced for imprisonment for five years or more (at any time);

● are believed to have criminal associations or are suspected of being likely to constitute a danger to New Zealand's security or public order.

The above restrictions also apply to Australians, who don't need a visa or visitor permit to visit to New Zealand.

Visitor's visas can be applied for at NZIS offices and New Zealand diplomatic missions. Like Australia, New Zealand operates a system whereby applications for visas in major cities such as London and New York can be cleared almost instantly via an electronic link with the NZIS computer in New Zealand.

Fees are usually charged for visas and permits, and vary according to the country where you apply. They must be paid in local currency by bank draft or money order (not in New Zealand) or in cash (if you're applying in person). Personal cheques and credit cards are accepted in New Zealand. Fees aren't refundable even if a visa isn't granted! Citizens of certain countries (mainly Austria, Finland, Iceland and Japan) aren't charged for certain types of visa.

Note that as a visitor to New Zealand you aren't entitled to use publicly funded health services unless you're a resident or citizen of Australia or a UK national or hold a permit valid for at least two years (e.g. long-term business visa). **Unless you belong to one of these categories, it's strongly recommended that you have comprehensive medical insurance for the duration of your visit** (see **Health Insurance** on page 211 and **Holiday & Travel Insurance** on page 213).

TRANSIT VISAS

Those from certain countries wishing to pass through New Zealand on their way to another country require a transit visa. If you're a citizen of Afghanistan, Bangladesh, Bulgaria, China (PRC), Ethiopia, Ghana, India, Iran, Iraq, Libya, Myanmar (Burma), Pakistan, Somalia, Sri Lanka, Syria, Turkey or Zaire travelling between New Zealand and the Cook Islands, Fiji, Marshall Islands, New Caledonia, Niue, Samoa, Solomon Islands, Tahiti, Tonga, Torelau, Vanuatu and (Western) Samoa, you will need a transit visa. This allows you to stay in New Zealand for up to 24 hours provided you remain within the transit area of the airport. If you wish to stay in New Zealand for more than 24 hours and/or leave the transit area of the airport, you will need a visitor's visa (see above).

WORKING HOLIDAY VISAS

There are special working holiday schemes for young people from several countries, including Canada, Chile, Denmark, France, Germany, Hong Kong, Ireland, Italy, Japan, Korea (South), Malaysia, the Netherlands, Singapore, Sweden and the UK, which allow you to look for seasonal, temporary and casual employment. Students from the USA can also spend up to six months working in New Zealand under the 'Work in New Zealand Programme' operated by the Council On International Educational Exchange (CIEE – see page 25 for their address). Applicants must be between 18 and 30 and not be accompanied by children, and must provide evidence of sufficient funds to purchase return travel and meet the conditions of the scheme they apply under. Applicants don't need an offer of employment and can take any casual job on arrival. You must apply for the visa from your local New Zealand Consulate or High Commission before arrival in New Zealand, unless you apply under the Canada, Malaysia, Netherlands or Singapore schemes, when you may apply at any NZIS branch in New Zealand. The number of visas available is limited and varies depending on the country, therefore you should enquire well in advance, e.g. in the autumn (i.e. September to November) of the year prior to that in which you plan to work.

WORK VISAS & PERMITS

A work visa allows you to travel to New Zealand in order to undertake a period of temporary work. It isn't usually applicable to those intending to take up permanent residence in the country and applies mostly to contract workers and other short-term employees. Work visas are granted to foreigners only when no suitable New Zealand citizen or resident is available to do a job. Their issue isn't based on a points system and each case is treated on its merits taking into account the availability of local labour. To obtain a work visa you must have a firm offer of a job in writing and apply to the NZIS, which can be done outside or within New Zealand (if, for example, you arrived as a visitor and then wish to work). The visa fee is around $160 (depending on where it's issued) and isn't refundable, even if your application is rejected! On arrival in New Zealand, you will be issued with a work permit, which applies only to one job for a specified period, usually a maximum of three years (but often for a much shorter period). Under certain circumstances a work permit can be issued while a residence application is pending.

STUDENT VISAS

Those wishing to study full-time in New Zealand on a course lasting longer than three months require a student visa. Like a work visa (see above), this is a temporary visa and applicable only for the course and duration to which it relates. Before applying for a student visa, you must have an offer of a place from a New Zealand educational institution confirmed in writing. You must also have paid the course fees or have proof that you're able to do so, and have evidence of sufficient funds to support yourself during your course of study. Sufficient funds usually means at least $1,000 per month for short courses and a minimum of $7,000 per year for longer courses. This doesn't mean that you will be able to live on this sum and you will almost certainly require more. If you don't have the money yourself, it's acceptable to be sponsored by someone (either in New Zealand or abroad), but you need to provide evidence of sponsorship. A student visa allows you to work to supplement your funds only if you're on a long-term study course and work for no more than 15 hours per week or during the Christmas period. However, if you can find a suitable job, you can apply for a work permit on the same terms as any other non-resident (see **Work Visas & Permits** above). If a period of work experience is part of your course, then (in most cases) the NZIS will grant you a work permit for that purpose.

SPECIAL VISITOR CATEGORIES

Certain categories of visitor to New Zealand require special visas or must meet certain conditions when visiting New Zealand. These include the following:

Business Visitors: If you intend to visit New Zealand to discuss and negotiate business deals and plan to stay no longer than three months in any year, you will need a visitor's visa and must meet the normal requirements. A visitor's visa allows you to undertake business discussions and negotiations, although it doesn't permit you to work in an employed or self-employed capacity.

Conference Delegates: If you're attending a conference in New Zealand, you should check with the organiser to see whether arrangements have been made for conference cards to replace visitor's visas.

Group Visitors: If you're travelling in a group, e.g. as an organised tour or part of an educational exchange, the group may be eligible for a group visa. To qualify for this, all members of the group must be travelling for the same purpose, have the same travel arrangements and have a leader who's responsible for travel, visa and arrival arrangements.

Medical Treatment: If you're travelling to New Zealand for medical treatment or consultation, you must apply for a visitor's visa and complete an 'Intended Medical Treatment' form. If this isn't possible (e.g. in an emergency), you should contact the NZIS, who may be able to make special arrangements for you. Note that, unless you're a citizen of a country with which New Zealand has reciprocal agreements (i.e. Australia, Canada, Denmark, Greece, Guernsey, Ireland, Jersey, the Netherlands or the UK) or hold a permit valid for two years or more (e.g. a long-term business visa), you aren't entitled to receive publicly-funded medical treatment in New Zealand and must pay the full cost yourself.

Professional Registration: If you've applied for residence and require New Zealand registration to work in your profession, you may undertake practical or educational training for up to three months with a visitor's permit. If you need more time to obtain your registration, you must apply for either a student or work visa before travelling to New Zealand (see above).

Returning Residents: A returning resident's visa is required by anyone who has been granted residence in New Zealand and then leaves the country with the intention of returning at a later date (e.g. for a holiday in their home country). If you wish to do this, you should apply for a returning resident's visa from the NZIS *before* leaving New Zealand in order to guarantee that you will be readmitted on your return. **If you don't have a visa, immigration officers are entitled to refuse you entry and insist that you apply for residence all over again!** If this happens, your application will be dealt with under current regulations, which may be different from those in force when you first obtained residence in New Zealand. The only circumstance under which you don't need a returning resident's visa is if you have New Zealand or Australian citizenship or are resident in Australia and hold an Australian Resident Return Visa.

The first returning resident's visa is valid for two years from the date of your first residence permit. The second and subsequent returning resident's visas may be for any period from 14 days to indefinitely and are issued according to your eligibility. Factors such as time spent in New Zealand, tax residence status and investments are taken into account. Note that the spouse/partner and children of the principal resident can be included on the same returning resident's visa, unless the children are over 20 or over 17 and non-dependent.

Single Parents: A single parent travelling with a child must provide evidence (e.g. custody or guardianship papers) that the child has the right to leave his country of residence.

RESIDENCE

Applying for residence means seeking the right to live and work in New Zealand permanently. Under the Immigration Act 1987, anybody who wishes to immigrate to New Zealand must apply for residence, which entitles you to live, study or work indefinitely in New Zealand. The only foreigners this doesn't apply to are Australian citizens, who need only produce their passports when entering New Zealand, although they're subject to the same good character requirements as other visitors (see page 57). Applications for residence are assessed by the New Zealand

Immigration Service (NZIS), which must adhere to the government's immigration policy and isn't allowed to 'bend' the rules or make exceptions. If your application is refused, you can appeal to the Independent Residence Appeal Authority. All applicants for residence must provide the information and documentation necessary to meet the current regulations. Most people apply for residence from outside New Zealand, although it's possible to apply for residence from within the country, provided you're there lawfully.

Health Requirements

You and your accompanying family members must be in good health, which means you mustn't be a danger to public health or be likely to become a burden on the public health system. You must undergo a medical examination and tests (including X-rays) in order to obtain the required NZ Immigration Service Medical and X-ray Certificates. The certificates must be presented with your residence application and should be no older than three months at the time of application. The X-ray certificate doesn't apply to pregnant women or children aged under 12. Note that in some countries there are specific medical panels who are the only professionals authorised to carry out the tests. Contact the NZIS for details.

Character Requirements

You and your accompanying family members must be of good character. In order to prove this you're required to provide a police certificate (for each person over 17) from your country of citizenship and any country where you have lived for 12 months or more (in total) in the last ten years. The certificate should be no older than six months when you apply for a visa. The residence pack provided by the NZIS explains how to obtain these certificates. Section 7 of the Immigration Act 1987 defines what constitutes good character.

Those who may be refused entry include:

● anyone who has been sentenced to imprisonment for five years or more (at any time) or for 12 months or more during the last ten years;

● anyone who has been deported from New Zealand or any other country;

● anyone who is believed to be associated with criminal groups or a danger to New Zealand.

English Language Requirements

New Zealand's two official languages are English and Maori (*Te Reo Maori*). English is the more common language, and the primary applicant must have a good level of English before applying for residence or state that they intend to pre-purchase English language training. This requirement isn't just to allow you to find and perform work, but so that you can integrate into society. You're exempt if you've been working lawfully in New Zealand for a minimum of 12 months and have used English in your job before lodging a residence application. Acceptable evidence of a good level of English includes the following:

- a certificate from the International English Language Testing System (IELTS), which must be no more than two years old at the time of application, showing that you have an 'Overall Band' score of 6.5 or more in the IELTS General or Academic Module;
- a certificate of completion of primary education and a minimum of three years' secondary education in English;
- a certificate showing completion of at least five years' secondary education in English;
- evidence that you've previously lived in an English-speaking country (including the duration);
- evidence that you've used English in your current or previous employment.

A full list of acceptable evidence is included in the *Guide to Applying for Residence in New Zealand* (NZIS).

Note that principal applicants may be required to produce an IELTS certificate even if they've provided evidence of an English-speaking background or circumstances. Principal applicants in the General Skills category who don't meet the minimum standard of English will be refused unless they've been working lawfully in New Zealand for the 12 months prior to the date of application, meet all other residence requirements and pre-purchase English language tuition (see below). Principal applicants under the Business categories must meet a specified standard of English. Accompanying family members aged 16 and over included in the application under the General Skills or Business categories can meet the specified standard of English or pre-purchase English language tuition.

The amount of English language (ESOL) tuition you need to pre-purchase is determined by your score in the IELTS Test Report Form; in early 2003 it varied from $1,700 to $6,650 in the General Skills category and from $1,500 to $6,000 in the Business category. ESOL tuition must be pre-purchased from Skill New Zealand (National Office, 3rd Floor, 34–42 Manners Street, PO Box 27-048, Wellington (☎ 04-801 5588, 🖵 www.skillnz.govt.nz) and the required fee must be paid to NZIS. If your application is approved but you need to purchase ESOL tuition, NZIS will advise you of the amount payable. You then have six months to pay the tuition charge and your residence visa or permit won't be issued until the tuition charge is paid. Note that failure to pre-purchase ESOL tuition on time may mean your application is refused.

FEES & FINANCE

A settlement information fee of $90 is charged to all successful principal or sole applicants in all categories except refugees and citizens of Samoa. There's a migrant levy of $235 (up to a maximum of $940 per application) for each person (principal applicant and family members) in the general skills, business investor, entrepreneur, employees of relocating businesses and residence from work categories. Those applying in the family, family quota and Pacific access categories pay a migrant levy of $125 per person (up to a maximum of $500 per application). If you're outside New Zealand, you're required to pay the equivalent amount in your local currency.

Income Requirements

If you include dependent children in your application, you must show that you can meet a minimum income requirement, i.e. to prove that you can support yourself and your dependants for at least your first four years in New Zealand. During this period, income support (New Zealand social security payments) will be granted only in exceptional circumstances. If your spouse/partner included in your application has an offer of employment in New Zealand, his salary may be included in the assessment of minimum income. In late 2001, minimum income (i.e. total family annual income) ranged from $30,946 for one dependent child to $47,586 for four or more dependent children.

RESIDENCE CATEGORIES

The are two main categories (or streams) of residence: the Skills/Business Stream, which is divided into two sub-categories, General Skills and Business, and the Family Sponsored category. There's also a special residence category for Pitcairn Islanders. Each of these residence categories is described below. Further details can be obtained from New Zealand consulates and embassies and from the NZIS, which publishes a useful *Guide to Applying for Residence in New Zealand*, which can be downloaded from its website (⌨ www.immigration.govt.nz).

Retiring To New Zealand: There's no special immigration category for those wishing to retire to New Zealand and those over 55 cannot apply for residence under the General Skills category. Most retirees seek residence under the Family category, although people with business experience and capital may qualify under the Business category.

General Skills Category

The General Skills category is used by most foreigners wishing to live and work in New Zealand and accounts for around 60 per cent of all visas issued. It admits migrants who, in the words of the official documentation, will "increase New Zealand's levels of human capital, enterprise and innovation and foster international linkages". This means that you can qualify under this category only if you have a skill or talent that's considered beneficial to New Zealand. Whether or not you're considered 'beneficial' is calculated using a system that allocates points for your various attributes, which are divided between 'employability' and 'settlement' factors, as detailed below. In order to be considered you must score a total number of points specified as the pass mark at the time of your application. The pass mark is set quarterly and is available from NZIS offices or via the Internet (⌨ www. immigration.govt.nz). In the first quarter of 2003 the pass mark was 28 points.

Employability Factors

Qualifications: You're allocated points for qualifications that are comparable to a New Zealand standard, as determined by the NZIS, although you may need to obtain a qualifications assessment from the New Zealand Qualifications Authority (NZQA) before the NZIS can make a decision. You can be allocated points for only one qualification and partially completed qualifications aren't accepted. You *must* score a minimum of ten points to qualify (the maximum score achievable is 12 points).

If you're claiming points for a qualification in an occupation where professional registration is required by law in New Zealand, you must gain full registration before points are awarded (see **Registration** page 77). Points are scored as follows:

Qualification	Points
New Zealand basic qualification or equivalent: a degree, diploma or trade certificate of a minimum of three years' training, study or work experience	10
New Zealand advanced qualification or equivalent: a minimum of one year's training, study or work experience which builds on a base qualification	11
New Zealand masters degree or higher (or equivalent)	12

If you're an IT specialist and don't hold qualifications of the standard required, you may be awarded ten points if you have a minimum of three years' full-time business experience in your field of specialisation (this experience cannot, however, also count towards points for business experience – see below), can provide evidence of some formal training in your area of specialisation and hold a letter of support issued by the Information Technology Association of New Zealand (ITANZ) confirming that your skills are in short supply, and have an offer of employment. Note, however, that three years' of points for work experience will be deducted.

Business Experience: You can claim up to ten points for professional or business experience (referred to as 'work experience'), which must be relevant to the qualification for which you're allocated points (see above). You must score a minimum of one point for business work experience and you cannot count experience which was an integral part (or a course requirement) of your training for the qualification for which you're allocated points (i.e. business experience must be entirely separate from your formal training or study). Points are allocated on the basis of business work experience of 30 hours or more per week, although experience of less than 30 hours per week may be awarded points on a pro rata basis. You can claim one point for each two complete years' business experience, i.e. one point for two years' experience, two points for four years experience, etc. up to a maximum of ten points for 20 years' experience.

Offer of Employment: You don't need to have found a job in New Zealand before you can apply for residence under this category. However, you can be allocated up to eight points if you have a genuine offer of employment, which will substantially boost your chances of acceptance. The offer of employment must be for permanent, full-time employment by a single employer or for one or more contracts totalling at least six months with an option of further terms, and must be current at the time of your application. Self-employment or employed paid by commission and/or retainer aren't acceptable. You must obtain registration if it's required by law (see above); if registration isn't required, employment must be relevant to the qualification for which you're allocated points or previous work experience. A non-relevant job offer scores two points and a relevant job offer up to five points.

Since March 2000, General Skills category applicants who meet the category requirements in all aspects but need an offer of employment to reach the pass mark have been allowed into New Zealand with a six-month work permit in order to look for a job.

Age: You can be allocated points for your age at the time that you submit your application. However, if you turn 25 while your application is being processed, you can qualify for maximum points. If you're 56 or over, an application for residence under the General Skills category cannot be made. Points are scored for age as follows:

Age	Points
18–24	8
25–29	10
30–34	8
35–39	6
40–44	4
45–49	2
50–55	0

Settlement Factors

You can be allocated a maximum of seven points for settlement factors, which include the following:

Settlement Funds: You can be allocated a maximum of two points for settlement funds, i.e. cash, shares, stocks or other assets. These funds must be transferred to New Zealand before residence can be granted and must be free of debt. You don't need to transfer funds to New Zealand until your application has been approved in principle and have six months from the date of approval to transfer funds. You can be allocated points if the funds are wholly owned by the principal applicant or spouse, or if they're jointly owned. One point is scored if you have $100,000 in funds and two points if you have $200,000.

New Zealand Business/Work Experience: You can be allocated a maximum of two points for professional or business/work experience gained lawfully in New Zealand. If no points are awarded for an offer of employment, this experience must be relevant to your qualification. You can be allocated points for New Zealand business experience under both this section *and* the business/work experience section (listed above under **Employability Factors**). Points are allocated on the basis of experience totalling 30 hours or more per week, although business experience of less than 30 hours may be awarded points on a pro rata basis. You can claim one point for one year's experience and two points for two or more years'.

Spouse Or Partner's Qualifications: You can be allocated a maximum of two points for your spouse or partner's fully completed qualification, provided it's comparable to a New Zealand qualification. The comparability rules are the same as for the principal applicant's qualifications (see page 21) except that your spouse or partner doesn't need to be registered before your application is processed (although he may need to be registered if he wishes to work in that occupation – see **Registration** on page 77). One point is scored for a basic qualification and two points for an advanced qualification, i.e. masters degree or higher.

Family Sponsorship: You can be allocated three points for family sponsorship. Your family sponsor must be aged 17 or over, a New Zealand citizen or permanent resident, lawfully living in New Zealand for at least three years immediately prior to the date of your application, and a parent, brother, sister or child of the principal applicant or the principal applicant's spouse. Family sponsors are responsible for providing information and advice about settling in New Zealand and providing you with financial support and accommodation for at least your first two years there. Your family sponsor must complete a *Sponsorship Form* available from NZIS offices in New Zealand.

Business Category

The objective of the Business category is to select migrants who will "increase New Zealand's level of human capital, enterprise and innovation, and also foster international links". The category is divided into the following four sub-categories:

Investor: To be granted residence under the Investor category (which replaced the Business Investor Category) you must score sufficient points to meet the pass mark applicable at the time your application is accepted, make an acceptable investment (see **Investment Funds** below), and meet other requirements such as good health, good character and age (25 to 84). Applications in the Investor category with a points score of 11 or less (or who don't score at least one point for investment funds – see below) will be refused. The pass mark is recalculated quarterly and can be obtained from NZIS offices or via the Internet (📖 www.immigration.govt.nz). In late 2001 the pass mark was 12 points.

Entrepreneur: This category is linked to the Long-term Business Visa and provides the opportunity for residence for people who have successfully established a business in New Zealand. Applications are accepted only if the business has been in operation for a least two years.

Long-term Business Visa: This is a multiple-entry work visa valid for up to three years and renewable. It's intended for those who wish to set up a business in New Zealand but not live there permanently.

Employees of Relocating Businesses: Key employees in a business relocating to New Zealand who don't qualify under other categories are considered in this category. Applications are assessed on a case-by-case basis.

Points

As with the General Skills category, points are awarded in all Business categories for various attributes, as detailed below.

Business Experience: You can be allocated up to five points for your business experience. Business experience is defined as a minimum of two years' ownership or management of a lawful business enterprise (estate agents and lawyers will be glad to hear that they aren't excluded) or senior management experience. For this purpose the definition of 'ownership' is that you own at least 25 per cent of the business. Points are allocated on the basis of business experience of 30 hours or more per week, although experience of less than 30 hours a week may be awarded points on a pro rata basis. You can claim one point for each period of two years' business experience up to a maximum of five points for ten years' experience.

Qualifications: You're allocated points for qualifications that are comparable to a New Zealand standard, as determined by the NZIS, although you may need to obtain a qualifications assessment from the New Zealand Qualifications Authority (NZQA) before the NZIS can make a decision. You're allocated points only for one or a series of qualifications that are comparable to one New Zealand qualification, and partially completed qualifications aren't accepted. Your qualification must be relevant to the business experience for which you're claiming points. Note that occupational registration isn't required for the allocation of points in this category. You can claim one point for a basic qualification and two points for an advanced qualification such as a masters or higher degree.

Age: You can be allocated points for your age, although if you're 65 to 84, points will be *deducted*. If you're over 84, an application cannot be made in the Business category – although you would hope to be retired by then anyway! Points for age are scored as follows:

Age	Points
25–29	10
30–34	9
35–39	8
40–44	6
45–49	4
50–54	2
55–64	0
65–74	-2
75–84	-4

Investment Funds: Up to 11 points can be awarded for funds and assets, which may be owned either solely by the principal applicant or jointly with his spouse. Points are scored according to the value of the funds as follows:

Funds	Points
$1,000,000	1
$1,500,000	2
$2,000,000	3
$2,500,000	4
$3,000,000	5
$3,500,000	6
$4,000,000	7
$4,500,000	8
$5,000,000	9
$5,500,000	10
$6,000,000	11

Funds must have been earned as a direct result of your business experience and/or accumulated as returns on the investment of funds earned by you as a result of your business experience. You must submit an 'accumulated earnings report' (compiled by a recognised agency) showing the link between your business experience and your funds and demonstrating that your business experience was in a lawful enterprise. You aren't required to transfer funds until your application has been approved in principle, after which you have six months in which to transfer your funds to New Zealand. If you're transferring direct investment funds, you have 12 months and can be granted a work visa so that you can come to New Zealand to decide how best to invest your funds. Your residence in New Zealand will be subject to the requirement that funds are invested in an acceptable way for a period of not less than two years. If you don't meet this requirement, your residence may be revoked and you may be required to leave New Zealand.

Family Sponsored Category

The objectives of the Family Sponsored category are to permit New Zealand citizens or residents to be joined by their spouses, partners, parents, siblings or children, and to allow New Zealand citizens or residents to sponsor family members and help them settle. The Family Sponsored category is therefore available to those who are in a genuine and stable married or de facto (including same sex) relationship with a New Zealand citizen or resident, or who have immediate family members who are New Zealand citizens or permanent residents. This category also includes the Family Quota available for relatives of New Zealanders who don't qualify under any other residence category. Good health and character requirements apply to the Family Sponsored category as to other residence categories (see page 63).

Sponsors: New Zealand citizens or residents sponsoring relatives to settle in New Zealand are required (since 10th October 2001) to make a declaration of undertaking under the Oaths and Declarations Act 1957 that they will provide their relatives with any necessary financial support and accommodation for at least the first two years after their arrival. Note that legal action can be taken to recover costs from sponsors who don't honour their obligations. Sponsors must also:

- be aged 17 or over;
- be a New Zealand or Australian citizen and, in some categories, have resided in New Zealand for 184 days or more in each of the three years immediately prior to the application.

Marriage & De Facto (including same sex) Relationships: You may be granted residence under the Family Sponsored category if you're married to and living in a genuine and stable relationship with a New Zealand citizen or resident or in a genuine and stable de facto relationship (i.e. living together, although unmarried, including same sex relationships), of at least two years' standing with a New Zealand citizen or resident. If you're married, you must provide your marriage certificate. If you're in a de facto relationship, you must present evidence that you've been living together for at least two years, such as proof of shared accommodation, letters of support from family and friends, proof of shared income, etc. The NZIS may verify any such documents. You and your partner may be called to an interview with the NZIS to assess whether you're living together and that your relationship is genuine and stable (if it's suspected that you're bogus, you will be split up and asked the same questions to see whether your answers match!).

If you've been in a de facto relationship for at least 18 months, you can apply for residence, but your application may not be granted until you've been in the relationship for two years (the authorities obviously believe that most relationships break up between 18 months and two years after they start!).

Parents: You may be granted residence if you have an adult child aged 17 or over who's a New Zealand citizen or resident living lawfully and permanently in New Zealand and who's prepared to sponsor you (see above), and the 'centre of gravity' of your family is in New Zealand. The centre of gravity of your family is considered to be in New Zealand if:

- you have no dependent children and all your adult children are living permanently outside your home country; *or*
- you have no dependent children and have an equal or greater number of adult children living lawfully and permanently in New Zealand than in any other single country, including your home country; *or*
- you have dependent children and have an equal or greater number of adult children living lawfully and permanently in New Zealand than in any other single country, including your home country. The number of dependent children must be the same as, or less than, the number of adult children living lawfully and permanently in New Zealand.

Siblings/Adult Children: You may apply for residence if you have a close family member, e.g. parent, brother or sister, who's a New Zealand citizen or resident living lawfully and permanently in New Zealand and who's prepared to sponsor you, and if you have an acceptable offer of employment in New Zealand.

Dependent Children: You may apply for residence under this section if:

- you're aged 17 to 24;
- you're single;
- you have no children;
- you're totally or substantially reliant on your parents or guardians for financial support, whether living with them or not;
- your parents live lawfully and permanently in New Zealand;

or

- you're 16 or younger;
- you're single;
- you're totally or substantially reliant on your parents or guardians for financial support, whether living with them or not.

If you were born or adopted before your parents applied for residence, you must have been declared on your parents' application for residence; if you were adopted after your parents applied for residence, your adoption must have taken place in New Zealand or been an overseas adoption recognised under New Zealand law. If your parents are separated or divorced, you must provide evidence that the custody or visitation rights of a parent living outside New Zealand won't be breached by your move to New Zealand.

Fees

A 'migrant levy' is charged to successful principal applicants and accompanying family members in the Family Sponsored category. The fee is $125 for each person included in the application, up to a maximum of $500 per application. There is also a one-off settlement information fee of $90.

Family Quota Category

The objective of the Family Quota category is to strengthen families and communities by providing New Zealand citizens and residents with an opportunity to sponsor family members who don't qualify under any other residence category. A number of people are chosen annually by ballot – the number of places (250 in the period 2002/03) available is announced annually by the Minister of Immigration. The non-refundable registration fee is $100 – if you're selected in the ballot the $100 is deducted from the normal fees payable.

If your parent, adult grandchild, adult sibling or adult child meets the sponsorship requirements (see **Sponsors** on page 68), he may apply for a Family Quota Category place. The application must be submitted during a specific period to a New Zealand branch of the NZIS; for example, for the quota applicable to the year 1st July 2001 to 30th June 2002, the application period is from 2nd to 30th April 2002. Applications received outside this period will be rejected. If you have a spouse/partner and/or dependent children, they must also be included in your application, or they won't be eligible for residence!

Other Quota Categories

The Humanitarian/International category was discontinued in 2001, although there are several special categories under which certain people can apply (see below), as well as categories relating to refugees. The principal applicant is the person assessed against the immigration criteria. A partner who's legally married to the principal applicant may be included, but a de facto partner may be included only if the applicant and partner have been living in a genuine and stable relationship for at least two years at the time of the application. Dependent children may be included in an application if they're single, aged 24 or under, have no children of their own, and are totally or substantially reliant on the applicant for financial support. If the applicant is divorced or separated from a child's mother or father, he or she must have the right to remove them from their current country of residence and provide documentary evidence of this. Adopted children can be included on an application irrespective of whether they've been formally adopted.

Refugee Family Policy: There are a number of places (the quota is announced annually) for the family members of residents who were refugees. A place is granted only if the family member couldn't obtain a place under any other category, with the exception of the family quota category.

Domestic Violence Policy: Ex-partners of New Zealanders can apply for residence when their relationship ended as a result of domestic violence and they can't return to their home country.

Samoan Quota: This quota (of up to 1,100 annually) applies to Samoan citizens living in Samoa who have an offer of employment in New Zealand. The scheme is administered by New Zealand High Commission, Beach Road, PO Box 2277, Apia, Western Samoa (☎ 685-21715), who can provide details.

Pacific Access Category: This quota allows for the grant of residence to a limited number of citizens of Toga, Fiji, Tuvalu and Kiribati aged between 18 and 45 with an offer of employment in New Zealand.

Pitcairn Islanders: New Zealand also has a special residence category for Pitcairn Islanders. This scheme operates in recognition of the fact that there are few employment opportunities on Pitcairn Island. Pitcairn Islanders are considered for residence on favourable terms providing they have a firm offer of employment in New Zealand. They must complete the standard residence form and attach supporting documents (two photos, birth certificate, passport, medical and X-ray examinations, and character reports), and pay the requisite fee.

RESIDENCE PERMITS

Once you've been granted residence, you have the right to live and work in New Zealand for an indefinite period and work in any job you wish. Unlike some countries, you aren't required to apply for separate work and residence permits after you've arrived in New Zealand. Note that if you apply for residence outside New Zealand, you will receive a residence visa valid for one year allowing you to travel to New Zealand, where you will be granted a residence permit on arrival. If you apply for residence within New Zealand, you will automatically receive a residence permit.

Note that residence permits expire once you leave New Zealand and if you wish to re-enter the country you must obtain a 'returning resident's visa' before leaving New Zealand in order to be re-admitted upon your return (see page 60). New Zealand residents retain the passport of their home country unless they become citizens (see **New Zealand Citizenship** on page 294).

4.

ARRIVAL

On arrival in New Zealand your first task will be to negotiate immigration and customs, which fortunately for most people presents no problems. You may find it more convenient to arrive in New Zealand on a weekday rather than at the weekend, when offices and banks are closed. If you arrive in New Zealand by ship, customs and immigration officials may board the vessel to carry out their checks (unless you're competing in a round-the-world yacht race). With the exception of Australians and visitors from countries who qualify under the visa waiver scheme (see page 56), anyone wishing to enter New Zealand for any reason requires a visa (see **Chapter 3** for information). **If you need a visa and arrive in New Zealand without one, you will be refused entry.**

There are also a number of tasks that should be completed on arrival, which are described in this chapter, where you'll also find suggestions for finding local help and information.

IMMIGRATION

When you arrive in New Zealand, your passport and other papers will be inspected by an immigration officer and (provided everything is in order) you will be given permission to enter and remain for the purpose and the period for which you've applied. It's worth noting that visitors can be refused entry (even with a valid visa) if an immigration officer believes that they could be a threat to public security or health, i.e. a visa doesn't automatically grant right of entry. Visitors arriving from countries that come under the visa waiver scheme (see page 56) can apply for a visitor permit on arrival using the form that is provided on the aircraft or ship. Do bear in mind that you may be expected to produce other documents to support your claim for entry, such as a return ticket and/or evidence of funds. New Zealand immigration officials are usually fairly amiable, although certain Asian visitors and young people on working holidays (who rank highly as potential illegal immigrants) may be subjected to greater scrutiny.

If you arrive in New Zealand at a location which isn't an authorised customs seaport or airport, you're required to report to an immigration officer within 72 hours of your arrival and must meet the usual visa requirements. The harbour master or airfield owner will tell you where to report. Special arrangements apply to yachts which arrive for the purpose of undertaking essential repairs or to wait out bad weather during the hurricane season (October to April), in which case a visitor permit may be granted for a longer period than usual.

CUSTOMS

New Zealand customs carry out checks at all points of entry into the country in order to enforce customs regulations, which apply to everyone entering the country, whether residents, visitors or migrants. There are no special concessions, even for visitors from Australia despite the 'closer economic agreement' with New Zealand (apparently they're not that close!). Prior to your arrival in New Zealand you will be given a New Zealand Passenger Arrival Card, which you must complete and hand in to customs when you arrive. This card includes a declaration stating whether you have any banned, restricted or dutiable goods (i.e. above your duty-free allowance – see below). Most ports of entry operate a red (goods to declare) and a green (nothing to declare) channel system. If you know (or think) you may have goods that should be declared, declare them on arrival. If you don't make a declaration, you may be subject to a random check.

Duty-free Allowances: Apart from personal effects (such as clothing) everyone entering the country aged over 17 is allowed certain duty-free allowances which include:

- 200 cigarettes *or*
- 250g of tobacco *or*
- 50 cigars *or*
- a mixture of all three not weighing more than 250g;
- 4.5 litres of wine or beer;
- a 1.125 litre bottle of spirit or liqueur.

You may also import other goods valued up to $700. New Zealand law allows you to purchase duty-free goods at a New Zealand airport on arrival, although if you exceed your allowance you can be charged customs duty plus goods and services tax (GST) at 12.5 per cent. If you're entering the country to take up residence, you can also import your used household effects and a car (see page 162), although it's unlikely you will be bringing these when you arrive at the airport! New Zealanders are entitled to the same allowances if they've been out of the country and living abroad for at least 21 months.

Restricted & Prohibited Goods: In addition to the usual items such as drugs, pornography, guns and explosives (which you cannot import without special permission), New Zealand customs are particularly sensitive about the import of anything with plant or animal origins. Breaches of the strict New Zealand Biosecurity laws result in an instant $200 fine as well as the prospect of an additional fine of up to $100,000 and of up to five years in prison. Food, plants, dried flowers, seeds and potpourri mustn't be imported into New Zealand under any circumstances. You can be fined for importing an apple or kiwi fruit, even if it came from New Zealand in the first place!

There are also special regulations governing the following:

- animals or items made from animal feathers, skin, fur, horns, tusks, etc;
- equipment used with animals, including riding tackle;
- biological specimens;
- garden tools, furniture and ornaments;
- lawn mowers, strimmers, etc;
- tents and camping equipment;
- golf clubs;
- vacuum cleaners, brooms and brushes;
- wicker and cane items;
- bicycles;
- walking/gardening boots.

It isn't recommended to import any of the items mentioned into New Zealand. If for some reason you wish to, you should seek advice from customs and declare them on arrival. Special inspection, cleaning and fumigation procedures are often required, for which you may be charged.

On your arrival card you're asked to declare if in the previous 30 days you've been camping or hiking in forest or parkland and if you've been in contact with animals other than domestic cats and dogs. You must also list the countries you've visited within the previous 30 days.

Pets and other animals shouldn't be imported into New Zealand without prior authorisation from customs. Should you wish to take your pet to New Zealand, you should entrust the job to a specialist pet shipping service. You require a health certificate provided by a vet in your home country and your pet will need to undergo a period of quarantine after it arrives in New Zealand (limited exemptions apply to pets imported from Australia, Hawaii, Norway, Sweden and the UK). The good news is that you won't be charged duty on your pet.

If you bring prescribed medicines with you, you should carry a prescription or letter from your doctor stating that the medicine is being used under a doctor's direction and is necessary for your physical well being. You should carry medicines in their original containers.

You must also declare amounts of cash in any currency to the value of $10,000 or more.

Information: If you have any doubts about whether anything you wish to import into New Zealand is banned or restricted, then you should make enquiries with a New Zealand Embassy, Consulate or High Commission, or directly to New Zealand customs (☎ freephone 0800-428 786 or 09 300 5399).

Customs also have a comprehensive website that you can visit for more information (🖥 www.customs.govt.nz) or alternatively you can contact the New Zealand customs office at your point of entry:

Auckland: Customhouse, 50 Anzac Avenue, PO Box 29 (☎ 09-359 6655)

Auckland International Airport: PO Box 73-003 (☎ 09-275 9059)

Christchurch: Drury Street, PO Box 14-086, (☎ 03-358 0600)

Dunedin: Investment House, 470 Moray Place, Private Bag 1928 (☎ 03-477 9251)

Invercargill: Business Centre, Ground Floor, Menzies Building, 1 Esk Street, PO Box 840 (☎ 03-218 7329)

Napier: 11 Station Street, PO Box 440 (☎ 06-835 5799)

Nelson: 10 Low Street, PO Box 66 (☎ 03-548 1484)

New Plymouth: 54–56 Currie Street, PO Box 136 (☎ 06-758 5721)

Tauranga: Nikau House, 27–33 Nikau Crescent, PO Box 5014 (☎ 07-575 9699)

Wellington: Head Office, The Customhouse, 17–21 Whitmore Street, PO Box 2218 (☎ 04-473 6099).

EMBASSY REGISTRATION

Nationals of some countries are required to register with their local embassy or consulate after taking up residence in New Zealand, and most embassies like to keep a record of their country's citizens who are resident in New Zealand (it helps to justify their existence).

FINDING HELP

One of the biggest difficulties facing new arrivals in New Zealand is how and where to find help with day-to-day problems, e.g. finding accommodation, schooling, insurance and so on. This book was written in response to this need. However, in addition to the comprehensive information provided in this book, you will also require local information. How successful you are at finding help will depend on your employer, the town or area where you live (e.g. residents of cities are better served than those living in rural areas) and your nationality.

There's an abundance of information available in English, but little in other foreign languages. An additional problem is that much information isn't intended for foreigners and their particular needs. You may find that your friends and colleagues can help, as they can often offer advice based on their own experiences and mistakes. But take care! Although they mean well, you may receive as much misleading and conflicting information as accurate (it won't necessarily be wrong, but may be invalid for your particular situation).

Your local community is usually an excellent source of information. As anywhere, it's often not what you know but who you know that can make the difference between success or failure. String-pulling or the use of contacts is invaluable when it comes to breaking through the layers of bureaucracy, where a telephone call on your behalf from a neighbour or colleague can work wonders. In fact, any contact can be of help, even a professional acquaintance, who may not even charge you for his time. Your local town hall, post office, council office, citizens' advice bureau and tourist office may also be able to help. Some companies employ staff to help new arrivals or contract this job out to a relocation consultant (see page 83), although most employers are unaware of (or don't understand) the problems and difficulties faced by foreign employees and their families.

There's a wealth of expatriate organisations in major cities, particularly Auckland and Wellington, where foreigners are well served by English-speaking clubs and organisations. Contacts can be found through local magazines and newspapers (see page 288), consulates and citizens' advice bureaux. Women living in country areas will find that a good network of support is offered by Country Women's Institutes. Most consulates also provide their nationals with local information, including details of lawyers, interpreters, doctors, dentists and schools.

CHECKLISTS

Before Arrival

The following checklist contains a summary of the tasks that should (if possible) be completed before your arrival in New Zealand:

- Look for a job, if appropriate. Even if you intend to look for a job after you've arrived, it's wise to make some preliminary enquiries about opportunities and possible employers.
- Obtain a visa, if necessary, for yourself and all family members (see **Chapter 3**). Obviously this must be done before arrival in New Zealand.
- Visit New Zealand prior to your move to compare communities.
- Find temporary or permanent accommodation (see **Chapter 5**).
- Arrange for shipment of your household and personal effects to New Zealand (see page 95).
- Arrange health and travel insurance for your family (see pages 211 and 213). This is essential if you aren't covered by a private insurance policy and won't be covered by New Zealand's public healthcare scheme.
- Open a bank account in New Zealand and transfer funds (you can open an account with many New Zealand banks while abroad). It's wise to obtain some New Zealand dollars before your arrival, as this will save you having to change money on arrival.
- Obtain an international driver's licence, if necessary.
- Obtain an international credit or charge card, which will be invaluable during your first few months in New Zealand, where almost everyone uses 'plastic'.
- Don't forget to bring your family's official documents, including birth certificates, driving licences, marriage certificate, divorce papers or death certificate (if a widow or widower), educational diplomas, professional certificates and job references, school records and student identity cards, employment references, medical and dental records, bank account and credit card details, insurance policies, and receipts for any valuables. You may also need the documents that were required to obtain your residence visa for other purposes, such as to enrol your children at school. It's also worthwhile taking numerous passport-size photographs (students should take at least a dozen for bus and student identity cards, etc.).

After Arrival

The following checklist contains a summary of tasks to be completed after arrival in New Zealand (if not done before):

- On arrival at a New Zealand airport, have your visa cancelled and your passport stamped, as applicable.
- You may wish to rent a car until you buy one (see page 169). Bear in mind that it's practically impossible to get around in rural areas without a car. Even if you're taking your own car, you will be unable able to drive it until it has been cleared through customs (see **Car Import** on page 162).
- Register with your local embassy or consulate (see page 77).
- Make courtesy calls on your neighbours within a few days of your arrival. This is particularly important in villages and rural areas if you want to be accepted and become part of the local community.

- Do the following in the few days after your arrival:

  - Check the availability of local doctors, dentists and hospitals (obtain advice and recommendations from your neighbours).

  - Open a bank account at a local bank and give the details to your employer (see page 224).

  - Arrange schooling for your children (see **Chapter 9**).

  - Obtain an Inland Revenue Department (IRD) number from your local Inland Revenue office (see page 233).

  - Arrange whatever insurance is necessary (see **Chapter 13**) including health insurance (see page 211), car insurance (see page 171) and household insurance (see page 212).

- Open a bottle of 'bubbly' to celebrate your arrival in New Zealand!

5.

ACCOMMODATION

In most areas of New Zealand, accommodation to buy or rent isn't difficult to find, depending on your requirements. There are, however, a few exceptions. For example, in Auckland, accommodation is relatively expensive (often as much as 50 per cent more than elsewhere) and can be in short supply in popular areas. Property prices rose sharply in New Zealand during the '80s, although the '90s saw more modest growth. In 2001, after a reduction in the Official Cash Rate and a fall in mortgage interest rates, the property market was booming and sales were on the increase. Prices were increasing again, with annual rises of around 9 per cent in Auckland and Wellington and almost as high in most of North Island. Average prices fell, however, in South Island and in the Wanganui area of North Island.

As in many other countries, there has recently been a increase in apartment living in city centres, and prices of apartments in some areas are comparable with those for houses, although most New Zealanders prefer a house with a garden. Home ownership in New Zealand is high at around 75 per cent (compared with some 40 per cent in Germany and 60 per cent in the UK) and most New Zealanders prefer to purchase their home rather than rent, although in recent years there's been a marked increase in the rental of property, particularly in Auckland. In addition, a significant number of New Zealanders also own a holiday home (called a 'bach' in North Island and a 'crib' in South Island), although it's often quite a modest property. New Zealanders are quite mobile and tend to move home much more frequently than people in some other countries, with around 90,000 domestic properties changing hands each year (a very large number for a country with less than 4 million inhabitants). During the last few years there has been a small but marked movement of people from the South to the North Island, and from throughout the country to Auckland, which has helped to fuel property shortages and accompanying higher prices in this part of the country.

TEMPORARY ACCOMMODATION

On arrival in New Zealand, you may find it necessary to stay in temporary accommodation for a few weeks or months, e.g. before moving into permanent accommodation or while waiting for your furniture and other possessions to arrive. Generally, you will find it easier to move into a hotel or motel initially and then look for somewhere permanent, rather than rushing into renting or purchasing a property which later turns out to be unsuitable, e.g. in the wrong place for work or much more expensive than you could have found by shopping around on the spot. Finding the right sort of property can take some time and you should allow up to six months between deciding to emigrate and moving into a purchased property, although a move can often be arranged in just a few weeks if you plan to rent a home.

Many hotels, motels and guest houses cater for long-term guests and offer reduced weekly or monthly rates. A motel can be a good choice, as many provide a kitchenette and some even have separate living and dining areas and one or two bedrooms. If you're planning to arrive during the winter (May to August), self-catering holiday apartments can be rented quite cheaply, although they're often located in remote places.

For lists of economic temporary accommodation it's advisable to obtain a copy of Jason's *Motels and Motor Lodges* or *Budget Accommodation*, which, although mainly intended for tourists, include several establishments offering long-term discounts, particularly out of season. For further information about hotels, motels, guest houses and hostels see **Chapter 15**.

RELOCATION CONSULTANTS

If you've got money to spare or you're fortunate enough to have your move to New Zealand paid for by your employer, you can arrange for a relocation consultant to handle the details. There are, however, few relocation consultants dealing with New Zealand and they mainly handle corporate clients with lots of money to pay their fat fees. They usually charge on a daily basis, plus expenses. The main service provided by relocation consultants is finding accommodation (either to rent or purchase) and arranging viewing. Other services include conducting negotiations, drawing up contracts, arranging mortgages, organising surveys and insurance, and handling the move itself. They may also provide reports on local schools, health services, public transport, sports and social facilities, and other amenities and services. Some companies provide an 'advice line' which you can call with queries and problems once you've moved in.

NEW ZEALAND HOMES

Most New Zealand families live in detached homes set on their own plot of land, known as a 'section'. This dates back to the pioneering days when the authorities divided great tracts of land into sections for house building. Each section was a quarter of an acre and hence the phrase 'quarter-acre paradise' was coined to describe the typical New Zealand home as well as the country itself. A quarter-acre section (or its metric equivalent, approximately $1,000m^2$) is still the standard plot size in New Zealand, although many sections have been subdivided and a second property built in the garden, or in some cases the original house has been demolished and several new properties built in its place. At one point this sub-division threatened to get out of hand, and the government has imposed a minimum plot size of $690m^2$.

Most New Zealand properties are single-storey bungalows (although they're usually called 'houses'), but two-storey houses are becoming more popular. If a property is described as a 'villa', don't expect a palace complete with columns, marble floors and a sunken bath worthy of Cleopatra, as they're usually quite modest homes made of wood with a corrugated iron roof (see below)i!. Semi-detached properties, terraced houses (known as townhouses) and apartments aren't as common as detached properties in most of New Zealand. The suburbs of most main cities have large townhouses from the Victorian area, many of which have been lovingly restored, and in recent years new smaller townhouses have been built. Apartments are largely confined to city centres. Apartment living went out of fashion in the '80s when many people moved out to the suburbs, although it's becoming fashionable again and apartments in the central areas of Auckland and Wellington are highly sought-after. Thankfully, there are hardly any high-rise apartment blocks in New Zealand, which does, however, boast a unique type of housing called a 'unit'. This is a single building containing a number (often four or six) of smaller properties, each having its own plot and therefore being part house, part apartment.

New Zealand homes often aren't built to the same standards as is common in Europe, and construction methods are similar to those used in Australia and many parts of the USA. Brick and stone are less common, except in more expensive properties, although cheaper properties may have a single wall in brick or stone to add a touch of 'elegance'. Older properties are built of wooden weather-boards (often Kauri wood) with corrugated iron roofs (instantly identifiable from the noise when it rains!). In newer properties, as hardwood has become not both expensive and environmentally unfriendly, the construction is usually a timber frame filled in by plywood panels sprayed with fibre cement and painted to give the impression of rendered brickwork. Modern roofs tend to be made of textured steel or concrete tiles rather than corrugated iron.

Although many new arrivals from Europe regard New Zealand home construction as 'flimsy', the materials used are adequate for the climate. An advantage of this type of construction is that there's a significant cost saving over brick and stone properties, and repair and maintenance costs are also lower. In addition, New Zealand is officially situated within an earthquake belt (it has been affectionately dubbed the 'shaky isles' or 'quakey isles'), where 'flimsier' construction has the benefit of being more flexible in the event of a quake, easier to repair, and also less likely to cause you serious injury if it comes tumbling down around your ears! (Earthquakes, or rather tremors, are fairly frequent throughout New Zealand, although most are too minor to be noticed and on average a serious earthquake happens only once every 210 years!)

The design and layout of New Zealand properties is fairly standard throughout the country. A typical home has a hall, kitchen, living area, dining area (which may be combined with either the living area or kitchen), bathroom and three bedrooms. Unless you're buying an individual, architect-designed property (rare, except at the top end of the price range) the layout of the homes you inspect will be monotonously predictable – it often seems as if every house in New Zealand was built from the same set of plans! The homes will, however, be functional and quite spacious. New Zealand homes are, on average, a little smaller than American homes but roomier than properties in most of Europe.

Most homes, except for the oldest, unrenovated properties, are well equipped and fitted. Fitted kitchens with cupboards and built-in appliances are standard, and many newer properties also have a utility or laundry room. Newer properties are also likely to have a bathroom attached to the principal bedroom as well as a main bathroom (often known as a family bathroom). Bedrooms often have fitted furniture, and some homes also have walk-in wardrobes. Some modern builders proudly boast that all you need to bring with you when you move in is a lounge suite and a bed! If you find an older property that hasn't been renovated, it will be in stark contrast to a modern home: leaky tin roofs, gaps in the windows and even holes in the weather-boarding are fairly common. It's wise to tread warily if you're offered a house at a tempting price that's described as 'needing TLC' (tender loving care), which is usually a euphemism for a dump!

BUYING PROPERTY

Buying a house in New Zealand is usually a good investment and preferable to renting in the long term. Most New Zealanders prefer to own their homes, and as mortgage interest rates have fallen in recent years the demand for properties has risen and prices have increased steadily. Currently, prices are rising by an average of 7 per cent per year and the average time a home spends on the market is just 37 days!

It's important to note, however, that most New Zealanders buy a house to provide themselves with a home and not as an investment, and there's little speculative buying as there is in some countries. You shouldn't, therefore, expect to get rich quick when buying a home in New Zealand. It's true that in recent years there have been cases of shrewd entrepreneurs making a killing by snapping up derelict ocean-front properties for renovation or buying townhouses in the 'wrong' districts of Auckland or Wellington, which then became 'yuppified' so that properties rocketed in value. However, these conditions are rare, and you can as easily lose money as make it by speculating.

Non-residents can buy a property on less than an acre (4,047m^2) of land in New Zealand without any restrictions. For property exceeding one acre, permission is required from the District Land Registrar or the Land Value Tribunal. Permission isn't required if permanent residence has been granted, in which case you can buy as much of New Zealand as you can afford!

Estate Agents

When looking for a house to buy, you can choose between visiting local estate agents (known as real estate agents in New Zealand), looking for a private sale in small advertisements in local newspapers, and touring the area looking for 'For Sale' signs. The easiest option is to visit an estate agent (or a number). There are both 'family' estate agents and a number of large national chains, including Bayleys (🖳 www.bayleys.co.nz) and Harcourts (🖳 www.harcourts.co.nz). If you wish to see what's available before you arrive in New Zealand, you can visit many agents' websites. The Real Estate Institute of New Zealand includes on its website (🖳 www.reinz.org.nz) details from a number of agents in the different parts of the country. The larger estate agencies also publish property newspapers or magazines advertising properties for sale. For example, Harcourts publish a 'Blue Book' series, which you can purchase in a number of countries or download from their website (see above).

All estate agents in New Zealand must be licensed and registered with the Real Estate Agents Licensing Board. You can check by contacting them at PO Box 1247, Wellington (☎ 04-520 6949). Don't deal with anyone who isn't registered, because if they cannot meet the standards for registration it's unlikely that they will abide by any other standards either. However, the fact that an agent is licensed shouldn't be taken as a guarantee that he's reputable. It's illegal for an estate agent to deliberately mislead you, but as in other countries, there are lots of little tricks of the trade which are perfectly legal, such as exaggerating the desirability of the local area or suggesting that other people are clamouring to buy a house that has been up for sale for months.

In New Zealand, estate agents' fees are entirely the responsibility of the vendor, and the buyer doesn't pay anything (although of course the fees are in effect 'built in' to the price of the property). This underlines the fact that the agent is working for the seller, not for you, so you cannot expect him to do you any favours. (In fact, most estate agents are working for themselves – i.e. trying to earn as much money as possible!)

Before visiting an agent, try to get an idea of the kind of property you're looking for (e.g. a house or an apartment), the price you can afford to pay and where you wish to live. The agent should then be able to give you a list of properties which fit that description. You should avoid the temptation to look at properties which are outside the areas you've chosen or which cost more than you can afford (agents will *always* send you details of properties outside your stated price range!). If a property you view seems suitable, you will be pressed to make a decision quickly (see **Purchase Contracts** on page 90).

When you see a property you like, don't hesitate to haggle over the price, which is standard practice, even when the seller or an agent suggests the price is firm or gives the impression that other buyers are keen to snap up a bargain. Usually, an offer of between 3 and 8 per cent under the asking price is 'acceptable', but there's nothing to say you cannot offer less if you think the price is too high or the vendor is anxious to sell. To get an idea of whether asking prices are realistic, you can check with Valuation NZ, a government agency that publishes monthly tables of likely minimum, maximum and average property prices on a region-by-region basis. Some estate agents also publish regular surveys and reports on the state of the New Zealand property market and current prices. For information contact the Real Estate Institute of New Zealand (🖳 www.reinz.org.nz).

When looking at estate agents' details, you will find a number of obscure terms and incomprehensible abbreviations, which the following list may help you to decipher:

Term	Meaning
B+T	Built from brick with a tiled roof
Bach	A holiday home (North Island)
Back section	A property built behind another with no road frontage
Brs	Bedrooms
Corr	Corrugated iron roof
Crib	A holiday home (South Island)
Dbrs	Double bedrooms
Ens	En suite bathroom
Rumpus room	Playroom
Sleepout	A garden room, similar in concept to a conservatory
TLC	Tender loving care required (estate agent-speak for derelict!)
T/H	Townhouse
Villa	Usually an older house, made of wood with a corrugated iron roof
Whiteware	Domestic appliances – often included in the price of new homes or offered for sale at a separate price in older houses
Section	A plot with a house or to build on
X-lease	Cross lease, i.e. a home built on part of a section (usually half) – see **Conveyance** on page 90
X-leasable	A section which could be divided and partly sold or leased for another property

Auctions

A small proportion of domestic properties in New Zealand (around 5 per cent) are offered for sale at public auction. These are usually properties whose value isn't easily determined, such as unique luxury properties and those requiring major renovation. Properties repossessed from those who've failed to meet their mortgage repayments are also sold by auction. If you have an eye for a bargain or enjoy the thrill of the auction room, you may wish to consider buying a property at auction. Before doing so you should:

● ascertain the true market value of the property. The best way to do this is to check on the selling prices of similar properties in the immediate area.

● pre-arrange your finance. You will probably be expected to pay a 10 per cent deposit as soon as your bid is successful and sign a contract within a day or two (if not immediately).

● inspect the property thoroughly. Never buy unseen no matter how low the price. If it seems too good to be true, it probably is!

If the property seems genuine, you could consider making a pre-auction bid of around 30 per cent less than its market value. Prices fetched at auction are notoriously unreliable, and sellers who are 'jittery' may (legally) agree to a deal before the auction, in which case you could have yourself a bargain!

Cost

In general, property prices in New Zealand are slightly lower than in Europe because of its small population (i.e. relatively low demand), low cost of land and generally low construction costs. There is, however, a huge gulf between Auckland and the rest of the country. Property is much more expensive in Auckland, mainly because most of the best paid jobs are to be found there. Auckland also has one of the best climates in New Zealand, and prices are further increased because a majority of immigrants make Auckland their first choice. Wellington is the country's second most expensive area for property purchase. Price variations are much less marked throughout the rest of the country, although the rural property market is also booming and average prices in rural areas have risen by around 14 per cent annually during the last few years. Figures from the Real Estate Institute of New Zealand show that the average price for a three-bedroom detached house is currently around $110,000 in Otago, $140,000 in Canterbury, $160,000 in Northland, $195,000 in Wellington and almost $260,000 in Auckland. The national average is around $180,000. Apartments are often as expensive as houses and townhouses (or even more so), as they're invariably located in city centres, whereas most houses are in suburbs or in the country. Advertised prices are usually around 3 to 8 per cent above a property's true market value and substantially above its rateable value (see **Property Taxes** on page 235).

When calculating your budget, you should also allow for lawyer's fees (see **Conveyance** on page 90) and bear in mind that banks charge a mortgage processing fee equal to 1 per cent of the mortgage amount and require a deposit (usually $500 minimum) on application.

Lifestyle Plots

The term 'lifestyle plot' or 'block' refers to a kind of smallholding – a large plot of (often) undeveloped land, usually in the country. Buyers of lifestyle plots tend to be independent, rustic types who yearn for a more rural way of life. They often build their own home on the plot (or have one built) and may keep horses or ponies or a few farm animals in addition to growing their own vegetables. Lifestyle plots are available in many areas and are usually temptingly cheap. When buying a lifestyle plot, the main points to check are that mains services are available nearby and the cost of connecting them, and that the land is suitable for agricultural purposes, e.g. the quality of the soil and whether water is available for irrigation. If you plan to keep animals, good fencing (preferably post and rail) should be included, as the cost of fencing a large plot can be high. Finally, you should check any development plans for the area, as there have been a number of cases where buyers planning a life of seclusion have found some years later that their plot adjoins an industrial park or is divided by a main road. You can expect to pay around $190,00 for a small lifestyle plot (around 5 acres/2ha) or up to $500,000 if it's within commuting distance of Auckland (the practice of working in Auckland and commuting to a 'farm' in the country has become popular in the last few years).

Buying Off Plan or Without Land

Buying 'off plan' means buying a property hasn't yet been built, which involves certain risks (as in other countries). The practice is becoming more common in New Zealand, but you should always check the procedure with a lawyer. (See also **Renovation, Restoration & Building** on page 92.)

One practice that's rare outside Australia and New Zealand is that of buying a house without land. In some cases, where developers have purchased a quarter-acre plot complete with a house, they will remove the house and put it up for sale without land. All you need to do is find yourself a plot and have your new home delivered to the site and installed there. This method of buying a house is much less common than it used to be, but it's still used and can be a way of buying a home cheaply. The main points to be aware of are not to buy a house until you have somewhere to site it, and to make sure that your plot has services (e.g. water and electricity) available. Also confirm the cost of moving the house and reinstalling it, which may exceed the cost of the house itself! The job needs to be done by specialist builders and hauliers who will literally cut the house into two or three sections and move it to your plot.

Choosing The Location

As when buying a property in any country, its location is an important factor in determining not only its value but how pleasant a home it will make. The most popular areas of New Zealand are the major cities of Auckland (particularly), Wellington and Christchurch, mainly because the vast majority of people live and work in these cities. Popular regions for retirement and second homes on North Island include the Coromandel Peninsula, the Bay of Islands, the Bay of Plenty and the Kapati Coast (north of Wellington). In South Island, the Southern Alps, the Glaciers, Mount Cook, Milford Sound and the northern Marlborough region (e.g. Blenheim,

Nelson and Picton, which are close to the inter-island ferry terminal) are all popular, as is Banks Peninsula south of Christchurch.

It's important, of course, not to allow the desirability of the area to cloud your judgement, but rather choose a property in an area that's well suited to your needs. Some points you may wish to consider are:

City or Country? Few places in New Zealand, except for central Auckland and Wellington, have a big city feel. On the other hand, there's a considerable difference between living in a town and living in a rural (and often remote) area. You may like the idea of living in seclusion in the country, but does the idea of hardly ever seeing anyone (except, occasionally, the postman) really appeal to you?

Accessibility: Most New Zealanders drive to work, as there are few commuter trains and no underground railways. Therefore, unless you plan to live close to a bus route, you will need to check the road links to your place of work. There aren't many multi-lane motorways in New Zealand, so journey times can be higher than you may expect.

Ethnic Areas: As in other countries, people of particular ethnic groups tend to prefer to live in the same area. Therefore, you will find some areas, particularly in the suburbs of Auckland, predominantly occupied by ethnic groups.

Climate. Broadly speaking, North Island is milder (the northern tip of the island can seem quite tropical), particularly in summer, while South Island is chillier and can be quite cold in winter. Rainfall varies only slightly across the country, except that in South Island it's more likely to fall as snow in winter.

Position: New Zealanders tend to place a great deal of importance on the position and orientation of their homes. Properties in positions that catch the sun usually sell at a premium over those in shady spots because they tend to be not only brighter but also warmer in winter. In Wellington, for example, any property that is sheltered from the wind and isn't forever in the shadows cast by the surrounding hills is likely to be worth significantly more and will also be more pleasant to live in. Also bear in mind that many areas of New Zealand, particularly in North Island, are susceptible to flash floods after torrential rain. It's therefore wise to avoid properties located near rivers and streams (which can quickly become raging torrents after heavy rain) or situated in hollows.

Schools: The availability of good local schooling is a major preoccupation of parents, and many families have even moved house to be close to the best state schools. Even if you don't have children, you will pay a premium for a property that's within walking distance of a school with a good reputation. You can, of course, buy a home in an inexpensive area and send your children to a school in a more up-market area, particularly since school catchment areas have been scrapped (previously, state schools had to draw their pupils from the surrounding area).

Services: It's important to check the local services in an area, particularly if you don't plan to drive. With the expansion of supermarkets, many areas don't have many (or any) local shops and you should also bear in mind that doctors don't usually make house calls in New Zealand. In rural areas, the nearest shop may be half an hour's drive away (or more) and even many city suburbs have been designed for those with cars.

Leisure Facilities: Wherever you live in New Zealand, you won't be far from various kinds of leisure facility, but not necessarily the kind that you enjoy. If you like dining out and cultural activities, you need to be located in a large town or you may be disappointed by the choice available locally. Keen 'yachties' and other water sports enthusiasts will find the slightly warmer waters in the north more to their taste, while South Island is favoured by skiers and hikers.

Parking: Although inner city apartment living has become fashionable in recent years, such properties rarely have much (or any) secure parking, an important consideration if you own a car. Even if you don't own a car and therefore don't require a parking space, you may find that the lack of parking will deter visitors if they cannot park nearby.

Crime: Overall, New Zealand has a low crime rate compared with many other countries, although some inner city suburbs have high rates of burglary, car theft, gang troubles, muggings and even shootings. On the other hand, most rural areas have very little crime, and a car break-in may make headline news.

Conveyance

Transferring the ownership of property (conveyance) is relatively straightforward in New Zealand, as it's easy to establish whether the title to a property is clear (i.e. there are no debts). As a result, it isn't mandatory to use a lawyer to do your conveyance, although given the thousand-and-one other things to be done when buying a house it's unlikely you would want to do it yourself. Conveyance by a lawyer, who is the only professional permitted to charge for conveyance, normally costs between $600 and $2,000. The fee may include the land transfer registration fee of $128. There's no fixed scale of conveyance charges, as this was abolished in 1984, so it's worth shopping around and haggling over the cost. It's possible to find a lawyer who will do the job for as little as $400.

Once you've instructed your solicitor to act on your behalf in a property purchase, his main task will be to conduct a title search, i.e. to established that the person selling the property is in fact entitled to sell it. This is usually carried out swiftly (the Department of Survey and Land Information is extremely efficient) and it's rare to discover hidden horrors in New Zealand, such as dozens of relatives laying claim to a property. One peculiarly local concept in property purchase is cross leasing (also known as X-leasing). This usually applies in a situation where the previous owner of a section has leased part of it for the construction of another home (e.g. the one you're planning to buy). In this case your ownership of the land is leasehold rather than freehold, usually for the balance of a period such as 100 years, at a nominal rent. To all intents and purposes your title to an X-leased section is as secure as freehold. Your lawyer will explain if there are any particular conditions of which you need to be aware.

You should also ask your lawyer to obtain a Land Information Memorandum (LIM) report from the local council, which describes the title of the land, outlines the official boundaries and buildings, changes allowed to these buildings and flood risks. This useful document (particularly for future reference) can cost anything from $2 to $1,500 depending on the property and the details included, so you should check the cost in advance.

Purchase Contracts

When you find a house you wish to buy, you need to make a formal offer in writing, and most estate agents have a standard form for this purpose. Note that a formal offer has to be made even if you wish to pay the advertised price. The offer is conditional and conditions may include the approval of finance (e.g. a mortgage), a satisfactory independent valuation, a satisfactory title search, the sale of another home, etc. Unless you've agreed to pay the asking price, there then follows a bargaining process which concludes when both parties have agreed a price for the property. As soon as you agree the price, you must sign a sales contract, which commits you to go through with the purchase. There are usually exclusions to this commitment (e.g. you aren't obliged to go ahead with the purchase if you find out that a new road is about to be built through the living room), but you cannot back out because you decide that you don't like the house or cannot afford it, unless you pay compensation. You also cannot subsequently reduce the price you've agreed to pay.

Many estate agents try to insist that purchasers sign a contract as soon as a sale is agreed, i.e. the day you view the property and say that you want it. **However, you shouldn't sign a contract before taking legal advice and confirming that the title is clear.** If you feel obliged to sign a contract before the conveyance checks are complete, you should ask your lawyer to insert a clause in the contract to the effect that the contract is null and void if any problems arise. However, there's no legal requirement to sign a contract immediately, provided it's done within a reasonable time, so don't allow yourself to be pressured into signing. It's usually better to pass up a property if, for example, the agent says that another party is keen to sign (which may in any case be a bluff), rather than buy a property that you aren't really sure about. The advantage of this system is that the seller cannot accept a higher offer after he has signed a contract with you, although most estate agents will try to push up the price to the highest possible level before pressing the highest bidder to sign a contract.

A deposit of 10 per cent is required when a sales contract is signed. This is usually non-refundable, but most contracts include a clause requiring its return if the title to the property isn't clear or the land is subject to government requisition (compulsory purchase). When buying a property in New Zealand, it's the exception rather than the rule to have a structural survey carried out. The main exception is if you're borrowing more than 80 per cent of the value of the property, when the lender will usually insist that a survey and valuation is carried out to protect its interests.

Because the time between viewing a property and being required to sign a contract can be short, you should have your finances arranged before you start looking. Most banks will give you an 'in principal' decision on a mortgage before you've found a suitable property and issue you with a mortgage guarantee certificate. This allows you to make an offer in the knowledge that, assuming the property is in order and your financial circumstances haven't changed, you will be lent the money to buy the property.

Property Income

In general there are no legal restrictions on letting a property. It's worth noting, however, that with such a large proportion of the population owning their own holiday homes and such a large number of hotels, motels, guest houses and campsites, there isn't a particularly buoyant market for rented property in New Zealand, and the limited demand is largely seasonal (i.e. during the summer in North Island and the winter in South Island), so you shouldn't expect to make a killing by letting a property.

RENOVATION, RESTORATION & BUILDING

Property renovation and restoration is a major pastime in New Zealand, where tens of thousands of people spend their evenings and weekends rebuilding, extending or redecorating their home (when they've finished rebuilding, extending or redecorating their holiday home, that is!). It may be something you wish to consider – there are plenty of older properties in need of renovation in New Zealand, and they're often offered at tempting prices.

It isn't particularly expensive to renovate a property in New Zealand, as the basic materials (weather-boarding and corrugated iron) are plentiful and cheap. The main difficulty is likely to be finding somebody who will do the renovation for you. As most New Zealanders are avid 'DIYers', there's a shortage of people to do odd jobs and small property repairs. On the other hand, if you're keen on DIY yourself, it could be the ideal solution. However, you should note that property in need of renovation is sometimes in a serious state of decline, with a rotten wooden frame or weather-boarding and a leaking tin roof. **Therefore, even if you intend to do much of the work yourself, you should take advice from a surveyor or builder as to whether a house is worth saving before committing yourself to a purchase.** Don't, whatever you do, believe an agent who says that a property will 'make a charming home with a little work'. Also bear in mind that you're unlikely to make a profit if you decide to sell a property you've renovated, but you could make a substantial loss, as it's easy to spend more than you could ever hope to recoup in 'added value'.

Any new building or significant addition to an existing building must comply with town planning regulations. Consent for the work can be obtained from your local council, who will send a building inspector to advise you on what you can and cannot do and monitor the works. If you intend buying an older building, you should check

that it isn't registered with the Historic Places Trust, as extensions and renovations to such properties are strictly controlled. Even many timber buildings which appear to have little or no historical interest are protected in this way, as they're considered part of New Zealand's heritage.

If you decide to build a house or renovate or extend an existing one, you should hire a builder who's a member of the Master Builders Federation (☎ 07-856 6660, 💻 www.buildonline.co.nz). The MBF operates a Master Builders' Five Year Guarantee Scheme, which does what it says: guarantees the work and materials for five years. The MBF website includes magazine features as well as tips and advice for anyone thinking of building a home. The New Zealand Certified Builders Association also guarantees that its members are qualified builders (☎ freephone 0800-222 845, 💻 www.certifiedbuilders.co.nz). Both associations strongly advise customers against paying any builder before work has been completed. According to the Institute of Valuers (💻 www.nziv.org.nz), the cost of building a house of average quality construction is around $950 per m².

SELLING PROPERTY

When it comes to selling a home in New Zealand, there's a choice between doing it yourself and engaging an estate agent to handle the sale for you. If you have an attractive house in a good area and it's in the average price band, you may get a fair bit of interest simply by planting a 'For Sale' sign in your garden. If, on the other hand, your property is tucked out of the way or is a highly individual or expensive home, an agent is probably the only realistic choice. Estate agents' charges have risen considerably in recent years and are higher than in many other developed countries, which leads many people to try to sell their own homes, although most are eventually forced to admit defeat and hand the job over to an agent.

There have been no fixed estate agent fees since the official 'Scale of Real Estate Agent's Commission' was abolished in 1985 and fees can vary between 2 and 4.5 per cent of the selling price of a property. It's wise to shop around agents and haggle over fees, as an agent who asks only 2 per cent may do just as good (or bad) a job as one who demands 4.5. It's common practice among New Zealand property sellers to add the agent's commission to the house value before fixing the asking price. It isn't unusual for a seller to put his property in the hands of several agents (a 'non-exclusive contract'), the commission going to the agent who finds the eventual buyer. Take care, however, that your agreement with each agent permits this (it usually does) and that an agent doesn't expect to be paid commission even if he doesn't sell the property. Agents also normally charge a higher percentage for a non-exclusive contract than an exclusive agreement.

RENTED ACCOMMODATION

You may wish to rent a property when you first arrive in New Zealand to give yourself time to look for a home to buy. Rental property of all sizes and descriptions is readily available in New Zealand, although only some 25 per cent of property is rented (including just 10 per cent of new properties). However, in recent years there's been a marked tendency among New Zealand households to rent rather than buy, particularly in Auckland (which accounts for nearly 40 per cent of the rental market), where rented properties can be in short supply. Rented property in towns and cities consists mainly of apartments and flats, although houses are available to rent. Unless an newspaper advertisement specifically states that a property is a house or cottage, you should assume that it's an apartment or flat. Two-bedroom apartments are the most highly sought-after property in the main towns and cities.

Finding a Rented Property: You can find property for rent through rental agencies, estate agencies, which sometimes handle rentals, and by looking at small advertisements in local newspapers. If you see anything advertised in a newspaper, you should arrange to view it straight away, as the best properties are snapped up quickly. Suffice to say, you should never rent anything without viewing it first. New Zealand landlords and agents are notoriously inventive in their descriptions (although legislation has been introduced to try to curb this) and they can make the shabbiest, most tumbledown 'villa' sound like the poshest place in town. Note that if you use an agency or estate agent to find a rental property, he will usually charge at least one week's rent as commission.

It's possible to arrange to rent a house or flat before you arrive in New Zealand, and several immigration consultants (and even some travel agencies) can arrange rentals for you. Bear in mind that properties obtained through these sources are often more expensive than those obtained locally. Another drawback of renting from abroad is that it's difficult to picture a property accurately from thousands of miles away and the location may prove to be inconvenient (although it may look ideal on a map).

Rental Costs: The main divide in rental costs is between Auckland and Wellington on the one hand and the rest of the country and the other. In these two cities you will pay significantly more to rent a property, particularly in the better areas. There's not a great deal of difference elsewhere and the national average rent of $190 per week has remained unchanged over the last two years. Apart from location, the size and facilities of a property are the main factors affecting the rent. Typical rental costs for a two-bedroom unfurnished apartment range from $135 per week in cheaper areas, such as Dunedina and Rotorua, to $250 per week in central Auckland and Wellington. The weekly rent for a three-bedroom unfurnished apartment ranges from $170 in Dunedin to $325 in central Auckland. Anything with a sea view will cost up to 50 per cent more, particularly in Auckland (there are lots of glorious views in New Zealand, but sea views are the only ones for which landlords charge extra). Basic properties are at a premium in any town with a university and may actually cost more than a good quality property elsewhere.

Most landlords prefer to let their properties for at least 12 months at a time and some won't let for less than this period; those who do tend to charge a higher rent, particularly for lets of less than six months. If you find a rental property through an estate agent or rental agency, you must usually pay a fee equal to one week's rent.

Tenancy Agreements: When renting property in New Zealand, it's usual to sign a tenancy agreement, although the Ministry of Housing issues a standard agreement for landlords and tenants. If your landlord uses this agreement and you're happy with the details, it isn't usually necessary to have it checked by a lawyer, as the terms and conditions are simple and written in non-legal language (other countries please take note!). Most tenancy agreements are on a periodic basis, which means that the tenancy continues indefinitely until either party gives notice. A tenant is required to give 21 days' notice to end a tenancy, but a landlord must give 90 days', except in exceptional circumstances, such as when he wishes to move into the property himself (in which case he need give 42 days notice only). It's also possible to have a tenancy agreement for a fixed period, in which case the tenancy lasts for the period agreed at the outset only, although it can be extended by mutual agreement.

When you take up a tenancy, you must pay a bond to the landlord, which is usually the equivalent of one or two weeks' rent, although legally it can be up to four weeks. The bond isn't held by the landlord but by the Bond Processing Unit of the Tenancy Services Department (Ministry of Housing) and the landlord must give your bond to the Unit within 23 working days of receiving it. At the end of the tenancy, the Bond Processing Unit refunds your bond less the cost of any damage (for which you're responsible under the standard tenancy agreement). Rent is usually paid fortnightly. The landlord must pay rates and home insurance, although your belongings may not be covered under the landlord's policy and you may need to take out separate insurance for these (see page 212).

If you have a dispute with your landlord, the Tenancy Services Department will advise you on your rights and responsibilities and help resolve the problem. The biggest causes of disputes in rented property, apart from tenants' failure to pay the rent on time, are landlords who don't maintain their premises (although they're legally required to) and neighbours (who may also be the same landlord's tenants) in, for example, an apartment block or units.

Inventory: Although you can find both furnished and unfurnished rental properties in New Zealand, the majority are offered on an unfurnished basis. However, kitchen appliances such as a stove, refrigerator and washing machine are usually included, and many bedrooms have fitted or walk-in wardrobes, so you will often find that you don't need a great deal of furniture. Whatever is provided with a house or apartment, it's important to obtain an inventory and check that everything listed in the inventory is actually provided. If appliances are included, check that they work properly and report any faults to the landlord immediately. If you don't, you may find that you're held responsible at the end of the lease. If you rent an unfurnished property and have no furniture, it's possible to rent furniture for between $260 to $420 per month for an average size house.

Public Housing: Public housing isn't the responsibility of the local council in New Zealand, where it's provided by the Housing Corporation, which builds and lets homes mainly to those on low incomes. Public housing comprises around a quarter of rented homes (less than 6 per cent of residential properties).

MOVING HOUSE

Once you've found a home, permanent or temporary, you can begin to consider the question of moving your possessions to New Zealand. This should be planned well in advance, as it can take anything from six weeks to six months (if moving from Europe or North America) depending on the efficiency of your shipping company and allowing for customs clearances. It's usually best to plan to arrive in New Zealand before your possessions, which will give you time to find a home and avoid storage costs. It also makes customs clearance easier if you're on the spot when your shipment arrives, which is essential if you haven't engaged someone to do this for you.

Although it's possible to ship every last possession to New Zealand, you should consider whether it's really worth the effort and expense, given that there's little that cannot be bought locally. It's generally unwise to ship bulky items of furniture and large domestic appliances, which may not even work in New Zealand (see **Electricity** on page 96). On the other hand, it's probably worthwhile taking all your clothes and personal items, together with larger items of great value or to which you're particularly attached.

Shipping the entire contents of a three-bedroom house from Europe or North America to New Zealand costs at least GB£6,000/US$9,000. Many companies offer international removals, although you should choose a company that specialises in shipping to New Zealand. Some companies will also pack your belongings in your home country and unpack them in New Zealand, which is naturally more expensive than doing it yourself, but saves a lot of hassle if you can afford it.

It's also important to make sure that your possessions are insured, the cost of which won't usually be included in the removal quote. The cost is likely to be up to 2 per cent of their value. If you have anything that's particularly valuable (such as antiques) you should agree an insurance value separately with the insurance company, rather than accept the 'guesstimate' which they usually make based on the likely value of the contents of an average house.

Make a complete list of everything to be moved and give a copy to the removal company.

Don't include anything that's illegal or restricted. As well as the usual items such as guns and explosives, bear in mind that New Zealand customs are particularly sensitive about the import of anything with plant or animal origins (see **Customs** on page 74). This includes not only live plants and animals, but things such as seeds, bulbs, furs and wicker goods, and even lawn mowers and golf clubs! Although you can sometimes import these, it makes it simpler if you leave them out of your shipment entirely. When packing your possessions, take care not to use any packing which is made from, or includes, plant products (such as straw). If you're travelling from Europe or North America also bear in mind that your shipment must pass through the tropics on its way to New Zealand, so packing things in plastic is to be avoided, as it will cause condensation to build up as your belongings sail through 95 per cent humidity and may lead to mildew.

UTILITIES

Electricity

The electricity supply in New Zealand is mostly generated by hydroelectric power plants (so conservationists can consume energy to their heart's content). The energy market in New Zealand is now completely privatised and most major areas have at least two electricity suppliers, so it's worth shopping around. The main companies are Mercury, Contact Energy, Genersis, Meridian Energy, OnPower and TrustPower. The supply is usually reliable, despite the catastrophic and well publicised cable failures in Auckland in early 1998, which left the centre of the city without full power for several weeks!

Connection & Payment: To have the electricity supply connected (or the bill transferred to your name when moving into a new home), simply call a local electricity company on the number shown in the telephone directory. Connection charges are around $35, although if the electricity hasn't been cut off you won't be charged. You may need to pay a bond, which can be $225 if you don't meet the company's credit criteria, $100 if you rent a property, or free if you own it. You will be billed every two months (most people pay by direct debit from a bank account). The typical bill for an average house is around $200 for two months (rates have been falling in recent years, although there was an 8 per cent rise in late 2001).

Power Rating: The mains current in New Zealand is 230 volts AC and appliances from countries with a 220V or 240V system (e.g. the UK and Europe) usually work. However, electrical equipment rated at 110V (for example, from the USA) requires a converter or transformer to convert it to 230V, although some electrical appliances (e.g. electric razors and hair dryers) are fitted with a 110/220V switch. Check for the switch, which may be located inside the casing, and make sure it's switched to 220V *before* connecting it to the power supply. Converters can be used for heating appliances but transformers, which are available from most electrical retailers, are required for motorised appliances (they can also be purchased second-hand). Add the wattage of the devices you intend to connect to a transformer and make sure its power rating *exceeds* the total.

Generally, all small, high-wattage, electrical appliances such as kettles, toasters, heaters and irons need large transformers. Motors in large appliances, such as cookers, refrigerators, washing machines, dryers and dishwashers, will need replacing or fitting with a large transformer. In most cases it's simpler to buy new appliances in New Zealand, which are of good quality and reasonably priced. Note also that the dimensions of New Zealand cookers, microwave ovens, refrigerators, washing machines, dryers and dishwashers differ from those in some other countries. If you wish to buy electrical appliances, such as a cooker or refrigerator, you should shop around, as prices vary considerably (choose those that have a high energy efficiency rating, which are cheaper to run) – see **Household Goods** on page 287. You shouldn't bring a TV or video recorder from any country other than Australia, as they probably won't work because of the different transmission system in use in New Zealand (see **Buying TVs & Videos** on page 127).

Frequency Rating: A problem with some electrical equipment is the frequency rating, which in some countries, e.g. the USA, is designed to run at 60Hz and not New Zealand's 50Hz. Electrical equipment *without* a motor is generally unaffected by the drop in frequency (except TVs). Equipment with a motor may run with a 20 per cent drop in speed, but automatic washing machines, cookers, electric clocks, record players and tape recorders are unusable in New Zealand if they aren't designed for 50Hz operation. To find out, look at the label on the back of the equipment. If it says 50/60Hz, it should work. If it says 60Hz, you may try it anyway, **but first ensure the voltage is correct as outlined above.** If the equipment runs too slowly, seek advice from the manufacturer or the retailer. For example, you may be able to obtain a special pulley for a tape deck or turntable to compensate for the drop in speed. Bear in mind that the transformers and motors of electrical devices designed to run at 60Hz will run hotter at 50Hz, so make sure that equipment has sufficient space around it for cooling.

Fuses: Most apartments and all houses have their own fuse boxes, which are usually of the circuit-breaker or 'trip' type in modern homes. When a circuit is overloaded, the circuit-breaker trips to the OFF position. When replacing or repairing fuses of any kind, if the same fuse continues to blow or trip, contact an electrician and **never fit a fuse of a higher rating than specified, even as a temporary measure.** When replacing fuses, don't rely on the blown fuse as a guide, as it may have been wrong. If you use an electric lawn mower or power tools outside your home or in your garage, you should have a Residual Current Device (RCD) installed. This can detect current changes of as little as a thousandth of an amp and in the event of a fault (or the cable being cut), will switch off the power in around 0.04 seconds.

Plugs: Unless you've come from Australia, your plugs will require changing or a lot of expensive adapters will be required. New Zealand (and Australian) plugs have three pins: two diagonally slanting flat pins above one straight (earth) pin, which are unique to these two countries. Plugs aren't fused. Most appliances purchased new in New Zealand, as in most other countries, are already fitted with plugs. Some electrical appliances are earthed and have a three-core flex – you must *never* use a two-pin plug with a three-core flex. **Always make sure that a plug is correctly and securely wired, as bad wiring can be fatal.** Note that for maximum safety, electrical appliances should be turned off at the main wall point when not in use.

Bulbs: Electric light bulbs in New Zealand are of either the Edison screw or the bayonet type. Low-energy light bulbs are also available and are more expensive than ordinary bulbs, although they save money by their longer life and reduced energy consumption. Bulbs for non-standard electrical appliances (i.e. appliances not made for the New Zealand market) such as refrigerators, lamps and sewing machines, may not be available in New Zealand (so bring extras with you). Plug adapters for imported lamps and other electrical items can be difficult to find in New Zealand, so you should bring a number of adapters and extension cords with you, which can be fitted with local plugs.

Rewiring: It's illegal in New Zealand for individuals to do anything more than the most basic electrical work in their homes, e.g. rewiring a plug or changing a light bulb. Anything else, such as rewiring or fitting a new socket, must be done by a qualified electrician.

Gas

Mains gas is available in most cities, towns and villages in North Island, with the exception of a few remote corners, but in South Island it's available only in Christchurch and Dunedin. As with electricity, it's supplied by local companies, which can be found in your telephone directory. Gas is popular for cooking (it costs less than electricity) in New Zealand, although it's less commonly used to provide heating and hot water (gas heaters are, however, becoming more popular). Note that there may be no gas supply in older homes, and modern properties may also be all-electric. If you're looking to rent a property and want to cook by gas, make sure it already has a gas supply (some houses have an unused gas service pipe). In country areas without mains gas, you can buy appliances that operate on bottled gas. On payment of a deposit for the bottle and regulator, a local supplier will provide you with gas bottles and replace them when they're empty. Large users can also have a storage tank installed and have gas delivered by tanker. If you need to purchase gas appliances, such as a cooker or fire, you should shop around, as prices vary considerably.

If you buy a home without a gas supply, you can usually arrange with a local gas company to install a line between your home and a nearby gas main (provided there's one within a reasonable distance; otherwise the cost will be prohibitive). If a home already has a gas supply, simply contact a local gas company to have it reconnected or transferred to your name (there's a connection charge of around $35). A security deposit (e.g. $100) is usually payable if you're renting. You must contact your gas company to obtain a final reading when vacating a property. In areas where mains gas is unavailable, some properties are plumbed for bottled gas. A 45kg bottle costs around $140 per year to rent and around $55 for each refill, although prices are higher in rural areas. Alternatively, you can buy 9kg gas bottles and refill them at most petrol stations for around $15 to $20.

Gas central heating boilers, water heaters and fires should be checked annually. Ask for a quotation for any work in advance and check the identity of anyone claiming to be a gas company employee (or any kind of 'serviceman') by asking to see an identity card and checking with his office. **Bear in mind that gas installations and appliances can leak and cause explosions or kill you while you sleep.** If you suspect a gas leak, first check to see if a gas tap has been left on or a pilot light has gone out. If not, there's probably a leak, either in your home or in a nearby gas pipeline. **Ring your local gas company immediately and vacate your home as quickly as possible.** Gas leaks are extremely rare and explosions caused by leaks even rarer (although often spectacular and therefore widely reported). Nevertheless, it pays to be careful. You can buy an electric-powered gas detector which activates an alarm when a gas leak is detected. Special controls can be fitted to many appliances to make them easier to use by the disabled and the blind or partially sighted (studded or Braille controls).

Water

Most of New Zealand usually has an abundant supply of water (see **Climate** on page 294). Over the last few years some north-western parts of North Island have suffered a relative drought, although this is rare. Mains water is available everywhere except in the most remote areas (where it sometimes shoots up in boiling form directly out of the ground!). All tap water is drinkable, although it's heavily chlorinated in towns (as in many other countries). Water is supplied and billed by a local water company, which may be a division of your local council. Usually, you pay an annual water rate, which is set according to the size and value of your property. In most areas, water rates are included in local property taxes (see page 235), but in some areas water is billed separately (e.g. in Auckland most households pay more than $800 per year). In some areas, properties (generally newer homes) have a water meter and you're charged according to use. Usually, it's cheaper to pay for your water on the rated system, although modest users living in large properties will find it cheaper to have a meter fitted. Mains drainage is found throughout New Zealand with the exception of remote rural areas, where properties usually have a septic tank.

HEATING & AIR-CONDITIONING

Although the weather in New Zealand is generally mild in summer , you shouldn't assume that you won't need heating at other times of the year. There are few areas of New Zealand where you won't need effective heating and good insulation (older properties aren't usually well insulated). Only a few areas, such as Northland (the northernmost tip of North Island), are warm enough to manage without good heating all year round, although you may want an air-conditioning system instead. Most newer homes (and many older homes) have central heating systems, consisting of heated water systems or ducted air. These are powered by electricity or mains or bottled gas and often double as air-conditioning in summer. Many homes also have a fireplace, as much for show as for effect. Older properties often have free-standing electric or gas heaters rather than a central heating system.

Older properties may have a wood burner, which is essentially a stove that heats the room but also provides hot water. Note, however, that although it's attractive, a wood burner requires a good deal of care and attention, and wood is relatively expensive.

6.

POST OFFICE SERVICES

The New Zealand Post Office (known as NZ Post) is a national institution and has a rich past, similar to the American 'Pony Express'; tales abound of how postmen in bygone days struggled through forests and mountains to ensure that the mail was delivered. Today the postal service remains a mainstay of New Zealand life, particularly for those living in remote regions. In addition to delivering (and collecting) letters and parcels, rural postmen deliver a variety of goods, including milk, newspapers, bread and even animals. They also offer a haulage service and, in some cases, carry passengers in their trucks and post buses to and from villages and isolated farms. In many ways, NZ Post lives in the past, and New Zealand is one of the few developed countries not to have a system of post (zip) codes, which makes life difficult for the poor New Zealand 'postie'. A lot of sorting is still done by hand, and postmen need to rely on their geographical and personal knowledge of who lives in their area. Nevertheless, the system is efficient enough, and NZ Post manages to deliver even poorly addressed letters on time (most of the time).

There are over 1,000 post offices throughout the country. Known as post shops, they're operated by NZ Post in major towns and cities. In small towns, post shops are run by private individuals, who also run another business (such as a grocery or dairy) and are paid either a salary or a commission by NZ Post. Some 80 per cent of New Zealand post shops are operated in this way. Post shops offer a friendly, personal service as well as providing a range of other goods and services such as bill payment (BillPay) and national lottery (Lotto) tickets, and acting as a focal point for the local community. Some post shops provide cheque cashing and deposit services (there's usually a sign indicating the services available). The spirit of private enterprise extends to rural postmen, who aren't NZ Post employees but self-employed individuals with a concession to deliver mail (they offer various other delivery and collection services to supplement their income).

Information about NZ Post services is available from post shops in a variety of leaflets, and also via Customer Service (☎ freephone 0800-501 501) or via NZ Post's (🖳 www.nzpost.co.nz), where there are numerous *Step by Step* guides to using the postal service.

New Zealand is one of the few countries in the world that allows private companies to compete with the nationalised postal service, and NZ Post encountered its first serious rival in 1998, when the Australian company Fastway launched a national private postal service, although their market share remains small.

General Information

Note the following general information regarding New Zealand postal services:

- As well as at post shops, stamps can be purchased from many shops.
- Post boxes are red and some are ornate cast-iron 'monuments' dating back to Victorian times. There are also special post boxes for FastPost in major cities and towns.
- When addressing mail, you should always state the name of the nearest large town, as there are several small places with the same name in New Zealand (and there are no post codes to distinguish between them). It isn't necessary to state which island your mail is intended for in your address, unless this is the main way of distinguishing between two towns with the same name. Take care when writing

Maori place names, as an extra letter added or dropped accidentally (or bad handwriting) can send your letter speeding off to entirely the wrong place, e.g. Whangara and Whangarei are 600km/370mi apart!

- The address for many isolated properties (usually farms) in New Zealand is often simply the name of the addressee, followed by RD (which stands for rural delivery) and a number (e.g. RD9), followed by the address of the nearest town. This form of address is adequate to ensure delivery of your mail, as the local postman will know everyone on his route.

- A postman is obliged to deliver your mail only as far as the roadside. If you have a long drive, you will need to provide a mailbox, which is usually fixed to a gate post or fence. There are specifications for mailboxes (information available from post shops), which must include a flag to indicate whether you have mail either for collection or for delivery. In rural areas the postman will collect your letters and parcels for posting when delivering mail.

- Many large mail users (i.e. businesses and government departments) have their mail delivered to a post office box (also called a private bag) at the main post shop in the town where they're located. This allows post to be collected from the box several times a day instead of delivered just once. If you're writing to a company with a PO box or private bag number, always use it even if you know the street address (which is intended for the use of visitors only).

- If you have reason to write to a government minister in New Zealand, all you need do is write his name, followed by 'Wellington' on the envelope and it will reach him. You don't even need to affix a stamp if posting your letter in New Zealand.

- When you're sending post overseas, be sure to mark it clearly with the country of destination, bearing in mind that many New Zealand places names are 'imported' from abroad. If you're sending a letter to Canterbury (UK), Canterbury (USA) or Canterbury (Australia), make sure the address makes this clear – if it doesn't, NZ Post will deliver it to Canterbury, New Zealand (where else?).

- NZ Post provides a mail redirection service and will redirect post to a new address within New Zealand or overseas for up to two months free of charge. Charges are made to extend the service for a further two, four, six or 12 months. If you wish to use this service, you must complete a *Change of Address Request* form available at most post shops. NZ Post also provides free pre-stamped change of address cards.

- A 'mail hold' service is available if you're planning to be away from your usual address for n extended period. Your local post shop will hold your mail for you until you return. If you wish to use this service, you must complete a *Mail Hold Request* form (of course).

- Philatelic products are available from NZ's Post Stamps Centre (60 Ridgway Street, Private Bag 3001, Wanganui, ▣ www.nzstamps.co.nz), which produces a bi-monthly *Focus On Line* magazine.

- The last posting dates for Christmas (for delivery by December 24th) for letters and parcels are displayed in post shops in October.

- Compensation is paid for loss or damage to mail (usually up to $250), plus reimbursement of postage for lost mail.

BUSINESS HOURS

Main post shops in towns and cities in New Zealand are usually open from 9am to 5pm, Mondays to Fridays, and are closed on Saturdays and Sundays. Post shop opening hours in small towns and villages vary considerably because they're usually privately operated, and opening hours aren't decided by NZ Post. Whatever the opening hours of the shop, you won't be able to obtain post shop services outside the 9am to 5pm period, and in some rural areas shops operate shorter hours or aren't open every day.

LETTER POST

There are two categories of domestic letter post in New Zealand, ordinary post (simply called Post) for non-urgent letters, which are usually delivered the next day within a city and in two to three working days to most other areas, and FastPost (air mail), which ensures delivery the next working day between major towns and cities. The cost of sending a letter weighing up to 1kg and measuring up to 5in x 9.25in (120mm x 235mm) within New Zealand is 40¢ (90¢ for larger envelopes) by Post and 80¢ ($1.20 for large envelopes) by FastPost, rising on a sliding scale according to weight. When using FastPost (air mail) you should affix a FastPost label or use one of the purpose made envelopes (with red and blue markings, as used for air mail in many other countries) and, where available, post letters in a FastPost post box.

International letters can be sent by AirPost (three to six days to Australia, six to twelve days to the UK, four to ten days to the USA) or EconomyPost (10 to 15 days to Australia and 15 to 20 days to the UK and the USA). Rates for a 20g AirPost letter are $1 to Australia, $1.50 to the USA and South Africa, and $1.80 to Europe. Postcards (which are sent by EconomyPost) and aerogrammes cost $1 to all destinations. CourierPost is can also be used for letters (see **Domestic Parcels** below).

REGISTERED POST

It isn't usually necessary to send mail by registered post unless it's valuable, as you can be fairly confident that ordinary mail will be delivered. However, NZ Post provides both recorded and registered post services. With recorded post, a signature is obtained on delivery and it's most suitable for important documents rather than valuable items (compensation is minimal if mail is lost). With registered post, you must use a pre-paid plastic envelope (available from post shops) sold in A5 ($7) and foolscap ($9.50) sizes, which have a weight limit of 1.5kg. With registered post you have the option to 'track and trace' your missive, and proof of delivery can be provided by e-mail, fax or post. There's an additional charge of $2.25 for Saturday or rural deliveries. Limited compensation is paid if registered post is lost or damaged. Note that registered post cannot be sent to a PO Box.

DOMESTIC PARCELS

Parcel deliveries in New Zealand are open to much wider competition than letter post. While NZ Post provides an efficient parcel delivery service, private operators are also allowed free access to the market. Therefore, while the easiest way to send a parcel may be to go to a post shop and send it by NZ Post, it may be faster to use a private courier firm as well as cheaper, particularly if you make frequent shipments. In some areas, post shops offer a choice of NZ Post and private couriers for parcel deliveries. Compensation of up to $250 is available for any lost or damaged parcels.

NZ Post's parcel service handles parcels up to 25kg (41in/1.05m in length and 98in/2.5m in length plus girth), which are charged at four rates depending on distance, as follows:

Distance	Delivery	Rate
Across town	Next day	$3
Short haul 150km/93mi within the same island)	1–2 days	$5.95 up to (up to 15kg $9.95 for 15–25kg
Within island (over 150km within the same island)	1–2 days	$7.95 up to 10kg plus $4.50 each additional 5kg
Between islands	2–3 days	$10.95 up to 5kg plus $9 for each additional 5kg

A nationwide parcel service is also available for parcels up to 2kg, which takes one to three days and costs $3.50 for parcels up to 1kg and $4.75 for parcels up to 2kg. NZ Post also provides a FastPost parcel service for parcels weighing up to 20kg. There are three rate bands (as for the standard service, but without the 'across town' rate), and charges range from $3 for a parcel weighing up to 500g short haul to a maximum of $34.40 for a parcel weighing 15 to 20kg between islands. Delivery is the next working day to most destinations, with the exception of some remote rural areas.

CourierPost is another NZ Post service for letters and parcels weighing up to 3kg. Delivery is guaranteed by 9am the next working day to local addresses, by noon the next day to residential addresses and within two days to rural addresses. The signature of the addressee can be collected for an additional $2.50. Compensation for loss or damage is provided up to $1,500 and additional insurance is available up to $50,000. CourierPost can be contacted on ☎ freephone 0800-268 7437 or via 🖳 www. courierpost.co.nz. Note that CourierPost no longer offers an international service

INTERNATIONAL MAIL

NZ Post provides four options for sending international mail: EMS, International Express, International Air and International Economy. In addition to NZ Post, a number of private companies (such as DHL and TNT) also offer fast (but expensive) courier services to many countries. Note that the pricing for parcels for international destinations is somewhat complex, as it increases in 10g increments; prices given below are a sample.

EMS International is an express mail service for urgent letters and documents to over 120 countries. It doesn't include parcels. It provides compensation of up to $250 for loss or damage, plus reimbursement of postage if lost. The maximum weight is 1kg and rates for sample rates for documents up to 500g are $15 to Australia, $31 to the UK and $33 to the USA. Documents weighing between 500g and 1kg cost $20 to Australia, $45.70 to the UK and $47 to the USA. Delivery times vary from one to ten days according to the destination.

International Express is for letters and parcels weighing up to 1kg. Delivery times vary from one to six days according to the destination. Compensation of up to $2,000 is paid for loss or damage (or up to $50,000 for an additional fee). Sample rates for documents weighing up to 500g are Australia $15, UK $31 and USA $33, and for documents weighing up to 1kg Australia $20, UK $45.70 and USA $47.

International Air is a fast service for letters (maximum weight 200g), small parcels (maximum weight 2kg) and customs parcels (maximum weight 20kg). Letter and document rates are based on three envelope sizes: medium (235 x 120 x 10mm), large (325 x 230 x 10mm) and extra large (385 x 260 x10mm). Letters cost $1.50 to Australia and the South Pacific, and $2 to the rest of the world. Compensation up to $250 is paid for loss or damage, plus reimbursement of postage if lost (insurance up to $1,500 is available for customs parcels for an additional fee). The 'track and trace' facility is available for parcels over 2kg to Australia, Japan, the UK and the USA. Delivery takes a maximum of seven days to most destinations.

International Economy is an inexpensive service for non-urgent mail using the same size and weight bands and offering the same compensation and insurance as International Air. However, International Economy isn't available for Australia. Letters to all other destinations cost $1.50 and the service takes three weeks to most destinations.

Note also the following when sending international mail:

● International parcels weighing less than 2kg or worth less than $620 require a green customs declaration form (OS8a). If a parcel weighs more than 2kg or is worth more than $620, you must complete form OS007. If a parcel forms part of a commercial transaction, you must also complete and attach form CP125, as well as an invoice. Information about customs regulations is available on ☎ freephone 0800-736 353.

● Post shops offer a wide range of packaging materials and NZ Post publishes a *Parcel Packaging Guide* (contact Customer Services on ☎ freephone 0800-501 501 or go to 🖳 www.nzpost.co.nz).

● It's illegal to send certain items by post, a list of which is available from post shops.

DELIVERY & COLLECTION

Post is delivered once daily in New Zealand, and delivery times vary from early in the morning to much later in the day, depending on the area. Note that delivery is from Mondays to Fridays and there's usually no Saturday delivery. If there's nobody at home when a large or bulky item (or something you need to sign for) is delivered, NZ Post won't leave the item, but will leave a card, which you should complete and return, stating when and where you would like the item re-delivered. You can have it delivered to a neighbour or another address (such as your work address) if you prefer. If you're travelling around New Zealand, post can be sent to you via the *poste restante* service to any main city post shop, from where you can collect it during normal business hours by presenting proof of identity (such as a passport or driving licence).

If you live in a rural area in New Zealand, in order to have your post delivered you must join the RuralPost Scheme. You should collect a customer pack from a post shop and sign a Rural Delivery Service agreement. You will then be assigned a Rural

Delivery number (e.g. RD3), which is your postal address. You're also required to purchase a mailbox of a specific size and type (information available from post shops), including a flag to indicate whether you have mail either for collection or for delivery. Your RuralPost postman will deliver and collect mail from your mailbox as well as sell stamps and range of other products.

OTHER SERVICES

NZ Post offers the possibility of transferring, sending and receiving money both within New Zealand and abroad. For domestic transactions, money order certificates costing $3 are available for amounts up to $1,000; for larger amounts electronic money orders can be purchased for $5. For the transfer of money to and from abroad, NZ Post uses the services of Western Union and charges $74 for amounts up to $1,000. Further information is available on ☎ freephone 0800-005 253.

In early 2002, NZ Post planned to launch a new banking service, under the name Kiwibank, through post shops, making it the largest branch network in the country. Banking services on offer are expected to include savings and current accounts, credit and EFTPOS card facilities, mortgages, and telephone and Internet banking. Banking facilities will be available during normal post shop hours, which, unlike those of banks (see page 223) sometimes include Saturdays (see **Business Hours** on page 106). Further information is available via the Internet (🖳 www.kiwibank.co.nz).

NZ Post provides a FaxLink service from over 160 post shops, whereby facsimiles (faxes) can be sent and received (see **Fax, Telex & Internet** on page 120).

Sadly, NZ Post no longer provides a 'traditional' telegram service where messages are delivered by hand, and in 2000 the telegram service from post shops was withdrawn because of lack of demand.

7.

TELEPHONE

New Zealanders are enthusiastic telephone users, and telephone ownership in New Zealand is among the highest in the world at around 450 lines per thousand people. This is largely because local calls are available free, long distances (or at least long travelling times) separate many communities and many New Zealanders are immigrants with family members and friends overseas. The telephone system in New Zealand has been extensively modernised in the last decade, and all areas are now served by modern digital exchanges (the last exchange on which subscribers could make calls only via the operator was closed in 1991).

The New Zealand telecommunications industry has been extensively deregulated in recent years. The main telecommunications operator in New Zealand is Telecom New Zealand (TCNZ), known simply as Telecom (💻 www.telecom.co.nz), which used to be state owned (and part of the post office) but was established as a separate company in 1987 and then privatised. In June 1990, Ameritech and Bell Atlantic of the USA purchased (for $2.5 billion) a 64 per cent stake in TCNZ, which was reduced to 49.6 per cent in 1993 under government direction. In 2000 the largest individual shareholder in Telecom was Bell Atlantic with around 25 per cent of shares. Although Telecom is essentially a private company, in effect it's the national telephone company and maintains around 1.7 million fixed lines and over 1 million cellular phone connections. Telecom is New Zealand's largest company and one of the country's most successful, recording profits of $300 million in the second half of 2000. AAPT, which operates in Australia, is part of the Telecom group and Telecom owns 50 per cent of the Southern Cross telecommunications venture, which will eventually boost New Zealand's international capacity greatly.

The deregulated environment has allowed Telecom to become much more than a telephone company and it maintains a number of other telecommunications services, including cable networks. After deregulation other telecommunications companies (such as Clear, Telstra Saturn and WorldxChange) have entered the marketplace, although they remain small fry compared with Telecom. Clear (previously known as Clear Communications, 💻 www.clear.co.nz) is the largest of Telecom's competitors and offers national and international phone services, Internet connection and, in partnership with the giant Vodafone company, a mobile telephone network.

INSTALLING A TELEPHONE

It's difficult to manage without a phone in New Zealand. In fact, many households have two or more lines, which enable them to connect a fax machine or modem, or to remain contactable when teenage children spend hours (and hours) gossiping to their friends (don't panic: as mentioned above, you can have free local calls!). Theoretically you're free to obtain your telephone service from any company you choose. In practice, however, there's little choice, as Telecom is the only company that can offer telephone services in most parts of the country. Some areas are served by other operators, e.g. Clear, which operates in Auckland, Wellington and Christchurch, although most serve business customers only. In Auckland and Wellington you can receive your telephone service via fibre optic cables (owned by First Media, yet another offshoot of Telecom), which also deliver TV signals. The easiest way to find out whether there's a choice of telephone companies in your area is to ask your neighbours. If a Telecom line and telephone are already installed in your property, you can usually take over the connection, but you aren't obliged to if an alternative is available.

To have a telephone connected, simply call your chosen telephone company (the number will be in your local telephone directory). Before connecting your line, Telecom (or another operator) will need your name and address, date of birth, proof of your address (e.g. driving licence), details of your previous address (and proof) and employer, and the address of a relative or friend in New Zealand (if applicable) whom you can use as a reference (plus six pints of blood or your first-born as security!). If you've just arrived in New Zealand, your immigration documents should be acceptable as proof of identity; otherwise ask your employer (if you have one) to confirm your identity. Once your application has been approved, your phone will be connected within 24 hours if your home has an existing line or within 48 hours if it hasn't but there are lines nearby. The fee is $62 to reconnect an existing line plus a $49 'visit' fee. If you need a line installed or you live in a remote area, you will be quoted a price for the labour costs and material involved.

Although you will probably need to rent your phone line from Telecom, you can no longer rent a telephone from them. However, you can choose from a wide variety of telephones of all shapes and sizes (plus answering machines and other equipment) at telephone and electrical shops, with prices starting at around $15, a cheaper option than renting anyway. Make sure that the phone you buy is a touch-tone (DTMF) phone (most are). Note that, although touch-tone phones purchased abroad usually work perfectly well in New Zealand, you aren't supposed to connect them unless they're Telecom approved.

ISDN/ADSL Access: If you spend a lot of time online, it's possible in some areas to have an ISDN (Integrated Service Digital Network) line or an ADSL (Asymmetric Digital Subscriber Line) installed at your home or office. These are available in all city and town centres and also where a cable telephone or TV service is provided. The advantage of an ISDN line or ADSL is that it allows data to be transmitted much faster than over a standard line (115.2 kilobytes of data per second) and you can also make and receive telephone or fax calls while a modem is in use, although the costs of installation and line rental are higher.

USING THE TELEPHONE

Using the telephone in New Zealand is simplicity itself. The numbering system was changed in 1990 and all standard telephone numbers now have nine digits. There are just five telephone regions in New Zealand, each with a two-digit regional code:

Region	Code
South Island	03
Wellington	04
South of North Island	06
Waikato/Bay of Plenty	07
Auckland and Northland	09

The remaining seven digits comprise a three-digit district code and a four-digit subscriber number. When calling a number in another region, you must dial the whole nine-digit number; when calling within a region, you can simply dial the seven-digit number (which you must do even when dialling within a district). The only drawback to the system is that many people don't quote the regional code in their numbers because they expect callers to know what it is.

In addition to the five regional codes, there are a number of other codes for special numbers. Numbers prefixed with 01 usually connect you to a telephone company service, such as the operator. Mobile telephone numbers are identified by the prefix 025. Numbers beginning with 0800 are freephone numbers, which are common in New Zealand where many businesses provide an 0800 number for their customers' use. When you dial a major company (such as a bank or airline) you dial the same number from anywhere in the country, rather than a local number. The telephone system then 'reads' your telephone number to find your location and routes your call, through what's known as a 'value added network', to the office dealing with your location. So, for example, when you dial an 0800 number from Christchurch you could end up speaking to someone in Christchurch or, equally, to someone in Auckland. Note that 0900 numbers are premium rate telephone numbers, where the cost of the call is inflated (typically $3 per minute but can be as much as $9 per minute!) to pay for the service, e.g. on an information line.

If you're unable to get through to the number you want, call the operator on 010. If you wish to make a reverse charge (collect) call, dial 010 for domestic and 0170 for international calls. For information about Telecom services dial 123.

Telephone Dials: All new telephones sold in New Zealand are of the push-button variety, although there are still many dial-operated phones to be found, mainly in homes (most public phones have buttons). One point to note is that buttons are numbered in reverse order compared with those in most other countries, i.e. the 9 is at the top and the 1 at the bottom!

Dialling Tones: Dialling tones are similar to those in the UK and different from American and other European tones. The ringing tone consists of two short rings followed by a pause, whereas the engaged (busy) tone consists of alternating beeps of the same length, each at a slightly different pitch.

Contacting Telecom: Telecom runs a Service Express open 24 hours a day, seven days a week for any queries regarding Telecom (☎ freephone 0800-000 000). For information about sales and service dial 123. To report faults dial 120. Telecom has numerous e-mail query forms on its website (🖳 www.telecom.co.nz) or you can write to Telecom New Zealand, PO Box 147, Christchurch.

OPTIONAL SERVICES

Telecom offers a range of optional services that can usually be ordered individually or as part of a package (a touch-tone phone is required). These include the following (Note that not all services are available in every area):

Call Display: Your telephone shows the number of the person calling you so that you know before you pick up the phone who's calling you (or you know that you don't know who's calling you). The caller's number appears on an LCD display, which is either built into the telephone or a separate unit. This service isn't available in all areas. Call Display costs $3.95 per month.

Call Minder: Call Minder is a phone message service (much the same as having your own answering machine) that allows callers to leave a message when you aren't at home or your line is busy. The call is automatically answered by the Call Minder service with your personal recorded greeting. Call Minder costs $9.95 per month.

Call Restrictions: This service allows you to restrict calls from your telephone to certain numbers, e.g. barring international calls and 0900 calls. To activate and deactivate the restrictions you have an access code and a four-digit PIN. The service is available only in certain areas and costs $3.50 per month.

Call Transfer: Call transfer allows you to divert calls to another telephone number automatically, e.g. from home to office (or vice versa) or to a mobile telephone.

Call Waiting: This lets you know when another caller is trying to contact you (through beeps on the line) when you're already making a call and allows you to speak to the caller without terminating your current call. You can suspend the call waiting beeps when using the Internet (otherwise your Internet connection is automatically broken). Call Waiting costs $3.95 per month.

Three-way Calls: This enables you to hold a three-way conversation, either within New Zealand or abroad and costs $3.95 per month.

Alarm Call: You can programme your telephone to ring at a certain time, e.g. to wake you or to remind you to stop filling the swimming pool. Alarm Call costs $3.95 per month.

Price Required: By dialling 010 before making a call and asking for this service, you will be informed of the cost of a call shortly after it ends. There's a charge per call for this service. Alternatively, dial 013 (016 for international calls) before making a call and the cost will be listed separately on your next bill. You can also calculate the cost of a call on the Telecom website (▣ www.telecom.co.nz).

'YABBA' Cards: Telecom YABBA cards are a prepaid calling card service with which you can make calls from any phone. Cards are available in $5, $15, $30 and $50 denominations and are 'rechargeable' by credit card.

CHARGES

New Zealand has a regulatory body which rules on whether telephone charges are fair and reasonable but otherwise leaves it to 'market forces' to keep charges competitive. When deregulation was first introduced, Telecom was accused of unfair practices and gross overcharging for the portion of Clear Communication's calls which pass through Telecom exchanges, thus hindering them from offering competitive rates. However, in October 2000 Telecom and Clear signed a public letter agreeing to end all disagreements (perhaps politicians could learn something from this).

Line Rental: Line rental charges vary according to the 'package' you choose. The monthly rental for a standard line under the HomeLine option is $36.34, which includes unlimited free local calls. The area which qualifies as 'local' is listed in your telephone directory and varies with the area and *doesn't* cover the whole of your regional code area. This arrangement is ideal for those whose friends and family live nearby and also for Internet addicts, who can stay online for hours at no cost, although you need to make sure that your service provider has an access number within your local calling area.

If you don't make many local calls (less than 14 a week on average), you can opt for the HomeLine Economy package (not available in all areas), whereby you pay a monthly line rental of $24.75 plus 20¢ for each local call up to two hours in duration and 20¢ for each additional two hours or part thereof. You may change from the HomeLine Economy option to HomeLine.

Calls: For non-local and non-freephone (0800) calls there are ten charge bands, with rates increasing with distance (the boundaries between bands are roughly 150km/93mi apart), although there isn't much difference in cost between the cheapest and the most expensive bands, particularly during off-peak times. The period during which you make a call has a far greater effect on the cost. The week is divided into four charging periods: morning (from 8am to noon on Mondays to Fridays); afternoon (noon to 6pm on Mondays to Fridays); economy (6pm to 10pm on Mondays to Fridays and 8am to 10pm on Saturdays, Sundays and public holidays); and night (10pm to 8am every day). With Telecom, a call over the longest distance lasting a minute costs 89.35¢ at the morning rate and 25.66¢ at the economy rate. However, calls are charged per second, so if a call lasts for less than a minute you pay the appropriate proportion of the minute rate.

Charge Plans: Telecom also offers a range of so-called 'plans' with reduced rates for non-local calls. For example in late 2001 the Neighbouring Area plan offered unlimited calls at any time to numbers just outside the free local call area for $19.95 per month, while the Favourite Place plan offered unlimited calls at economy and night times (i.e. 6pm to 8am every day) to a particular area in the country for a monthly fee of $29.

Alternative Networks: Although most people rent their telephone line from Telecom, there's no obligation to make all your calls via the Telecom network. Under deregulation, other companies can provide your telephone service even when you have a Telecom line. This is achieved by entering an access code before calls, which routes calls to your local exchange via Telecom lines, but uses the alternative company's lines for the long-distance part of its 'journey'. The cost is charged to your account by the alternative company (usually debited to a credit card) and doesn't appear on your Telecom bill.

The main alternative network is Clear, who provide long-distance calls and plans that are often cheaper than Telecom's. To use the service you must register your telephone number with them and then dial 050 before a call (you can also make calls from any telephone by entering an access code) for a short period (usually around a week) while your account is set up, after which all long-distance calls will automatically be charged to your account with Clear without your needing to dial the prefix. It's worth considering an alternative company to Telecom if you make a lot of international calls, as calls may be significantly cheaper. Short distance calls cost the same, so there's no advantage in using another operator for these (unless you rent your line from them, which is possible in some areas).

BILLS

Telephone bills are issued monthly in New Zealand and you have around a week to pay before a reminder is sent. You can pay bills by post, at post shops and some other outlets that are Telecom agencies, or pay your bill by direct debit from a bank account. All telephone bills in New Zealand are itemised, although it's possible to request a non-itemised bill if you wish. You can also decide the level at which itemisation begins, e.g. calls over 50¢, $1 or $5. This is handy if you just want to keep an eye on the more expensive calls and don't want to receive reams of paper listing all your calls (other telephone companies please take note!). Telecom runs a Credit Management scheme (☎ 128), under which you can choose how you pay your phone bill. Bill

Online is a new system whereby you can receive and pay your phone bill via the Internet and includes the option to schedule when and how much you pay each month. To use this system you must register online (⌨ www.telecom.co.nz).

INTERNATIONAL CALLS

It's possible to direct dial international calls from private and public phones in New Zealand through the ISD (International Subscriber Dialling) system. A full list of country codes is shown in the information pages of your telephone directory. To make an international call, dial the international access code of 00, followed by the country code (e.g. 1 for the USA, 44 for the UK) and number you want, usually omitting the initial 0. For international operator assistance dial 0170.

International telephone calls via Telecom are charged according to the time of day (see **Charges** above) and the part of the world (zone), Australia being in the cheapest zone and the UK in one of the most expensive (I wonder why!). Other companies (such as Clear) charge a separate rate for each country. It's usually much cheaper to use a company other than Telecom to make international calls. Telecom does, however, have periodic special offers, e.g. in 2001 the Weekends and Weeknights plan offered a call lasting up to two hours (!) made after 6pm any day for $4 to Australia and $8 to the UK or Ireland.

If you're travelling overseas, you can use Telecom's Direct service to call New Zealand. By dialling the relevant local access number you can speak to an operator in New Zealand and charge the call to your Telecom account or a calling card or credit card, or place a reverse charge (collect) call. For information and access numbers contact Telecom.

It's possible to make Home Country Direct (HCD) calls in New Zealand by dialling 0009 followed by the country code of the country you wish to call. You will then be connected directly to an operator in the country you're calling, who will place the call for you and charge it to either the number you're calling or your bill, assuming you have a telephone account in that country. It's quite expensive, however, and much more expensive than paying for the call yourself. Travellers visiting New Zealand from the USA and holding a calling card from a US telephone company can use HCD and have the cost charged to their account. If you have an MCI calling card in the USA (or a card issued by a company with which MCI has an agreement), simply dial 000 912 from any telephone; if you have an account with BT in the UK, you can dial 000 944. You can then dial the number yourself and no operator intervention is necessary.

DIRECTORIES

You're entitled to a free copy of the telephone directory (called a telephone book in New Zealand) for your local region, which is delivered when your line is connected and annually thereafter. Directories for other regions can be ordered for a nominal cost and charged to your telephone bill. If you live outside the Auckland region, it's wise to order the Auckland book, as most important businesses (e.g. airlines and banks) are located there. Subscribers are divided into private and business customers and there's also a separate yellow pages for each region (a copy is delivered with your local telephone book). If you don't have a directory handy (or cannot be bothered to look a number up) the number for directory enquiries (known as directory assistance) is 018 for domestic numbers and 0172 for international numbers. A fee is charged for both services, e.g. $1.33 for international numbers.

PUBLIC TELEPHONES

Public telephones can be found in the streets of towns and villages and at various other locations, including post shops, bus stations and airports. All payphones allow local, national and International Subscriber Dialling (ISD) calls. International calls can also be made via the operator or the Home Direct Service (see **International Calls** above). Most traditional telephone boxes have been replaced by kiosks with push-button phones. Call boxes are different colours to indicate that they accept coins (blue), PhoneCards (green) or credit cards (yellow); no boxes accept more than one method of payment! Credit card phones are found mainly in cities. The majority of public phones (over 4,000) accept only PhoneCards (see below). This is to save Telecom money by not having to empty coin boxes (or to repair phone boxes that have been broken into for the cash) rather than for customer convenience. Local calls aren't free from public phones (as they usually are from a private telephone) and the minimum charge is around 50¢ per minute.

Coin Phones: Phones in blue boxes usually accept 10¢, 20¢ and 50¢ coins. You must lift the receiver and insert at least 50¢ before dialling (the minimum cost of even the shortest local call). In older coin boxes you should insert only small coins (one at a time), because if you speak for less than the time you've paid for, you won't receive any change. In newer boxes (where the amount in reserve is shown on a digital display) you can insert as much money as you like, as completely unused coins are automatically refunded at the end of the call. However, you still won't receive any change from a partly used coin, e.g. if you insert a $1 coin but make only a 50¢ call. Making an international call from a coin phone can be difficult, as you need to insert at least $3 (the minimum charge) in coins. Even if you plan to use the Home Direct Service, you must insert 20¢ (which isn't refunded) to access the service.

PhoneCard Phones: Telecom PhoneCards are available from post shops, petrol stations, Telecom Centres and various shops (such as dairies) displaying a Telecom PhoneCard symbol (a green, yellow and blue illustration of a card being inserted into a telephone receiver). Cards are sold in denominations of $5, $10, $20 and $50 and have different designs, usually scenic views of New Zealand (many people collect them and some issues are much sought-after and therefore worth far more than the face value!). PhoneCards save you from having to find change or carry around lots of coins. The procedure when using a PhoneCard in most public phones is as follows:

1. Lift the receiver and check for the dial tone.

2. Insert your PhoneCard into the slot.

3. Wait (while your card is checked).

4. When your card's remaining credit is displayed, you can dial your number.

5. Hang up when you're finished and **don't forget to remove your card**.

Credit Card Phones: In some places, mainly city centres and airports, there are public phones that accept international credit cards (e.g. American Express, Bankcard, Diners Club, Mastercard and Visa), where the cost is automatically debited to your credit card account. Credit cards cannot be used in PhoneCard payphones and vice versa. There's a minimum call charge of $2.

Private Payphones: There are private payphones in hotels, bars, shops and other businesses. They're usually portable units rather than phone kiosks and operate like any other phone, except that they don't usually give change so you should insert only the amount that you expect to spend. The main point to note is that the owner of the phone can set whatever rates he wishes, which are usually much higher than Telecom's (and he has no obligation to display what the charges are). The same applies to calls from hotels, which charge as much as twice normal rates.

Calling Cards: If you do a lot of travelling, you can obtain a Telecom calling card. Calls can be made with a calling card from any phone, public (including credit card phones) or private (including mobile phones), and are charged to your home or business Telecom account or a credit card. You can also use the card to make calls to New Zealand from overseas, using the NZ Direct service. A calling card can be limited to 20 pre-selected numbers or to numbers with a particular prefix. Additional cards can be allocated to family, friends or business associates. Although cards are free, call charges are high. A Personal Identification Number (PIN) protects you against misuse of your card.

MOBILE PHONES

Given the remoteness of many parts of New Zealand, mobile (cellular) telephones are popular and there are well over 2 million mobile phones in operation. Coverage is surprisingly good despite the difficult terrain in many places, and New Zealand has both analogue and digital networks. Recently, however, there have been scare about the risks to health from both mobile phones themselves and the antennae towers (one garage owner who planned to mount a tower on his land adjacent to a primary school received death threats!).

The main cellular network is operated by, you guessed it, Telecom Mobile with some 56 per cent of the market, although Clear has teamed up with Vodafone in a major cellular network and their aggressive marketing policy means their market share had risen spectacularly to 43 per cent in late 2001 and is expected to reach 50 per cent in the near future. Competition for business is fierce so prices are keen, and it's no longer necessary to have a contract. Offers with a contract in late 2001 included a mid-range phone for $99 plus $14.95 per month including 50 free minutes (Telecom) or a top-of-the-range phone for $199 with a contract of $30 per month including 200 free minutes (Vodaphone). Pre-pay ('pay as you talk') phones are increasingly popular in New Zealand, as elsewhere, and you can buy cards for $20, $30 and $50 in many shops, including post shops. You can buy a mobile telephone directly from Telecom or Vodafone or from a mobile phone shop, where you can be connected to a network. It's also possible to rent mobile phones by the day or week, starting at around $17 per day. Calls to and from mobile phones are generally expensive, e.g. Telecom charges 63¢ for the first minute and 1.05¢ per second afterwards. A recent development is a voice-activated mobile phone, which is ideal for use in the car. Unfortunately, these machines can only recognise a New Zealand accent, so if you don't have one you will need to dial manually!

FAX, TELEX & INTERNET

Facsimiles (faxes) can be sent from a variety of locations in New Zealand, including post shops, stationers, newsagents and many other businesses, who can also receive them on your behalf. NZ Post provides a FaxLink service from over 160 post shops from where a fax can be sent for a flat fee of $2.50 plus 25¢ per page within the same town or city or $1.50 per page nation-wide. International charges are $1.60 per page for Australia, $2.50 for the South Pacific, $3 for North America and $4 for the rest of the world. NZ Post will also receive faxes for $2.50 when collected from a post shop (they can be delivered by CourierPost for $5). For more information ☎ freephone 0800-501 501. Fax machines (Groups 2/3) imported from abroad usually function properly in New Zealand, although you aren't supposed to connect them unless they're Telecom-approved.

Telex machines aren't widely used any longer in New Zealand, although many major hotels, banks, government offices and large businesses still have them.

The Internet is extremely popular in New Zealand where most companies and all government bodies are online and Internet time is free (provided you have free local calls and your service provider has a local access number). There are numerous Internet service providers (ISPs) mainly based in the large cities, including Telecom's Xtra and Clear's Clear Net. Other smaller companies are iHug and Paradise. Most companies also offer broad-band fast connection via ISDN lines or ADSLs, although these aren't yet available in all areas. Prices are competitive and limited free access (e.g. two hours per month) is available from $2 per month or unlimited access for around $28 per month. The monthly magazine *NZ PC World* often publishes a comparison of rates and packages, which can also be viewed online (🖥 www. pcworld.co.nz). The Consumers Organisation also offers an online comparison of ISP rates for the whole of New Zealand (🖥 www.consumer.org.nz).

EMERGENCY NUMBERS

The only emergency number you need to know in New Zealand is 111. This can be dialled free from any telephone and will connect you to the nearest emergency operator, who will connect you to the police, fire or ambulance service as required. You don't need any money, even when calling from a public phone, whether it accepts coins, PhoneCards or credit cards. Be ready to tell the emergency operator which service you require and your name. You don't need to give your location, as the telephone from which you're calling automatically 'sends' its identity.

8.

TELEVISION & RADIO

Broadcasting in New Zealand, as well as the ownership of TV and radio stations, used to be strictly regulated by the government, although since 1991 it has been deregulated to a certain extent and a number of new companies (particularly huge, foreign media corporations) have entered the market, making the broadcasting industry somewhat volatile. New companies are constantly starting up, both in radio and TV, buying existing stations and, just as frequently, closing down. (It doesn't pay to become too attached to a particular programme, as you may find that the next time you sit down in front of 'the box' your favourite station has disappeared!) However, the situation has stabilised in recent years and, despite the influx of foreign companies into New Zealand, television programming is still highly regulated by the Broadcasting Standards Authority and evening programmes receive a classification according to their suitability for younger viewers, e.g. PG (parent guidance). Television is popular in New Zealand, where over 1.2 million households own at least one television set and it's estimated that 99 per cent of the population watches some television every day.

TELEVISION

Stations

There are four terrestrial, national free TV stations in New Zealand, imaginatively named TV One, TV2, TV3 and TV4; TV One and TV2 are state owned, while TV3 and TV4 are privately owned by the Canadian company, CanWest. All stations, even those that are state owned, carry advertising, although the amount of revenue the state-funded channels can raise from advertising is limited. As in all countries, the TV advertising market in New Zealand is lucrative, and total annual revenue from advertisements is almost $500 million. There are also both state and privately owned regional TV stations in some areas (e.g. Triangle TV in Auckland, Channel 7 in Wellington, Christchurch TV and Channel 10 in Dunedin), although TVNZ, the state broadcasting company, has closed its five Horizon Pacific regional channels. The government has long-term plans to sell off TVNZ, although this has been delayed for years.

TV One is TVNZ's main channel and provides a staple diet of news broadcasts, home-produced and imported dramas and the ubiquitous 'lifestyle' programmes. TV One is New Zealand's most watched channel and has an audience share of around 38 per cent. TV2 broadcasts children's programmes, drama series and films. TV3 claims to target the 18 to 49 age range and offers mainly home-produced and international series. TV3 had 24 per cent of the audience share in the 1999/2000 season and this is expected to increase, as in late 1999 CanWest signed a sports deal with Sky TV and now offers major sporting events. TV4, which was set up in 1997, targets a younger, urban audience and offers comedy and lifestyle programmes (no getting away from these!).

Terrestrial TV is short on the New Zealanders' passion – sport – because the major sporting events have been sold to the highest bidder, namely satellite or cable TV, although this has changed to some extent following the agreement between Sky TV and TV3. Otherwise, if you like watching sport, you will need to invest in a satellite dish or cable connection to watch the big matches, although you can watch them free at hotels (pubs) that show live sport on large-screen TVs (the drinks aren't free!).

Programmes

Television in New Zealand doesn't have a particularly good reputation, as most people New Zealand admit. The small population and limited budgets mean that there are relatively few home-made programmes (around 20 per cent, the lowest percentage in the developed world – a cause for growing concern among certain groups), even fewer good ones, and TV stations prefer to import programmes from other English-speaking nations (mainly Australia, the UK and USA). Lovers of America's 'Friends' and 'South Park' and the UK's 'Coronation Street', 'Eastenders' and 'Changing Rooms' will be delighted to hear that they're all shown on New Zealand TV. The quality of documentary programmes is high, and wildlife programmes such as 'Meet The Real Penguins' and 'Mount Cook' have won New Zealand programme makers top awards in Asia and Europe. News programmes are also presented professionally, although they tend to focus on national rather than international news, and coverage can also be rather superficial (making CNN and Sky News good value for those who want to know what's happening in the wider world).

Viewing figures show that New Zealanders have better taste in TV than their European or North American counterparts. News or documentary programmes usually comprise the top five programmes (rather than soap operas) ranked by audience figures, although one of New Zealand's most popular programmes is the American 'Survivor'. Rugby matches regularly make the top five programmes, particularly the Super 12 games. A TV gardening programme, 'Maggie's Garden Show' is also regularly in the top five. The British soap 'Coronation Street' usually makes the top five, and when TVNZ bosses once announced plans to cut the weekly showings of 'Corrie' from three to two they received a petition of 20,000 signatures in protest! New Zealanders also have their own soaps, of which the most popular is the hospital drama 'Shortland Street', now in its tenth year, although the programme rarely appears in the top ten. Other popular home-produced programmes are 'Te Tutu', a drama series on TV One, 'Captain's Log', a series about famous voyages around New Zealand, and 'Inside New Zealand', a documentary produced by TV3. Most programmes are broadcast in English, but a small number are broadcast in Maori including 'Te Karere' (meaning news).

The government-funded organisation NZ On Air aims to promote New Zealand culture and provides funding for home-produced programmes. Home-produced documentaries, drama series and children's programmes account for some 20 per cent of total broadcasting, although in a recent survey more than 60 per cent of New Zealanders claimed they would like to see the proportion substantially increased. (This percentage is even higher among the Maori population, whose culture is given top priority by NZ On Air.) More information on indigenous television can be found on the NZ On Air website (⌨ www.nzonair.govt.nz).

New Zealand TV stations claim to show the same amount of advertising and other 'promotional messages' as TV stations elsewhere in the English-speaking world and TVNZ has a policy of showing no more than 12 minutes' advertising per hour, an amount they claim is less than in Australia and the USA.

Most daily newspapers and many magazines contain TV sections giving details of programmes for terrestrial, cable and satellite stations. A magazine called *TV Guide* ($1.50) has the most extensive listings, including in-depth features on forthcoming films and other programmes allowing you to plan your viewing (it also happens to be New Zealand's largest-circulating weekly magazine, selling over 230,000 copies a week). *TV Guide* has recently started to include show business news in addition to TV information. The *Listener* is an upmarket magazine of comment and criticism (similar to the British publication of the same name) which also contains TV programme listings. TVNZ also runs a website (⌨ www.nzoom.com, voted New Zealand's best in 2001) providing, among other things, TV programme listings. Women's magazine publishers often produce weekly TV programme guides.

Cable

Cable television has made slow but steady progress in New Zealand and is currently available in Wellington and Kapiti Coast, Greymouth, Gisborne and several suburbs of Auckland. The main operators are Pacific Satellite Cable TV in the Greymouth and Gisborne areas and Telstra Saturn Cable TV in Wellington and along the Kapiti Coast. Cable TV is very much the poor relation of satellite TV and, despite initial optimistic predictions, isn't very popular; the sparse population in many parts of the country means that universal cable coverage is unlikely. However, Telstra Saturn have an ambitious expansion programme to include the areas of Auckland, Hamilton and Dunedin. The company is currently laying a 1,000km (625mi) high-capacity fibre optic cable connecting Auckland, Wellington and Christchurch with an investment of $1.2 billion. This expansion is expected to be even greater if Telstra Saturn merges with Clear (see **Chapter 7**) in 2002. The easiest way to find out whether cable TV is available in your area is to ask your neighbours. The presence of cable 'pillars' (junction boxes) and unsightly, subsiding trenches in the roads and pavements of Auckland and Wellington's smartest suburbs are also a good indication!

Cable TV provides exclusive cable channels as well as terrestrial TV broadcasts and satellite programmes such as CNN. Eventually, over 50 channels will be available on cable. Telstra Saturn operates a pick-and-choose menu pricing system, with a basic package costing around $32 per month and including the principal sports, news and movie channels. It's also possible to choose which channels you wish to receive and the days on which you wish to receive them, paying as little as $1.50 per day for one channel, which works out cheaper if (for example) you just want to watch films at weekends. If you subscribe to cable TV, you can also obtain your telephone and Internet service via cable, which costs around $60 per month.

Satellite

Sky satellite TV is well established in New Zealand, where it's owned by a consortium of international communications and media companies (TVNZ also has a stake in the enterprise). Foreign investors have pumped millions of dollars into satellite TV, confident that it's the way ahead in a country where long distances and a sparse population have slowed the sprawling trenches of cable networks. However, although Sky TV has over 400,000 subscribers in some 30 per cent of households, it remains a loss-making enterprise for TVNZ.

You can take out a subscription by calling your nearest dealer and have a dish installed within a few days. If you live in a remote or mountainous area, you may need a large dish in order to receive transmissions. A start-up package to receive Sky TV, including a large dish, receiver/decoder and installation costs around $300, although Sky have occasional special offers. Sky viewers pay a monthly subscription fee of

$38, although an increasing number of programmes, such as films and top sporting events, are on a pay-per-view basis, which is in addition to the basic cost, e.g. an extra $19 for the movie option and $8 for sports, and can make satellite TV expensive. Sky TV provides three channels: Sky News, Sky Movies and Sky Sports. Sky News incorporates BBC and CNN transmissions into its programmes and is similar to equivalent Sky stations in other countries, as is Sky Movies. Sky Sports' trump card has been to secure exclusive broadcasting rights to many top sporting events in New Zealand, including the All Blacks' rugby matches. As sport (especially rugby and *particularly* the All Blacks) is something which few New Zealanders can live without (literally), it may account for the impressive following that satellite TV has made.

Buying TVs and Videos

It isn't worth shipping a foreign TV or video recorder to New Zealand, as they're available locally at reasonable prices. Also, a TV made for a foreign market is unlikely to be compatible with the New Zealand transmission system (a PAL variant) and voltage, particularly if it's designed for the US system (you will be able to receive a picture or sound, but not both), although Australian equipment will work. A small portable TV costs between $400 and $550.

Like a TV, a video recorder has become an essential item of equipment in the majority of New Zealand homes in the last few decades. The cheapest video recorder costs around $350 and the cheapest DVD player around $400. There are video cassette rental stores in cities and towns and a night's rental of a popular film costs around $10. Purchase prices of videos start at around $10 for the oldest releases, although recent films and major sporting events cost more.

Licence

There's no longer an annual TV licence fee in New Zealand, which was abolished in 1999. Non-state funding for television and radio programmes on TVNZ now comes from NZ On Air and from advertising.

RADIO

Radio broadcasting in New Zealand follows the model established for the TV industry in that there are both state-operated and commercially run stations. Radio New Zealand (RNZ) runs two national stations, Concert FM and the National Programme, which are similar to the BBC's Radio 3 and 4. They have a good reputation for the quality of their broadcasting, although both are rather staid and mainly have an older (and declining) audience. Both stations entirely state-funded and don't broadcast advertising. RNZ also operates a network of local radio stations throughout the country, which are partly state-funded and partly funded from advertising. They broadcast mainly rock, pop and easy listening music, local and regional news, and sport. CanWest (the owner of TV3 and TV4) runs RadioWorks, the second largest national radio network, which broadcasts mainly pop music.

There's a wealth of national commercial radio stations in New Zealand, mainly broadcasting pop music such as Classic Hits, Easy Listening, Radio Hauraki, Radio Pacific and Wolf. There are also several special interest stations, such as Radio Sport (whose commentaries have been widely acclaimed), and Life FM and Radio Rhema, both broadcasting for Christians. A student station, b.NET, broadcasts from universities and polytechnics around the country. There's also an abundance of local commercial radio stations, with almost 100 FM stations alone plus others broadcasting on the AM frequency. Stations are closely involved with their local communities and play pop or easy listening music plus local news and sport. Because there are so many commercial stations competing for a limited amount of advertising money, stations often go to extraordinary lengths to attract listeners. Most radio stations broadcast in English, although there are a number of state and private radio stations broadcasting in Maori, particularly in areas with large Maori communities such as Auckland and the north-west tip of North Island.

The BBC World Service is re-broadcast on a local frequency in several main cities, including Auckland and Wellington. It can also be received direct. To obtain a free BBC World Service programme guide and frequency information write to BBC Worldwide, BBC World Service, PO Box 76, Bush House, Strand, London WC2B 4PH, UK (☎ 020-7752 5040). The BBC publishes a monthly magazine, *BBC Worldwide*, containing comprehensive information about BBC World Service radio and TV programmes, which is available on subscription from the above address.

9.

EDUCATION

New Zealand has always had an effective and respected educational system, although few areas of New Zealand life have gone through more upheaval in the last ten years. In 1987, the prime minister launched a major review of education with the aim of developing a system that would improve educational opportunities and prospects for all. Until the '90s, education in New Zealand was highly centralised and under the control of the Department of Education. However, the review set out to achieve its objectives by creating something of a commercial market in the state educational system, schools being given increased autonomy and the freedom to set their own rules and to spend their budgets in a way that most benefits their students. To encourage each school to strive for excellence, parents have been given greater freedom of choice as to which school their children attend.

Most of the changes made during the '90s have been in the primary and secondary sectors, which were formerly the responsibility of the Department of Education via regional or local authority school boards (who managed all schools in their districts in the same way). Today, these schools are mainly run by boards of trustees, comprising members of staff, politicians, business people and other worthy citizens. The trustees have considerable leeway in how a school is run, but they're responsible to the Education Review Office for their actions and for meeting the standards laid down by the government. The Education Review Office monitors their progress and reports directly to the Minister of Education. The latest change in education is a change in the school qualifications from the age of 16 onwards, which aims to give students the opportunity to study a wider range of subjects and to provide a more detailed picture of their achievements.

There have been many critics of educational reforms over the last ten years, although most are forced to admit that they've been largely successful. The New Zealand education system is regarded as one of the best in the world and, when ranked alongside their counterparts from other developed countries, New Zealand students often have superior levels of numeracy and literacy. In December 2001 the OECD released a survey comparing education standards for 15-year-olds in more than 32 countries. New Zealand came third overall (only Finland and Canada performed better) with excellent results in numeracy and literacy.

Education is compulsory in New Zealand for children aged between 6 and 16 (the school leaving age was increased from 15 to 16 in the 1980s), although most children start school at five. In addition to state and private school education, over 6,000 children are actually educated at home, by either parents or tutors (permission is required from the Ministry of Education). Secondary students can also take courses via the Correspondence School (see page 146) if these aren't offered by their secondary school. School enrolments have begun to decline in the primary sector as a result of the falling birth rate, and this decline is due to affect secondary schools from 2006.

Enquiries about education in New Zealand should be directed to the Ministry of Education, Box 1666, Wellington (☎ 04-463 8000, 🖥 www.minedu.govt.nz).

STATE OR PRIVATE SCHOOL?

If you're able to choose between state and private education, the following checklist will help you make your decision:

- How long are you planning to stay in New Zealand? If you're uncertain, it's probably better to assume a long stay. Possible integration problems mean that enrolling a child in a New Zealand state school is recommended only for at least a year, particularly if he isn't a native English speaker.

- Bear in mind that the area where you choose to live will affect your choice of school(s). For example, it's usually more convenient to send a child to a state school near your home, and if you choose a private day school you must take into account the distance from your home to the school.

- Do you know where you're going when you leave New Zealand? This may be an important consideration with regard to a child's language of tuition and system of education in New Zealand. How old is your child and what age will he be when you plan to leave New Zealand? What plans do you have for his education and in which country?

- What educational level is your child at now and how will he fit into a private school or the New Zealand state school system? The younger he is, the easier it will be to place him in a suitable school.

- How does your child view the thought of studying in New Zealand? If you aren't from an English-speaking country, what language is best from a long-term point of view? Is schooling available in New Zealand in his mother tongue?

- Will your child require your help with his studies, and more importantly, will you be able to help him?

- Is special or extra tutoring available in New Zealand for other subjects, if necessary?

- What are the school hours? What are the school holiday periods? How will the school holidays and hours affect your family's work and leisure activities?

- Is religion an important aspect in your choice of school? Usually only private church-run schools offer a comprehensive religious education and are run according to their respective religious values.

- Do you want your child to go to a co-educational or a single-sex school? New Zealand state schools are usually co-educational.

- Should you send your child to a boarding school? If so, in which country?

- What are the secondary and further education prospects in New Zealand or another country? Are New Zealand examinations or the examinations set by prospective New Zealand schools recognised in your home country or the country where you plan to live after leaving New Zealand? If applicable, check whether the New Zealand Higher School Certificate and University Bursary examinations are recognised as a university entrance qualification in your home country.

- Does a prospective school have a good academic record? Most schools provide a glowing prospectus, but you should also check the exam pass rate statistics.

- How large are the classes? What is the pupil-teacher ratio?

Obtain the opinions and advice of others who have been faced with the same decisions and problems as yourself, and collect as much information from as many different sources as possible before making a decision. Speak to teachers and the parents of children attending the schools on your shortlist. Finally, most parents find it pays to discuss alternatives with their children before making a decision. See also **Choosing a Private School** on page 142.

STATE SCHOOLS

The New Zealand state school system educates around 95 per cent of children and is one of the government's largest expenses, consuming well over 10 per cent of the national budget. There are state schools throughout New Zealand, where most children attend a day school, although around 10,000 attend state boarding schools. Many of these are children whose homes are in remote areas and for whom boarding school is the only way of receiving a full secondary education. However, state boarding schools in the cities with reputations for academic excellence also attract local day students. Most state schools are co-educational, including a number of single-sex schools that have opened their doors to the opposite sex in recent years, particularly in the higher grades. State schools are organised on the comprehensive system and attract students with a wide range of abilities. There's much less distinction between 'good' and 'not-so-good' schools compared with many other countries, with schools striving to maintain and improve standards within the terms of their charter. However, as is the case in other countries, schools in wealthier areas where parents can afford to provide extra finance and support, tend to have better academic records than schools in poorer areas.

Curriculum & Facilities: Most state schools follow a balanced curriculum based around the sciences, mathematics, the humanities, practical or vocational skills and modern languages. The study of the Maori language and culture is undertaken in all schools, although some Polynesian schools focus on this more than others. The majority of schools recognise New Zealand's strengthening links with Polynesian and Asian countries, rather than with Europe. For example, the study of Japanese (and recently Chinese) has been added to the curriculum and often replaces the study of French and German. All state schools have good sports facilities and are usually set amidst extensive sports fields and offer a variety of sports, of which (as would be expected) rugby is the most popular.

Teaching: In general, the standard of teaching is high and teachers have a good reputation among their peers abroad. However, the country suffers from a shortage of qualified teachers (there are around 700 teacher vacancies at any given time) and it has been estimated that several thousand children in primary education don't have a permanent class teacher. The problem tends to be worse in schools in poorer areas, rural areas and areas with large Maori communities. To try to solve the problem the government has set up an organisation called TeachNZ offering a package of enhanced pay and benefits to tempt teachers from other countries to come and work in New Zealand, and to encourage New Zealand teachers who have gone abroad (often in search of higher salaries) to return home (⌨ www.teachnz.govt.nz) – see also page 29.

Discipline: The standard of discipline is good in most state schools, although some schools in poor or ethnic areas have problems with race relations and gangs. Most schools have strict anti-violence policies where verbal or physical violence isn't tolerated, although the level of enforcement is variable. The latest threats to discipline in New Zealand schools are alcohol and drugs, which have prompted some schools to introduce drug and alcohol testing for students. Corporal punishment isn't permitted in New Zealand schools in any form (it was banned some years ago), although there have been calls to reintroduce it.

Language

To get the most out of the New Zealand educational system, students must be able to communicate in English. This is a basic requirement imposed by the government and one that's taken into account when prospective migrants apply for residence. For children whose mother tongue isn't English, most schools (at least in areas attracting a significant number of immigrants) provide extra English language tuition. However, the amount of tuition provided varies with the school and may be insufficient for some children. Many educationalists agree that while children in New Zealand have a similar level of ability in most subjects to children of a similar age in other English speaking countries, they're generally more advanced in reading and writing than children in Australia, the UK and the USA. In many areas, children of both Maoris and other Polynesians, who receive only minimal Maori tuition at school, attend Maori language 'nests' (known as *Kohanga Reo*) where they learn the Maori language and culture.

Enrolment

Parents are responsible for ensuring that their children are enrolled in the most suitable school. Finding the 'best' school is something that you will need to do largely unaided, as there's no central body which will allocate your child to the most appropriate or best available school. Indeed, the concept of parental choice is crucial to the new 'market' which now operates in education. The Education Review Office (ERO, 💻 www.ero.govt.nz) publishes a booklet entitled *Choosing a School for a Five Year Old*, which is available from their offices (its general principles also apply to choosing a school for older children). The ERO will also supply a list of suitable schools in an area on request. All schools have a charter, and many have either a prospectus or brochure setting out their aims and objectives.

Parents don't have to enrol children in their nearest school, as used to be the case, but most children in New Zealand attend the school nearest their home for the sake of convenience, and in any case, in some areas there's only one primary or secondary school. The above-mentioned ERO booklet suggests that parents take into account the following criteria when choosing a school: the proximity of a school to their home, how safe it is to walk there, and where the child's siblings or friends attend school. It also suggests that parents should take into account whether a school operates individual age group or composite classes (where several age groups are taught in the same class by one teacher). Composite classes are found in some rural schools and are generally thought to be detrimental to a child's progress. Official policy apart, visiting schools and discussing their merits with parents are both highly recommended before making a decision. You should telephone the schools you're interested in and ask to visit.

If a school has too many children wishing to enrol, the Ministry of Education allows it to operate an enrolment scheme to prevent overcrowding. Under the scheme each school must have a clearly defined catchment area, known as 'home zone' or 'zoning' in New Zealand, and children who live in the catchment area have a right to attend the school. If you live outside the catchment area, you must apply for enrolment. There's a priority order to enrolment and children with siblings currently or formerly at the school have priority over others. Priority is also given to children of board employees. If after priority has been allocated there are still more children than places, a ballot is held. Schools with enrolment systems must advertise in local newspapers the number of places available and the enrolment dates. Note that, if you live in the catchment area of a school with an enrolment scheme and you want to enrol your child, then the school is obliged to accept him. If, however, you want to enrol your child in a school with an enrolment scheme outside your catchment area you may need to wait until the school organises the next ballot.

The ERO recommends that parents take a child's last report from his current school and also examples of his work (if it's in English) to help teachers assess his level of ability as accurately as possible.

Details of schools, universities and polytechnics in New Zealand are contained in a publication entitled *Excellence: NZ Education Directory*, which is published in January each year and can be purchased in bookshops in New Zealand or consulted in public libraries.

School Hours & Holidays

Schools are allowed a certain amount of freedom to set their hours, but these are usually from 8.30 or 9am until 3pm in primary schools (until 3.30 or 4pm in secondary schools), Mondays to Fridays. There's normally an hour's break for lunch and short breaks mid-morning and mid-afternoon. The New Zealand academic year follows the calendar year, in common with Australia but unlike the autumn-to-summer system that operates in most of Europe and North America. This system creates a frantic situation for parents and children alike, as the main school holidays coincide with the Christmas period.

The Ministry of Education stipulates that schools must open for a minimum period each academic year; this varies from year to year, although it's usually around 394 half-days for primary schools and 380 half-days for secondary schools. The ministry has also declared that there must be four terms each year and sets fixed term dates for state schools throughout the country, although schools are allowed some freedom to take half-term breaks and occasional days off. Term dates vary from year to year and in 2002 and 2003 are as shown below. Dates are for both primary and secondary schools unless different, in which case secondary dates are shown in brackets (Secondary schools usually close a week earlier at the end of the year because of examinations).

Term	Period
1	30th January (28th January) to 28th March 2002
	29th January (27th January) to 11th April 2003
2	15th April to 28th June 2002
	28th April to 4th July 2003
3	15th July to 20th September 2002
	21st July to 19th September 2003
4	7th October to 19th December (6th December) 2002
	6th October to 16th December (5th December) 2003

Costs

Educating children can be an expensive business in any country, no less so in New Zealand. The cost of educating a child in New Zealand is estimated to be around $30,000, assuming he starts at the age of five and leaves at 16. This can be considered a modest estimate for a child attending a state school where no tuition fees are charged. The cost of a private education, including tuition fees and expenses, is reckoned to be around $200,000 for the same period. This is broadly similar to costs in other developed countries.

State schools aren't allowed to charge fees of any kind, but there are extra expenses associated with educating your children. Many schools suggest that you donate a set amount at the start of each year or term to boost their finances. This is set by individual schools and varies from modest sums in poorer areas to larger solicitations in wealthier areas and is unlikely to be less than $170 annually. Although it's entirely voluntarily, parents may feel obliged to pay for fear that they may harm their child's education if they don't. If you want your child to take part in any extra-curricular activities, such as specialist sports coaching or music tuition, then you also need to allow for the cost of this. Of course, schools provide a basic education in these areas, but many parents like their children to pursue extra interests. A year's tuition in a musical instrument can easily cost $1,000. In addition, there are the inevitable (sometimes expensive) school trips, in which most parents wish their children to participate. Many schools organise residential trips where the entire class spends a week together, for example, studying the environment or participating in adventure sports. The cost of such a trip is likely to be at least $200 and possibly more if special clothing or equipment needs to be bought or hired.

There are some expenses which are unavoidable even in the 'free' state sector. Schools are entitled to charge for items such as stationery (which includes subject workbooks), for which around $100 per year should be allowed (more for students studying in the higher grades). School textbooks are generally free for primary and secondary school students in the state system. Parents are also expected to pay for school uniforms (where these are worn) and other special clothing such as sports kit. The cost of a full, new school uniform is at least $500 to $700 which, depending on how fast your child is growing, may last less than one school year. Parents on a limited budget can buy these items second-hand from local shops.

Class Grading System

In 1998, New Zealand introduced a new system of grading school years based on a 'year of schooling' system. This is similar to the system that has been used in Australia and the USA for many years and which is also common in the UK. It measures the number of years a student has spent in the educational system as a whole, rather than the number of years spent in each school, as was previously the case. Students in their first year of compulsory education are classified as 'year one' and when they move on to secondary school for their first year of secondary education, usually at 13, they're classified as 'year nine'. Students who start a New Zealand school after the age of six (for example those who've migrated) are allocated to the same year grade as the majority of children their age.

Students usually progress from one grade to another at the end of each academic year irrespective of their level of attainment. A student who has failed to make sufficient progress in one year may be required to repeat the previous year's study, but this is rare. If for some reason your child is absent from the New Zealand educational system for all or most of an academic year, the new system permits them to rejoin the grade they were in when they left.

Early Childhood Education

More than 90 per cent of children in New Zealand attend some kind of nursery school before the compulsory school starting age of six; this is known as 'early childhood education'. If you can afford to, you can send your child to a nursery or similar school almost straight from birth and they may attend whatever establishment you choose. The government has a policy of partly funding early childhood education, which means that it subsidises the facilities but doesn't provide all children with free schooling. If you cannot afford to pay, your choice is more restricted and you may need to join a waiting list with the result that your child may not be able to begin his early childhood education until at least the age of four and probably not until five.

Early childhood education is provided in various centres, including kindergartens (known as 'kindys' in New Zealand), play centres, crèches, childcare centres and community playgroups. Kindergartens take children from two upwards and usually charge a small fee (around $5 to $10 a week), although space is limited. There's a kindergarten waiting list of 10,000 in Auckland alone and it's recommended to register your child as soon as possible (preferably before conception) in order to secure a place. Where private kindergartens are available, they're likely to charge around $800 per term. Play centres, childcare centres and community playgroups are often run by voluntary organisations or groups of parents on a non-profit basis and either are free or charge a small daily fee to cover expenses. Crèches take children at any age (from babies upwards) and tend to be more upmarket. They can, however, be quite expensive, although those that are registered and employ qualified staff are state-subsidised.

Primary School

Primary schools educate children aged between five and ten. Your child is required to attend primary school from the age of six, although many schools take children from five, which is a considerable relief for parents who have been paying private kindergarten fees. Indeed, enrolling a child at five is often the only way to ensure that your child attends the school of your choice, as there may be no places remaining for the admission of six-year-olds. If you want your child to attend one of the better primary schools, it's wise to make enquiries well in advance rather than waiting until he's almost six.

Primary school education in New Zealand concentrates on studying spoken and written English (reading, writing and spelling) plus maths, social studies, sciences, art, health education, music and physical education (PE). The standard of New Zealand primary reading and writing education is particularly high. Some say that this is because it still relies heavily on 'old fashioned' methods such as learning by rote and making children read aloud to teachers and classroom assistants.

Primary school pupils don't wear uniforms, although some schools have a school T-shirt or sweatshirt, which they sell to raise funds, for pupils to wear on a 'voluntary' basis (try telling your kids that it's voluntary when all their friends wear them).

Intermediate School

Intermediate school caters for children aged 11 and 12 and, as the name implies, serves as a bridge between primary and secondary schools. In some country areas an intermediate school education has traditionally been provided within the local primary school, and it's becoming common in many areas for students to remain at primary school until the age of 12 and then move directly to secondary school, or even for secondary schools to take students at 11. This is thought to be beneficial to children, as they suffer only one upheaval in their schooling, rather than two changes of school within two years. Students at intermediate and secondary schools wear uniforms which parents must pay for.

Intermediate school education in New Zealand concentrates on studying spoken and written languages (reading, writing and spelling) plus maths, social studies, sciences, art, health education, music and PE, as well as more practical skills such as wood and metalwork and domestic science. The main difference from primary school is that subjects are taught by specialist subject teachers in their classrooms, with students rotating between them rather than being taught all lessons by one class teacher.

Secondary School

At secondary school students study a core curriculum consisting of English, mathematics, social studies, general science, health and PE, music, home economics, arts and crafts. They can also study other optional subjects, e.g. history and geography, economics, and languages such as French and German or, increasingly, Japanese. Exactly what subjects a student studies is decided in conjunction with parents and teachers. There's also some variation in the range of optional subjects from school to school, individual schools competing in the educational marketplace to offer subjects which are regarded as either beneficial to students' future careers or fashionable, such as information technology and Chinese. While all secondary schools must offer the core curriculum, there's a tendency for some to specialise in certain areas such as business, sciences or vocational skills. This means that choosing a secondary school requires more thought and planning with regard to a child's future career than it did previously.

Examinations

Until 2002, New Zealand senior school students took the School Certificate (usually in year 11), Sixth Form Certificate (year 12), Higher School Certificate and University Entrance, Bursaries and Scholarships (year 13). From 2002, examinations for senior school students will start to change and be renamed the National Certificates of Education Achievement (NCEA). NCEA can be achieved in a wide range of courses and subjects and their main objective is to combine academic and vocational learning and to offer students a wider variety of subjects. Each certificate will be achieved through internal (at school) and external assessment. NCEA are as follows:

Level 1: The NCEA Level 1 will replace the School Certificate in 2002 and will be taken by most students after three years at secondary school at the age of 16. It's awarded after a written examination, an internal assessment or a combination of the two, and students may study courses in any number of subjects (usually six), depending on their ability and interests. A student's result for each subject (sometimes known as 'standards') is shown according to the following grading (credit) system: 1 (achieved the standard), 2 (achieved the standard with merit) or 3 (achieved the standard with excellence). NCEA Level 1 is equivalent to Australia's School Certificate (SC), the UK's General Certificate of Secondary Education (GCSE) and the level reached by students who graduate from tenth grade in the USA.

NCEA Level 2: The NCEA Level 2 will replace the Sixth Form Certificate from 2003 and will be awarded to students after they've studied a subject at a more advanced level than NCEA Level 1 for a year. Any number of subjects can be studied, which must include English, although it isn't compulsory to take an English exam. Results are shown as Level 1 (see above).

NCEA Level 3: The NCEA Level 3 will replace the Higher School Certificate from 2004 and will be awarded to pupils who have studied an advanced course for two years in at least three subjects (chosen by students), and there are minimum requirements for literacy and numeracy for university entrance. It's similar in standard to the HSC in Australia, the UK's 'A levels' and the standard required to graduate from twelfth grade in the USA.

NCEA Level 4: The NCEA Level 4 will replace the university bursaries examination from 2004 and is for students wishing to go to university. Students passing Level 4 may earn not only a place on a their chosen course but also a scholarship (bursary). Scholarships are awarded in two classes: class 'A' worth up to $250 per year, for students with a total of at least 300 marks; and class 'B', worth up to $200 per year, for students with marks between 250 and 299. Details of NCEA Level 4 have yet to be finalised. University entrance can also be achieved by gaining NCEA Level 3 (or Higher School Certificate) and at least three C grades in the bursary examination.

The Ministry of Education produces a series of pamphlets called *What's New* outlining the changes in examinations as well as the latest curriculum developments. The pamphlets are available from Learning Media Customer Services, PO Box 3293, Wellington. Information can also be obtained from the New Zealand Qualifications Authority (NZQA), PO Box 160, Wellington (☎ freephone 0800-623 243, 🖳 www.nzqa.govt.nz).

PRIVATE SCHOOLS

New Zealand has a flourishing private school sector, although it serves only some 5 per cent of the school population. In recent years, a number of state schools have effectively become private schools, as the government now gives greater autonomy to state schools and several have been encouraged to join the commercial market. Private schools range from nursery schools (see **Early Childhood Education** on page 138) to secondary schools, both day and boarding, and from traditional-style schools to those offering 'alternative' education such as Montessori and Rudolf Steiner schools. Private education includes schools sponsored by churches and religious groups (known as parochial schools), educational foundations and private individuals, and schools for students with learning or physical disabilities and for gifted children. In addition to mainstream parochial (e.g. Catholic) schools, there are also schools for religious and ethnic minorities, for example Muslims, where there's a strict code regarding the segregation of boys and girls. Most private schools are single sex, although some have become co-educational in recent years. There are also private boarding schools, although few accept only boarders and many accommodate both day students and boarders.

Most private schools provide a similar curriculum to state schools and set the same examinations. However, some private schools offer the International Baccalaureate (IB) examination, an internationally recognised university entrance qualification, which may be an important consideration if you intend to remain in New Zealand only for a short period.

Fees vary considerably according to a variety of factors, including the age of students, the reputation and quality of a school, and its location (schools in major cities are usually the most expensive). Private schools receive some government funding, although most of their spending is financed by fees paid by parents. The average fee for boarders is around $4,800 per term. Some schools offer reduced fees to parents with two or more children attending a school. To the fees must be added another $2,200 or so per year for uniforms (around $1,500), books, building levies, special equipment (e.g. for sports), excursion charges, computers and assorted surcharges.

The advantages of private schools are manifold, not least their excellent academic record, which is generally better than those of state schools. Private schools place the emphasis on traditional teaching, including hard work, good manners, consideration for others, responsibility, and not least, a sense of discipline (values which are sadly lacking in some state schools). They provide a broad-based education (aimed at developing a pupil's character) and generally provide a more varied approach to sport, music, drama, art, and a wider choice of academic subjects than state schools. Many private schools have resolutely embraced new technology, and the use of computers and the Internet are widespread. Their aim is dedicated to the development of the child as an individual and the encouragement of his unique talents, rather than teaching on a production-line system (as is often the case in state schools). This is made possible by small classes (an average of around 15 to 20 pupils or as little as half that of some state schools), which allow teachers to provide pupils with individually tailored lessons and tuition. Private schools are also better equipped to cater for special needs, including gifted children, slow learners or those who suffer from dyslexia, children requiring boarding facilities, and children whose parents want them to be educated in the customs of a particular religious belief. Don't, however, send your child to a school with high academic standards unless you're sure that he will be able to handle the pressure. Neither should you assume that all private schools are excellent or that they all offer a better education than state schools, which certainly isn't true.

You should make applications to private schools as far in advance as possible. The best and most popular schools have a demanding selection procedure and long waiting lists (in some cases many years), and parents register a child for entry at birth at some schools. Obviously, if you've just arrived in New Zealand, you may not be able to apply a long time in advance. However, if possible, start planning long before arriving in New Zealand. Don't rely on enrolling your child in a particular school and neglect the alternatives, particularly if your preferred school has a rigorous entrance examination. When applying, you're usually requested to send previous school reports, exam results and records. Before enrolling your child in a private school, make sure that you understand the withdrawal conditions in the school contract.

For information on private schools in New Zealand contact the Independent Schools Assocation of New Zealand at PO Box 5222, Wellington (☎ 04-471 1924, 🖳 www.independent.school.nz).

Choosing a Private School

The following checklist is designed to help you choose an appropriate private school in New Zealand:

- Does the school have a good reputation? How long has it been established?

- Does the school have a good academic record? For example, what percentage of students obtain good examination passes and go on to university? All the best schools provide exam pass-rate statistics.

- What does the curriculum include? What examinations are set? Are examinations recognised both in New Zealand and internationally? Do they fit in with your education plans? Ask to see a typical student timetable to check the ratio of academic to non-academic subjects. Check the number of free study periods and whether they're supervised.

- How large are the classes and what's the student/teacher ratio? Does the stated class size tally with the number of desks in the classrooms?

- What are the classrooms like? For example, their size, space, cleanliness, lighting, furniture, furnishings and equipment such as computers. Are there signs of creative teaching, e.g. wall charts, maps, posters and pupils' work on display?

- What are the qualification requirements for teachers? What nationalities are the majority of teachers? Ask for a list of the teaching staff and their qualifications.

- What is the teacher turnover? A high teacher turnover is a bad sign and may suggest inadequately paid teachers with poor working conditions.

- What extras must you pay for? For example, lunches, art supplies, sports equipment, outings, clothing, health and accident insurance, text books and stationery. Most private schools charge parents for absolutely everything.

- Which countries do most students come from?

- Is religion an important consideration in your choice of school?

- What provision is available for children whose mother tongue isn't English?

- What standard and kind of accommodation is provided? What is the quality and variety of food provided? What is the dining room like? Does the school have a dietician?

- What languages does the school teach as obligatory or optional subjects? Does the school have a language laboratory? (Some private schools focus on French and German which are of minimal use in New Zealand, whereas state schools are tending to teach Asian languages which students may find more useful in their future lives.)

- What is the student turnover?

- What are the school terms and holiday periods?

- If you're considering a day school, what are the school hours? Is transport provided to and from school?

- What are the withdrawal conditions, should you need or wish to remove your child? A term's notice is usual.

- What sports instruction and facilities are provided? Where are the sports facilities located?
- What are the facilities for art and science subjects, for example, arts and crafts, music, computer studies, biology, science, hobbies, drama, cookery and photography? Ask to see the classrooms, facilities, equipment and some students' projects.
- What sort of outings and school trips are organised?
- What medical facilities does the school provide, e.g. infirmary, resident doctor or nurse? Is medical and accident insurance included in the fees?
- What punishments are applied and for what offences? Private schools are likely to be strict, although corporal punishment is forbidden.
- What reports are provided for parents and how often?
- Last but not least, unless someone else is paying, what are the fees?

Before making a final choice, it's important to visit the schools on your shortlist during term time and talk to teachers and students (if possible, also speak to former students and their parents). Where possible, check out the answers to the above questions in person and don't rely on a school's prospectus or principal to provide the information. If you're unhappy with the answers, look elsewhere. Finally, having made your choice, keep a check on your child's progress and listen to his complaints. Compare notes with other parents. If something doesn't seem right, try to establish whether the complaint is founded or not; if it is, take action to have the problem resolved. Never forget that you or your employer are paying a lot of money for your child's education and you should ensure that you receive good value. See also **State or Private School?** on page 132.

APPRENTICESHIPS

A system of apprenticeships operates in New Zealand, where it's usually known as industry training, whereby you can undergo a period of training that meets industry standards. Currently, there are some 45,000 people undertaking industry training throughout the country. There's no rigid format to industry training, which is offered by both large and small employers, but by no means all employers. Some employers provide on-the-job training, whereas others provide training both in the workplace and at a polytechnic or other college. The range of industry training options is being widened and made more flexible in order to suit the needs of different employees and employers, e.g. the sports, fitness and recreation industry has recently introduced standards for industry training and has enrolled more than 1,000 new trainees.

HIGHER EDUCATION

Higher education and further education (see page 146) are known as post-compulsory education in New Zealand. Higher education is provided by seven universities, 25 polytechnics, and a number of colleges of education specialising in teacher training. Higher education institutions are expected to operate on a 'free market' basis and compete with one another for students. They're funded partly by student fees and partly by government subsidies, which are allocated according to student numbers rather than on the basis of need.

Universities: Universities are the most prestigious educational establishments in New Zealand. They include the University of Auckland, the University of Waikato (located at Hamilton), Massey University (at Palmerston North, Wellington and in Albany near Auckland), Victoria University (Wellington), the University of Canterbury (in Christchurch), Lincoln University (near Christchurch), and the University of Otago at Dunedin. Auckland also has a University of Technology.

All universities offer a wide choice of courses, although each tends to have certain specialities in which it's regarded as a 'centre of excellence'. For example, the University of Otago specialises in medicine, dentistry, surveying, home science, physical education (PE) and pharmacy, and Lincoln University specialises in agriculture and horticulture. The University of Auckland specialises in architecture, planning, engineering, medicine, optometry and art, and the University of Canterbury in engineering, fine art and forestry. Victoria University is the main institution for public administration and social work, whereas Massey University is well known for agriculture and horticulture and also produces most of New Zealand's veterinary surgeons.

No university is regarded as better or worse than any other, although a degree in a subject from a university that's a centre of excellence in that subject is more highly valued than a degree from a university which isn't. Auckland is the largest university in terms of student numbers (26,000) and offers the widest range of courses. It's also more cosmopolitan whereas the others, both geographically and intellectually, are more provincial.

Honours degree programmes last for three or four years. Entry requirements depend on the individual course, and some courses, such as medicine, demand nothing less than the best grades. Each university handles its own admissions and most distribute an enrolment pack in the first week of September. Applications must be submitted by the end of the first week of December at the latest (the date usually coincides with the end of the secondary school term). The university and polytechnic academic year runs from February until November.

Polytechnics: While universities specialise in academic study, polytechnics tend to specialise in applied studies. They don't compete directly with universities, although some subjects (e.g. accountancy) can be studied at both university and polytechnic. Polytechnics tend to offer diploma or certificate courses rather than degrees and provide mainly short courses or courses for those who are already in work and wish to study part-time.

Accommodation: All universities provide accommodation in halls of residence for a proportion of students, either on campus or nearby, although many students live in shared houses or as boarders in private homes. Given their financial situation (see below), it's much more cost-effective for students to live at home with their parents, although (not surprisingly) few choose to do so.

Student Finances: Higher education in New Zealand isn't provided free and students must pay tuition fees, which go towards funding their course of study, and also support themselves during their studies. The fee for the least expensive standard, full-time course, such as Bachelor of Arts, is around $11,000 per year; specialist courses (such as medicine) cost substantially more and can cost as much as $38,000 per year. Basic living expenses (including accommodation and food) are unlikely to be less than $250 per week, in addition to the cost of books, transport and entertainment.

Very few students are fortunate enough to have parents who can afford to pay all their expenses or are able to find jobs to finance their studies. Students can apply for a Student Allowance, which is income tested although the income limits are relatively low in New Zealand terms and most students don't qualify. If the combined parental income (or student income if they're 25 or over) is less than $28,079 per year, students living at home qualify for a weekly payment after tax of up to $103, and those who live away can get up to $129. However, this allowance is reduced progressively as combined income increases and reaches zero once income reaches $55,545, and even the maximum allowance doesn't cover all of the cost of higher education. Universities offer a number of scholarships to promising students, although the number is limited and few students can depend on these to finance their studies.

Loans: As a result, most students obtain a loan to cover the difference between their allowance or their parents' contribution and their tuition fees and living expenses – a gap that is set to increase further in the next few years, as many universities are planning to drastically increase their fees. New Zealand introduced a system of student loans in 1992, which allows students to borrow up to $10,500 per year. Factors such as age, income, parental income and credit rating don't affect your entitlement to a loan, nor is it necessary to provide security or a guarantee, but loans are restricted to New Zealand citizens and permanent residents.

There are four elements to a student loan: a contribution towards compulsory fees, course related costs (such as books), living costs and an administration fee. To qualify for a loan, students must be studying a course that's either funded by the Ministry of Education or recognised as a qualifying course. The latter category refers to courses run by private organisations rather than state colleges and universities, and these must consist of full or part-time study for at least a year. Students can usually take out a loan for living costs even if the course they're following isn't Ministry-funded. Those who receive a student allowance can also apply for a student loan (indeed they usually need to) but aren't entitled to the part of the loan that applies to living costs.

Student loans must be repaid through deductions from your salary once you're working. Your employer deducts a fixed monthly amount and sends it to the Inland Revenue Department (IRD). The repayment rate is 10 per cent of your income above $15,132. You have the option of repaying more or the entire loan at any time. Loans attract an annual interest rate (7 per cent in 2001/02), although you can apply for an interest 'write off' if you're a full-time student or a part-time student earning no more than $25,073 a year.

Since 1992 some 310,000 students have taken advantage of loans, the average student having to repay around $12,600, although some students on longer courses, such as medicine, accumulate debts of $60,000 or more. However, if the graduate leaves New Zealand and earns no money there, compulsory payments cease, with the result that many graduates with large student debts emigrate. The problem is particularly serious among health professionals, and New Zealand suffers a doctor 'brain drain'. The government is working on an amendment of the law, which will mean that graduates must repay their student loan regardless of their location. A government committee has also been set up to address the problem of student debt amongst medical students, and the New Zealand Medical Assocation is calling for significant financial help for current and future medical students. The Council of Trade Unions is campaigning vigorously for the abolition of the student loan system.

If the financial situation for New Zealand students isn't good, it's much worse for foreign students, who don't qualify for a student loan and are charged much higher fees by universities and colleges. Two organisations offer information and advice to overseas students wanting to study at higher education institutions in New Zealand: Education NZ, PO Box 10-500, Wellington (☎ 04-472 0788, ⌨ www.education nz.org.nz) and Study in New Zealand (⌨ www.study-in-newzealand.co.nz). It's generally estimated that you need between $9,000 and $11,000 per year for living expenses apart from tuition fees.

Postgraduate Studies: All universities offer facilities for postgraduate study, usually within their subjects of speciality only. Students who climb this far up the academic ladder are rewarded by much lower tuition fees than for first degree courses. This reflects the contribution that postgraduate studies make towards a university's reputation and prestige. It's also common for New Zealand students to undertake postgraduate studies at foreign universities, usually in Australia, the UK or the USA, particularly when their area of expertise isn't well catered for in New Zealand. Foreign postgraduate students are also welcomed at New Zealand universities and are offered the same favourable rates as local students.

FURTHER EDUCATION

It's government policy to encourage New Zealanders to study and learn at all stages of their lives. A keystone of the government's further education programme is The Correspondence School in Wellington, which is in fact the largest 'school' in New Zealand with some 18,000 students. The Correspondence School was established in the 1920s and is something of a New Zealand institution. It provides correspondence courses catering for adults wishing to gain qualifications in order to obtain a job or those who just want to improve their academic ability, and courses are taken by people throughout New Zealand as well as overseas. Secondary students can also take courses if these aren't offered by their secondary school, and New Zealand children abroad can follow primary and secondary school programmes. The school is manned by a team of student advisers and clerks who offer pre-enrolment advice, course counselling and student support. Students receive tuition by means of written courses, by telephone and Internet, and at seminars. There are academic, vocational and general interest courses, including the full range of secondary school subjects, as well as more practical and general interest courses. Course fees range from $40 to $80. For information contact The Correspondence School, Private Bag 39992, Wellington (☎ within New Zealand freephone 0800-659 988 or 04-473 6841, ⌨ www. correspondence.school.nz).

LANGUAGE SCHOOLS

Obtaining a working knowledge or becoming fluent in English while living in New Zealand is relatively easy, as you will be constantly immersed in the English language and will have the maximum opportunity to practise. However, if you wish to speak or write English fluently, you will probably need to attend a language school or find a private tutor. Note that it's usually necessary to have a recognised qualification in English to be accepted at a college of higher or further education in Australia. If you speak English fluently (or you wish to learn another language) you can enrol in a language course at one of the many language schools in New Zealand. Many languages are spoken in New Zealand (see **Language** on page 135), so there's plenty of opportunity to learn and practise foreign languages with immigrants.

English-language courses at all levels are offered by universities, language schools, foreign and international organisations, local associations and clubs, private colleges, the Correspondence School (see page 146) and other distance learning organisations, and private teachers. New migrants can enrol at special 'migrant education colleges' through a programme run by Skill New Zealand (see page 62). Classes range from language courses for complete beginners to special business or cultural courses and university-level seminars leading to recognised diplomas. There are language schools in cities and large towns in New Zealand, many equipped with computers, language laboratories, video studios, libraries and bookshops.

Most language schools offer a variety of classes according to your ability, how many hours you wish to study per week, how much money you want to spend and how quickly you wish to learn. Full-time, part-time and evening courses are offered by most schools, and many also offer residential courses or accommodation with local families (highly recommended to accelerate learning). Courses that include accommodation (often half board, consisting of breakfast and an evening meal) are usually good value. Bear in mind that if you need to find your own accommodation, particularly in Wellington or Auckland, it can be difficult and expensive. Language classes generally fall into the following categories:

Category	Hours per Week
Compact	10–20
Intensive	20–30
Total immersion	30–40+

Most schools offer compact or intensive courses and also provide special courses for businessmen and professionals (among others), and a wide variety of examinations, most of which are recognised internationally. Course fees vary considerably and are usually calculated on a weekly basis. Fees depend on the number of hours' tuition per week, the type of course, and the location and reputation of the school. Expect to pay up to $550 per week for an intensive course and around $350 per week for a compact course.

Total immersion or executive courses are provided by some schools and usually consist of private lessons. Fees can run to $2,000 or more per week and not everyone is suited to learning at such a fast rate (or has the financial resources). Whatever language you're learning, don't expect to become fluent in a short period unless you have a particular flair for languages or already have a good command of a language. Unless you desperately need to learn a language quickly, it's better to arrange your lessons over a long period. Don't commit yourself to a long course of study (particularly an expensive one) before ensuring that it's the correct one. Most schools offer a free introductory lesson and free tests to help you find your appropriate level. Many language schools offer private and small group lessons. **It's important to choose the right course, particularly if you're studying English in order to continue with full-time education in New Zealand and need to reach a minimum standard or gain a particular qualification.**

10.

PUBLIC TRANSPORT

Although the population of New Zealand is dispersed over a wide area, it has a good public transport service, which is centred around road, rail and air links, plus the essential umbilical ferry link connecting the North and South Islands. Unless you live in a remote country area, you shouldn't find it too difficult to get around without your own transport. Probably the most impressive feature of public transport is that the different elements are closely integrated and if you start a journey by bus, continue by rail and then take to the air, you will usually find that services are planned and timed to connect.

Although car ownership and usage in New Zealand are high (see **Chapter 11**), this shouldn't be taken as a sign that public transport is unreliable (although it does have a few shortcomings, such as finishing too early in many cases), but rather that the roads are relatively uncongested and therefore that driving still has many advantages over public transport. Even in metropolitan Auckland and Wellington, commuters travelling into the centre often drive – the relatively modest rush hour traffic hasn't induced them to let the bus or train take the strain.

Note that all public transport timetables in New Zealand use the am/pm time system rather than the 24-hour clock. Note also that, if your luggage is lost, stolen or damaged on public transport in New Zealand, you should make a claim to the relevant authority, as you may receive an ex-gratia payment.

Disabled Travellers: Like many countries, New Zealand has started to take the needs of the disabled seriously only within the last decade. Domestic airlines and trains cater fully for disabled travellers, but you should tell them that you need special assistance when booking. As most taxis are simply converted saloon cars, you can use them only if you can gain access to a standard car. There are wheelchair-accessible taxis in cities, although you need to book in advance (particularly for the return journey), as their number is limited. There are no special facilities for the disabled on coach and bus services, although discounts on fares are widely available. Further information can be obtained from the Disability Information Service, 314 Worcester Street, Christchurch (☎ 03-366 6189).

TRAINS

New Zealand's rail network is privatised and operated by a consortium called NZ Rail, which includes American owners. It's operated under the name Tranz Rail, or Tranz Scenic for the more picturesque services aimed at leisure travellers. The network is limited, mainly because of the mountainous terrain in many parts of the country and, of course, the fact that lines cannot cross the Cook Straits (until a bridge or tunnel is built). The service itself is modern and comfortable (part of the Auckland-Wellington line has recently been electrified), but neither frequent nor fast, although stops at many small stations on long-distance lines have been eliminated making journey times shorter. As a result, rail services are widely promoted as a tourist attraction rather than a day-to-day amenity. In this regard the rail service is excellent, as many lines pass through native forests, past volcanic peaks and through alpine passes giving spectacular, panoramic views. NZ Rail is criticised by New Zealanders for its disorganisation and timekeeping, although foreigners rarely seem to complain.

The Tranz Rail timetable is simple, as there's only one train a day on most routes, with the exception of Auckland-Roturua where there are three daily return services, and Auckland-Wellington where there are two. Special day return excursion trips run on the Tranz Alpine Express, which is a popular tourist route. Most services commence their outward journey between 8 and 8.30am. There are eight main railway routes, each with a colourful name, as follows:

The Geyserland	Auckland-Hamilton-Rotorua
The Kaimai Express	Auckland-Hamilton-Tauranga
The Overland	Auckland-Wellington (day service)
The Northerner	Auckland-Wellington (overnight service)
The Bay Express	Wellington-Napier
The Southerner	Christchurch-Dunedin-Invercargill
The Coastal Pacific	Christchurch-Picton
Tranz Alpine Express	Christchurch-Greymouth

Fares range from $32 for the cheapest rail trip (Hamilton-Tauranga) to $135 for the most expensive (Auckland-Wellington). There's only one class of travel whichever service you choose. If you're a student, an International Youth Hostel Association (IYHA) member or over 60, you qualify for a 30 per cent discount. Disabled passengers receive a 50 per cent discount. You may need proof of identity (e.g. student card, IYHA membership card, pension book or passport) and must book in advance.

All services provide free refreshments with a free lunch on the Overlander service, although there are also buffet cars selling more substantial meals and a bar on all services except the Northerner. All trains have guided tourist commentaries (whether you're a tourist or not). If you wish to take a bicycle on a train, check when booking, as they aren't allowed on many services and only limited space is available when they are. Smokers may also have a tough time travelling by train in New Zealand, as smoking isn't permitted on any train, even though some of the journeys can take ten hours or more.

Timetables & Information: Enquiries about services and a copy of the latest timetable can be obtained from travel agents or Tranz Rail travel centres or by calling ☏ freephone 0800-802 802 or 04-498 3303 from overseas. Tranz Rail also have a comprehensive website (🖥 www.tranzrailtravel.co.nz). As the sole daily departure on most routes changes by just a few minutes from year to year, you will soon have committed the timetable to memory if you're a regular train traveller.

Buying Tickets: The easiest way to book a trip by train is to call Tranz Rail on ☏ freephone 0800-802 802 and pay by credit card, although you can also book at travel agents (a booking fee is charged) or free at stations. Tranz Rail also have numerous agents overseas where you can book tickets, and you can book online (🖥 www.tranzrailtravel.co.nz). If you travel on a train without a ticket (or with an invalid ticket or pass), you must pay the full fare plus a modest surcharge, but you won't be made to get off the train in the middle of nowhere!

Discounted Tickets: Given the limited nature of the rail system, there are no season tickets on Tranz Rail, although there are a limited number of discounted tickets available on each journey. Super Savers entitle you to a 50 per cent discount, Savers to 30 per cent and Economy to 15 per cent for travel at off-peak times. Note that discounted tickets are available only if you book in advance. If you expect to do a lot of travelling, you should consider buying a Best of New Zealand pass (see page 159), which allows you to travel on trains, coaches and the Interislander ferry. Tranz Rail also runs packages known as Great Train Escapes, which include train travel and accommodation, and Ski Specials during the skiing season.

Stations: Tranz Rail stations have few facilities. This is mainly because, in many cases, there's only one arrival or departure per day and hence no demand for buffets, bars and the range of other services you usually find at major railway stations. There's an enquiry office open from before the first train leaves (or at least 7.30am) until 5.30pm for information and reservations. Taxis and buses don't stop at stations throughout the day, but tend to congregate there as each train arrives. This means that you may have to wait in a queue, although you're unlikely to be left stranded, as there's usually a connecting bus service timed to meet the last train. Stations aren't always conveniently situated for city centres: for example Auckland's is on Beach Road, a 15-minute walk from the city centre, and isn't on a regular bus route; Wellington's is on Waterloo Quay on the edge of the central area, near one of the city's bus stations and served by the city's commuter railway services (it's also connected by shuttle bus to the Interislander ferry terminal).

Commuter Railway Services

There are no underground services anywhere in New Zealand. There are fast and reliable commuter rail networks in Auckland and Wellington known as Tranz Metro, although they don't run underground. In Auckland there are two lines running from the railway station, one to Waitakere in the west and the other to Papkura in the south. Wellington's main station has three Tranz Metro lines, one to Johnsonville, one to Paraparaumu and the third to Upper Hutt. Tranz Metro services are popular with commuters and offer frequent trains. Timetable and fare information can be obtained from Tranz Metro (☎ 04-366 6400, 🖥 www.tranzrailtravel.co.nz).

BUSES & TRAMS

Most towns and cities have a good public bus service, and some cities operate double-decker buses, like those in the UK. Bus services have been deregulated and privatised to some extent in recent years, although in many cases the original public bus company is still the largest operator on a majority of routes. In Auckland, the main operator is Rideline. One of the drawbacks of the public bus service is that it ends early, and on Saturdays and Sundays the last services leave at around 5pm. Even during the week in Auckland you won't find a bus running after 11.30pm (many routes finish much earlier) and some services are discontinued altogether at weekends.

Auckland bus services include the Link, which runs at ten-minute intervals around the main parts of the city in a loop. There's also a free bus service introduced during the America's Cup (yacht race), which serves the central area (where the 'Cup Village' is set up). For information telephone ☎ 09-366 6400. In Wellington the bus system is run by Stagecoach with frequent services, including an after-midnight service from the entertainment district to outlying suburbs. Timetables and other information are available from ☎ freephone 0800-801700. Christchurch buses are among the best in the country with cheap and frequent services. A free Shuttle runs around the city centre at ten-minute intervals. Information is available from Bus Info

(☎ 03-366 8855). On New Zealand buses you usually buy your ticket from the driver as you enter the bus. Some buses accept the exact fare only.

One benefit of bus deregulation is that small private firms have been allowed to enter the public transport business, and many operate services late into the evening and at weekends when the main operators have suspended their services. Some services, using minibuses and cars, can be ordered by phone when required. As several companies now operate in most towns, there's no centralised place to obtain timetable information. Check your telephone directory for details of where to obtain information about services and a copy of the timetable. In larger cities there's more than one bus station serving the different companies and routes. In Wellington, the main stations are at Waterloo Quay and Courtenay Place. In Auckland, buses use the Downtown and Midtown terminals (although Midtown is only a series of lay-bys rather than a proper terminal).

Bus Fares: Fares for town bus services are calculated on a zone basis and depend on how many zones you travel through. In Auckland, bus journeys within the city cost from 50¢ and a journey on the Link $1. In Wellington, it costs $1.10 to ride within one zone (known as a section) and $1.70 for two. Bus fares in Christchurch start at 90¢. Most areas offer daily and weekly passes, which work out much cheaper if you plan to do a lot of travelling by bus. The cheapest pass in Auckland costs $8 for unlimited rides on bus and ferry, while in Wellington a Daytripper pass costs $5. In both cases you cannot begin your journey until 9am on weekdays, although there are no restrictions at weekends. In Christchurch a Big Red Bus Pass giving unlimited travel costs $5 per person or $10 for a family of four.

Trams: Trams operate in several cities in New Zealand, including Wellington, where they're called trolley buses and operate on several routes in the city centre and inner suburbs. The cost is the same as for buses (see above), and the Daytripper pass issued for buses can also be used on trams. Wellington also has a cable car operating between Lambton Quay and the Botanic Gardens in Kelburn. This is a popular tourist attraction, but is also used daily by commuters, as it's an easy way to travel up one of Wellington's steepest hills. Trams operate on a city centre loop in Christchurch, stopping at nine points along the way, and mostly attract tourists but are handy for commuters and shoppers in the city centre. You can buy a one hour, half-day or full day ticket from the conductor on board (the service operates between 9am and 6pm).

COACHES

New Zealand has a comprehensive and reliable long-distance coach service, which is the main way of travelling long distances for those who don't have a car or who cannot afford or don't want to fly. Services are provided by two major companies. InterCity Coachlines is a subsidiary of NZ Rail operating countrywide and serving over 1,000 destinations (and therefore a much more comprehensive and useful service than its parent company's rail service). Newmans is its main competitor in North Island but doesn't operate in Northland or on South Island. There are also around a dozen smaller companies, such as Northliner and Pioneer Coachlines, which operate their own services but mainly provide services on a sub-contract basis for InterCity.

Coach services, even of competing companies, are well co-ordinated so that they connect not only with other coach services but also with other modes of transport. So, for example, if you take the train from Auckland to Wellington, the Interislander ferry across the Cook Strait and then a coach to Christchurch, it's possible to plan a route which connects smoothly allowing just enough time to get from one terminus to another. Unlike the train, there are several coach services per day on the main routes such as Auckland-Wellington.

Coaches are modern and provide facilities such as toilets, reclining seats and air-conditioning. On routes that are popular with tourists the driver usually provides a commentary on sights and places of interest. On services operating in more remote areas, you may find that half the coach is given over to freight and parcels. Snacks and drinks aren't available on board coaches but they stop regularly for refreshments, although drivers tend to choose the more expensive places (so it pays to take your own snacks with you). Smoking isn't permitted on coach services.

Bookings: It's usually possible to just turn up and travel by coach except at busy times such as summer and public holiday periods. However, if you know when you want to travel, it makes sense to book as it costs no extra when booking direct. Bookings can be made by telephone or via the Internet; the telephone numbers and website addresses of the three main companies are:

- InterCity Coachlines: ☎ Auckland 09-913 6100 or Christchurch 03-379 9020, 🖳 www.intercitycoach.co.nz
- Newmans ☎ freephone 0800-733 500, 🖳 www.newmanscoach.co.nz
- Northliner ☎ 09-307 5873, 🖳 www.newzealandnet.com/northliner

You can also book at InterCity Travel Centres in the main towns or with a travel agent (where you're charged a $3 booking fee).

When booking, take note of exactly where your service operates from, which will depend on the coach company and isn't necessarily the same location as the departure point of local city buses. In Wellington, Newmans services operate from the Interislander ferry terminal, while InterCity services operate from near the railway station. In Auckland, InterCity services depart from Hobson Street, whereas Newmans' operate from Quay Street.

Fares: Coaches are the cheapest way of travelling long distances in New Zealand. For example, the standard one-way adult fare from Auckland to Wellington is $94 (around ten hours), from Rotorua to Wellington $75 (eight hours) and from Picton to Christchurch $57 (6 hours 15 minutes). If you're travelling from North to South Island or vice versa, it's worth noting that the Interislander ferry fare (see below) isn't included in the coach price and you need to pay separately for the North and South Island legs of your trip (although you can book them together and services are timed to connect).

Special offers are available when travelling at off-peak times, e.g. Super Saver Fares with a reduction of 50 per cent and Saver Fares with a 25 per cent discount. 'Golden Age' passengers (men over 65 and women over 60) qualify for a 25 per cent discount on production of appropriate identification.

Children under two travel free if they don't occupy a seat, and there are reductions of 33 per cent for children aged between 2 and 11. You can take one large and one medium size suitcase per person on coach services, and excess baggage incurs a small fee. Bicycles can be carried for a flat fee of $10 per journey, irrespective of the length of the trip (you must remove the pedals and wrap the chain, e.g. in newspaper).

Each of the main coach lines offers a travel pass allowing unlimited travel for a set period. InterCity Coachlines offer passes on a zone basis, with several options for either North or South Island, or allow you to combine any two passes into a 'Combo' pass. These include Auckland to Wellington and all points between for $99 (adult) and $66 (child), and Christchurch to Milford via Mount Cook for $132 (adult) and $88 (child). Passes are usually valid for three months and bookings cost $3 per zone. Newmans have Newmans Stopover Passes, such as the North Island pass for $95 and the South Island pass of $129. Northliner offers passes for Northland, such as the Bay of Islands Pass ($49) and the Loop ($79). If you want to combine coach and train travel, you can purchase a Best of New Zealand pass (see page 159).

Timetables: You can obtain a copy of coach timetables from InterCity Travel centres (for InterCity Coachlines), which are found in cities and large town, Visitor Information Network (VIN) centres or by calling the numbers listed under **Bookings** above.

Backpackers' Buses: An economical way of travelling for young people are backpackers' buses which operate throughout New Zealand (similar to those in Australia). Backpackers' buses are operated by a number of companies, of which Kiwi Experience and Magic Bus are the best known. Services operate on a pass basis whereby once you've bought a ticket you can switch buses and stop off along the route, whether for a few hours for or a few days. Sporting and adventure activities are also sometimes offered along the way, such as white-water rafting or kayaking. These services tend to be cheap and cheerful and aimed at those aged between 18 and 35. You must pay extra for accommodation, although this is usually low-cost and there's also the option to camp. Fares are around $425 for a 12-day trip and at least $950 for 25 or more days. Booking is essential in summer.

FERRIES

As a country consisting mainly of two large islands, North and South, separated by Cook Strait, New Zealand is highly reliant on the ferry service between the two. In addition to the Interislander, there are several smaller ferry services linking the two main islands, as well as serving smaller islands.

Interislander

The Interislander ferry service is highly efficient and employs two roll-on roll-off ferries most of the year, the Arahura (the larger) and the Aratere (the newer), which carry passengers, vehicles and railway carriages. They sail between Wellington in North Island and Picton in South Island, which takes areound three hours. (The ferry route is 96km (60mi), although the Strait is only 20km (12mi) wide at its narrowest point.) The Arahanga, a freight vessel, also operates across the Strait.

The number of daily sailings varies between summer and winter. In summer (December to April) there are five daily sailings (but only four on Sundays and Mondays), but in winter the service is usually reduced to two or three crossings per day, as one of the vessels is taken out of service for maintenance. Summer timetables vary only slightly from year to year: ships leave Wellington at 1.10am, 9.30am, 1.00pm and 5.30pm, and Picton at 5.30am, 8am, 12.30pm, 4pm and 8.30pm.

Bookings & Fares: It isn't essential to book ahead for the Interislander ferry except at busy times, such as the beginning of school holidays, although it's cheaper, as discounted tickets can only be purchased in advance. If you turn up without a ticket, you must pay the full fare, even if you are travelling off-peak. Reservations can be made up to six months before travel at any Tranz Rail-appointed travel agent, by calling ☎ freephone 0800-802 802 or via the Internet (🖳 www. tranzrailtravel.co.nz/interislander). The standard single fare is $49 for adults and $175 for a vehicle up to 6.6m (21ft 7in) in length.

Discounts range from 15 to 60 per cent depending on the time of travel and the availability of discounted tickets. Children from 4 to 14 are entitled to a discount of 40 per cent and children under four travel free. There are extra charges for excess luggage, bicycles ($10 each), canoes and windsurf boards, unless they can be dismantled. Prominent notices at the terminals also state that 'Excess Charges Are Involved for Lawnmowers', so it pays to think twice before taking your lawnmower on holiday with you. Pets travel free in vehicles, but otherwise a charge is made for use of on-board kennels, as they cannot be taken on deck (unfortunately, a similar facility isn't available for children).

Inter-Island Terminals: Interislander ferries depart from the Inter-island terminals in Wellington and Picton, both of which are well signposted. There are terminal buildings at both terminals where tickets can be purchased and where foot passengers can check in their luggage for the journey rather than carry it aboard. There are also car parks and car hire facilities and if you have a hire car or are staying on the other island for a short time only, it's cheaper to leave your car on one island and hire another when you arrive (see **Car Rental** on page 169). A free bus service (the Interislander Shuttle Bus) runs between Wellington railway station and the Inter-island terminal, leaving around 35 minutes before ferry departures. A bus departs from the Inter-island terminal and arrives at the railway station in time to catch the evening Northerner train to Auckland. At Picton, shuttle buses operate from the Inter-island terminal to the station to meet the arrival and departure of trains, which run directly to Christchurch.

The latest check-in time is 30 minutes prior to departure for foot passengers and one hour for those with vehicles. Foot passengers may take only two pieces of luggage weighing a maximum of 30kg and no more than 200 'linear' centimetres in size (a combination of the height, width and breadth).

Interislander ferries are well equipped, which is just as well given the length of the crossing, and include a cinema, telephones, several bars, children's nursery and play areas, Visitor Information Network (VIN) centres and a number of eating places, including fast food outlets. There are also fruit machines, something of a novelty in a country where gambling is so tightly controlled. For a supplement you can also use the club class lounge which provides free drinks and snacks, newspapers and an oasis of peace before boarding the ship (children under 18 aren't permitted!).

Other Ferry Services

Lynx: Tranz Rail operates a high speed ferry between Wellington and Picton known as the Lynx. The journey is half an hour quicker than with the Interislander (2 hours 30 minutes) but considerably more expensive. There are two crossings each day in each direction for foot passengers and cars. The Lynx departs from Wellington at 8am and 3pm, and leaves Picton at 11.30am and 6.30pm. The standard single fare is $63 for adults and $199 for cars, although it's possible to obtain discounted tickets at off-peak times and by booking in advance. Foot passengers don't usually require a booking, but if you want to take a car at busy periods (December to February and public holidays) it's best to make one. You can make a Lynx booking at any travel agent or by calling Lynx direct on freephone ☎ 0800-834 596.

There are several ferry services to various small islands, particularly in Auckland's Hauraki Gulf (e.g. that operated by Fuller's ☎ 09-367 9111). As few of these islands have a large population, ferries mainly attract tourists.

TAXIS

Taxis are plentiful in most cities and towns in New Zealand. They're usually ordinary saloon cars (or minibuses) painted in distinctive colours, which vary with the town or city. You can pick one up at a taxi rank or order one by telephone. Taxis cannot be hailed in the street and will pick you up only if they're stopping to drop a passenger (so you had better be quick!). All taxi fares are metered; you pay a standard charge of $2 plus $1.60 per kilometre. You pay the amount showing on the meter only and aren't expected to tip (Americans please note!). An extra charge is made for telephone bookings, items of luggage, and when travelling during the evening and at weekends, when taxis are most in demand due to the curtailment of bus services. There's also a surcharge for waiting and at airports ($1).

AIRLINE SERVICES

Air travel is a popular form of domestic travel in New Zealand, but it certainly isn't cheap. Domestic air fares are on a par with European scheduled services (i.e. expensive) and nothing like as good value as US services. In spite of this, New Zealanders travel by air as frequently as possible (or as frequently as they can afford) as it's by far the fastest way to cross the country.

Airlines: New Zealand is served by some 25 international airlines, most of which fly to Auckland or Christchurch. New Zealand's main domestic airline (and also its international airline) is Air New Zealand (☎ freephone 0800-737 000 or 🖥 www.airnz.co.nz), which was previously state-owned but is now privatised and regularly acclaimed as one of the world's best airlines. In 2001 Air New Zealand (ANZ) came near to bankruptcy when it attempted to buy the remaining 50 per cent of Ansett Australia (it already owned 50 per cent), which went into liquidation in mid-2001. The New Zealand government, in an attempt to save the airline, announced a $500 million rescue package, which effectively makes the government the majority shareholder in the company. (Many New Zealanders believe that the airline shouldn't have been privatised in the first place.) ANZ has a comprehensive route network operating over 3,000 individual flights throughout the country each week. Its domestic services are sold under the name of ANZ National (major domestic routes) and ANZ Link (minor domestic routes).

ANZ's only significant competitors are Ansett New Zealand on (☎ freephone 0800-803 146, 🖥 www.ansett.com.au), itself a subsidiary of Ansett Australia, and Origin Pacific (☎ freephone 0800-302 302, 🖥 www.originpacific.co.nz), a relatively new player. Ansett New Zealand operates quiet BAe146 whisper jets and competes with Air New Zealand on a comprehensive network, although flights linking Auckland, Wellington and Christchurch are its mainstay. Origin Pacific operates flights linking major centres between Auckland and Christchurch. Mount Cook

Airlines also operate domestic services, although it's a partner airline to ANZ (operating services on their behalf) rather than a real competitor. A number of other competitors have started up or been proposed over the years, including the inappropriately named Kiwi Air (considering that the kiwi is a flightless bird!), although most have fallen by the wayside. Many domestic services provide in-flight bar facilities, which is something of an innovation in New Zealand where the sale of alcohol is subject to strict licensing hours. Smoking isn't permitted on the domestic services of any airline. Surprisingly, however, the health-conscious New Zealanders haven't banned that other risk to the well-being of air travellers – airline food!

Southair (☎ freephone 0800-505 005) operates between Wellington and Picton. This short flight is the fastest and cheapest route between North and South islands and at $50 compares favourably with ferry prices (see **Ferries** above). There are also a number of mini-airlines serving minor destinations often using aircraft with as few as four seats. Great Barrier Airlines (☎ freephone 0800-900 600) and Mountain Air (☎ freephone 0800-222 123) both operate a service to Great Barrier Island (a paradise-like island, likened to Fiji or Tahiti) in the Hauraki Gulf off Auckland with Auckland, Tauranga, Whangarei, Pauanui, Whitianga, Thamas, Coromandel and Matarangi.

Fares: ANZ's services were notoriously expensive until Ansett arrived on the scene a few years ago, which prompted more competitive pricing. However, standard fares are still high, and it's necessary to shop around and compare prices to obtain the best deal. Of the three airlines, Ansett and Origin Pacific are most likely to have special offers and cut-price deals. The cheapest fares are to be had by booking at least seven days ahead. Sample fares are Auckland-Wellington (one hour) for $305, Auckland-Christchurch (1 hour 20 minutes) $430 and Rotorua-Christchurch (the longest domestic service at 2 hours 10 minutes) $390. These are full-fare one-way prices and are the most you should pay. Discounts of up to 40 per cent are available for one-way flights and up to 70 per cent for return flights.

A departure tax of $25 is levied on passengers on departing international flights, which should be paid before you pass through immigration. At Auckland International Airport it can be paid at the Bank of New Zealand offices on the ground and first floors.

Airports: New Zealand's main international airport is Auckland, which is connected by direct flights to most main cities in Asia, several cities in the USA and Europe (particularly London), plus several Polynesian destinations. The airports at Wellington and Christchurch also dub themselves 'international', but offer a much smaller number of international flights, mainly to Australia, although Christchurch serves some other countries, including the UK. Wellington is the country's domestic air hub, as many flights from all points north and south stop at Wellington to allow passengers to change planes. There are also airports at Blenheim, Dunedin, Gisborne, Hamilton, Hastings, Hokitika, Invercargill, Kaitaia, Te Anau, Mount Cook, Napier, Nelson, New Plymouth, Palmerston North, Queenstown, Rotorua, Taupo, Tauranga, Wanganui, Whakatane and Whangerei. These serve mainly domestic flights and private planes, and their facilities range from a modest but modern terminal building to a motley collection of huts.

Auckland International airport is 21km (13mi) south of the city at Mangere. There are three separate terminals, one for ANZ international flights and foreign airlines, and separate mini-terminals for ANZ and Ansett New Zealand's domestic services. There's an AirBus shuttle connecting the airport with the city centre every 50 minutes costing $10 single and $16 return. The privately operated Johnston's Shuttle Link and the SuperShuttle also run to the city centre taking 35 minutes and costing $15 one way. Airport information is available on ☎ 09-256 8899 or 🖳 www.auckland-airport.co.nz.

Wellington International Airport is 7km (5mi) south of the city at Rongotai. It has been designated a 'low noise' airport and may be used only by the quietest planes, which, even so, aren't permitted to arrive or depart at night. Wellington's airport is also notoriously windy and renowned among pilots as a difficult place to land or take off. As with Auckland, there are three terminals serving international, ANZ domestic and Ansett domestic flights. The two airport shuttle buses, again privately operated by Johnston's Shuttle Link and SuperShuttle, cost $8 and take 20 minutes to reach central Wellington. Airport information is available on ☎ 04-388 5123 or 🖳 www.wellington-airport.co.nz.

Christchurch International Airport, whose facilities have recently been greatly improved, is 11km (7mi) north of the city centre and is easily reached by bus for a fare of $2.70 (half price at off-peak times). For information ☎ 03-358 5029 or 🖳 www.christchurch-airport.co.nz.

HOLIDAY & VISITORS' PASSES

The most comprehensive travel pass available for travel within New Zealand is the Best of New Zealand Pass, which offers travel to some 1,100 destinations within the country on InterCity, Tranz Scenic, and Interislander and Lynx ferries. The pass works on a system of points known as Best Points. You can purchase 600, 800 or 1,000 Best Points. With 600 points ($462 for an adult) you may travel anywhere within one island and with 1,000 points ($725 for an adult) anywhere in the whole country. Each journey you make has a points value, e.g. Christchurch to Greymouth on the Trans Alpine Express train is worth 76 points. If you use all your points, you can buy a top up of 100, 200 or 300 points. The pass is valid over 180 days and if you're doing a lot of travelling it represents good value. Family and group passes are also available.

Comprehensive information as well as route planning is available from Tranz Rail (☎ freephone 0800-692 378 or 04-498 3303, ✉ bestpass@tranzrail.co.nz, 🖳 www.tranzrailtravel.co.nz). The Best of New Zealand pass can be purchased through most travel agents, both world-wide and in New Zealand, and at most Tranz Rail/Tranz Scenic or InterCity Coachlines Travel Centres. There are other passes for coach travel only (see page 154).

11.

MOTORING

In the absence of a comprehensive rail system, the road network is the mainstay of both public and private transport in New Zealand, covering 92,300km (around 57,000mi), of which some 60 per cent are sealed (tarmac). The country has no national motorway (freeway) network, and those motorways that exist are short, e.g. in and around cities such as Auckland and Wellington, although more are planned. Most New Zealand roads have just one lane in each direction, but they're invariably well surfaced and maintained, even when they pass through areas with difficult terrain (which is frequently). All New Zealand roads are toll-free.

New Zealand has one of the highest rates of vehicle ownership rates in the world, and car registrations increase by some 17 per cent annually, with nearly 17,000 new registrations a month. The main reason for this devotion to the motor vehicle is that driving is simply the most convenient way of getting around the country, where many places aren't accessible by public transport or services are infrequent. A car is highly recommended if you live in a rural area, where you will find getting around difficult without one. Even in Auckland and Wellington people make use of their cars a great deal, as traffic congestion and parking aren't yet bad enough (in this fairly sparsely populated country) to make driving a headache. However, traffic density is increasing, along with the resultant pollution, which is an important issue in this environmentally-minded nation, and the government and motoring associations are now considering traffic reduction measures for Auckland. Motoring is more expensive than taking a coach or train, but much cheaper than flying, particularly over long distances.

The travel brochures portray motoring in New Zealand as an idyllic pursuit, where roads are uncrowded and passing scenery breathtaking. To some extent this is true in rural areas, particularly outside the tourist season, when it's possible to drive for miles without seeing another motorist (or having to crawl behind a caravan). **However, this disguises the fact that New Zealand is one of the most dangerous countries for motorists in the world.** The country has one of the highest rates of road accidents (and deaths) per head of population anywhere in the world, which is even more surprising given the width of the roads. Your chance of being involved in a road accident in New Zealand is nearly twice that in the UK (which has some of the safest roads in the world), substantially higher than in Italy and slightly below France, Spain and the USA, none of which are noted for their safe driving. Much has been done to make motoring safer in the last decade, and a recent survey found that the accident rate in New Zealand was falling faster than in any other country. But, be warned, it's still very high and taking to the open road in New Zealand is a risky business!

CAR IMPORT

The long sea crossing from most countries means that it's usually cheaper to buy a car on arrival in New Zealand than to import one. Note also that some vehicles don't comply with New Zealand registration requirements (see below) and therefore cannot be used in the country. If you own an unusual car (e.g. one made from a kit), you should check in advance. New Zealand also has a competitive used car market, and importing your car can often prove uneconomical, especially when you consider the cost of shipping, duty and tax (see below). However, if you have a collector's car or a vehicle to which you're attached (or you're making the comparatively short trip across the Tasman from Australia), you may wish to import your own car.

Left-hand Drive Cars: New Zealanders drive on the left, so vehicles used there need to be right-hand drive. Consequently there's a restriction on importing and registering left-hand drive cars, such as vehicles from the USA. If you wish to import a left-hand drive car, you should first make enquiries with the LTSA (see below). Left-hand drive cars aren't usually permitted for ordinary daily use (unless they're left-hand drive for practical purposes, e.g. plant or agricultural machinery).

Shipping: As there are no regular ferry services to New Zealand, vehicles must be shipped on cargo vessels. Most international shipping companies can arrange this for you. It takes at least five weeks to ship a vehicle from Europe and three weeks from the west coast of the USA, although it can take much longer when loading, unloading and customs clearance are included. Note that you're advised not to pack belongings in your vehicle when it's shipped because of the risk of theft, and many shippers won't accept vehicles for shipment if they contain personal items.

Arrival: The following documents are required in order to clear a vehicle's arrival in New Zealand:

- invoice receipt showing total price paid and date of purchase;
- registration papers, e.g. Certificate of Permanent Export (UK), Certificate of Title (USA);
- invoice showing freight and insurance costs to New Zealand;
- bill of lading;
- odometer reading at time of purchase or export to New Zealand;
- odometer reading at time of import into New Zealand.

Duty & Tax: If you're coming to New Zealand for the first time to take up residence, you're permitted to import one car, motorcycle or other motor vehicle (other than a motor home – see below) free of customs duty provided:

- you have legal authority to take up permanent residence in New Zealand (a valid visa or permit is required as proof);
- you've never previously lived in New Zealand (short stays as a non-resident are excluded);
- you've owned and used the vehicle yourself for at least a year before arriving in New Zealand. A purchase invoice or registration document is required as proof.
- you're importing the vehicle for your own use and not with the intention of giving it away or selling it (nor may it be used in a business);
- you intend to keep and use the vehicle for at least two years. You must give a written undertaking that if you sell it or give it away during this period you will pay taxes and charges on its full value.

You may be allowed to import more than one vehicle duty-free, provided the same conditions are met for each. Note that these conditions are strictly applied and there are heavy penalties, including fines and confiscation of a vehicle, for false or misleading declarations. If you're unable to comply with the conditions, or if you wish to import a motor home, you must pay customs duty at 17.5 per cent on each vehicle imported into New Zealand. Duty is calculated according to a vehicle's local market value and not its value in your home country. Briefly, the local market value of a vehicle is determined by calculating the purchase price paid or payable overseas by the importer minus any overseas duties or taxes included in the price which have been refunded before the vehicle arrives in New Zealand. There's an allowance for depreciation ranging from 13 per cent for vehicles owned for more than three months to 75 per cent for vehicles owned for over four years. The net value is the amount on which customs duty is levied. Below is an example of how customs duty is calculated on a vehicle costing $27,500 and owned for over six months but less than nine:

Value for duty of vehicle	$27,500.00
Value for duty after depreciation (-27.5%)	$19,937.50
Customs duty (17.5%)	$ 3,489.06

All imported vehicles are subject to goods and services tax (GST) at 12.5 per cent, which is levied on the sum of the dutiable value and the duty (if applicable) plus the cost of shipping the vehicle to New Zealand (including insurance). For the same vehicle, this would be calculated as follows:

Shipping and insurance costs	$ 4,500.00
GST value (value for duty + duty + shipping costs)	$27,926.56
GST (12.5%)	$ 3,490.82

You should check what the tax and duty will be in advance, which will prevent any unexpected tax demands after the vehicle has arrived in New Zealand. The Collector of Customs publishes a booklet entitled *Advice on Private Motor Vehicle Imports*, which explains how tax is calculated and how to calculate your tax liability, or you can ask customs to assess the tax due. You can contact the Collector of Customs (☎ freephone 0800-428 786 or 09-300 5399, 🖳 www.customs.govt.nz) or any regional customs office (see page 76).

Testing & Registration: After a vehicle has been cleared by customs, it must be taken to a Transport Services Delivery (TSD) agent, who will inspect it to determine whether it complies with approved standards and is safe. To locate your nearest TSD agent, call the Transport Registry Centre on ☎ freephone 0800-108 809 or contact a TSD agent directly. TSD agents include:

- New Zealand Automobile Association (☎ 09-309 4563);
- On Road New Zealand (☎ 09-444 6921);
- Vehicle Identification New Zealand (☎ 09-573 3055);
- Vehicle Testing New Zealand (☎ 04-495 2500).

All motor vehicles must be certified by the Land Transport Safety Authority (LTSA) that they comply with New Zealand legal requirements before they can be registered for use. You must provide documentation proving the vehicle's original compliance with approved standards, which will be checked. Note that some vehicles (e.g. kit cars) don't comply with New Zealand registration requirements and therefore cannot be used in the country. This may also be the case for vehicles whose manufacturers are unable to supply information about compliance with approved standards. You're therefore advised to contact LTSA and obtain the necessary information and documentation *before* making arrangements to import a vehicle into New Zealand.

The LTSA publishes two useful factsheets, which can be downloaded from its website, *Bringing a Light Vehicle into New Zealand* and *Certification of Imported Motor Vehicles*. The LTSA can be contacted at PO Box 2840, Wellington (☎ freephone 0800-699 000, ⌨ www.ltsa.govt.nz). See also **Car Inspections** and **Registration & Road Taxes** below.

Steam Cleaning: In line with New Zealand's strict policy of trying to exclude plant and animal pests, vehicles imported into New Zealand are subject to an inspection on arrival. If a vehicle is found to be contaminated with soil, plant or animal material, it must be thoroughly steam cleaned before it will be admitted. The charges for inspection and cleaning are paid by the importer. Vehicles arriving from Australia don't need to be steam cleaned unless they're found to be dirty on arrival.

REGISTRATION & ROAD TAXES

Registering a brand new or imported car attracts an initial registration fee of $160. This entitles you to a Vehicle Registration Certificate (VRC) and a pair of number (licence) plates, which must be displayed at the front and rear of your vehicle. Number plates in New Zealand have up to six characters, e.g. ZZ1357 and personalised plates are available. All motor vehicles are also subject to an annual registration fee, which is collected by the Land Transport Safety Authority (see above). This is essentially a road tax, although it's known as a registration fee in that it entitles your car to be registered and display the relevant number plates for the coming year. The fee for cars and small trucks is $202.85 and for motorcycles over 60cc it's $188.70. GST is included in the registration fee. You can pay your registration in person at post shops, New Zealand Automobile Association (AA) offices, LTSA offices or by post, for which you need the re-registration application forms that are automatically sent to owners around a month before your registration expires.

Road User Charges are payable for diesel-powered vehicles, and the cost varies with the weight of the vehicle. For cars (under 2 tonnes) the cost is $194.16 for 10,000km, which must be paid in advance and the tickets displayed in your windscreen along with the registration fee. Tickets can be bought from the LTSA (see above) or from post shops. For further information, ☎ freephone 0800-655 644.

CAR INSPECTIONS

All vehicles used on public roads in New Zealand are subject to an official inspection test, after which (assuming they pass) they're awarded a Vehicle Inspection Certificate (VIC), more commonly known as a Warrant of Fitness (WOF), an old term still in widespread use. All vehicles require a new VIC annually until they're three years old and every six months thereafter, unless they were first used before 1st December 1985, in which case they require a VIC every six months. As an incentive to support local industry, cars assembled in New Zealand are granted an annual VIC until they're six years old. VICs are issued at official government testing stations and approved garages (most garages are approved). Many garages offer a VIC service while you wait. A VIC inspection costs $33 for a car and checks are made only for basic roadworthiness covering such things as brakes, lights and tyres, similar to vehicle inspections carried out in most US states. The test isn't as stringent as either the British MOT or German TUV inspections. As well as a VIC you will receive a sticker, which must be displayed behind the windscreen of the vehicle (the penalty for failing to display a valid sticker is $200).

BUYING A CAR

There have never been any indigenous New Zealand cars. (Honda, Mitsubishi, Nissan and Toyota used to have plants in New Zealand where cars were assembled from imported parts in order to get round duty and tax on imported vehicles, but these have now closed, making New Zealand entirely reliant on imports.) Since the government's policy of restricting imported cars was abandoned, the New Zealand car market has been dominated by Japanese vehicles. This isn't surprising given New Zealand's proximity to Japan and the fact that Japanese cars are well made, reliable and offer good value. Japanese car dealerships (particularly Honda, Nissan and Toyota) are found in most towns and offer most models, including family and luxury saloons, estate cars (station wagons) and sports cars. It's possible to buy most European makes in New Zealand, although these are expensive and so most family cars are Japanese. The main non-Japanese makes are Ford, which are variants of American (rather than European) models, and Holden, which are made in Australia by General Motors (and sold in Europe as Opels and in the UK as Vauxhalls). In 2001 Toyota dominated the new car market with an almost 25 per cent share, followed by Holden and Ford. Lovers of classic cars will be delighted to see many old British-made cars such as Minis and Morris Minors still in daily use in New Zealand. These date back to the days when 'patriotic' local car buyers bought mainly British cars and kept them for 'ever' because of the high cost of new vehicles.

New Cars

New cars used to be astronomically expensive in New Zealand. However, reductions in import taxes in the last decade or so have brought prices down to a more reasonable level and in recent years on-the-road prices of some models have fallen by almost 10 per cent. In general, cars are still more expensive than in the UK and other European countries, and substantially more expensive than in the USA, even for identical models. However, further tax reductions and fierce discounting by Japanese manufacturers have led to lower prices so that many more people can now afford a new car, which was previously something of a luxury. New cars prices start at around $18,000 for a small Japanese car and $30,000 for a small European family car, up to around $80,000 for a quality European car such as an Audi, BMW or Saab.

You should shop around when buying a car in New Zealand and be prepared to haggle over the price. Although cars are officially sold at list price, there's usually a discount to be had somewhere, whether by inflating the allowance paid for your part exchange vehicle or in the form of a cash discount. Ensure that the price you're quoted includes GST (12.5 per cent) and registration (see page 165). The new car market is covered by a magazine entitled *Auto Car* which reports motor industry news, previews new models, performs road tests and provides an update on prices. The AA magazine *Directions* also provides a comprehensive listing of new car prices at the back of each issue.

Used Cars

Price reductions in the new car market in New Zealand have had the knock-on effect of reducing used prices (and also accelerating depreciation). The easiest way to buy a used car is from a dealer, although it's wise to ask a colleague or neighbour if they can recommend one. When buying a car from a dealer, you should check that he's a member of the Motor Vehicle Dealers Institute (look for the MVDI logo). The Institute (🖳 www.mvdi.co.nz) has around 2,250 members, who must comply with fair trading practice and abide by a strict code of ethics. Anyone who sells or exchanges more than six vehicles within a 12-month period must be licensed, although small dealers without MVDI membership often pose as private sellers (which is illegal). An alternative is to check the local newspapers (*NZ Herald* on Wednesday and *The Dominion* on Saturday) or the *Trade & Exchange* and *Auto Trader* magazines, which list hundreds of cars for sale (most accompanied by a photograph), both private and from dealers. Used car dealers and private sellers also advertise cars for sale on the Internet (e.g. 🖳 www.autonet.co.nz). In some towns there are weekend car markets where private sellers offer their cars for sale, such as the Manukau and Ellerslie Racecourse car fair in Auckland (arrive before 9am for the best choice). Car auctions, often held several times a week, are also popular venues for used car buyers.

Important Precautions: As in most other countries, buying a used car in New Zealand requires a great deal of caution, and both the vehicle and seller should be carefully scrutinised, including the following:

- Ensure that the seller owns a vehicle or is entitled to sell it. If it's a private sale, ask to see the vehicle registration certificate together with some other proof of the seller's address. If the addresses match, this gives you some indication that the seller is probably who he says he is.

- Inspect the bodywork carefully for damage, as a lot of cars in New Zealand have been involved in accidents. A car with a few minor cosmetic knocks is preferable to one that looks immaculate, but which has been repaired following a major accident.

- Try to confirm that the odometer reading is correct, as odometer tampering is common. Service records from a main dealership and repair invoices showing the km reading are a good way of doing this.

The LTSA publishes an excellent factsheet, *Buying a Used Car,* which includes exactly what to look for inside and out, as well what sort of sounds the engine should make. The factsheet is available from LTSA offices and can be downloaded from the website (☎ freephone 0800-699 000, 🖳 www.ltsa.govt.nz).

If you know little or nothing about cars, it's wise to arrange an inspection by a competent engineer. The AA provides this service, and often there are car inspection services available at car fairs and auctions. An inspection costs from around $85. The Ministry of Justice maintains an Autocheck register (☎ 0900-909 777, calls cost around $5 – you must provide the licence and chassis numbers), which lists vehicles that are subject to a hire purchase or leasing arrangement or have been pledged as security. Alternatively you can go to your nearest court with the vehicle details and obtain a certificate confirming that the vehicle is free of debt. Always check the

Autocheck or court registers before buying a used car. This doesn't, however, guarantee that a vehicle hasn't been stolen or suffered accident damage, or that the kilometre reading is correct. If a vehicle is diesel powered, you should check there are no Road User Charges owing (☎ freephone 0800-655 644) – see **Car Registration & Road Taxes** on page 165.

Warranties & Guarantees: Used car dealers offer warranties and guarantees. All car sellers (including private sellers) are legally obliged to sell cars in a roadworthy condition. If you buy a car and find that it isn't roadworthy, a threat to report the seller to the police may receive you a refund (always assuming that you can find him!). If you have a complaint about a new or used car purchased from a dealer, you can take it up with the Motor Vehicle Disputes Tribunal. If the tribunal finds that your complaint is justified, they can order the dealer to fix the problem, award compensation (up to $12,000) or take the car back and refund your money. Around 66 per cent of cases dealt with in this way result in a successful outcome for buyers, but it applies only to cars costing up to $30,000. The Institute of Motor Vehicle Dealers also has a fidelity fund which compensates buyers when a dealer cannot pay, e.g. when he has gone bust.

Imported Used Cars: A particular area of concern for buyers of used cars in New Zealand is that of imported used cars, i.e. vehicles that have been used in another country and then exported to New Zealand, as opposed to used cars which were purchased new in New Zealand. There have been problems in recent years with cars which have been stolen, usually in the UK, and shipped to New Zealand and resold. This mainly applies to prestige and executive cars. If you're offered a used vehicle such as a Mercedes or BMW at a temptingly low price, you should check its history particularly carefully. A popular (and probably apocryphal) bar-room tale in New Zealand tells of the Pom (Briton) who emigrated and bought back his BMW which had been stolen in London six months previously!

A problem can also occur with used cars imported from Japan, which are imported legally by dealers and sold at low prices (used cars are worth little in Japan), often with low mileage (kilometres). However, several dealers have been convicted for winding back the odometers of cars on their sea journey from Japan, thereby defrauding buyers. Even with genuine used cars imported from Japan, there's often concern that the wear and tear on the engine is greater than the kilometre reading may suggest (Japanese cars spend most of their life crawling in traffic jams). On the other hand, several dealers have been caught winding the odometers of imported used cars *forward*, in order to reduce their value and cut the import taxes payable (thus defrauding customs). In summary it's fair to say that buying a used car in New Zealand is something of a mine-field, although it's no different from most other countries in this respect.

SELLING A CAR

Before selling a car in New Zealand, you must obtain a new Vehicle Inspection Certificate (VIC – see **Car Inspections** on page 165), from a local garage, unless your current VIC was issued in the previous month. When you find a buyer, simply give him the VIC, which he will need to register the car in his name. Registration can be done by post or in person at a postal shop. Other things to do when selling a car include the following:

● Inform your insurance company.

● Notify the Transport Registry Centre (☎ freephone 0800-108 809, ✉ info @tregistry.co.nz) of the sale by lodging an MR13A form within seven days of the sale. Don't rely on the buyer to lodge the form because if he doesn't (accidentally or on purpose) you will be liable for parking tickets and fines. Many New Zealanders have found themselves liable for $hundreds worth of fines and it's expensive in lawyer's fees and time-consuming to sort out.

● When selling a car privately, insist on payment in cash or with a banker's draft (cashier's cheque), which is standard practice in New Zealand. If you accept a personal cheque, make sure that it clears before you part with your vehicle.

The best places to advertise a car for sale are in local newspapers or the *Auto Trader* magazine. Some people try to sell it at a car market or put a 'for sale' notice in their car window with a phone number and park it in a prominent place.

CAR RENTAL

A variety of companies in New Zealand rent cars by the day or week, including the ubiquitous multinationals such as Avis, Budget and Hertz, and a large number of local firms. The multinationals offer better insurance and the newest cars but are more expensive than local firms, which usually offer older cars (sometimes with 100,000km or more on the clock). One big advantage of renting from a national firm is that you can pick up a car in one town and drop it off in another, whereas local firms usually insist that a car is returned to the same place. Note that many car rental firms don't allow you to take a car from North to South Island (or vice versa) on the ferry and those that do impose a stiff surcharge. This, together with the cost of taking a car on the ferry, means it's usually cheaper to drop a rental car off at the ferry terminal (where major rental companies have offices), travel as a foot passenger, and rent another car on the other island. Auckland has the most competitive car hire rates in the country.

Typical car brands and daily rental costs (including GST) from a multinational are: Ford Festiva 1.3 around $70, Toyota Corolla 1.6 $100, Ford Falcon 4.0 Station Wagon $95 and Toyota Previa $110. The above rates (from multinationals for brand new vehicles) include basic third-party insurance and unlimited kilometres, but exclude fuel or personal accident insurance. There's an extra charge for damage excess waiver (DEW) of around $10 per day, which removes any liability for damage caused to a rented vehicle. If you don't have DEW (called collision damage waiver/CDW in many other countries), you must leave a cash or credit card deposit of $700 or more. It's important to note that no matter how comprehensive the insurance cover, you're unlikely to be covered for damage caused by driving off tarmac roads (i.e. unsealed roads), even if a vehicle is of the four-wheel-drive type. Some companies forbid their cars to be driven on unsealed roads. Extras that can be ordered with a rental car include mobile phones, roof/ski racks, child seats (compulsory in New Zealand) and snow chains (recommended when venturing into a mountainous area during winter).

The minimum age for renting a car in New Zealand is usually 21 and a full licence must have been held for at least 12 months, although some rental companies have a minimum age of 25. Other rental companies levy a supplement for larger vehicles when the driver is under 25, and under 25s incur a larger insurance excess with most rental companies. Popular car rental companies include Maui, which has offices in Auckland and Christchurch (☎ freephone 0800-651 080) and Budget Rent-a-Car with offices in various locations (☎ freephone 0800-652 227). Rent-a-Dent (Auckland and Christchurch ☎ freephone 0800-736 823) have bargain-priced (i.e. well-worn) cars for rent from around $35 per day excluding insurance.

DRIVING LICENCE

The minimum age for driving in New Zealand is 15, although this may increase to 17 in the future, as the 15 age limit dates back to the days when the school leaving age was 15 and school-leavers were often required to drive vehicles on farms. However, 15-year-olds are entitled only to a Learner Licence and don't receive a Full Licence until at least two years later. The driving licence system in New Zealand is unique and has three stages: Learner Licence, Restricted Licence and Full Licence, each of which has to be passed by prospective drivers.

A Learner Licence is awarded after you've taken a theoretical and practical test. With a Learner Licence, you can drive a car only when accompanied by an experienced driver and the car must display 'L' plates. Learner Licence drivers under the age of 20 are subject to additional licence restrictions, including a lower blood alcohol limit (30mg of alcohol per 100ml of blood, which in practice means they cannot drink and drive legally). The second stage, the Restricted Licence, is reached after a minimum of six months as a learner driver and an additional practical test. With a Restricted Licence you can drive alone but can carry no passengers other than your spouse and/or dependants (the only ones considered brave enough?) and you can't drive at night. The Full Licence is the third and final stage awarded after you've held a Restricted Licence for six months if you're aged 25 or over, or for 18 months if you're under 25, and after you pass further theoretical and practical tests. To obtain a Full Licence therefore takes at least a year and costs $246 (excluding driving lessons). Note that you require an eyesight test in order to obtain a New Zealand driving licence (see page 195).

If you already have a driving licence, it can be used in New Zealand for up to a year, provided it's written in English. If it isn't, it must be accompanied by an international driver's permit, which you can obtain from a motoring organisation in your home country. After a year, your foreign driving licence must be exchanged for a New Zealand licence. If your driving licence was issued in Australia, Canada, the European Union, Norway, South Africa, Switzerland or the USA, you may be eligible for exemption from the practical test but must take a theory test. Driving licence holders from other countries must also take a practical test. Licences are issued in paper form and last until your 80th birthday, after which they're renewable every two years subject to a driving assessment and a medical examination. You're required to carry your driving licence or car papers with you when driving in New Zealand.

Before taking to the road in New Zealand, you should familiarise yourself with the official guide to driving rules and regulations known as the *Road Code*, which is available from book shops and is New Zealand's best selling book (amazing, considering that nobody reads it!). It's also available on a CD-ROM, which includes details of the driving tests, practice tests, first aid information and demonstrations of how to manoeuvre a vehicle.

CAR INSURANCE

In most countries, motorists are required to have at least third-party insurance so that, if they injure or kill another road user, their insurance company pays compensation. This isn't legally required in New Zealand because of the country's innovative Accident Compensation Scheme (see page 202), whereby anyone who suffers an accident or injury is compensated directly by the government. This system works reasonably well, although it isn't free, as everyone pays for it through their taxes. One effect of this system is that it isn't possible to sue anyone who causes an accident or injury for compensation.

The scheme doesn't, however, compensate other drivers for damage to their cars and it's therefore wise to have insurance which covers at least this. Most people with anything other than a worthless heap take out insurance. The cost of car insurance varies according to the extent of the cover (e.g. fully comprehensive, third-party fire and theft, third party) make and type of vehicle, the driver (you can obtain a 20 per cent discount if you don't insure any driver under 25) and where you live (Aucklanders pay up to 30 per cent more than country dwellers), the average fully comprehensive insurance premium being around $650 per year. With most insurance policies, you must pay an excess (deductible) of around $300. Note that a no-claims bonus system operates in New Zealand and you should take documents showing your no-claims bonus with you.

MOTOR BREAKDOWN INSURANCE

It's important to bear in mind that motor breakdown insurance isn't included in most New Zealand motor insurance policies. When you buy a new or used car from a dealer, you will usually receive an insurance-based warranty package as part of the deal, which covers the costs of a breakdown (e.g. garage fees and towing) and the cost of repairing most major components of a vehicle. However, these warranties are riddled with loopholes and even if you get past the exclusions and excesses, you will probably find that the pay-out is minimal. The cheapest way to insure against breakdowns is to join the New Zealand Automobile Association (see page 182) who will attend to minor repairs on the spot or arrange for a vehicle to be taken to a garage.

GENERAL ROAD RULES

First time visitors may be forgiven for thinking that there are no road rules in New Zealand. However, there are, and some of the main ones are as follows:

● Among the many odd customs of New Zealanders is that of driving on the left-hand side of the road, as in Australia, Japan and the UK (and many other countries). You may find this a bit strange if you come from a country which drives on the right; however, it saves a lot of confusion if you do likewise. It's helpful to have a reminder (e.g. 'think left!') on your car's dashboard (many rented cars have a fluorescent sticker stating 'DRIVE ON THE LEFT' on the dashboard). Take extra care when pulling out of junctions, one-way streets and at roundabouts. Remember to look first to the *right* when crossing the road on foot. If you're unused to driving on the left, you should be prepared for some disorientation (or blind panic), although most people have few problems adjusting to it.

- At crossroads and junctions where no right of way is assigned, traffic coming from the right has priority (as on the continent of Europe). At major junctions, right of way is indicated by a triangular 'GIVE WAY' (yield) sign or an octagonal red 'STOP' sign. There are also usually road markings. When faced with a stop sign, you must stop completely (all four wheels must come to rest) before pulling out onto a major road, even if you can see that no traffic is approaching. At a give way sign, you aren't required to stop, but must give priority to traffic already on the major road. You must also give way to traffic coming from your right when entering a motorway or dual carriageway from a slip road.

- At roundabouts (traffic circles), vehicles on the roundabout have priority and not those entering it. Traffic flows clockwise around roundabouts and not anti-clockwise, as in countries where traffic drives on the right. Some roundabouts have a filter lane which is reserved for traffic turning left. You should stay in the lane in which you entered the roundabout, follow the lane markings and signal as you approach the exit you wish to take. There are many roundabouts in New Zealand, which, although they are a bit of a free-for-all, speed up traffic considerably and are usually preferable to traffic lights, particularly outside rush hours (although some busy roundabouts also have traffic lights).

- The use of seatbelts is compulsory for front and rear-seat passengers when they're fitted, and children must be properly restrained by an approved child restraint or adult seatbelt if fitted to a vehicle. In the absence of an approved restraint or seatbelt, they must travel in the back of a car. A child must *never* travel in the front seat without using a child restraint or seatbelt, even when the back seat is full. Seatbelts or restraints must be approved (to the requisite New Zealand standard) and be appropriate for the age and weight of a child. Babies up to six months must be carried in an infant seat and children up to four must be carried in a child seat. Older children may use either a child seat or an adult seatbelt.

  It's estimated that seatbelts would prevent around 75 per cent of deaths and 90 per cent of injuries suffered by those involved in accidents not wearing seat belts. In addition to the risk of death or injury, you can receive a fine for ignoring the seatbelt laws. Note that it's the driver's responsibility to ensure that children are properly restrained. If you're exempt from using a seatbelt for medical reasons, a safety belt exemption certificate is required from your doctor.

- Be particularly wary of cyclists, moped riders and motorcyclists. It isn't always easy to see them, particularly when they're hidden by the blind spots of a car or when cyclists are riding at night without lights. **When overtaking, ALWAYS give them a wide . . . WIDE berth.** If you knock them off their bikes, you may have a difficult time convincing the police that it wasn't your fault; far better to avoid them (and the police).

- If you needed spectacles or contact lenses to pass your sight test, you must always wear them when driving. It's wise to carry a spare pair of glasses or contact lenses in your car.

- White or yellow markings are painted on the road surface in towns and cities, e.g. arrows to indicate the direction traffic must go in a particular lane. You should stay in the centre of the lane in which you're driving or, where there are no lane markings, keep to the left side of the road. White lines mark the separation of traffic lanes. A solid single line or two solid lines means no overtaking in either direction. A solid line to the left of the centre line, i.e. on your side of the road, means that overtaking is prohibited in your direction. You may overtake only when there's a single broken line in the middle of the road or double lines with a broken line on your side.

- Headlights must be used when driving between sunset and sunrise or at any time when there's insufficient daylight to be able to see a person wearing dark clothing at a distance of 100 metres (so keep an eye out for people in dark clothing). It's illegal to drive on side (parking) lights, and headlights must usually be dipped (low beam) when driving in built-up areas where there's street lighting. Headlamps must also be dipped within 200 metres of an approaching vehicle, immediately an oncoming vehicle has dipped its headlights and when travelling within 200 metres behind another vehicle.

  Headlight flashing has a different meaning in different countries. In some countries it means 'after you', while in others it means 'get out of my way'. It can even mean 'I'm driving a new car and haven't worked out what the switches are for yet'! **In New Zealand, headlamp flashing has only one legal use – to warn another vehicle of your presence**, although most people use it to give priority to another vehicle, e.g. when someone is waiting to exit from a junction. Note that it's illegal to warn other vehicles that they're approaching a speed trap or police road block by flashing your lights (although many drivers do it). Hazard warning lights (all indicators operating simultaneously) are used to warn other drivers of an obstruction, e.g. an accident or a traffic jam.

- The sequence of New Zealand traffic lights is green, amber, red and back to green. Amber means stop at the stop line; you may proceed only if the amber light appears after you've crossed the stop line or when stopping may cause an accident. A green filter light may be shown in addition to the full lamp signals, which means you may go in the direction shown by the arrow, irrespective of other lights showing. Cameras may be installed at busy traffic lights to detect motorists driving through red lights (a favourite pastime of many New Zealand motorists).

- Always approach pedestrian crossings with caution and don't park or overtake another vehicle on the approach to a crossing. At some crossings a flashing amber light follows the red light, to warn you to give way to pedestrians before proceeding. **Note that pedestrians have the right of way once they've stepped onto a crossing without traffic lights and you MUST STOP (it isn't optional as in many other countries). Motorists who don't stop are liable to heavy penalties.** Where a road crosses a public footpath, e.g. at the entrance to a property or car park bordering a road, motorists *must* give way to pedestrians.

- Tail-gating (driving close to the vehicle in front) is commonplace in New Zealand, where few drivers have any idea of safe stopping distances (including thinking distance, i.e. the time it takes a driver to react). In good conditions you should leave a gap equal to three seconds between your vehicle and the one in front in order to be able to stop in an emergency. Note that the three-second rule applies to cars with good brakes and tyres, on dry roads, in good visibility and with an *alert driver*. If you're half asleep and driving an old banger on a wet or icy road, you had better not exceed 20kph (12mph), or you will never stop in an emergency! As a safety precaution, try to leave a large gap between you and the vehicle in front. This isn't just to allow you more time to stop, should the vehicles in front decide to come together, but also to give a 'tail-gater' behind you more time to stop. **The closer the car behind you, the further you should be from the vehicle in front.**

- Watch out for pedestrianised streets in city centres (which are closed to traffic during certain periods indicated by a sign). Note that bicycles may not be ridden (or sometimes even wheeled) in pedestrianised streets.

- Keep a look out for animals on roads in country areas, where fields are often unfenced and livestock are free to graze at will. Many motorists are injured following collisions with animals, particularly at night.

- Snow chains may be used on snow-covered roads, but should be removed as soon as the road is clear.

ROAD SIGNS

Road signs in New Zealand can be extremely variable. In most cities and towns there are extensive road signs to most destinations and local facilities such as schools, swimming pools and car parks. However, outside towns, signposting can be vague and you will frequently not find any (or many) signs at junctions. The main reason for this is that there's often only one major road between cities and towns. For example, if you leave the Interislander ferry at Picton heading for Christchurch and keep to the major road at every junction, the only place you can end up is Christchurch! If you're stuck for directions, simply stop and ask. Most locals will be pleased to help you and, unlike some countries, it's usually quite safe to stop anywhere at any time of the day or night.

On short stretches of motorway, signs usually indicate the street to which an exit leads, rather than a town or suburb. For example, when heading north into Auckland on the southern motorway and wishing to travel to the suburb of Newmarket, you're advised to take the exit marked Broadway, the main road that passes through Newmarket. Therefore check the name of the street before setting out. Some roads are promoted as tourist attractions (indicated by blue and white signs), for example the Pacific Coast Highway, which runs from Auckland to Hastings.

Roadside information signs in New Zealand traditionally contained written instructions, for example 'SHARP BEND' or 'MAJOR ROAD AHEAD', and there are still many of these signs around (which may puzzle visitors from America who must wonder how a bend can be sharp). However, international pictorial signs are becoming commonplace, although in some cases they are still accompanied by written explanations, e.g. 'no entry' signs consist of a red circle with a white bar accompanied by the words 'No Entry'. An inverted red triangle on a white background means give way or yield and is marked 'Give Way' just to remind you (not that most New Zealand motorists take too much notice of it!). One sign that's peculiar to New Zealand is the 'LSZ' sign, consisting of black lettering on a white border surrounded by a red circle. This means Limited Speed Zone and is found where a major road runs through a town or village (often so small that you don't notice it, which is why the sign is there to remind you). The sign generally means slow down, take care and look out for pedestrians and animals. Instructions are also sometimes marked on the road, but in the reverse order so that motorists can read the message in the correct sequence, e.g. 'Give' followed by 'Way' a little further down the road means that you're approaching a junction where you must yield right of way.

SPEED LIMITS

The speed limits in New Zealand couldn't be simpler: 50kph (31mph) in built-up areas and 100kph (62mph) in rural areas, except where (rarely) a different limit is indicated. The rural limit is reduced to 90kph (55mph) for buses and heavy lorries, and to 80kph (50mph) for school buses and vehicles towing trailers. In some areas there's an LSZ sign (Limited Speed Zone), which means that the speed limit is reduced to 50kph (31mph) under certain conditions such as bad weather. Although speed limits are low compared with many other countries, although speeding is the direct cause of more than one in five road deaths n New Zealand, where the authorities are taking increasing steps to reduce and control vehicle speeds. Speed traps are commonplace and employ a variety of methods to detect speeders, including radar and laser.

One device that the road safety authorities have taken to enthusiastically in their bid to persuade (or force) motorists to slow down is the speed camera, which measures the speed of passing vehicles and takes a photograph of the number plate of those that are speeding. These devices exist, of course, in other countries, but they aren't usually employed with the fervour they are in New Zealand, where they raise $75 million for the government annually ('spotting the speed camera' has become a national pastime). Speeding has been dramatically reduced since the introduction of cameras, as have speed-related crashes (some 5.5 per cent a year). Even so, New Zealanders aren't about to be beaten by 'big brother' and it isn't uncommon for a friendly local to put up a hand-written 'Speed Camera Ahead' sign by the side of the road.

There are heavy fines for speeding as well as demerit points and, if you're caught driving at more than 50kph above the speed limit, your licence is suspended immediately for 28 days. Demerit points for speeding range from 10 points for exceeding the speed limit by up to 10kph to 50 points for exceeding the speed limit by 36kph or more. If you receive a total of 100 demerit points in two years, you're suspended from driving for three months.

TRAFFIC POLICE

The policing of road traffic and drivers in New Zealand comes under the auspices of the Traffic Safety Service (TSS), which is jointly operated by the police and the Ministry of Transport. TSS officers drive black and white cars to distinguish them from police officers and like most police officers aren't armed. In late 2000, Specialist Highway Patrols were introduced in order to clamp down on speeding on main roads, which are patrolled by some 180 units. These and other officers deploy a range of radar and laser apparatus to detect speeding motorists, and they carry out frequent roadside checks and mount random roadblocks (stopping motorists or filtering out 'suspicious looking' ones), checking documents and vehicles, and administering breath tests (see **Driving & Drinking** on page 179).

Officers cannot impose on-the-spot fines other than for minor violations (such as illegal parking or not displaying a valid VIC), and traffic offenders are usually issued with a traffic infringement notice and summoned to appear at a district court. Fines can be up to $1,000 for 'minor' offences and up to $6,000 for serious offences, for which you can also be imprisoned for up to two years. The fine for not wearing a seatbelt is $150. See also **Speed Limits** above.

NEW ZEALAND ROADS

Roads in New Zealand are divided into three main categories: motorways, state highways and secondary roads. Motorways are found only in the major cities where they provide a direct route from the suburbs into the centre. They consist of two or more lanes in each direction, although motorways entering Auckland have three lanes in each direction, and are known by names rather than numbers: for example, in Auckland the Northern, Southern and North-western motorways radiate from the city centre in their respective directions, and the Wellington Urban Motorway runs northwards from the city centre.

Special rules apply on motorways, which cannot be used by pedestrians, cyclists, animals or small-engined motorcycles. You may stop only in an emergency, when you must use the near-side verge or hard shoulder. Motorways are identified by signs with white lettering on a green background, and junctions are numbered. A new system has been proposed which will number junctions according to their distance in kilometres from a given point of the motorway, rather than in numerical order. For example, junction ten would be 10km (6mi) from the given point. This system is hoped to be in place by 2003 – it has long been delayed, mainly because no one can agree on where the given point is!

State highways are major trunk roads with usually just one lane in each direction, on which you can expect to average around 55 to 65kmh when travelling cross-country. They're marked in red on maps and identified by a shield symbol, both on road signs and maps. There are eight principal state highways in New Zealand:

Highway No.	Route
1	Awanui–Auckland–Wellington–Picton–Christchurch–Invercargill
2	Auckland–Tauranga–Gisborne–Napier–Wellington
3	Hamilton–New Plymouth–Palmerston North
4	Te Kuiti–Wanganui
5	Putaruru–Napier
6	Blenheim–Invercargill (via the Southern Alps)
7	Greymouth–Waipara (near Christchurch)
8	Timaru–Milton (inland route)

Secondary routes are marked in yellow on most maps and by a shield symbol on maps and road signs. They're identified by a two-digit number and in most cases the first digit indicates that the road starts or finishes (as the case may be) on the state highway with the same number. All other roads are unclassified and unnumbered and indicated by white lines on most maps, but have no special identification or road signs. They're usually of reasonable quality and sealed (tarmacked) unless they're specifically marked on a map or signposted as 'unsealed' or 'not tar sealed' which means that they're gravel or compacted earth. They're passable by standard two-wheel-drive cars in good weather and four-wheel-drive vehicles at any time.

New Zealand's roads rarely have special facilities such as service areas or rest stops, although they're well served by petrol stations, cafes, restaurants and motels (most state highways pass through towns rather than bypassing them) where you can stop for fuel, food, accommodation and mechanical services. The only exception to this is in remote parts of the country, mainly in South Island, where you should use a map to plan overnight stays, refuelling and rest stops.

Parking is never easy in city centres, but unlike many other countries it's at least possible. Rush hour in the cities is between 7.30 and 9am and 4.30 and 6.30pm, when it takes a little longer to make a journey, although outside cities there's no such thing as a rush hour. Roads are naturally busier during holiday periods, particularly between December and February. The beginning of summer school holidays (the end of the first week in December) and the week before Christmas are the only times when it's advisable to think twice before making a long journey by road, as everyone else will be doing the same.

Most roads are passable year round, except in the more inhospitable areas of the South Island, where some roads, particularly state highway 6 through the Southern Alps, are rendered impassable by snowfalls and icy conditions. In the winter you should check to make sure that you can reach your destination before setting out. On some roads there are automatic warning signs to warn you of a road closure further along the highway. Don't be tempted to ignore them, as each year many people are stranded and a number lose their lives by doing this. In the North Island, several main roads are subject to flooding during heavy rain, particularly where they pass through the volcanic plateaux.

NEW ZEALAND DRIVERS

In normal circumstances New Zealanders are friendly and polite. However, this changes the minute they get behind the wheel of a car, when they become uncharacteristically aggressive, intolerant and discourteous. The average New Zealander's attitude is to reach his destination as fast as possible with little regard for whoever he may maim or kill in the process. There are, on average, around nine road deaths each week in New Zealand, together with 20,000 convictions annually for careless or dangerous driving. Being a foreigner doesn't exempt you from this carnage, although the Land Transport Safety Authority estimates that less than 3 per cent of fatal accidents are *caused* by foreign drivers.

The three greatest threats to road safety are drunk driving (see page 179), excessive speed (see page 175) and reckless overtaking. Another problem is lane changing and pulling in or out without looking or without leaving sufficient room. This is a significant problem in New Zealand where there are few multi-lane roads and many drivers have no lane discipline. Young men tend to be the worst offenders, although even young women and mature drivers compete in New Zealand's 'drink the pub dry and get home first at all costs' road race. Road rage is the latest trend to emerge in New Zealand and there have been several cases of motorists who, after having been hit by a car, have remonstrated with the offending driver only to be hit again – this time in the face! It's best never to drink and drive in New Zealand (and never to accept a ride with anyone who has been drinking), and it pays to regard speed limits as an absolute maximum and, if necessary, drive slower, particularly in towns. Finally, avoid overtaking except where there's enough clear road ahead to land a jumbo jet!

All this shouldn't put you off driving in New Zealand, as you will pass through some breathtaking scenery (best admired by stopping the car), even on the most routine trips to the office or the shops. Best of all, roads are relatively uncrowded outside cities, so your chances of meeting many kamikaze drivers are slim.

MOTORCYCLES

Motorcycling is popular in New Zealand, both as a means of transport and a leisure pursuit. It is, however, a relatively dangerous undertaking, partly because drivers of other vehicles have little regard for motorcyclists (usually they don't even notice them) and partly because many motorcyclists take advantage of New Zealand's wide open roads to reach some incredible speeds. Crash helmets must be worn and riders must use dipped headlamps at all times. It also pays to wear bright, fluorescent or reflective clothing but, even then, don't expect car drivers to see you. In recent years motorcycle deaths and injuries have been reduced thanks to helmets, better bikes and protective riding gear, better training and defensive riding by bikers. In general, laws that apply to cars also apply to motorcycles.

It's possible to buy (or rent) a wide range of motorbikes in New Zealand ranging from lovingly preserved British classics to the latest German and Japanese superbikes. A motorcycle can be imported duty-free on the same terms as a car (see page 163).

ACCIDENTS

New Zealanders aren't generally perturbed by road accidents, and many people delight in recounting the details of their latest scrape over dinner or in the pub. If you're unfortunate enough to be involved in a car accident in New Zealand (perhaps that should be *when* you're involved in your first accident), the procedure is as follows:

1. Stop immediately. Switch on your hazard warning lights. In bad visibility, at night, or in a blind spot, try to warn oncoming traffic of the danger by sending someone ahead to flag down oncoming cars.

2. In the case of minor accidents, try to move your car off the road immediately. Many serious accidents are caused by other drivers running into vehicles that have had a minor bump.

3. If anyone is injured, call an ambulance and/or the fire service immediately by dialling 111. If there isn't a mobile or public phone, just ask at the nearest house.

4. Don't move an injured person unless it's absolutely necessary to save him or her from further injury and don't leave him alone except to call an ambulance. Cover him with a blanket or coat to keep him warm.

5. If there are no injuries and damage to vehicles or property isn't serious, it's unnecessary to call the police to the accident scene. Contacting the police may result in someone being fined or prosecuted for a driving offence. If another driver has obviously been drinking or appears incapable of driving, call the police. **Note that you must never leave the scene of an accident, however minor, as this is a serious offence.**

6. If either you or the other driver(s) involved decide to call the police, don't move your vehicle or allow other vehicles to be moved. If it's necessary to move vehicles to unblock the road, mark their positions with chalk. Alternatively, take photographs of the accident scene or make a drawing showing the position of all the vehicles involved before moving them.

7. Check whether there are any witnesses to the accident and take their names and addresses, particularly noting those who support your version of what happened. Write down the registration numbers of the vehicles involved and their drivers' names, addresses and insurance details. If asked, give any other drivers involved your name, address and insurance details. Bear in mind, however, that motorists aren't legally required to have insurance, so don't be too surprised if the other driver doesn't have any!

8. If you've caused material damage, you must inform the owner of the damaged property as soon as possible. If you cannot reach him, contact the nearest police station (this also applies to damage caused to stationary vehicles, e.g. when parking).

9. If you're detained by the police, ask someone you're travelling with to contact anyone necessary as soon as you realise you're going to be detained. Don't sign a statement unless you're certain you understand and agree with every word.

10. In the case of an accident involving two or more vehicles, it's normal practice for drivers to complete a standard accident report form provided by most insurance companies. Each driver completes a form, which is then countersigned by the other and a copy exchanged. It isn't necessary for the two drivers' versions of the event to agree.

11. Your insurance company must be notified of an accident as soon as possible.

Claims for personal injury where the other driver is wholly or partly at fault can be directed to the government's Accident Compensation Corporation (ACC – see page 202). If your claim is complex, you may need to engage a lawyer to help with this. You must, at the very least, have the registration number of the other vehicle if you're to succeed with a claim.

DRIVING & DRINKING

It's estimated that a large proportion of road accidents in New Zealand are due to drunken driving (and also a fair number due to drunken walking), which is acknowledged as one of the country's most pressing social problems. It's still socially acceptable in New Zealand to drive after a 'few drinks' and the limited licensing hours for 'hotels' (pubs) often encourage people to travel in search of a drink when their local pub is closed on a Sunday or in 'dry' areas. Drunken driving is endemic at all levels, from older drivers who consider they're experienced enough to drive a car after drinking to bravado young drivers who may even encourage their mates to drive when drunk. Drunk drivers in New Zealand are often very drunk indeed. One driver who ended up in court on a drunk driving charge was reported to have 1,863mcg of alcohol per litre of breath – over four times the legal limit (a medical expert at his trial reckoned he should have been 'brain dead' after consuming so much alcohol!).

Police and TSS officers can breathalyse drivers at any time in New Zealand without a reason, and drivers involved in accidents, however minor, are routinely breathalysed. Random breath tests are common, and roadblocks can be set up or moved at a few moments' notice. All motorists stopped are tested and a reading above 400mcg of alcohol per litre of breath leads to a blood test, after which, if you're still over the limit, you're charged with drunken driving.

In recent years the government has made great efforts to reduce drinking and driving through public education campaigns and stricter laws. These have had some effect, although drunken driving remains a serious problem and is one of the main causes of accidents. It's estimated that at least 20 per cent of drivers killed on the roads each year were over the legal limit. The alcohol limit for motorists in New Zealand is 80mg per 100ml of blood (0.08 per cent), similar to the UK but higher than many European countries. For motorists under 20 years of age the limit is 30mg. Drunk driving is a serious offence and motorists caught over the legal limit can be fined up to $1,500 or imprisoned for up to six months; the penalty for a third offence can be a fine of up to $6,000, a two-year prison sentence and a one-year disqualification from driving. Your car can also be confiscated, although this usually applies only to repeat offenders. Each year over 30,000 New Zealanders are convicted of drunken driving, although few are jailed.

The latest threat on New Zealand's roads is driving under the influence of drugs. Although there are no official figures, a significant number of drivers are believed to be under the influence of illegal drugs (mainly cannabis) when driving and the government plans to introduce roadside drug testing when a reliable test becomes available.

CAR THEFT

Usually when you leave your property unattended in New Zealand, you can expect it to be in the same place when you return. This, however, doesn't always apply to cars (nor to motorcycles and bicycles for that matter), as New Zealand has a surprisingly high incidence of car theft considering the fairly low crime rate in general. There's a huge variation in the incidence of car crime between city and country areas, and while Auckland is the car crime capital of New Zealand, in most country areas car theft is rare and even a theft *from* a car may make headline news. It's rare for a stolen car to disappear completely in New Zealand, however, as there's no easy way for a thief to take a car abroad and most are unlikely to pay the inter-island ferry fare to spirit your car to the other island. Therefore, if your car is stolen, you're likely to get it back. The bad news, however, is that many cars are stolen by joy-riders or petty criminals, so when you do get it back it may be damaged or completely wrecked.

To reduce the chance of theft, don't take unnecessary risks and always lock your car, engage your steering lock and completely close all the windows (but don't leave pets in an unventilated car). Never leave your keys in the ignition, even when filling up at a petrol station or when parking in your drive. Put any valuables (including clothes) in the boot or out of sight and don't leave your vehicle registration papers or any form of identification in the car. If possible, avoid parking in commuter (e.g. railway station) and long-term (e.g. airport and shopping centre) car parks, which are favourite hunting grounds for car thieves. When parking overnight or when it's dark, always park in a well-lit area, which helps deter car thieves.

Car theft has spawned a huge car security business in the (losing) battle to prevent or deter car thieves. These include a multitude of alarms, immobilisers, locks, wheel clamps, window etching with a car's registration number, locking wheel nuts and petrol caps, and removable/coded stereo systems (a favourite target of thieves). If you drive a new or valuable car, it's wise to have it fitted with an alarm, an engine immobiliser (preferably of the rolling code variety with a transponder arming key) or other anti-theft device, and to use a visible deterrent such as a steering or gear change lock. Although a good security system won't stop someone from breaking into your car (which usually takes a 'professional' a matter of seconds) or prevent it being stolen, it will make it more difficult and may prompt a thief to look for an easier target. If you plan to buy an expensive stereo system, buy one with a removable unit or control panel/fascia (which you can pop in a pocket), but *never* forget to remove it, even when stopping for a few minutes. If your car is stolen, report it to the police and your insurance company as soon as possible. Don't, however, expect the police to find it or even take any interest in your loss.

PETROL

There are no fewer than six kinds of motor fuel sold in New Zealand: petrol (or gasoline) is available in unleaded grades of 91 and 96 octane, as well as super and regular leaded grades. Most new and recent cars are equipped with catalytic converters and run on unleaded fuel. However, super and regular are still available at most petrol stations for older cars and should never be used in cars equipped with a catalytic converter, as they will destroy it. Fortunately the fuel nozzles and filler caps on 'cat' equipped cars are smaller than those for leaded, so a mistake is unlikely (they're also usually coloured green). The cost of unleaded 91 octane fuel is around 90¢ per litre, a litre of unleaded 96 (intended for high performance cars) or leaded costing around at 95¢. In recent years supermarkets have opened petrol stations selling fuel at discount prices, which has created something of a price war in some areas.

Diesel fuel is also available at most petrol stations at around 60¢ per litre, which means that running a diesel vehicle can work out much cheaper, as they also usually offer more kilometres per litre, although diesel users have to pay a Road User Charge (see page 165). New Zealand doesn't have a great number of diesel powered cars and it's mainly used in commercial vehicles, although many campervans are diesel powered. In recent months there has been a problem with locally refined diesel leading to the malfunction of filters. There's a national Diesel Help Line, which compensates drivers for the cost of replacing a filter (☎ freephone 0800-003 002). Another kind of fuel available is Liquid Petroleum Gas (LPG) or Compressed Natural Gas (CNG), which can be used only in specially converted cars. Liquid gas is cheaper than petrol and provides slightly better fuel consumption, although it's currently used only in North Island and its availability may decline over the next few years if petrol remains below $1 per litre.

There are plenty of petrol stations in towns and cities, but they can be few and far between in rural areas, particularly in South Island. It's wise to plan your fuel stops on long trips using a reliable map – when you see a 'last fuel for 70 miles' sign, it may well be true and not just a cynical marketing ploy! Also note that many petrol stations close at 6pm and are closed on Saturday afternoons and all day Sundays, although now it's at least *possible* to buy petrol in New Zealand on Sunday (a fairly recent development).

GARAGES

When buying a car in New Zealand, you would be wise to take into account local service facilities. There are plenty of Ford, Holden, Honda, Mazda and Toyota dealers in large towns, although dealers in other makes may be few and far between. It's difficult to find garages that can repair many European cars (which are often considered specialist or luxury cars) and the nearest dealer may be located a long way from your home or workplace. If you drive a rare car, it's wise to carry a basic selection of spare parts, as service stations in New Zealand may not stock them and you may need to wait several days (or even weeks) for them to arrive from Auckland or abroad. Kiwi mechanics, however, have a reputation for being able to improvise a repair on virtually any vehicle given a few nuts and bolts and a couple of pieces of wire!

Garages in New Zealand usually charge an hourly rate for their work, which varies considerably between main dealers and small country garages. Some franchised dealers operate a 'menu pricing' system, charging a fixed fee for a particular job irrespective of how long it takes. However, it's generally much cheaper to have your car serviced at a local country garage than at a main dealer, although they may lack expertise in such areas as automatic transmissions and ABS. If you have an accident and you car needs body repairs, it's usually best and cheaper to take it to a specialist body shop, of which there are many in New Zealand (not surprisingly!).

Note that when a car is under warranty, it must usually be serviced regularly by an approved dealer in order not to invalidate the warranty. However, if you need urgent assistance, particularly with an exotic foreign car, you're more likely to receive sympathetic help from a small local garage than a large dealer. Garages in New Zealand generally open from 8am to 5pm Mondays to Fridays and may also open on Saturday mornings, but are closed on Saturday afternoons and all day Sundays. In most areas there's a 24-hour breakdown service, although it's expensive, and it may pay you to join a motoring organisation such as the AA (see below).

Service stations in New Zealand don't usually provide a free 'loan car' while yours is being serviced or repaired, although some garages are agents for local hire services which are cheaper than national companies. Some garages will collect your car from your home or office and deliver it after a service, or will drop you at a bus station or in a local town and pick you up when your car is ready for collection.

MOTORING ORGANISATIONS

The Automobile Association (AA, PO Box 1, Wellington, ☎ freephone 0800-500 444, 🖥 www.nzaa.co.nz) is the main motoring organisation in New Zealand. It's similar to the British organisation of the same name (it even uses the same logo of black 'AA' letters on a yellow background), but shouldn't be confused with Alcoholics Anonymous! The AA provides technical and legal advice, route planning, traffic information and a variety of maps and books on motoring, as well as an emergency breakdown service. Visitors who are members of most major foreign motoring organisations can use all AA services *except* the breakdown service. Basic annual membership costs $66 in the Auckland area and $54 in the rest of New Zealand, plus a one-off $25 'registration' fee. In return the AA will send a mechanic to repair your car at the roadside or, if this proves impossible, have it taken to the nearest garage. Extra services, such as a 'get you home' service, loan car and hotel accommodation can be provided for an extra fee. Membership of the AA also entitles to you to free maps and accommodation guides. The AA publishes a magazine (also available online) which is useful for keeping up with the latest motoring news.

Several other organisations in New Zealand provide motoring breakdown cover, although most won't send a mechanic when you break down. Instead you must arrange your own repairs and the service then pays the bill up to a maximum amount.

ROAD MAPS & GUIDES

A variety of motoring maps is available in New Zealand, including the *AA New Zealand Road Atlas*, which is the best selling general map. The AA also publishes 1:350,000 district maps, which are free to members. If you want a more comprehensive guide, one of the best maps available is the *Explore New Zealand Motoring Guide* (New Holland Publishers), which shows motorways, state and secondary highways and unsealed roads, town maps with one-way streets, railway lines and stations, airports, public toilets and hospitals. It also provides historic information about a number of towns and cities, geological features, national and forest parks, campervan and camping sites, hot springs and skiing areas. Good maps are also produced by the major oil companies (available from petrol stations) and many publishers. Free maps of New Zealand are also available from Visitor Information Network (VIN) centres, libraries and car rental companies. Local town maps are available from tourist offices. Maps are also available on the Internet, including those showing major roads and towns produced by LINZ (🖳 www.linz.govt.nz/services) and one produced by the AA of the whole country with driving distances and times (🖳 www.aahost.co.nz).

There are several books on driving in New Zealand including *Signpost Guide New Zealand: Your Guide to Great Drives* by G. Powell (Thomas Cook Publishing), *4WD North Island* by Andy Cockroft and *4WD South Island* by Sibly & Wilson.

PARKING

Parking is rarely a problem in New Zealand, except in Auckland and Wellington. Street parking can also be difficult in other city centres during the day, although there are off-street (including multi-storey) car parks. Many hotels and public buildings have underground car parks which are open to the general public. Car parks are indicated by the internationally recognised 'P' symbol, and several cities publish a *Guide to Parking*, which you can pick up at local VIN offices. Parking is usually either pay-and-display, where you buy a ticket and display it behind the windscreen of your car, or a 'pay on exit' system. Most public car parks have extra-wide, easy-access spaces for disabled drivers, offering free or reduced cost parking; you need a Mobility Parking Scheme card, which is available from New Zealand CCS Inc., PO Box 6450, Auckland (☎ freephone 0800-227 225, 🖳 http://ccs.nzl.org). Applications must be supported by a certificate of disability from a doctor.

No Parking Zones: Restricted on-road parking zones are indicated by yellow lines painted at the roadside. A nearby sign will explain whether parking is banned at all times or only within certain hours and whether a time limit applies. Where parking is restricted rather than being prohibited at all times, restrictions usually operate between 8am and 6pm, Mondays to Fridays. Restrictions don't apply on Sundays but are usually in force on Saturdays, e.g. from 8am to 1pm. In areas where there's late night shopping or night-time entertainment (e.g. restaurants or theatres), parking limitations often apply until 9pm. If so, expect them to be enforced with the same vigour as they are during the day. Where parking is permitted, you should park on the left-hand side of the road facing the direction of the traffic flow.

Charges & Fines: Most city and town centres have meter zones. The charge, together with the time you may stay, varies according to the location but is usually around $1 per half hour (a nearby sign will explain the charges). Meters take 20¢, 50¢ and $1 coins. Some cities (such as Wellington) are experimenting with free weekend parking in an attempt to entice shoppers back to city centres and away from out-of-town shopping centres. Check carefully, however, as schemes are always changing. Car parks are expensive and cost from $2 to $3.50 for half an hour and from $7 to $14 for a whole day depending on the city.

Parking offenders receive fines up to a maximum of $60 for individual offences (e.g. parking on yellow lines) and for exceeding time limits. Note that town and city councils have veritable armies of parking wardens who are keen to give you a ticket or tow your vehicle away.

PEDESTRIAN ROAD RULES

Given the state of New Zealand driving, the best advice for pedestrians is to stay off the road completely. However, as this obviously isn't practical, you should take great care when crossing the road. Pedestrian crossings in towns are indicated by white stripes and yellow flashing beacons. Once you're on the crossing, drivers *should* stop, but it's wise to make sure they have before venturing into the road. There are also crossings controlled by traffic lights. Take extra care when with children, many of whom are killed or injured by speeding, drunk or dangerous drivers each year. Never let them play on a road, however quiet. Bear in mind that young children are unable to judge traffic speeds accurately and should usually be escorted to and from school. Take particular care in country areas where there are no footpaths, and wear bright coloured clothing and carry a torch (flashlight) at night. It's best to step off the road (jump into the ditch!) when you hear or see a vehicle approaching, even though it's legal to walk on a road without a footpath.

Take care when using pedestrianised streets, some of which allow access to vehicles at certain times or may be used by delivery vehicles and buses (cyclists also use pedestrianised streets, although it's illegal). When using footpaths, keep an eye open for skateboarders and rollerbladers (as well as cyclists). Many city authorities have banned skateboarding on footpaths and roads, but it remains a hazard despite the fact that offenders face a fine of up to $500.

12.

HEALTH

The quality of healthcare in New Zealand is excellent and comparable with other developed countries. Most illnesses and chronic conditions can be treated in New Zealand hospitals with the exception of a few highly specialist areas (such as certain transplants), when it may be necessary to travel abroad. The standard of public health is generally high, although there are some differences between racial groups, with Maoris in particular suffering from ill health more often than people of European origin. New Zealanders tend to suffer more from alcohol-related diseases than Europeans, but less from smoking-related diseases. A disturbing trend in recent years is that diseases associated with poverty, such as rickets and TB in children, are on the increase after being virtually wiped out. The infant mortality rate is around nine deaths per 1,000 live births (relatively high compared with other OECD countries) and average life expectancy at birth some 77 years.

New Zealand provides 'free' or subsidised healthcare to its citizens, permanent residents and certain visitors. The system is comparable to those in European countries such as France or Germany, where the state covers the bulk of the cost of medical treatment but expects most patients to make a contribution. 'Free' care isn't as comprehensive as under the British National Health Service, which aims to provide free care to almost everyone, including emergency treatment for visitors. On the other hand it's nothing like that in the USA, where every last pill, potion and sticking plaster must be paid for.

The New Zealand Ministry of Health is responsible for funding and providing state healthcare, which it delegates to District Health Boards (DHBs) whose job is to meet the government's health objectives by spending their budgets in the most cost-effective way. DHBs use their funding to 'buy' healthcare services from various 'suppliers', including family doctors, hospitals, nursing homes and other health organisations. This system has been in existence since 1993 and introduced the commercial market into the public healthcare sector. It has seen most hospitals reformed as Crown Health Enterprises (CHEs or 'cheeses' in local slang), which are effectively in competition with each other to provide the best healthcare at the lowest cost. As each of the 21 DHBs has substantial freedom to adopt its own system and framework, there tends to be a lack of national consistency in the health system.

The state healthcare system has come under huge pressure in recent years due to an increasing demand for services amid severe financial constraints, as politicians have sought to reduce the spiralling health budget in order to fund tax cuts. A number of hospitals have been closed and the number of people on waiting lists for non-emergency treatment, once unknown in New Zealand, has soared to almost 100,000. There has also been disruption to healthcare as successive governments have experimented with various measures aimed at providing a better service for less money (a formidable task). The latest measure is the Health Strategy, launched in December 2000, which provides a framework within which DHBs will operate and highlights government health priorities such as reducing smoking and ensuring access to child healthcare. However, the government has yet to provide adequate funding for DHBs and much public and media attention is concentrated on the general lack of funds behind New Zealand's state healthcare. Medical staff generally feel that they're underpaid and obliged to work with over-stretched resources. There have been several high-profile cases of people needing urgent treatment having to wait too long. The New Zealand Medical Association (NZMA) also highlights the shortage of rural GPs and professionals in some specialist areas, such as psychiatry, as well as the 'brain drain' of doctors from New Zealand who have accumulated vast student debts and are attracted by salaries and working conditions abroad.

Although you won't be denied medical attention in New Zealand (assuming you don't mind waiting), alternative treatments are also popular. A recent survey by *Consumer* magazine claimed that half of New Zealanders have tried alternative therapies, usually for conditions for which they had been seeing a 'traditional' doctor. The most popular alternative therapies are chiropractic, herbal medicine, homeopathy and osteopathy. New Zealand doctors are generally sympathetic to these therapies and occasionally refer patients to alternative practitioners.

EMERGENCIES

In a medical emergency in New Zealand simply dial 111 and ask for an ambulance, which will be despatched to take you to the nearest hospital. The ambulance service is free and is provided by different organisations depending on the region (e.g. Wellington Free Ambulance in the capital). In most regions, the ambulance service has paramedic teams and also uses helicopter ambulances. In remote areas, specially trained search-and-rescue teams are available and usually include a doctor who can administer treatment and perform minor operations on the spot.

If you're physically able, you should make your own way to the accident and emergency department of your nearest hospital. When you move to a new area, it's wise to find out where your nearest emergency hospital is situated, as a number have closed or merged their accident and emergency departments in recent years or operate them only part-time. Therefore, while there will always be an accident and emergency facility in your area, not every hospital is equipped to handle emergencies. If your condition isn't serious enough to warrant a hospital visit, you should consult your family doctor. In towns and cities there are 'after-hours' clinics where you can see a doctor concerning minor ailments when your doctor's surgery is closed (see **Doctors** on page 191).

A private company called Accident Info Services operates a telephone information service and advises callers on how to access New Zealand's health system. It can advise you on local doctors and hospitals and arrange for a doctor to visit you at home and is particularly useful when medical attention other than immediate hospital treatment is necessary. You can contact Accident Info Services on ☎ freephone 0800-263 345 or ☎ 09-529 0488.

STATE HEALTHCARE

New Zealand doesn't deduct social security health contributions from salaries, and the cost of providing public health services is largely met from general taxation. All citizens and permanent residents are automatically entitled to state healthcare, and it isn't necessary to establish a contributions record. If you're a visitor or temporary migrant but a national of a country with which New Zealand has a reciprocal agreement (such as Australia, Canada, Denmark, Greece, Guernsey, Ireland, Jersey, the Netherlands and the UK), you can also receive state health benefits. Otherwise you must pay the full cost of healthcare.

The basic principle of state healthcare in New Zealand is that hospital in-patient treatment is provided free, whereas the cost of out-patient and non-hospital treatment (e.g. consultations with a family doctor and prescribed medicines) must be paid for by patients (although services are subsidised). Those on low incomes can apply for a Community Services Card (CSC) which entitles them to a discount on healthcare costs (☎ freephone 0800-999 999 for information). There's no automatic reduction in charges for special groups, although free doctor's services are provided for children under six. Pensioners aren't automatically entitled to reduced-cost services unless they have a low income. Note that dental treatment and optical services are largely outside the scope of the state health scheme (see pages 194 and 195).

For information about public health services in New Zealand contact the Ministry of Health, PO Box 5013, Wellington (☎ 04-496 2000, ⌨ www.moh.govt.nz). See also **Social Security** on page 205.

Accident Compensation Scheme

Medical treatment necessary as the result of an accident isn't covered by the state healthcare scheme but by the accident compensation scheme run by the Accident Compensation Corporation (ACC – see page 202). Medical benefits paid by the ACC are more comprehensive than the basic state health scheme and include all treatment, including surgery, hospital care, specialists, doctor's fees and medicines, irrespective of where or how the accident occurred and who was to blame. The Injury Prevention and Rehabilitation Act passed in 2000 means that medical expenses are paid in full and claimants are paid a weekly allowance but must go through comprehensive monitored rehabilitation before they receive any lump sum compensation. This compensation is paid only after the claimant's condition has stabilised or after two years and if the claimant has 'whole person impairment'. The advantages of this scheme, which is unique, are that you don't need to buy private accident insurance (although you can if you wish) or sue a guilty party for compensation (in fact the law forbids you to do this). The main disadvantage is that the benefits aren't usually as generous as they would be with private insurance or compensation as great as you could receive as a result of taking legal action against someone who causes an accident.

PRIVATE HEALTHCARE

Private health practitioners operate both hand-in-hand with the public health service and independently of it. In addition to specialist appointments and hospital treatment, people commonly use private health treatment to obtain second opinions, health checks and screening, and for complementary medicine (which isn't usually available under the public health service). If you need to see a GP or specialist privately, you (or your insurance company) must pay the full fee. Most patients who receive private health treatment in New Zealand have private health insurance (see page 211), usually in order to circumvent the public health waiting lists for non-emergency specialist appointments and hospital treatment. Private patients are free to choose their own specialist and hospital and are usually accommodated in a single hotel-style room with a radio, telephone, colour TV, en suite bathroom and room service.

Make sure that a doctor or medical practitioner is qualified to provide the treatment you require and, when choosing a private specialist or clinic, you should be extremely cautious and only go to one that's highly recommended. It's sometimes wise to obtain a second opinion, particularly if you're diagnosed as having a serious illness or require a major operation (but don't expect your doctor or specialist to approve). Although not common in New Zealand, unnecessary operations aren't unknown.

Note that the quality of private treatment isn't any better than that provided by the public health service and you shouldn't assume that because a doctor (or any other medical practitioner) is in private practice he's more competent than his public health counterpart. In fact you will often see the same specialist or be treated by the same surgeon under the public health service and privately.

DOCTORS

New Zealand has a community-based system of healthcare, where your first point of contact for any medical problem is your family doctor or general practitioner (GP), who treats minor conditions and refers more serious cases to specialists or hospitals. It's wise to find and register with a doctor as soon as you arrive in a new area, although it isn't compulsory to do so and you can just turn up at any doctor's surgery, where you will usually receive prompt attention. You're allowed to choose any doctor, although it's obviously more convenient to use one near your home. Telephone directories contain a list of local doctors in the preface.

Most doctors' surgeries are well equipped and often take the form of health centres or group practices where several doctors practise together and specialise in different areas, such as obstetrics or paediatrics. Many also have their own nurses whom you can consult for minor problems and treatment, which is cheaper than seeing a doctor. New Zealand nurses are highly trained and qualified and are authorised to prescribe certain drugs and administer treatments (such as intravenous injections) which aren't permitted in many other countries.

Under the state healthcare scheme, a flat rate is charged for each visit to a doctor, irrespective of the nature of the visit. The basic consultation fee is from $35 to $45 for adults and $20 for children over five (or $10 for a visit to a nurse), plus the cost of any medicines prescribed (see **Medicines** below). Weekend and evening appointments usually cost between $5 and $10 extra. Under a scheme introduced in 1997, children under six were entitled to free doctor's visits and prescriptions. However, the subsidy paid to doctors by the government hasn't increased since then and many doctors are considering making a 'part charge' for the treatment of children under six. If you hold a Community Services Card (see page 190), a doctor's visit costs $20 for an adult and $15 for a child over five. If you need to visit the doctor frequently (at least 12 times a year), you can apply for a High Use Health Card, which entitles you to the same reductions as a CSC, through your doctor.

Surgery hours are usually 8.30am to 5.30pm Monday to Friday, although it's necessary to make an appointment and a doctor may not always be available (e.g. he could be out on a house call). Some family doctors provide a service outside surgery hours and make house calls, although this is rare; in cities, calls outside surgery hours are directed to an after-hours clinic. If you don't know where your nearest after-hours clinic is located, call your doctor's regular number and your call will be diverted (or a recorded message will tell you where the clinic is).

Healthline is a pilot scheme currently working in four areas of New Zealand providing 24-hour health advice from trained nurses. The scheme, similar to those in

Australia, the UK and the USA, is under a two-year trial due to finish in July 2002, when it may (or may not) be expanded to include the whole country. Healthline can be contacted on ☎ freephone 0800-611 116.

MEDICINES

Medicines are sold in pharmacies, known in New Zealand as chemists', which may be part of another business. They sell prescription and non-prescription medicines, and other products such as cosmetics and toiletries, but don't usually carry such an extensive range of goods as an American drugstore. Normal opening hours are 9am to 5.30pm Mondays to Fridays (occasionally later on Thursdays or Fridays) and sometimes on Saturday mornings. In most areas there's a duty chemist who's open longer hours or an emergency contact number is provided for those needing medicines in an emergency (details are shown in chemists').

The cost of prescribed medicines is subsidised by the government agency, Pharmac, and should be no more than $15 per item for adults and $10 for children or $3 per item if you have a CSC or High Use Health card (see above). After you've paid for 20 prescription items in a year, you're entitled to apply for a Pharmaceutical Subsidy Card (PSC), irrespective of your income, which entitles you to receive further prescriptions for as little as $2 each for the rest of the year (or free if you have a CSC). The PSC is applied for through your chemist. Note that PSC and CSC holders always have to pay manufacturers' charges over and above the Pharmac subsidy, and the full price for non-prescribed medicines. Pharmac periodically adds and removes medicines from its subsidised list, e.g. several new AIDS-inhibiting drugs such as Ritonavir have recently been added to the list, while a number of acne treatments have been removed. If you're obtaining a prescription item from a chemist, you will pay the same price everywhere. However, the cost of non-prescription items can vary considerably and items such as toiletries are considerably cheaper at supermarkets.

Most chemists provide general advice as to the best medicines for particular conditions and some are specially trained to provide individual consultations and advice to customers under the Comprehensive Pharmaceutical Care Service. Many patients use this system as a cheaper alternative to visiting a doctor, with the result that some pharmacists have begun charging $30 to $50 for consultations, plus the cost of the medicines! It's still possible, however, to find chemists who dispense free specialist advice; in the case of minor ailments this can save you a great deal of money compared with the cost of a visit to a doctor, as chemists will also tell you which drugs can be purchased over the counter for less than the $15 prescription charge.

HOSPITALS & CLINICS

Members of the public can use hospitals without a doctor's referral only in the case of accidents and emergencies. In all other cases your first point of contact is your family doctor, who will refer you to an appropriate hospital as necessary. The main criticism of the healthcare reforms in recent years has related to the increase in hospital waiting lists, which are long and growing longer. There have been many horror stories of patients requiring urgent hospital treatment having to wait ten hours or more for a bed (not that this makes New Zealand any worse than many other countries). Under the current system, regional health authorities must 'buy' the services you require (e.g. an operation) from the most cost-effective source, which will usually be your local hospital. However, if you're willing to travel to another (or any) hospital, you should inform your doctor, as he may be able to book you into a hospital where the waiting list is shorter.

Once you're given a bed in a public hospital, the standard of medical and nursing care is as good as you're likely to find anywhere. New Zealand hospitals provide free in-patient healthcare, which includes medical and nursing care, medicines and accommodation. (The government experimented with a $50 per day 'hotel charge' in hospitals between 1991 and 1993, but this was dropped after public opposition.) Out-patient treatment in accident and emergency departments isn't free and is paid for in the same way as visits to a family doctor (CSC holders pay reduced fees).

It can be difficult to identify hospitals in New Zealand since the 1993 changes to the state healthcare system, when they became known by various euphemisms such as 'healthcare centres', 'mental care units' (mental hospitals) or 'elder care units' (geriatric hospitals). In addition to public hospitals there are also many private hospitals in New Zealand, which allow the wealthy and those with medical insurance to avoid the waiting lists in the public sector. Many private hospitals are owned by the medical insurance companies (as public hospitals don't accept private patients) and accommodation may be more luxurious than in public hospitals, although the standard of medical care is the same and they're often staffed by the same doctors. Some private hospitals receive government subsidies and there are a number of projects where the public and private sectors co-operate to provide specialist services such as coronary care. Some charities also provide health services, e.g. community clinics, which are partially funded by the government. Some private hospitals and clinics specialise in non-essential cosmetic surgery.

The New Zealand Ministry of Health helpfully publishes hospital death rate statistics to help you choose a hospital, although this won't do you much good if you're rushed to the nearest hospital in an emergency!

CHILDBIRTH & ABORTION

The first port of call for pregnant women in New Zealand is their family doctor, who can undertake preliminary tests and checks and refer you for ante-natal and (subsequently) post-natal care, either within the practice itself or at a nearby clinic, where you're attended to by a 'lead maternity carer' who may be either a midwife or doctor. It's usual for a birth to take place in a local hospital, where you can stay for up to five days, although it's possible to have a baby at home attended by a midwife. This is more usual in rural areas, where the nearest hospital may be a considerable distance away. All maternity and childbirth treatment within the state system is free.

Abortion is legal in New Zealand under certain conditions, such as when continuing with a pregnancy would pose a threat to the physical or mental well-being of the mother, or when a child is likely to be born seriously handicapped. Two specially approved doctors or counsellors must authorise an abortion.

CHILDREN'S HEALTH

Family doctors provide a health service for children and where necessary refer them to consultants and specialists at an appropriate hospital. Child immunisation is free and actively encouraged for HIB, hepatitis B, diphtheria, tetanus, whooping cough, poliomyelitis, measles, mumps and rubella. Public health nurses visit primary schools to conduct regular hearing and eye tests. The national non-profit organisation Plunket also provides free check-ups for children, advice and information as well as support. Plunket, which is run by professionals and volunteers and aims to provide New Zealand children with access to the best health care and the organisation, fills the many gaps in the state child healthcare system. Plunket also works closely with Maori and ethnic groups. Further information can be obtained from Plunket, PO Box 5474, Wellington (☎ 04-471 0177, 🖳 www.plunket.org.nz).

New Zealand's leading children's hospital (with a similar status there to London's famous Great Ormond Street Children's Hospital) is Auckland's Starship Children's Hospital, which caused an outcry among doctors and dieticians for allowing McDonald's to open a fast food outlet in the foyer (although it went down well with the kids)!

New Zealand has a tradition of promoting access to the great outdoors for children and there are 'health camps' throughout the country for children under 13 with special needs, who can attend for up to six weeks. Children are referred to the camps by doctors, social workers and teachers, and they undertake a programme of remedial education, health education, sports and games, in addition to learning 'life skills'. Camps also have psychologists who counsel children with behavioural problems. Health camps are largely financed by special 'health postage stamps' issued by NZ Post in the spring, from which a donation is made to help fund camps. Health authorities also operate various health education and development programmes for children, including a recent screening programme for Auckland teenagers to try to minimise future incidence heart disease.

DENTISTS

There are excellent dentists throughout New Zealand; indeed New Zealanders travelling abroad often search high and low in cities such as London or New York for a New Zealand dentist. If you wish, you may be able to find a British or American dentist in Auckland or Wellington, although they all inflict the same sort of torture irrespective of nationality! Most dentists in New Zealand are in private practice, as the public health scheme doesn't extend to dentistry, except in the case of children. Children at primary schools see a school dental nurse and many primary schools have a dental surgery on the premises. Children are entitled to see a school dentist every 12 months, although a backlog has been developing for several years resulting in most children seeing a dentist only once every 18 months (they don't seem to mind!). All children up to the age of 16 (18 if still at school) are entitled to free treatment by the dentist of their choice, assuming that he participates in the 'free dental scheme' (many dentists have withdrawn from the scheme because of the 'inadequate' fees paid by the Ministry of Health).

To find a dentist, ask for recommendations from neighbours, colleagues and friends, or consult your local telephone directory. It's wise to shop around, as charges can vary considerably, particularly for extensive repair work. However, most dentists, unless they target wealthy patients, charge fees that are affordable to the average person (although it can still be an expensive business). It's wise to obtain a quotation before having any 'expensive' treatment – many dentists have 'menu pricing', although this should be regarded only as a guide. Typical dental fees include $65 for an examination, $110 for an examination and scaling, and $90 for a small filling, while a set of dentures (including extractions and fitting) is likely to set you back from $780 to $2,000. Information about dentists can be obtained from the Dental Council of New Zealand, PO Box 10 448, Wellington (☎ 04-499 4820, 🖳 www.dental council.org.nz).

It's possible to take out special insurance against dental costs, and cover for dental treatment may also be included in general medical insurance policies, which can be purchased from medical insurance companies and from dentists (see **Chapter 13**).

OPTICIANS

Opticians in New Zealand are known as optometrists and have 'surgeries' (more often shops) in most towns and cities, where they provide eye tests and sell spectacle lenses and frames and contact lenses. Optometry is an entirely private business in New Zealand and outside the scope of the public health system. You can save money by shopping around and buying spectacles and contact lenses somewhere other than the fancy optometrists found in modern shopping centres. A standard pair of spectacles and lenses costs around $300 to $400 plus $48 for the cost of an eye test, although a basic deal is available countrywide for $180 for glasses and $48 for the eye test required for a driving licence. (When the requirement was introduced many New Zealanders were shocked to discover that not only couldn't they see well enough to drive but also they had to pay for new glasses!) If you think that you have a medical problem affecting your eyes (such as glaucoma), you should ask your family doctor to refer you to a specialist at a hospital, in which case treatment will be provided free.

COUNSELLING & SOCIAL SERVICES

Counselling and assistance for health and social problems is available under the public health system, and from many local community groups and volunteer organisations, ranging from national associations to small local groups (including self-help groups). Local authorities provide social workers to advise and support those requiring help within their community. If you need to find help locally, you can contact your local council, local voluntary services or a Citizens' Advice Bureau (☎ freephone 0800-367 222, 🖳 www.consumer.org.nz). A list of 24-hour emergency services (including many counselling services) is included in telephone directories, plus community help and welfare services, and help for young people.

Many colleges and educational establishments provide a counselling service for students, and general hospitals usually have a psychiatrist on call 24 hours a day. Problems for which help is available are numerous and include drug rehabilitation, alcoholism (e.g. Alcoholics Anonymous), gambling, dieting (e.g. Weight Watchers), smoking, attempted suicide and psychiatric problems, homosexual related problems, youth problems, battered children and women, marriage and relationship counselling, and rape. A number of voluntary organisations and local authorities run refuges for battered wives (and their children) or maltreated children whose conditions have become intolerable (some provide 24-hour emergency phone numbers). If you or a member of your family are the victims of a violent crime, the police will put you in touch with a local victim support scheme. For information about help and advice to disabled people, see below.

HELP FOR THE HANDICAPPED

Official government statistics show that around 20 per cent of New Zealanders have some kind of 'handicap', varying from a serious physical disability to a minor visual impairment (curiously the rate is higher in South Island than in North Island). All public offices and businesses are required to make special provision for handicapped people (e.g. special access ramps, facilities for the hard of hearing, etc.), although provision of these services is patchy, as a lot of older buildings cannot be modified. Most buses cannot accommodate those with mobility problems, although a small number of taxis can (see **Chapter 10**). There are several organisations that provide help to the handicapped in New Zealand, which includes practical help, financial assistance and advice (including advice on state benefits). The main organisations are:

- Enable New Zealand (formerly the Disability Resource Centre, ☎ freephone 0800-171 981 or 06-952 0011, 🖥 www.nzdrc.govt.nz/enable);

- New Zealand CCS Inc., PO Box 6450, Auckland (☎ freephone 0800-227 225, 🖥 http://ccs.nzl.org);

- New Zealand Disability Information Service (314 Worcester Street, Christchurch, ☎ 03-366 6189).

Invalids benefit is payable to those unable to work because of a physical or mental disability (see page 207); those who are handicapped as a result of an accident receive payments from the Accident Compensation Corporation (see page 202).

SEXUALLY TRANSMITTED DISEASES

Like most countries, New Zealand has its share of sexually transmitted diseases (STDs), including the deadly Acquired Immune Deficiency Syndrome (AIDS). Fortunately, New Zealand has one of the lowest incidences of AIDS in the developed world and only around 30 people a year are found to have the disease, down from a peak of 79 in 1989, although the incidence among women has risen sharply. AIDS is transmitted by sexual contact, needle sharing among drug addicts, and less commonly, through transfused blood or its components. All blood used in transfusions in New Zealand is screened for HIV (human immunodeficiency virus), the virus which usually leads to AIDS.

The furore over AIDS has died down in the past few years, which many fear may cause those most at risk to be lulled into a false sense of security (many teenagers still practise unprotected sex). The explosion of AIDS predicted by 'experts' in many countries hasn't materialised, particularly among the heterosexual population, although the number of heterosexual cases is increasing. In an attempt to combat AIDS, the use of condoms has been widely encouraged through a comprehensive (if obscure) advertising campaign, although it has taken a long time to get the message across about safe sex. Condom machines can be found in various public places (there's an on-going debate about whether they should be installed in secondary schools) and purchased from chemists and other outlets (but they aren't cheap). Some positive news for sufferers is that several AIDS-inhibiting drugs have been placed on the subsidised drugs list in recent years (see **Medicines** on page 192).

Family doctors in New Zealand can provide basic information about STD prevention and can refer those with particular problems and worries to specialists. Gay and other organisations are also active in providing help and advice.

SMOKING & DRUGS

New Zealand has become one of the leading countries in the battle against smoking, which has resulted in a significantly lower death rate from lung disease and other smoking-related diseases than, for example, in most European countries. Cigarettes have become increasingly expensive thanks to sharp tax rises in the last few years. The government spends around $20 million per year on anti-smoking programmes aimed principally at children and Maoris, although this represents only a fraction of the amount raised in tobacco taxes (a strange situation, in which the government is spending money in order to try to *reduce* its income!). Cigarette packets contain bi-lingual (English and Maori) warnings about the perils of smoking. Those under 18 are prohibited from purchasing tobacco products, and the penalty for selling tobacco to those under age is $2,000, although there's no fine for the purchaser. The government plans to ban retailers from selling tobacco if they have several convictions for selling tobacco to minors. There's a national Quitline providing advice and support for those trying to give up smoking (☎ freephone 0800-778 778).

Smoking is officially banned in most public places, and you may not smoke in most public buildings or on buses, coaches, trains and aircraft. Most workplaces have banned smoking altogether, although the more tolerant have a small smoking area, and the majority of restaurants are entirely non-smoking (if they aren't they must have a non-smoking area). Quite apart from the anti-smoking legislation, smoking is considered socially unacceptable in New Zealand. You would be extremely unwise to smoke in a non-smoking area and even when indulging in the evil weed perfectly legally you may attract angry glances, remarks, or even requests to stub it out if your smoke is causing annoyance to others. The main government objective for 2002 is to ban smoking completely in bars, restaurants, casinos and clubs, and initial legislation was passed in 2001.

'Recreational' smoking of cannabis, which is widely grown in New Zealand, and marijuana is widespread, although it's illegal, and the use of ecstasy and hard drugs such as heroin and cocaine is on the increase. However, drug abuse is less of a problem than in many other countries, and New Zealand's border controls are relatively effective in keeping out illicit substances.

BIRTHS & DEATHS

Births in New Zealand must be registered within seven days at your local registry office for births, marriages and deaths. You will be provided with a copy of the entry in the register, otherwise known as a birth certificate (necessary for official purposes such as claiming benefits and school registration). Deaths should be registered at the same office (also within seven days) with a copy of the death certificate provided by the hospital or doctor attending the death. This is usually carried out by the undertaker. As anywhere, dying is a major expense in New Zealand where an average funeral and burial costs around $1,600 and possibly much more with 'extras' such as cars and flowers. The cost of shipping a body to another country for burial is considerable and is to be avoided if at all possible. Most medical insurance policies provide cover for funeral expenses (with the amount of benefit linked to the cost of the policy). It's also possible to take out a funeral plan to cover these expenses. For those without insurance or private means, a government funeral grant of up to $1,182 is available, which depends on the means and assets of the deceased and his next of kin (it's generally only available to those who already receive social security benefits).

MEDICAL TREATMENT ABROAD

If you're a visitor to New Zealand and a resident of a country with a reciprocal health agreement with New Zealand (including Australia, Canada, Denmark, Greece, Guernsey, Ireland, Jersey, the Netherlands and the UK), you can take advantage of public healthcare services in New Zealand, including free hospital in-patient treatment and free medicines while in hospital. When visiting a doctor, you will be charged at the same rate as New Zealanders for consultations (see page 191) and will also be able to purchase subsidised prescriptions (see page 192). To claim these benefits, simply show your passport to the doctor or chemist. There's no entitlement to subsidised dentistry (except for children) or optical services and you aren't entitled to free treatment for conditions which existed before you entered New Zealand (if you knew or could reasonably have been expected to know about them). It's important to note that citizens of countries without a reciprocal health agreement with New Zealand aren't entitled to free hospital treatment or subsidised doctor's consultations or prescriptions, and must pay the full cost of treatment (which is substantially higher than the subsidised rate). Therefore it's essential for citizens of those countries to have private medical insurance when visiting New Zealand.

If you're entitled to social security health benefits in New Zealand, you can take advantage of reciprocal healthcare arrangements in other countries with which New Zealand has such an agreement. These include Australia, Canada, Denmark, Greece, Guernsey, Ireland, Jersey, the Netherlands and the UK (but not the USA), where you're entitled to the same public health benefits as citizens and residents simply by producing your New Zealand passport or migration documents. In Australia you receive free hospital treatment and subsidised prescriptions through the Medicare system, while in the UK you receive most medical treatment free, paying only prescription and subsidised dental charges.

13.

INSURANCE

New Zealand has an innovative approach to insurance, which is quite different from that in, for example, the USA and most western European countries. As in those countries, there are state schemes which pay health, sickness and unemployment benefits. Unlike those of most other countries, however, New Zealand's system isn't largely insurance based, and individuals aren't required to make contributions in order to benefit (although, as the substantial costs are funded by general taxation, they cannot be said to be free to tax payers). New Zealand has also taken the concept of state insurance a step further than most other countries and provides universal accident benefits to all citizens, residents and visitors (see below). **Note, however, that the situation regarding 'free' insurance in New Zealand doesn't mean that you don't need to take out private insurance.** The state schemes don't, by any means, cover every eventuality and neither are the benefits necessarily generous, making private insurance provision recommended, if not essential.

See also **Car Insurance** on page 171 and **Motor Breakdown Insurance** on page 171.

ACCIDENT COMPENSATION SCHEME

If you have an accident at work or on the roads, you will be compensated by the government-operated Accident Compensation Corporation (ACC), irrespective of who was to blame or whether you've paid any contributions. The ACC operates what's essentially a mandatory accident insurance system, financed both through taxes and (unlike most other state benefits) by a levy on earnings. However, entitlement to benefits isn't based on contributions as it would be with a commercial insurance scheme. Visitors are also covered by the ACC scheme without the need to make contributions. If you should suffer an accident and make a claim on the scheme, it will cover your medical and associated expenses in New Zealand, but it won't cover repatriation or medical expenses arising abroad in connection with an accident or loss of earnings abroad. Note that, as the ACC isn't a social security scheme, continuing to pay into the social security scheme in your home country (which you're usually entitled to do) doesn't exempt you from paying the ACC levy on your earnings in New Zealand.

The aim of the accident compensation scheme was originally to provide New Zealanders with superior accident insurance at low cost by taking the commercialism out of insurance. The scheme has gone through many changes in recent years, including a period of two years when employers were permitted to take out accident compensation insurance with private companies instead of with the state ACC. However, since 2000 workplace insurance can only be provided by ACC. Payments made under the ACC scheme used to be extremely generous and consisted of lump sum payments on a fixed scale, but this resulted in large amounts of money being paid to people with relatively minor injuries. The Injury Prevention and Rehabilitation Act passed in 2000 has resulted in a general tightening of the ACC budget and the emphasis now lies on injury prevention and rehabilitation rather than the payment of compensation as was previously the case. Compensation ranges from a minimum of $2,500 to a maximum of $100,000. The aim of the Act, which also establishes a 'code of claimants' rights', is to prevent fraud and to ensure that the more seriously injured claimants receive greater compensation than the less seriously injured. The Act has come in for much criticism, particularly from employers, but the ACC scheme is much more generous than most other countries' public schemes, most of which don't pay out a penny to accident victims, certainly not without a long legal struggle.

Note that suing the party who caused an accident isn't usually possible under New Zealand law – a situation that that would have grossly overpaid personal injury lawyers in the USA gasping in horror! You must simply accept the payment awarded by the ACC, which, although it means that you're unlikely to receive a multi-million dollar payout (as you may in the USA), ensures that a lot of money isn't wasted on long drawn out court cases (and it prevents fraud, reduces premiums, etc.). However, if you wish, you can take out personal injury insurance, which is likely to pay considerably higher compensation in the case of an accident and may also compensate you for damage to property (which the ACC doesn't).

Expenses covered by the ACC are comprehensive and include medical and hospital treatment, hospital surgery, loss of earnings, loss of future earnings, physiotherapy, home nursing care, expenses involved with rehabilitation or future disability, and an allowance if you're unable to work. For information about ACC health benefits, see **Accident Compensation Scheme** on page 190. For further information, contact the Accident Compensation Corporate Office (☎ 04-918 7700, ▣ www.acc.org.nz).

Contributions: Although New Zealand doesn't require employees to make social security contributions, you must contribute to the ACC scheme. Employee ACC contributions, known as the 'earner's levy', are used to pay compensation for accidents occurring outside the workplace. They're fixed annually and are deducted from your salary by your employer, who will automatically register you for the ACC levy when you start work in New Zealand. ACC contributions (which are changed periodically) for employees are currently $1.10 for each $100 of liable income up to a maximum amount of liable earnings of $85,795 (i.e. a maximum contribution of $943.75). Unlike self-employed people, employees don't have a choice of ACC schemes, although they may take advantage of the TimeOut option (see below).

Your employer also makes a contribution to the scheme, known as the 'employer's levy', which is used to provide compensation for accidents in the workplace. It's illegal (punishable by a $5,000 fine) for an employer to try to recover the employer's levy from employees, either by a direct deduction or any kind of informal agreement. The ACC offers employers the option of ACC Workplace Cover (standard) or ACC Workplace Safety Management Practices, which provides premium discounts in return for a safer workplace.

All self-employed people must also belong to the ACC scheme and have three options: ACC CoverPlus, which provides basic cover; ACC CoverPlus Extra, which allows you to choose the weekly compensation you'd receive if injured; and ACC TimeOut, which gives continued income protection cover to the self-employed who are planning to take a break from work. The self-employed pay the same ACC levy as employees, although they're exempt if their liable earnings are less than $14,560 per year ($11,256 for those under 20), and expenses are deductible.

Further information and advice about ACC contributions can be obtained from your local Inland Revenue Department (IRD) office.

INSURANCE COMPANIES

There are numerous insurance companies to choose from in New Zealand, either providing a range of insurance services or specialising in certain fields only. You can buy insurance from many sources, including traditional insurance companies selling through their own salesmen or independent brokers, direct insurance companies (selling directly to the public), banks and other financial institutions, and motoring organisations. An increasingly common trend in New Zealand is for banks to offer property, life and even motor insurance to their customers, which they do on an agency basis, i.e. they don't compare prices from various companies to find you the cheapest policy, although their premiums are usually competitive. The major insurance companies have offices or agents (brokers) throughout the country, most of whom will provide a free analysis of your family or business insurance needs. Two organisation provide useful information and advice about insurance: The Insurance Company of New Zealand, which publishes a comprehensive *Guide to Insurance* brochure (PO Box 474, Wellington, ☎ 04-472 5230, 💻 www.icnz.org.nz), and the Citizens' Advice Bureau (CAB), which has offices in most large towns and cities (☎ freephone 0800-367 222, 💻 www.consumer.org.nz). New Zealand also has an insurance ombudsman who is there to deal with any complaints about insurance companies and services (PO Box 10-845, Wellington, ☎ 04-499 7612, 💻 www.iombudsman.org.nz).

Brokers: If you choose a broker, you should use one who's independent and sells policies from a wide range of insurance companies. Some brokers or agents are tied to a particular insurance company and sell policies only from that company (which includes most banks). An independent broker should research the whole market and take into account your individual requirements, why you're investing (if applicable), the various companies' financial performance, what you can afford and the kind of policy that's best for you. He mustn't offer you a policy because it pays him the highest commission, which, incidentally, you should ask him about (particularly regarding life insurance).

Direct Insurance: In recent years many insurance companies have begun operating by 'direct response' (i.e. bypassing brokers), which has resulted in huge savings for consumers, particularly for car, building and home contents insurance. Direct response companies give quotations over the phone and often you aren't even required to complete a proposal form. Compare premiums from a number of direct response insurance companies with the best deals from brokers before choosing a policy.

Shop Around: When buying insurance, you should shop 'til you drop and then shop around some more! Premiums vary considerably (e.g. by 100 to 200 per cent), although you must ensure that you're comparing similar policies and that important benefits haven't been omitted. Bear in mind that the cheapest policy isn't necessarily the best, particularly regarding the prompt payment of claims. Many analysts believe that it's better to pay for independent insurance advice rather than accept 'free' advice, which may be more expensive in the long run. You should obtain a number of quotations for each insurance need and shouldn't assume that your existing insurance company is the best choice for a new insurance requirement. Buy only the insurance that you *want* and *need* and ensure that you can afford the payments (and that your cover is protected if you're sick or unemployed).

INSURANCE CONTRACTS

Read insurance contracts carefully before signing them. If you don't understand everything, ask a friend or colleague to 'translate' it or obtain professional advice.

Policies often contain traps and legal loopholes in the small print. If a policy has pages of legal jargon and gobbledegook in *very* small print, you have a right to be suspicious, particularly as it's common practice nowadays to be as brief as possible and write clearly and concisely in language which doesn't require a doctorate in law. Note that an insurance certificate or schedule won't list all the conditions and exclusions, which are listed only in the full policy document. Many of the new direct response companies handle quotations, enquiries and claims by phone on a paperless basis, so you may never see a form or document explaining your policy. This saves companies money, which they allegedly pass on to policyholders in the form of lower premiums. Take care how you answer questions in an insurance proposal form; even if you mistakenly provide false information, an insurance company can refuse to pay out when you make a claim.

Most insurance policies run for a calendar year from the date on which you take out a policy. All insurance policy premiums should be paid punctually, as late payment can affect your benefits or a claim, although if this is so, it should be noted in your policy. Before signing an insurance policy, you should shop around and take a day or two to think it over (never sign on the spot, as you may regret it later). With some insurance contracts, you may have a 'cooling off' period (e.g. 10 to 14 days) during which you can cancel a policy without penalty.

Claims: Although insurance companies are keen to take your money, many aren't nearly so happy to settle claims. As in other countries, some insurance companies will do almost anything to avoid paying out in the event of a claim and will use any available loophole. Fraud is estimated to cost the insurance industry $millions a year (particularly motor insurance fraud) and staff may be trained to automatically assume that claims are fraudulent. If you wish to make a claim, you must usually inform your insurance company in writing by registered letter within a number of days of the incident (possibly within 24 hours in the case of theft). **Failure to do so will render your claim void!** Don't send original bills or documents regarding a claim to your insurance company unless it's essential (you can send a certified copy). Keep a copy of bills, documents and correspondence, and send letters by recorded or registered post so that your insurance company cannot deny receipt.

Don't bank a cheque received in settlement of a claim if you think it's insufficient, as you may be deemed to have accepted it as full and final settlement. It's also unwise to accept the first offer, as many insurance companies try to get away with making a low settlement (if an insurer pays what you've claimed without a quibble, you probably claimed too little!). When dealing with insurance companies, perseverance often pays. Insurers are increasingly refusing to pay up on the flimsiest of pretexts, as they know that many people won't pursue their cases, even when they have a valid claim. Don't give up on a claim if you have a good case, but persist until you have exhausted every avenue.

SOCIAL SECURITY

New Zealand has a comprehensive social security system that provides a wide range of benefits to cover sickness and invalidity, unemployment and old age. Around one in four New Zealanders receives some sort of social security payment. As in many other countries, the social security system has suffered a funding crisis in recent years and (in real terms) benefits are being reduced, even though they're officially increased each year (benefits are reviewed annually, with increases taking effect in

January). The government spends over $10 billion annually on social security benefits, most of which aren't based on contributions or previous earnings but on a flat rate set by the government. On average this provides claimants receiving benefits with around 40 to 50 per cent of the average annual weekly wage, which is barely enough to live on.

The government has introduced a number of schemes in recent years to try to ensure that benefits are paid only to those in genuine need and, even then, only for as long as they need them. An increasing number of benefits are paid only after means-testing (an appraisal of an applicant's savings and other financial circumstances). In other cases, claimants are regularly called to account and expected to prove that they still need a benefit and cannot manage without it. Despite this increasingly tough stance on paying out government (or rather taxpayers') money, the authorities still encourage people to claim benefits to which they may be entitled on a 'we may turn you down but you're welcome to try' basis. Applications for benefits should be made to the Income Support Service or, in some cases, the Inland Revenue Department, the addresses of which can be found in your local telephone directory.

Eligibility

New Zealand nationals, permanent residents and foreign workers temporarily employed in New Zealand are covered by social security without the need to make social security contributions. (They must, however, make contributions to the ACC scheme – see page 202.) Benefits are normally paid only after a minimum period of residence, e.g. unemployment benefit is available only after you've lived in New Zealand for two years, and national superannuation (state pension) usually requires a ten-year residence period. However, New Zealand has reciprocal agreements with certain countries (including Australia, Canada, Denmark, Greece, Guernsey, Ireland, Jersey, the Netherlands and the UK), under which those migrating from these countries can apply for New Zealand social security benefits as soon as they arrive to take up permanent residence. It's important to note that a reciprocal agreement entitles you to only *apply* for benefits; whether or not a benefit is paid may depend on other criteria. Not all residents are eligible for all benefits, as various 'tests' (e.g. income and other means) may be used to determine whether you're entitled to them. For example, under a recent change in the immigration rules, prospective immigrants are excluded from state benefits if they don't have sufficient resources to support themselves for at least 12 months without claiming state benefits. For further information contact WINZ Head Office, Level 8, Bowen State Building, Bowen Street, PO Box 12-136, Wellington (☎ freephone 0800-559 009 or 09-913 0300, ▪ www.winz.govt.nz).

Benefits

Social security benefits are paid (where appropriate) at a flat rate, irrespective of your previous income. Benefits are taxable (assuming you earn enough to pay tax), and the Department of Social Welfare deducts tax due (if applicable) before paying benefits. If you receive a benefit for the first time and aren't registered for tax, you should contact your local IRD office, which will issue you with an IRD number. This is required by Work and Income New Zealand (WINZ) in order to deduct tax before paying your benefits. Those who receive no income other than benefits receive an 'M' tax code.

Health Benefit: Your entitlement to health benefit in New Zealand doesn't depend on your having established a contributions record. If you're either a New Zealand citizen or a permanent resident you're automatically entitled to state healthcare (see page 189). If you're a visitor or temporary migrant but a national of a country with which New Zealand has a reciprocal agreement (such as Australia, Canada, Denmark, Greece, Guernsey, Ireland, Jersey, the Netherlands and the UK), you can also receive health benefit. Otherwise you must pay the full cost of healthcare.

Sickness & Maternity Benefits: Sickness benefit is payable to those who are unable to work due to illness on a temporary basis, whereas invalids benefit (see below) is a permanent or semi-permanent benefit. In social security terms pregnancy also counts as a 'sickness' in that expectant mothers can apply for sickness benefit when they're unable to work, both during and after a pregnancy. In mid-2001 legislation was introduced under which maternity leave will be paid, for up to 12 weeks, as from 1st July 2002. The rate will be a maximum of $325 per week before tax, although as yet some sectors, such as self-employed women, don't qualify. Sickness benefit is payable weekly at three gross rates: $121.21 for single people under 20 living at home; $181.84 for single people under 20 living away from home, single people aged 20 to 24, and single people aged 25 or over; and $151.52 (each) for couples. The benefit is increased slightly if you have dependent children.

Accidental Injury Benefit: If you have an accident at work or anywhere else in New Zealand (including when motoring), all expenses and appropriate compensation are paid by the ACC scheme (see page 202).

Invalids Benefit: Invalids benefit is payable to those permanently unable to work because of a physical or mental disability, and provides a weekly payment equivalent to around half the average wage. Invalids benefit is granted following a medical examination and is based on the opinion of the examining doctor. As in other countries, there has been concern that many people receiving this kind of benefit aren't incapable of work. The eligibility criteria have therefore been tightened and the cases of claimants who receive this benefit are periodically re-examined to ensure that they still qualify. Gross weekly rates are $230.66 for a single person over 18 and $189.91 each for a married couple.

Family Support: Family support is a social security benefit available to those with children under 19 who are living at home and financially dependent. Entitlement to this benefit and the rate at which it's paid depend on your family's income and the number of children you have. A family with one child whose total annual income doesn't exceed $30,000 qualifies for family support and if you're in the happy (or unhappy?) position of having six children you can earn up to $58,500 and still receive family support. Family support is paid at a rate of $47 per week for your first child and $32 for each subsequent ($40 if they're aged 13 to 15 and $60 if they're 16 to 18). The threshold limits and amounts payable are increased annually.

To apply for family support contact your local IRD or WINZ office, which will require proof of your income (e.g. a pay slip), the ages of your children (their birth certificates) and your bank account details. IRD pays family support if your total income is over $20,000; otherwise it's paid by WINZ. Depending on your other income and benefits, you may receive your family support as a direct payment into your bank account or as a credit against income tax deducted from your salary (known as an 'independent family tax credit').

Domestic Purposes Benefit (DPB): Domestic purposes benefit is mainly intended for single parents with dependent children who don't receive maintenance or support from a partner, although it's also sometimes paid to eligible widows and widowers and those caring for sick or disabled relatives at home. It's generally payable only to those on low incomes (although there are various eligibility criteria) and only to New Zealand citizens and permanent residents, although under a reciprocal agreement those moving from Australia and the UK can apply for the benefit immediately. In late 2001 DPB was available at the following rates:

Category	Gross Weekly Rate ($)
Woman or single adult	189.91
Single parent with one child	266.34
Single parent with two or more children	291.83

Widow's Benefit: Widow's benefit is payable to women whose husband or partner has died. The benefit is mainly to help widows with children to support. It's a means tested benefit payable only to those of limited means and if the widow remarries, she's no longer eligible for the benefit. Rates are the same as Domestic Purposes Benefit (see above).

Funeral Grant: A funeral grant of up to $1,182 is payable to those who suffer a death in the family. It is, however, a means tested benefit payable only to those with limited resources; the assets of the deceased person are also taken into account when assessing whether it's payable.

Independent Youth's Benefit: The independent youth's benefit is for young people aged 16 and 17 who are looking or training for work, at school or can't work because of sickness or pregnancy. To qualify for the benefit you must either have the support of your parents or live with a partner. The gross weekly rate is $151.52.

Unemployment Benefit: Some 5.2 per cent of the working population is registered as unemployed in New Zealand. Both New Zealand citizens and permanent residents are entitled to apply for unemployment benefit (or 'dole') and no history of contributions or tax deductions is required to make a claim. However, newcomers must wait 12 months before they can apply for unemployment benefit, and those who resign from their jobs or are dismissed must wait 13 weeks before they can receive benefits.

The New Zealand unemployment benefit service is run by Work and Income New Zealand (WINZ), the arm of the Department of Labour that provides a job-finding (or 'vacancy-filling') service to employees and employers (see page 22). A much tougher approach than in the past is being taken to unemployment benefit, and claimants are required to register with WINZ and make a 'Job Seeker Commitment', under which they're obliged to look for full-time work or training and take a suitable job if offered one. Claimants are also required to have regular meetings with Income Support Services to determine what they're doing to find work (and to ensure that they aren't working while claiming benefit!). Those who fail to meet their obligations without a good reason may have their benefit suspended. On the third failure, benefit may be stopped for 13 weeks. There are exceptions for those with children under 14 or anyone caring for a disabled or dependant relative.The benefit is paid at a flat rate irrespective of your previous income, although there are variations according to age and family status and you may be eligible for other rates. Rates in late 2001 were as follows:

Category	Gross Weekly Rate ($)
Single under 20, living at home	121.21
Single under 20, living away from home	151.52
Single, 20 to 24	151.52
Single, 25 or over	181.84
Couple (each)	151.52
Single parent with one child	266.34
Single parent with more than one child	291.83
Couple with one or more children	161.01 (each)

Transitional Retirement Benefit: Transitional retirement benefit is for those who have retired and have a low income but haven't yet reached the qualifying age for superannuation, i.e. 65 (see below). Gross weekly rates are $230.66 for a single person over 18 and $189.91 each for a married couple.

National Superannuation: New Zealand provides an old age retirement pension known as national superannuation or 'super' for short. It's funded from general taxation rather than individual contributions. In order to be entitled to it you must:

- be 65 or over;
- be a legal resident of New Zealand and normally live there;
- have lived in New Zealand for ten years since the age of 20 (five of those years must have been since your 50th birthday).

If you come to New Zealand from a country with a reciprocal social security agreement (including Australia, Canada, Ireland and the UK), you can claim national superannuation without a minimum period of residence, provided you would have been entitled to a state pension in your home country, although your overseas pension will probably be deducted from New Zealand superannuation. WINZ have special freephone contact numbers for overseas entitlements (for Australia ☎ 0800-777 227; for Ireland and the UK ☎ 0800-771 001; for other countries ☎ 0800-777 117).

National superannuation payments are made every two weeks and in late 2001 were at the following rates (before tax):

Status	Fortnightly Benefit ($)
Married (both partners qualify)	428.76
Married (only one partner qualifies)	407.34
Single (living with others)	520.24
Single (living alone)	565.98

Superannuation is intended to provide a basic standard of living only. In a recent survey the Retirement Commission found that most pensioners would require a weekly income of at least $370 in order to maintain the standard of living that they enjoyed before retirement. There are, however, several additional allowances available for 'superannuitants' (those on superannuation), including Disability Allowance, Accommodation Allowance, a Community Services Card (entitling the holder to reduced doctor and prescription costs), a High Use Health Card (for a reduction in doctor costs if you visit the doctor more than 12 times a year) and a Pharmaceutical Subsidy Card (see also **Chapter 12**). Contact WINZ for further details. If you don't qualify for superannuation, you may be eligible for Transitional Retirement Benefit if you're nearly 65 (see above) or Domestic Purposes Benefit if you're a woman over 50 and living alone (see above).

There were plans to abolish the national superannuation scheme and replace it with a system of private pensions, under which employees would be required to join a company superannuation scheme or take out a private pension. Employees would be able to contribute as much as they liked (or could afford) to this scheme and the government would guarantee that they would receive at least a basic minimum pension on retirement (payments would also be protected if a private pension company failed). However, a referendum on introducing such a scheme was held in 1997 and was rejected by an overwhelming 90 per cent of the 2 million people who voted. Nevertheless, the cost of funding pensions from tax revenue is so high (and unsustainable without tax increases) that plans for compulsory private pensions will inevitably surface again. For further information about national superannuation contact WINZ (☎ freephone 0800-552 002, ⌨ www.winz.govt.nz), which publishes a useful booklet *Guide to Superannuation* (also downloadable). There are Super Centres in most large towns and cities where superannuitants can obtain information and advice. Superannuitants are issued with a Super Card, which can be used as proof of age and to get discounts offered by private organisations (e.g. transport).

Note that, if you're an employer, you must make contributions to employee superannuation funds, which are subject to a superannuation contribution withholding tax.

PRIVATE PENSIONS

Private pensions are common in New Zealand, as national superannuation (see above) provides only enough income to maintain a basic standard of living. Many companies provide contributory pension schemes for their employees, but if your employer doesn't do so you would be well advised to consider taking out a private pension. These are available from a variety of insurance companies and are also offered by many banks (shop around). Most private pensions are based on a savings scheme which accumulates a lump sum that, on retirement, is used to purchase an annuity providing a regular income. In a recent survey the Retirement Commission found that men would need a lump sum of $119,000 and women $139,000 in order to purchase an annuity that would increase their state pension to the average level of income. Tax relief on private pension contributions was abolished in 1987, although in 2001 the Minister of Finance stated that he was in favour of the re-introduction of tax relief on private pension contributions.

If you don't intend to remain in New Zealand indefinitely, you should ensure that you can take your private pension with you when you leave. Note that, generally, you cannot 'export' a private pension from New Zealand to another country unless you've been paying contributions for at least two years.

HEALTH INSURANCE

Everyone who's either resident in New Zealand or a visitor from a country with which New Zealand has a reciprocal agreement is covered by the national healthcare scheme, which provides either free or reduced cost medical treatment. However, while treatment under the state health scheme is considered adequate, many people also have private health insurance. The main purpose of this is to pay the cost of doctor's consultations, prescriptions and dentistry (which aren't covered by the state healthcare system), and also to pay for treatment in private hospitals, thus circumventing public hospital waiting lists. Private health insurance schemes also provide other benefits such as cover for loss of earnings due to illness. Around 40 per cent of New Zealanders have some form of private health insurance, which can be purchased from a variety of insurance companies of which the largest is Southern Cross Medical Care Society, Private Bag 99-934, Newmarket, Auckland (☎ freephone 0800-800 181, 💻 www.southerncross.co.nz).

The cost depends on what's covered and which company you insure with. For a family of four a hospital-only policy costs from $450 to $1,360 per year and a comprehensive policy from $500 to $3,800 per year. Southern Cross' most popular family insurance is their RegularCare policy and monthly premiums are $18.69 for a child under 20 and $39.35 for an adult aged between 20 and 46. Private health insurance costs have rocketed in recent years as more people make claims to avoid waiting for treatment at public hospitals, and they're likely to continue increasing at a rate well above inflation, particularly for the elderly. The Consumers Organisation (💻 www.consumer.org.nz) publishes helpful information on health insurance, including advice on whether you really need it!

Checklist

When comparing the level of cover provided by different health insurance schemes, the following points should be considered:

- Does the scheme have a wide range of premium levels and are discounts or special rates available for families or children?

- Is private hospital cover available and are private rooms available at local hospitals? What are the costs? Is there a limit on the time you can spend in hospital?

- Is dental cover included? What exactly does it include? Can it be extended to include extra treatment? Dental insurance usually contains numerous limitations and doesn't cover cosmetic treatment.

- Are there restrictions regarding hospitalisation, either in New Zealand or abroad?

- What is the qualification period for special benefits or services?

- What level of cover is provided outside New Zealand and what are the limitations?

- What is the cover regarding pregnancy, hospital births and associated costs? What is the position if conception occurred before joining the insurance scheme?

- Are medicines included?

- Are convalescent homes or spa treatments covered when prescribed by a doctor?
- What are the restrictions on complementary medicine, e.g. chiropractic, osteopathy, naturopathy, massage and acupuncture? Are they covered? Must a referral be made by a doctor?
- Is life insurance or a disability pension included, possibly as an option?
- Are possible extra costs likely, and if so, what for?
- Are spectacles or contact lenses covered, and if so, how much can be claimed and how frequently?
- Is the provision and repair of artificial limbs and similar health aids covered?

If you're planning to change your health insurance company, you should ensure that no important benefits are lost. If you change your health insurance company, it's wise to inform your old health insurance company if you have any outstanding bills for which they're liable.

DENTAL INSURANCE

With the exception of school children (see page 194) and emergency dental treatment for people on low incomes, dental treatment isn't provided free under the state healthcare system. It's possible to take out special insurance against dental costs, although it's unusual to have full dental insurance in New Zealand, as the cost is prohibitive. The cost of dental insurance varies according to the state of your teeth and what treatment is covered. Most people find that it's cheaper not to have dental insurance, but to put a little money aside for dental costs and pay bills from their own pocket. However, cover for dental treatment may be included in general health insurance policies, which can be purchased from medical insurance companies and from dentists. Basic dental care such as check-ups, X-rays and cleaning are usually included in the standard premium, and some companies offer more comprehensive dental cover as an optional extra. Some international health policies also include basic dental care, and most offer optional (or additional) dental cover, although there are many restrictions, and cosmetic treatment is excluded. The amount payable by a health insurance policy for a particular item of treatment is usually fixed and depends on your level of dental insurance. A detailed schedule of refunds is available from insurance companies.

HOUSEHOLD INSURANCE

As when living anywhere, it's important to ensure that your home and its contents are fully insured in New Zealand. Premiums are modest in most areas, particularly for home contents insurance (a reflection of the country's modest crime rate). However, your insurance company will probably claw back the savings on buildings insurance, as damage caused by severe weather (particularly flooding) isn't uncommon in certain parts of the country, and subsidence can also be a problem in some areas.

When insuring your home (rather than its contents) you're offered a choice between fully comprehensive insurance (known as 'accident damage insurance'), which covers all risks, and 'defined risk insurance', which covers specified risks only. Defined risk insurance is the cheaper option, particularly in an area subject to subsidence or flooding, where these risks would be expensive to insure against and can be excluded from a policy (although you should ask yourself why you want to live there in the first place!). You're also offered a choice between a policy that pays out at replacement value and one that pays at indemnity value. Under a replacement value policy, a destroyed home is replaced with a new building of similar quality, while an indemnity value policy simply pays out the market value of your home. As the market value of your home is usually less than the cost of rebuilding, an indemnity value policy is cheaper, although it should cover the purchase of a property of similar age and quality. In all cases the value of the land on which your home is built is excluded.

Contents Insurance: Home contents insurance is usually separate from buildings insurance, although most people have buildings and contents insurance with the same company. It covers home contents up to a specified figure against risks such as theft, fire and accidental damage. If you have particularly valuable possessions, you should take out extra cover, which normally requires high-value items to be detailed and photographs and documentation (e.g. a receipt or valuation) provided. You should also consider putting serial numbers on your appliances and valuable possessions so that they can be returned to you if recovered by the police. 'Operation Snap' introduced in Auckland in 1999 has been particularly successful in the return of stolen goods with serial numbers on them to their owners. When claiming for contents, you should produce the original bills if possible (always keep bills for expensive items) and bear in mind that replacing imported items may cost more than their original price. Note that contents policies usually contain security clauses and, if you don't adhere to them, a claim won't be considered. Most policies don't cover possessions (such as cameras and musical instruments) when they're used outside your home, although you can usually pay an extra premium to cover this.

Earthquake Insurance: New Zealand is within an earthquake zone and minor (usually unnoticeable) tremors occur almost monthly, although records show that serious earthquakes occur, on average, only once every 210 years. As the consequences of a major earthquake would be catastrophic and no insurance company could possibly cover them, the New Zealand government assumes the responsibility of providing earthquake insurance. The Earthquake Commission operates an insurance scheme, which is funded through a small levy on property insurance policies. In the event that an earthquake devastates your property, the Earthquake Commission will pay you compensation up to a maximum of $100,000 for a property and $20,000 for contents. If your property is insured for less, you will receive only the sum insured. The Earthquake Commission pays no compensation for vehicles, boats, jewellery, money or works of art. This scheme ensures that, in the event of an earthquake, most property owners are compensated, even if the government goes bust as a result! Because $100,000 is unlikely to be sufficient to rebuild anything other than a modest home, most insurance companies offer top-up insurance to cover the difference between the $100,000 paid by the government and the value of your home, which is a must for owners of valuable properties. Further information is available from the Earthquake Commission, PO Box 311, Wellington (☎ 04-499 0045, 🖳 www.eqc.govt.nz).

HOLIDAY & TRAVEL INSURANCE

Travel insurance is recommended for those who don't wish to risk having their holiday or travel spoilt by financial problems or to arrive home broke. As you're no doubt aware, many things can and often do go wrong with a holiday, sometimes before you even reach the airport or port (particularly when you don't have insurance). In addition, New Zealand has some of the world's most dangerous roads, is home to dangerous (and downright suicidal) sports and is in an earthquake zone (see above). If you don't fall victim to bungee jumping or a crazed New Zealand motorist, there's always the possibility of falling into boiling mud (it has happened to hapless hikers on a number of occasions)!

Travel insurance is available from many sources, including travel agents, insurance agents, motoring organisations, transport companies and directly from insurance companies. Package holiday companies also offer insurance policies (some are compulsory), although most don't provide adequate cover. Before taking out travel insurance, carefully consider the level of cover you require and compare policies. Most policies include cover for loss of deposit or holiday cancellation, missed flights, departure delay at both the start and end of a holiday (a common occurrence), delayed and lost baggage and personal effects, medical expenses and accidents (including repatriation if necessary), loss or theft of money, personal liability, legal expenses and, in some cases, a tour operator going bust. However, in 2001, the Insurance Council of New Zealand alerted the public to the fact that some travel insurance doesn't cover you for costs or losses arising from the failure of travel agents, tour operators, accommodation providers, airlines or other carriers. You should check your policy carefully.

Medical expenses are an important aspect of travel insurance, and you shouldn't rely on reciprocal health arrangements, assuming you're entitled to them (Americans, among others, aren't). It's also unwise to depend on travel insurance provided by charge and credit card companies, household policies or private medical insurance, none of which usually provide adequate cover (although you should take advantage of what they offer). The minimum medical insurance recommended by experts when travelling to New Zealand is $2 million. If applicable, check whether pregnancy-related claims are covered and whether there are restrictions for those over 65 or 70 (pregnancy restrictions don't usually apply to pensioners).

Check any exclusion clauses in contracts by obtaining a copy of the full policy document (all relevant information won't be included in the insurance leaflet). Skiing and other winter sports aren't usually covered unless you take out a policy specifically for this purpose (widely available but expensive). Dangerous activities such as bungee jumping and parachuting are never covered by standard travel insurance, and it's often difficult to obtain cover at any price. When participating in a dangerous sport, check what (if any) insurance cover the organisers provide, as many include (or will sell you) dangerous sports insurance, although it may cover you only for third party liability (e.g. if you sky-dive through someone's roof) and may not cover personal injury. You may be covered under New Zealand's ACC scheme (see page 202) if you have an accident, but the pay-out may be inadequate if your injuries are serious, and it won't pay for repatriation and medical expenses or loss of income abroad.

Although travel insurance companies gladly take your money, they aren't so keen to pay claims and you may need to persevere before they pay up. Be persistent and make a claim irrespective of any small print, as this may be unreasonable and therefore invalid in law. Insurance companies usually require you to report a loss (or any incident for which you intend to make a claim) to the local police (or carriers) within 24 hours and obtain a written report. Failure to do this may mean that a claim won't be considered. If you're travelling on holiday, take out insurance before you arrive. Bear in mind that it's difficult or impossible to sue for compensation for personal injuries in New Zealand, although if you have taken out insurance in another country you may have a slightly better chance of obtaining compensation.

LIFE INSURANCE

Although there are worse things in life than death (like spending an evening with a life insurance salesman), your dependants may rate your death *without* life insurance high on their list. You can take out a life insurance policy with dozens of companies in New Zealand, although it's important to shop around before doing so. Be extremely wary of insurance sales people (whose credibility is on a par with used car salesmen, estate agents and politicians), some of whom use dubious soft and hard-sell methods to hook customers. You have no guarantee of receiving good or independent advice or indeed any advice at all from them. When buying life insurance, you're usually better off dealing with an independent insurance adviser or broker who does business with a number of insurance companies. Most banks are unable to give independent advice on life policies and many are tied to a particular insurance company. Some companies provide free life insurance as an employment benefit (although it may be accident life insurance only), and a private pension scheme may provide a death-in-service benefit. A life insurance policy can be used as security for a bank loan and can be limited to cover the period of the loan. Most companies offer a variety of life insurance policies, e.g. term, whole life and endowment (which pays out even if you don't die). It's usually necessary to take out an endowment policy if you have an interest-only mortgage, which can be used to repay the capital at the end of the mortgage.

Note that although it's often referred to as life *insurance*, life policies are usually for life *assurance*. Assurance is a policy which covers an eventuality which is certain to occur (for example, like it or not, you must die one day). Thus a life assurance policy is valid until you die. An insurance policy covers a risk which *may* happen, but isn't a certainty, for example, accident insurance (unless you're exceptionally accident prone).

Commissions & Charges: One disadvantage of life insurance policies is the large commissions paid to salesmen, which may be equivalent to a year's premiums, so it pays to shop around and ask salesmen or brokers about their rates of commission. Added to commissions are expenses, including management and administration fees. Performance tables are published regularly in financial magazines showing the best-performing unit trusts, pension funds and other long-term investments. You would be wise to consult them and other independent sources of information before taking out a policy from which you expect either a lump sum on maturity or a regular income, as choosing the wrong investment can be *very* costly. Try to ensure that you have a cooling-off period, during which you can cancel a policy without incurring a penalty.

Health: Whether you need to undergo a medical examination depends on the insurance company, your age, state of health and the amount of insurance required. You must complete a medical questionnaire and, depending on your age and health record, your GP may be required to provide a medical report. If you have no family doctor or previous medical history, you may be required to have a medical examination. Many policies don't pay out when death is the result of certain illnesses, e.g. an AIDS-related illness. If you're a clean living, non-smoking teetotaller, you may be able to obtain cheaper life insurance than an alcoholic, sensation-seeking, chain-smoker (although you will probably die early of boredom!).

Finally, it's wise to leave a copy of all insurance policies with your will (see page 237) and with your lawyer. If you don't have a lawyer, keep a copy in a safe deposit box. A life insurance policy must usually be sent to the insurance company upon the death of the insured, with a copy of the death certificate.

14.

FINANCE

Although lagging behind Australia, most European Union countries and the USA, New Zealand is a relatively wealthy country with a Gross Domestic Products (GDP) per head of around US$13,800 in 2001. A period of recession followed the Asian economic crisis in the late '90s and two successive droughts, which caused the country's export market to fall dramatically. However, the economy is now on an upward trend and GDP growth was around 2.2 per cent in 2001, with an inflation rate contained within the Reserve Bank of New Zealand's target range of 0 to 3 per cent (around 2 per cent in 2001). New Zealand has fewer extremes of wealth and poverty than many other developed countries, with a large middle class and comparatively few poor people, while incredibly wealthy people are rare enough for them to be 'famous' (or notorious). New Zealanders are generally restrained when discussing money, much the same as the British, although the '80s saw the creation of a 'yuppy' class who did well in business and the professions and didn't mind flaunting their wealth.

The New Zealand banking and financial sector is modern and efficient. For example, it's possible to clear cheques virtually instantaneously in New Zealand – something which isn't even possible in the UK or USA (although this is a deliberate policy on the part of banks in these countries). Wide use is made of electronic banking, rather than shuffling pieces of paper around the country, and New Zealanders have taken enthusiastically to the cashless economy – the use of credit, debit and electronic-funds-transfer-at-point-of-sale (EFTPOS) cards is widespread, while cheques are becoming much less popular. This isn't because New Zealanders are enthusiastic about credit, but simply that it's so convenient. The banking sector is dominated by a relatively small number of large institutions, although competition for your business is healthy.

When you arrive to take up residence in New Zealand, it's best to have a bank account established with funds on deposit, plus some New Zealand currency for immediate use. If you're planning to invest in property or a business in New Zealand financed with funds from abroad, it's important to consider both the present and possible future exchange rates (don't be too optimistic). On the other hand, if you earn your income in New Zealand dollars, this may affect your commitments abroad, particularly if the New Zealand dollar weakens. If you plan to live and work in New Zealand you should ensure that your income is (and will remain) sufficient to live on, bearing in mind the cost of living (see page 238). If you're receiving a pension from abroad, you should be cautious, as you will be at the mercy of not only exchange rate fluctuations but also the fact that pensions are usually calculated according to the cost of living in your *home* country and may be inadequate to support you in New Zealand.

NEW ZEALAND CURRENCY

The New Zealand unit of currency is the New Zealand dollar, affectionately know as the 'Kiwi dollar' or just the 'Kiwi' (New Zealanders gave up the British-style pounds, shillings and pence in 1967). The New Zealand dollar is usually identified by the international $ sign and is rarely prefixed by NZ, except in some banking documents involving currency exchange and in international trade (in this book a $ sign refers to NZ$, unless otherwise stated). It isn't one of the world's strongest currencies but has a reputation for stability, although it fell to a 12-year low against the US$ in 1998 as a result of the crisis in world (particularly Asian) financial markets. You cannot spend foreign currency in New Zealand, although there are a few duty-free and tourist shops that will accept both Australian and US dollars (at an unfavourable exchange rate). The New Zealand dollar is divided into 100 cents. Banknotes are issued in denominations of 100, 50, 20, 10 and 5 dollars (Americans should note that there's no $1 bill), and coins are minted in 1 and 2 dollars, 50, 20, 10 and 5 cents. (The 5 cent coin is colloquially known as the 'pest'.) The cent is identified by the symbol ¢, although occasionally you will see it expressed as a decimal, e.g. $0.75, or values in dollars expressed as cents, e.g. 115¢, neither of which is officially correct. Until 1992, Her Majesty Queen Elizabeth II appeared on all New Zealand banknotes, but she was 'retired' (despite protests from many people) and now appears only on the $20 note. Famous New Zealanders have been installed on other notes: Lord Rutherford ('Father of the Atom') on the $100, Apirana Ngata (a Maori statesman) on the $50, Kate Sheppard (a suffragette) on the $10 and Sir Edmund Hillary (one of the first men to climb Mount Everest) on the $5 note.

Note that 20¢ and 10¢ coins are difficult to distinguish from Australian coins of the same value, and Australian coins occasionally turn up in your change in New Zealand (you can either save them for a trip to Oz or use them in parking meters).

It's wise to obtain some New Zealand currency before your arrival in the country. However, because international *bureaux de change* don't usually handle coins, the smallest unit of currency you will be able to obtain outside New Zealand is $5. Ask for a selection of $5, $10 and $20 notes, which are the most useful. Many shops, taxi drivers and small businesses are reluctant to accept $50 and $100 notes; legally they cannot reject any notes or coins, but if you proffer a $100 note, they're likely to have no change. These notes also attract most scrutiny, as they're more likely to be the target of forgers, although counterfeit currency isn't a serious problem in New Zealand.

FOREIGN CURRENCY

Exchange controls operated in New Zealand between 1938 and 1984 but have since been abolished and there are now no restrictions on the import or export of funds. A New Zealand resident is permitted to open a bank account in any country and to export unlimited funds from New Zealand. It's also possible to transmit funds to New Zealand without being hindered by bureaucratic procedures.

Transferring Money: When transferring or sending money to (or from) New Zealand, you should be aware of the alternatives. One way to do this is to send either a personal cheque or a bank draft (cashier's cheque), which should both be sent by registered post. Money shouldn't be treated as having been paid until the cheque or draft has cleared the system, which is usually within seven days of receipt. Note, however, that a bank draft shouldn't be treated as cash, and you cannot be sure that payment has been made until it has cleared. A safer method of transferring money is to make a direct transfer or a telex or electronic transfer between banks. A direct transfer involves a process similar to sending a cheque or bank draft and usually takes at least seven days (but can take much longer). A telex or electronic transfer can be completed within a few hours. However, bear in mind that (because of the time difference) banks in New Zealand close for the day before they open in Europe or the USA, so it will be at least the next day before funds are available in New Zealand. The transfer process is usually faster and less likely to come unstuck when it's between branches of the same or affiliated banks (in any case, delays are more likely to be overseas than in New Zealand). The Commonwealth Bank of Australia, which has branches in Europe and the USA, can transfer funds almost instantaneously to its branches in New Zealand, although its branch network there (around 130) isn't the most extensive.

NZ Post offers the possibility of transferring, sending and receiving money both within New Zealand and to and from overseas. For domestic transactions, money order certificates costing $3 are available for amounts up to $1,000 and for larger amounts electronic money orders can be purchased for $5. For the transfer of money to and from overseas, NZ Post uses the services of Western Union, which charges $74 for sums up to $1,000. Further information is available on ☎ freephone 0800-005 253.

The cost of transfers varies considerably – not only commission and exchange rates, but also transfer charges (shop around and compare rates). Usually the faster the transfer, the more it will cost. Transfer fees also vary with the amount being transferred, and there are usually minimum and maximum fees. For example, banks in the UK charge from £5 to process a cheque for up to £50, and up to £40 for a cheque worth the equivalent of £10,000 (most banks in the UK charge in the region of £10 to £45 for electronic transfers). If you routinely transfer money between currencies, you should investigate Fidelity Money Funds, which operate free of conversion charges and at wholesale rates of exchange. In emergencies, money can be sent via American Express offices by Amex card holders.

When you have money transferred to a bank in New Zealand, ensure that you give the name, account number, branch number and the bank sort code. Bear in mind that the names of some New Zealand banks (and towns) are strikingly similar, so double check your instructions. If you plan to send a large amount of money to New Zealand or overseas for a business transaction such as buying property, you should ensure that you receive the commercial rate of exchange rather than the tourist rate. Check charges and rates in advance and agree them with your bank (you may be able to negotiate a lower charge or a better exchange rate). If you send a cheque or bank draft to New Zealand, it should be crossed so that it can only be paid into an account with exactly the same name as shown on the cheque.

Changing Money: Most banks in major cities have *bureaux de change*, and there are banks and *bureaux de change* with extended opening hours at both Auckland and Wellington international airports, plus other airports when international flights arrive (which may be just a few times a week). At *bureaux de change* you can buy and sell foreign currencies, buy and cash travellers' cheques, cash personal cheques, and obtain a cash advance on credit and charge cards.

There are private *bureaux de change* in the major cities and tourist resorts with longer business hours than banks, particularly at weekends, e.g. they open on Saturdays from 9.30am to 12.30pm when banks are closed, and there are 24-hour, automatic, money-changing machines in some major cities (e.g. outside the Downtown Airline Terminal, Auckland). Most *bureaux de change* offer competitive exchange rates, low or no commission (but always check) and are easier to deal with than banks. If you're changing a lot of money, you may be able to negotiate a better exchange rate. Note, however, that the best exchange rates are usually provided by banks. The New Zealand dollar exchange rate against most major international currencies is displayed in banks and listed in daily newspapers.

Travellers' Cheques: If you're visiting New Zealand, it's safer to carry travellers' cheques than cash. Travellers' cheques in major currencies, including US$ and £ sterling, are easily exchanged in New Zealand but aren't usually accepted by businesses, except perhaps some luxury hotels, restaurants and shops, which usually offer a poor exchange rate. You can buy travellers' cheques from any New Zealand bank, which will charge a minimum commission fee of $5 or 1.25 per cent. Shop around, as fees can vary, particularly on larger amounts. Some banks exchange travellers' cheques free of commission, although their charges are usually built into the (inferior) exchange rate, so always compare the net amount you will receive. Keep a separate record of cheque numbers and note where and when they were cashed. American Express provides a free, three-hour replacement service for lost or stolen travellers' cheques at any of their offices world-wide, provided you know the serial numbers of the lost cheques. Without the serial numbers it can take three days or longer. Most companies provide freephone telephone numbers for reporting lost or stolen travellers' cheques in New Zealand, e.g. American Express (☎ freephone 0800-442 208).

Note that there isn't a lot of difference in the cost between buying New Zealand currency using cash, travellers' cheques or a credit card. However, many people simply take cash when travelling overseas, which is asking for trouble, particularly if you have no way of obtaining more cash locally, e.g. with travellers' cheques or a credit card. **One thing to bear in mind when travelling anywhere, is *never* to rely on only one source of funds!**

BANKS

There are officially just two kinds of financial institution in New Zealand: registered banks and what are euphemistically known as 'other financial institutions'. The main exception is the Reserve Bank of New Zealand, which doesn't fit into either of these categories and is the country's central bank, performing a role similar to the Bank of England or the Federal Reserve Bank in the USA. It has a range of functions, including managing the money supply, supervising commercial banks, implementing the government's financial policy, controlling the exchange rate, providing a banking service to the government and acting as a registrar for government stocks.

Savings banks in New Zealand were traditionally mutual organisations owned by their members or investors, which concentrated on accepting personal savings and granting mortgages for residential property. In this respect they were much like building societies in the UK and savings and loan organisations in the USA. However, deregulation in the financial sector during the '80s allowed commercial banks to enter this market. With their greater financial clout and marketing expertise they've managed to largely take it over, and as a result many savings banks have either converted to commercial or registered banks or been taken over by them.

Changes in the banking system over the last few years have meant that most individuals and businesses in New Zealand carry out their banking, including savings, loans, mortgages and day-to-day transactions, with one of the registered commercial banks. Banks operating in this sector include: Australia New Zealand Bank (ANZ), the country's second-largest bank; ASB, formerly the Auckland Savings Bank, which has its strongest presence in Auckland but is also popular throughout the rest of the country; the Bank of New Zealand (BNZ), which is New Zealand's largest bank in asset terms and, despite its name, wholly Australian-owned; the National Bank, which is the third-largest and the only major bank operating in New Zealand not owned by Australians (it's British-owned); and Westpac Trust (formed from the merger of the Westpac Banking Corporation and Trustbank), which probably has the biggest market share in the country and is also the government's banker. It's estimated that only some 12 per cent of the New Zealand banking market is operated by indigenous banks. Note that the New Zealand banking operations of Australian banks are completely separate, so customers of Australian Westpac, for example, cannot access their Australian accounts at Westpac in New Zealand, or vice versa. The National Bank is associated with Lloyds Bank in the UK, although it also operates independently.

Several banks are mainly telephone and Internet-based, such as AMP (currently the only New Zealand bank losing money), Bankdirect (a subsidiary of ASB), and TSB. PSIS is a financial institution owned by its customers, which offers banking services administered by the Bank of New Zealand, although it isn't a bank and as such isn't a member of the Banking Ombudsman scheme nor subject to supervision by the Reserve Bank. The large insurance group AMP also offers banking services, and in 2002 the New Zealand Post Office is due to start offering banking services at post shops under the name Kiwibank (see page 109).

In addition to locally registered banks, you will also find many international banks in New Zealand, which are mainly located in the financial district of Wellington and don't have extensive branch networks around the country. Other financial institutions that aren't registered banks include merchant banks and leasing companies, which mainly serve the business sector. They aren't authorised to accept deposits from the public and, in any case, registered banks offer a more comprehensive range of services to the public and business community. Finance companies aren't registered banks, but provide consumer credit such as loans and hire purchase (or time purchase as it's also known in New Zealand).

All New Zealand banks are efficient and highly automated. You'll find that staff, who are generally friendly and informal, work behind low counters or desks rather than armoured glass. This isn't to say that banks in New Zealand aren't robbed (they most certainly are), but the transition towards cashless banking has done much to reduce the amount of cash shuffled across bank counters (or used in shops and other businesses).

A Citizens' Advice Bureau (CAB) 2001 survey among its members showed the best-performing banks as far as customer satisfaction is concerned were ASB and National Bank. At the other extreme were the BNZ, Westpac Trust and ANZ, who were highly criticised in the survey for bad customer service and high bank charges.

Opening Hours: Normal banking hours are from 8.30 or 9am until 4.30pm, Mondays to Fridays, although banks may stay open for half an hour later one evening a week (which is the exception rather than the rule). Banks don't open at weekends and are also closed on public holidays, although *bureaux de change* open longer at weekends.

Opening an Account: You can open a New Zealand bank account from outside the country or after your arrival, although given the widespread use of cashless transactions in New Zealand, it's better to open an account before you arrive. To open an account while overseas, you need to find the nearest office of a New Zealand bank, e.g. by looking in the telephone directory or asking your bank for assistance. You probably won't find a great deal of choice, but there are branches of New Zealand banks in most major cities in Europe, North America and Asia. You don't usually need to visit a branch in person, as an account can be opened by telephone or post. Note that most banks require an opening balance of at least $200 and up to $500 in some cases, so it's advisable to transfer the necessary funds before your planned arrival date.

To open a bank account in New Zealand, simply choose any of the registered banks. Most people choose a bank branch that's most convenient for them. Different banks require different documentation, so you should check exactly what's required beforehand; typically you will need two forms of identification, your IRD number (see page 233) and possibly statements from your current or previous bank. Note that if you don't have an IRD number when you open an account, you will be charged resident withholding tax (RWT) at 33 per cent (see page 235). If you think that you may apply for an overdraft, loan or mortgage in New Zealand at some time, it's wise to obtain a reference from your overseas bank manager to the effect that your account has been maintained in good order.

Current Accounts: The normal account for day-to-day transactions in New Zealand is a current or cheque account. You'll receive a cheque book within a week of opening your account. This is worth having even though cheque books are becoming less widely used in New Zealand, where most people pay bills in shops with debit cards and pay their regular household bills by direct debit. There are no cheque guarantee cards in New Zealand, which is why you may be asked to produce a driving licence or credit card as proof of identity when paying by cheque. Not surprisingly, many shops and businesses are reluctant to take personal cheques (there may be a notice to this effect).

The design of cheques is basically the same as that in most other countries; you enter the name of the payee, the date, the amount in words and figures, and sign it. All cheques should be crossed, although crossed cheques are a fairly recent innovation in New Zealand. A crossed cheque can only be paid into a bank account in the name of the payee and cannot be cashed. The use of a cheque incurs cheque duty (a kind of stamp duty) of 5¢, which is automatically deducted by your bank (which makes it difficult to reconcile cheques you've written with the amounts that appear on your bank statement) and needn't be paid separately.

Cheque clearing in New Zealand is highly efficient, and a cheque paid into your account is usually credited the next day (occasionally the same day if it's at the same branch or bank). A cheque drawn on your account and given to someone else may also be debited from your account on the same or next day and there isn't a delay of between three and ten days as in some other countries. Nevertheless, when paying a cheque into your account, it's probably best to wait a few days to spend the money just in case the drawer didn't have enough money to cover the cheque (in which case the cheque will be returned to you by post, which may take a couple of days). On the other hand, you should assume that a cheque drawn on your account is debited from it on the same day.

Account statements are usually provided monthly, although you can ask to have them sent weekly. It's also possible to obtain details of your most recent transactions, request a mini-statement or make a balance enquiry at an automated teller machine (ATM), commonly referred to as a cash dispenser. Although you can withdraw cash from your account at any branch of your own bank by writing a cheque, it's much easier to use an EFTPOS card in an ATM (it's also possible to pay cash or cheques into your account at some machines).

Savings Accounts: You can open a savings (or deposit) account with any registered or savings bank. Over the last few years registered banks have become more competitive in this sector and have largely taken over the functions of the savings banks. Most financial institutions offer a range of savings accounts with interest rates varying with the amount deposited, the period for which the money must be left on deposit, and the notice which must be given before you can withdraw it. An account with a minimum deposit period is known as a term deposit account, and terms range from one month to five years, with a correspondingly higher rate of interest the longer the term. The interest rate may fluctuate according to the bank rate, be fixed for the entire term, or escalate (where the rate of interest paid rises annually irrespective of general interest rates).

Bank Charges: As in many countries, banks in New Zealand make charges for most transactions, which are highly unpopular with clients (a recent survey showed that some 75 per cent of bank customers find bank charges excessive) and are the main reason why people change banks. Most banks charge a monthly base fee of at least $3 unless you meet certain conditions, such as maintaining a minimum monthly balance. Electronic transaction fees range from 25¢ to 45¢ and manual transactions cost from 50¢ to $1.15, depending on the bank. Most banks also charge at least 50¢ for the use of another bank's ATM.

In order to reduce your bank charges, the Citizens' Advice Bureau offers the following advice:

- Reduce the number of transactions you make (e.g. when you pay with an EFTPOS card, get some cash out at the same time).

- Use electronic banking which is cheaper than over-the-counter.

- Ask if there's a flat-fee option, which may be cheaper if you have a lot of monthly transactions, and negotiate the best deal with your bank.

General Information: The following points are applicable to most New Zealand banks:

- All regular bills such as electricity, gas, telephone, mortgage or rent, can be paid automatically by direct debit from your bank account. The creditor or your bank will provide the necessary form for you to complete and return to them. You're protected against loss as a result of error or fraud in the system.

- To stop a cheque contact your bank. If your cheque book or EFTPOS card(s) is lost or stolen, contact your bank immediately.

- Safety deposit boxes are provided at most branches and are effective (although expensive) way of keeping your valuables secure. The average annual rental charge for a small box is $250, and you must usually pay a key deposit (bond) of around $80. Most banks conduct extensive security checks, including fingerprinting, when you use a deposit box.

- Registered banks offer a range of investments in addition to regular savings accounts, including stocks and shares, bonds and securities. Although you can also buy these through a stockbroker, banks offer competitive fees, particularly for smaller transactions. You don't need to use your own bank and may be able to find a cheaper stock and share service elsewhere (e.g. the Internet).

- Most registered banks offer a range of non-banking services, such as insurance, including life insurance, and pensions. Charges and premiums are usually competitive compared with similar products available from other sources such as insurance brokers. However, it's important to shop around, as some banks sell only their own products or those from certain companies, rather than choosing the best deal from the whole range available.

DEBIT CARDS

When opening a bank account, you should request an 'electronic funds transfer at point of sale' (EFTPOS) card, also known as a debit card, which can be used to pay for goods and services, with payments debited from your account, usually on the same day. The use of debit cards is widespread in New Zealand, much more so than in many European countries, and most hotels, garages, restaurants and even small shops accept them. An EFTPOS card can also be used to withdraw cash from ATMs throughout the country and overseas, for which you need a PIN number (which is usually sent automatically and separately from the card itself).

Guard your EFTPOS card and PIN number carefully, and if the card is lost or stolen inform your bank immediately so that it can be cancelled. It's common practice in New Zealand for people to give their EFTPOS card and PIN to other people (e.g. partners, children or friends) to enable them to withdraw money on their behalf. This practice is discouraged by banks, and if a card is misused they will hold you responsible for any debits charged to the card, whether you authorised them or not. If your card is lost or stolen, you won't be responsible for any more than a token amount (and even then it isn't usually charged), provided you've used your card properly and informed your bank as soon as you discovered it was missing.

You aren't usually charged a fee when using an EFTPOS card in a shop or other outlet, although it's legal for shops to charge a fee to cover their costs. Those that do must display a notice advising you of the fee, which is usually 50¢ or $1. When using an EFTPOS card to withdraw cash from a cash dispenser, you aren't usually charged a fee if the cash dispenser belongs to your own bank. Many banks have mutual arrangements with other banks whereby their EFTPOS cards can be used in other banks' ATMs, although where this is possible you may be charged a fee of up to $2.

The Mondex system, a kind of debit card that is 'topped up' with a sum of money, which is used to purchase goods and services, has recently been introduced in New Zealand, although it isn't yet in widespread use.

CREDIT & CHARGE CARDS

New Zealanders are enthusiastic users of credit and charge cards, although many prefer to use debit cards, where payments are immediately debited from their account. Credit and charge cards are issued by most banks (although some will only give you a credit card if you have a certain type of account with them e.g. a mortgage loan), are accepted almost anywhere, and can also be used to withdraw cash from ATMs or over the counter at banks (note that this service costs from $1 to $3 and interest is charged from the day of the withdrawal). To use ATMs you require a PIN number.

Most international credit and charge cards are widely accepted in New Zealand, including Visa, Mastercard, Diners Club and American Express, plus the local

Bankcard, which is also widely accepted in Australia. Most businesses in New Zealand accept major credit cards, so you're unlikely to be stuck if you possess only one card.

Annual fees start at $15 for a Visa Classic and $80 for a Visa Gold. Most credit cards offer loyalty schemes with various bonuses, such as frequent flyer points with Qantas or Air New Zealand or cash rewards ('cashback'). These loyalty schemes are extremely popular, particularly those offering air miles, and in late 2001 BNZ was forced to change its GlobalPlus scheme from one point per $1 spent to one point per $2 spent, as it was becoming too expensive for the bank! Interest rates on credit cards in late 2001 ranged from 17 to 19.5 per cent.

Some large store groups in New Zealand issue their own charge cards, to which you can charge purchases made in their stores, branches and associated shops. However, you should note that they usually charge a significantly higher interest rate than the main credit cards.

Note that credit card fraud is a big problem in New Zealand. If you lose your credit or charge card, you must report it to the issuer immediately by phone. The law protects you from liability for any losses when a card is lost or stolen unless a card has been misused with your consent (e.g. by a friend), in which case you're liable.

LOANS & OVERDRAFTS

To apply for a loan or overdraft you must have both a permanent address in New Zealand and a regular income. The amount of a loan or overdraft, the interest rate and the period of repayment depends on your financial status, which a bank appraises using a credit scoring system. You can expect banks to be cautious (or even to refuse you altogether) unless you've lived in the same place for at least three years. Some banks offer a 'buffer' overdraft (e.g. $100 or $200) automatically to new customers, which is intended to cover you against minor overspending and isn't a permanent overdraft facility (they may charge high fees for this privilege).

It pays to shop around for a loan, as interest rates vary considerably with the bank, the amount and the period of the loan. Don't neglect banks other than your own, as it isn't always necessary to have an account with a bank to obtain a loan. Ask your friends and colleagues for their advice. If you have collateral, e.g. New Zealand property (or you can get someone to stand as a guarantor for a loan), you will be eligible for a secured loan at a lower interest rate. It's also possible to take out payment protection insurance which covers your payments in the event of illness or death, and may entitle you to a lower interest rate. To compare the interest rate on different loans, check the annual percentage rate (APR). Borrowing from finance companies, such as those advertising in newspapers and magazines, is usually much more expensive than borrowing from banks.

A popular form of loan in New Zealand is a 'revolving loan', where you make a fixed repayment each month according to your income. You can borrow up to a set multiple of the monthly payment, e.g. if you can repay $200 per month the lender may allow you to borrow up to 20 ($4,000) or 30 times ($6,000) this amount. The advantage of such a scheme is that you have access to loan finance whenever you need it and don't need to borrow the entire amount all at once. As you make repayments, the money you've repaid again becomes available for you to borrow up to your limit. The disadvantage is that it's easy to be constantly in debt! A revolving loan can also be linked to a mortgage (see **Types of Mortgage** below).

MORTGAGES

Mortgages (home loans) are available from New Zealand banks, mortgage bankers, mortgage brokers and some direct response (i.e. via telephone or Internet) lenders. Generally, there's little difference between the interest rates charged, although there's a variety of mortgage plans with different repayment methods, terms (i.e. periods) and fees (see below), so it's worth shopping around for the best deal. Mortgage brokers are increasing in popularity and in 1999 accounted for some 17 per cent of the mortgage market compared to 1 per cent in 1991. If you decide to use the services of a mortgage broker, ensure that he's a member of the New Zealand Brokers Association, whose members must have professional indemnity insurance and work with at least six different lenders. You can contact the Association at PO Box 33.1568, Takapuna, Auckland (☎ 09-489 8414).

By and large, New Zealand financial institutions are accommodating when it comes to granting mortgages and put a great deal of effort into gaining your business. Banks are keen for you to take out a mortgage with them and many can offer competitive deals. Some banks don't even require you to attend an interview at their local branch but offer mortgages by phone or via the Internet. All you need to do is telephone a freephone number (or send an e-mail) and provide details of the property you wish to purchase and your personal details, and you will receive an 'in principle' decision virtually immediately. The main direct response mortgage companies are BankDirect and AMP Banking. Telephone mortgage companies are highly competitive (although they offer a 'no frills' service) and are particularly suitable if you know exactly what kind of mortgage you require. If you don't, you'd be advised to visit your local bank, where staff will explain the different types of mortgage on offer.

There are no fixed lending criteria in New Zealand, although generally the maximum mortgage you can obtain is where the repayments equal no more than 30 per cent of your net income (which is combined for a couple). It's sensible, however, to take a mortgage on which the repayments constitute no more than 20 to 25 per cent of your income. The most you can usually borrow is 90 per cent (some lenders set the limit at 80 per cent) of the value of a property, although a high percentage mortgage may be based on the lender's own valuation (rather than what you're actually paying to the property) and you may be required to take out mortgage guarantee insurance (which guarantees that the lender get its money back if you default on your repayments). It's customary in New Zealand for a property to be held as security for a loan taken out on it, i.e. the lender takes a first charge on the property.

Mortgages can be obtained for any period up to 25 years, although the trend nowadays is for people to take 20 or even 15-year mortgages. The reason for this is that many New Zealanders take out a second mortgage in order to pay for their children's education or a holiday home before they retire. Although the repayments on a shorter mortgage are higher, you pay much less interest.

Types of Mortgage

The two main kinds of mortgage offered are a 'table mortgage' (equivalent to a repayment mortgage in other countries), where you make equal repayments of capital and interest throughout the period of the loan, and an interest-only mortgage, where you pay only the interest on the sum borrowed and are required to repay the original capital sum at the end of the term. Most lenders require you to take out an insurance policy to guarantee repayment of the loan, and in this way an interest-only mortgage is similar to an endowment mortgage offered in some other countries. Some lenders allow you to take out an interest-only mortgage without insurance, which makes the repayments temptingly low, but unless you make lots of money (or win the lottery) during the period of the mortgage, you may need to sell your home at the end of the term in order to repay the capital! A third kind of mortgage that's sometimes offered is a 'straight line' mortgage, where you repay capital and interest throughout the term and repayments reduce over the years as the amount of capital owed reduces.

The interest rate on a New Zealand mortgage is either 'floating', so that it varies with interest rates generally, or fixed for the period of the loan, the repayment period being adjusted accordingly. A recent trend is for lenders to offer mortgages that are fixed (usually at a 'bargain' rate) for a period such as one to five years and then revert to a floating rate. These offer a temptingly cheap opportunity to get a foot on the property ladder, provided you budget for the fact that your repayments are likely to increase after the fixed rate period expires, depending on how interest rates change in the meantime. A New Zealand mortgage usually provides a high degree of flexibility. Many lenders allow you to convert from one type of mortgage to another, increase or decrease your payments, take a payment 'holiday' for a few months, or repay part of the capital early (thus reducing your repayments or the term of the mortgage). It's even possible to transfer your mortgage to another property. In fact, provided you keep making repayments, you're likely to find your lender accommodating. In late 2001, floating mortgage interest rates ranged from 6.4 to 6.7 per cent and fixed mortgage rates for the first year ranged from 5.85 to 6.4 per cent.

As you work your way through the mortgage maze, you should bear in mind that banks and financial institutions in New Zealand are experts at dressing up mortgages in a user-friendly way and creating a variety of seemingly too-good-to-be-true packages. At the end of the day your mortgage can, however, only be either a table, straight line or interest-only mortgage, with either a fixed or floating rate – no matter what fancy marketing name may be given to it. Make sure that you compare interest rates and calculate how much you're going to have to repay at the end of the day.

Should you need to, it's usually quite easy to remortgage your property and gain access to some of the equity capital you've built up in it (assuming that property prices have risen since you purchased it!). It's also possible to have a mortgage linked to a revolving loan facility (see **Loans & Overdrafts** on page 228), where the difference between the capital borrowed and the value of your property can be advanced for other uses, such as home improvements, a car purchase or a holiday. This is a cheap way of borrowing, as the mortgage interest rate is usually much lower than that for a loan, although interest on a mortgage cannot be claimed as a tax allowance in New Zealand. Many New Zealanders use one of these methods to finance the purchase of a holiday home (bach or crib), which, because of their often flimsy construction, don't qualify for a full mortgage.

Conditions & Fees

Once a loan has been agreed in principle, a lender will provide you with a conditional offer of a loan outlining the terms. You need to provide proof of your income and outgoings, such as other mortgage payments, rent, other loans and regular commitments (e.g. bills). Proof of income includes three months' pay slips for employees; if you're self-employed, you require an audited copy of your trading accounts for the past three years. If you decide to accept the offer, you must usually pay a deposit (likely to be at least $500) to your mortgage lender. If the sale doesn't go ahead for any reason, the deposit should be refundable, although many lenders charge a 'discontinued application fee' which is deducted from the deposit, so it isn't wise to accept a mortgage offer unless you're certain you want to go ahead with a property purchase.

There are various fees associated with mortgages. All lenders charge an application fee for setting up a loan, usually 1 per cent of the loan amount or $400 (you won't be charged all of this sum if your application is rejected). There's usually a minimum fee and there may also be a maximum, although many mortgage lenders will negotiate the fees. In addition, there's a land transfer registration of $150. It isn't usually necessary to have a survey unless you're borrowing more than 80 per cent of the value of a property.

If you fail to maintain your mortgage repayments, your property can be repossessed and sold at auction, although this rarely happens in New Zealand, as most lenders are willing to arrange lower repayments when borrowers get into financial difficulties. It's best to contact your lender immediately if you have repayment problems rather than wait until a huge debt has accumulated. You may be offered the chance to transfer to another type of mortgage or may be able to remortgage entirely and gain access to some of the equity in your property.

Foreign Currency Mortgages: It isn't unusual in New Zealand for property buyers to take out a foreign currency mortgage, i.e. in a currency other than New Zealand dollars, particularly if interest rates are lower in another country. However, you should be extremely wary of doing so, as interest rate gains can be wiped out overnight by currency swings and devaluations. When choosing between a New Zealand dollar loan and a foreign currency loan, be sure to take into account all costs, fees and possible currency fluctuations. Note that if you have a foreign currency mortgage, you must usually pay commission charges each time you transfer money into a foreign currency to meet your mortgage repayments, although some lenders will do this free of charge. **Taking out a foreign currency mortgage is a risky business and, while it can save you a small fortune, it can just as easily cost you one.**

GOODS & SERVICES TAX

A goods and services tax (GST) is levied in New Zealand, which is essentially the same as the value added tax levied in European Union countries but isn't a sales tax as in the USA. GST is the second largest component of tax revenue and is expected to raise some $11.7 billion for the government in the 2001/02 financial year. GST is levied at a single rate of 12.5 per cent on most goods and services, although some are exempt (e.g. the letting of residential accommodation). When you import goods into New Zealand, GST (and in some cases also customs duty) is assessed on their value, unless they're exempt or imported under a tax-free arrangement. Immigrants can import their personal possessions free of duty and tax, provided they've been owned and used prior to their arrival. This also applies to used cars, provided you meet the import criteria (see page 162).

All businesses with a turnover of $34,000 or more within a 12-month period must register for GST with the Inland Revenue Department and must levy GST on goods and services supplied (unless they're exempt). Similarly, businesses can reclaim GST paid on goods and services used in their business. A GST return must usually be filed every two months, although businesses with a turnover of less than $250,000 per year can choose to file a return every six months, and those with an annual turnover of over $24 million must file monthly. A penalty of 10 per cent of the tax due is levied if a return isn't filed by the due date, plus a cumulative penalty of 1 per cent per month. For further information on GST contact the Inland Revenue on ☎ freephone 0800-377 776.

INCOME TAX

Generally speaking, income tax in New Zealand is below average for a developed country. During the '90s most people saw their income tax reduced, but the Labour government elected in 1999 has increased income taxes. Most New Zealanders are resigned to paying taxes (tax evasion isn't a national sport as it is in some countries) and in any case the country has a system of pay-as-you-earn (PAYE) that ensures that tax is deducted at source from employees' salaries. The tax system in New Zealand isn't particularly complicated, and the only contact most people have with the tax man is when they complete their annual tax return using information taken from pay slips. The system is designed so that most people can prepare and file their own tax returns, although if your tax situation is complicated you may need to seek advice from an accountant.

Information: The IRD runs a comprehensive help service and publishes numerous factsheets and brochures for taxpayers. The following helplines are available:

- Income tax and general enquiries: ☎ freephone 0800-377 774 or 04-381 9439;
- Overdue tax and returns: ☎ freephone 0800-377 771;
- Student loans: ☎ freephone 0800-377 778;
- Family Assistance: ☎ freephone 0800-227 773;
- INFOexpress: ☎ freephone 0800-257 772 (to order tax packs);
- Forms and stationery: ☎ freephone 0800-257 773.

The IRD also has a comprehensive website (🖳 www.ird.govt.nz) that includes downloadable factsheets and forms or can be contacted by post at PO Box 3754, Christchurch, PO Box 1535, Hamilton or PO Box 39-050 Wellington.

Liability

Your country of domicile determines whether you're liable to pay New Zealand income tax. New Zealand residents are taxed on their world-wide income, while non-residents are subject to income tax only on income derived from New Zealand. To determine 'domicile' the tax authorities apply what's known as the 'permanent place of abode test', although this is arbitrary and isn't enshrined in New Zealand tax law. Usually anyone who's present in New Zealand for more than 183 days in a 12-month period is considered resident there and liable to pay taxes. You don't need to be a permanent resident to be liable, and the existence of financial and social ties (including bank accounts and club memberships) may be taken as evidence of domicile. You can usually be considered exempt from New Zealand taxes only if you aren't present in New Zealand for 325 days in a 12-month period. However, if you maintain a home in the country, you cannot be considered non-resident, no matter how brief your stay. If you decide to leave New Zealand, you should inform your local IRD office. Note that the 325-day time limit doesn't start until the IRD have confirmed that you've ceased to become a resident.

Income that's subject to tax in New Zealand includes salary and wages, profits or gains from a business, commissions, rents, royalties, trust distributions, interest and dividends.

Double Taxation: New Zealand has double taxation treaties with several countries, including Australia, Belgium, Canada, China, Denmark, Fiji, Finland, France, Germany, India, Indonesia, Ireland, Italy, Japan, Korea, Malaysia, the Netherlands, Norway, the Philippines, Singapore, Sweden, Switzerland, Taiwan, Thailand, the UK and the USA. Double taxation treaties are designed to ensure that income which has been taxed in one treaty country isn't taxed again in another. A treaty establishes a tax credit or exemption on certain kinds of income, either in the taxpayer's country of residence or in the country where the income is earned. Where applicable, a double taxation treaty prevails over local law.

Tax Code

Every taxpayer in New Zealand is required to fill out a Tax Code Declaration (form IR 330) when they start employment and if there are any changes in their employment circumstances, e.g. if working hours are reduced. You should be given the form by your employer, who returns the completed form to the IRD. The tax code for most employees is M. It's important that you fill in the form correctly, since the amount of tax you pay is based on the information provided.

Tax Return & Tax Bill

When you start work in New Zealand, you should register with your local IRD office, who will issue you with an IRD or tax file number, which must be quoted on tax documents and enquiries. To apply for your IRD number you need to complete an IRD form and send a copy of your passport (☎ freephone 0800-227 774, 🖥 www. ird.govt.nz). IRD numbers are usually issued within five working days.

Recent changes in tax legislation have made tax calculations simpler and more accurate, and tax returns easier to complete. Until recently, everyone who earned an income in New Zealand had to file an income tax return annually with the Commissioner of the Inland Revenue Department. However, under new tax legislation tax returns have been eliminated for individuals who receive income from employment subject to PAYE or from interest and dividends subject to Resident Withholding Tax (RWT – see page 235). All individuals who derive income that isn't taxed at the time of payment or who are in business must file an annual return. The return, known as an IR5, is sent to you automatically each year. The New Zealand tax year runs from 1st April to 31st March of the following year, and returns must be filed by 7th July. The IRD then issues a tax assessment (i.e. a tax bill) showing the amount of income tax payable.

Payments for due tax can be made in a variety of ways, including by cheque, by electronic payment or direct debit from your bank, by cash or cheque at any branch of the Westpac Trust bank, or online through the Internet banking facility at any major New Zealand bank.

Personal Tax Summaries: Employees whose income tax is deducted at source by their employer under PAYE and who don't have any other income, receive a Personal Tax Summary from the IRD based on information provided by employers and shouldn't have any more income tax to pay. The Personal Tax Summary states your tax code and you should check with the IRD that you're using the correct tax code (see above).

You will also receive a Personal Tax Summary if you receive family assistance payments from IRD, if you receive family assistance payments from WINZ and earn over $20,000, if you have a student loan and qualify for an interest write-off, and if you have paid too little or too much tax. The Personal Tax Summary shows whether you're entitled to a tax refund or have tax to pay. If you have tax to pay, you must pay it by 7th February. If you're entitled to a refund, this will be paid when you've confirmed your Personal Tax Summary or within 30 days if the amount owing is less than $50. If you wish to claim certain rebates, such as a child or low income earner rebate (see **Allowances** below), or if you earn under $38,000 but your dividend income was taxed at 33 per cent, you should request a Personal Tax Summary.

Tax Rates

It has become common practice in recent years for the rate of income tax to be adjusted annually in the July budget. There are three tax rates in New Zealand, which were as follows for the tax year 2001/02:

Taxable Income ($)	Tax Rate (%)	Cumulative Tax ($)
0–38,000	19.5	7,410
38,001–60,000	33	14,670
over 60,000	39	

Under recent tax changes, if you receive a lump sum payment (e.g. bonuses, back pay or retirement) and your annual income is over $60,000, you can elect to pay the higher tax rate of 39 per cent on the lump sum and therefore avoid 'squaring up' your tax at the end of the year. If you receive a redundancy payment which together with the annual value of your income for the previous four weeks is less than $38,000, you will pay a flat rate of 21 per cent tax on the redundancy payment.

Allowances

Before you're liable for income tax, you can deduct certain allowances (known as rebates) from your gross salary, which serve to reduce your tax bill. Some income rebates, such as the low income earner rebate, are built into the PAYE rates but others, such as the housekeeper, childcare and donations rebates, must be claimed from the IRD on separate forms. Key rebates include:

- **child taxpayer rebate** ($156), available for children under 15 or still at school;
- **housekeeper rebate** ($310), which generally includes childcare costs for working parents;
- **donations rebate** ($500);
- **low income earner rebate** (4.5 per cent of net income up to $9,500 and 1.5 per cent of income above $9,500);
- **transitional tax allowance** ($728, reduced by 20¢ per $1 of earnings over $6,240), which is available to full-time earners working at least 20 hours per week.

Tax rebates must be claimed by 30th September following the end of the relevant tax year. Expenses associated with employment (such as clothing or travel to work) cannot usually be claimed as a tax allowance in New Zealand. However, the self-employed can claim legitimate business expenses. Note also that interest on a mortgage cannot be claimed as a tax allowance in New Zealand.

Resident Withholding Tax

Interest on bank and other savings accounts is paid after deduction of resident withholding tax (RWT) at a rate equivalent to the standard rate of income tax (19.5 per cent). If, however, you don't provide your IRD or tax file number (see page 233) to a bank when opening an account, it's taxed at the higher rate (33 per cent). This means that taxpayers who pay only the standard rate of income tax have no further tax liability on their investment income at the end of the tax year. Those who pay tax at the higher rate are subject to additional tax on investment income.

Businesses & Self-employment

Income tax for the self-employed and small businesses is broadly similar to wage and salary earners. You're sent a tax return (form IR3) at the end of your financial year, which you must complete and return by the 7th day of the fourth month following the end of your financial year. If your financial year is the same as the tax year (April to March), your tax return must be filed by 7th July each year. You can apply to have a financial year that differs from the tax year. The self-employed are required to pay a proportion of their estimated tax on a monthly basis, which is based on their previous year's liability. When your tax return is submitted, the IRD reconciles the tax due with the sum already paid and issues a tax assessment for any tax payable or a refund if you've over-paid. Company tax is levied at a flat rate of 33 per cent, whether a company is resident or non-resident.

PROPERTY TAXES

Property taxes (rates) are levied by local authorities and are based on the rateable value of properties. Bills are sent out at the beginning of the financial year and are payable by whoever occupies the property, whether it's the owner or a tenant. If you occupy a property for just part of a year, then only a proportion of the tax is payable. The annual bill for an average family house is between $1,000 and $2,000

(Auckland's average is $1,200). It isn't uncommon for residents, either individually or collectively, to appeal against their property valuation in order to obtain a tax reduction.

Property taxes pay for local services such as street cleaning, lighting, and subsidies paid to local public transport companies. They usually include rubbish collection (although an extra charge is levied in some areas), recycling collection and water, although in some areas such as Auckland, water is billed separately. Auckland residents have been protesting against water charges and rates for the last few years, because although water charges were recently excluded from their rates, these weren't reduced! As a result, Auckland residents pay more or less the same as before in rates as well as expensive water charges (most households pay more than $800 per year).

OTHER TAXES

There are no local income taxes, wealth tax, capital gains tax or estate taxes (inheritance taxes) in New Zealand. However, income tax may be levied on income derived from any undertaking or scheme entered into or devised for the purpose of making a profit. For example, income from the sale of property and land if the principal purpose of purchasing it was to resell it or if your business is dealing in property. In addition, gains resulting from certain investments, such as debentures and some preference shares, options and leases, may be taxable irrespective of whether the nature of the gain is capital or income.

Gift Tax: Gift tax (known as gift duty) is imposed at fixed rates on certain gifts, including property in New Zealand or elsewhere if the donor was domiciled in New Zealand at the time of the gift. Gifts that aren't dutiable include those made to charities, gifts for the maintenance or education of your immediate family, and gifts of up to $2,000 per year to an individual if they're made as part of the donor's normal expenditure, e.g. birthday and Christmas presents. The rates of gift duty range from 5 per cent on amounts over $27,000 to 25 per cent plus $5,850 on amounts in excess of $72,000.

Fringe Benefits Tax (FBT): FBT is payable by employers on the value of most fringe benefits paid to employees in New Zealand. From 2000, employers can choose to pay FBT at a flat rate of 64 per cent on all benefits provided or attribute fringe benefits to individual employees and pay FBT at rates based on the employees' marginal tax rates, which range from 17.65 per cent on net earnings of less than $8,075 to 64 per cent on net earnings over $45,331. Examples of fringe benefits are:

- vehicles, which are subject to FBT at 24 per cent of their cost or market value;

- subsidised or low-interest loans or mortgages, which are subject to FBT at rates revised quarterly (in the first quarter of 2001 the rate was 8.5 per cent);

- employer contributions to medical insurance, which are subject to FBT for the whole amount of the contribution.

It's important to note that income such as interest, rents, dividends and royalties are taxable under income tax in New Zealand, rather than separately as is the case in some other countries.

WILLS

It's an unfortunate fact of life, but you're unable to take your worldly goods with you when you take your final bow (even if you have plans to return in a later life). Once you've accepted that you're mortal (the one statistic you can confidently rely on is that 100 per cent of all human beings eventually die), it's wise to make a will leaving your estate to someone or something you love, rather than leaving it to the government or leaving a mess which everyone will fight over (unless that's your intention). Many people in New Zealand die intestate, i.e. without making a will, in which case their property is subject to New Zealand's intestacy laws. In general, these divide your estate equally between your spouse and children. If you die in New Zealand without making a will and aren't domiciled there, the intestacy laws of your home country will apply to the disposal of your estate.

As a general rule, New Zealand law entitles you to make a will according to the law of any country and in any language. If you're a foreign national and don't want your estate to be subject to New Zealand law, you may be eligible to state in your will that it's to be interpreted under the law of another country. To avoid being subject to New Zealand inheritance laws, you must establish your country of domicile in another country. If you don't specify in your will that the law of another country applies to your estate, then New Zealand law will apply. A legal foreign will made in an overseas country dealing with overseas assets is valid in New Zealand and will be accepted for probate there. However, you should have a New Zealand will to deal with your New Zealand assets.

It isn't a legal requirement in New Zealand to use a lawyer to prepare your will, although the relatively small fee (e.g. $150) may save problems later. If you want to make your own will, you can simply write your instructions and sign them, which is known as a holographic will and doesn't need to be witnessed. If your circumstances change dramatically, e.g. you get married, you must make a new will, as under New Zealand law marriage automatically annuls an existing will. Husband and wife should make separate 'mirror' wills. Similarly, if you separate or are divorced, you should consider making a new will, although divorce doesn't automatically annul a will. A new bequest or a change can be made to an existing will through a document called a codicil. You should check your will every few years to make sure it still fulfils your wishes and circumstances (your assets may also increase dramatically in value). A will can be revoked simply by tearing it up.

You'll also need someone to act as the executor of your estate, which can be relatively costly for modest estates. Your bank, building society, solicitor, or other professional will usually act as the executor, although this should be avoided if possible, as fees can be *very* high. If you appoint a professional as executor of your estate, check the fees in advance (and whether they could increase in future). **It's best to make your beneficiaries the executors; they can instruct a solicitor after your death if they need legal assistance.** The good news about dying in New Zealand (at least for your beneficiaries) is that there's no inheritance tax or death duties.

Keep a copy of your will in a safe place (e.g. a bank) and another copy with your solicitor or the executor of your estate. It's useful to leave an updated list of your assets with your will to assist the executor in distributing your estate. You should keep information regarding bank accounts and insurance policies with your will(s), but don't forget to tell someone where they are!

COST OF LIVING

It's useful to try to estimate how far your dollars will stretch and how much money you will have left (if any) after paying your bills. The inflation rate in New Zealand is low; it was around 2 per cent in 2001, and the government is committed to maintaining it at this rate (or lower). Prices of many imported goods have fallen in real terms in recent years, particularly cars and electrical appliances. In general, New Zealanders enjoy a high standard of living, although salaries are lower than in Australia, North America and many European countries.

It's difficult to estimate an average cost of living in New Zealand, as it depends on where you live as well as your lifestyle. If you live in Auckland, drive a BMW and dine in expensive restaurants, your cost of living will be much higher than if you live in a rural part of the South Island, drive a small Japanese car and live on lamb and kiwi fruit. You can live most economically by buying New Zealand produce when possible and avoiding expensive imported goods, which are more expensive not only because of the distance they have to travel but also because they're considered fashionable.

The following gives a *rough* idea of the monthly cost of living for two people in New Zealand. Note that the list doesn't include 'luxury' items such as alcohol, and if you live in Auckland the cost of living is around 20 to 30 per cent more higher.

Item	Amount ($)
Housing	140
Transport (including a car)	140
Food	130
Utilities and furniture	100
Other goods	95
Health	60
Leisure	40
Clothes	30
Total	735

Examples of typical salaries, housing costs and the price of many everyday items can be obtained from Statistics New Zealand (⌨ www.stats.govt.nz), the statistical office of the New Zealand government.

15.

LEISURE

When it comes to leisure, New Zealand is a country where full advantage is taken of the natural environment and the great outdoors. New Zealanders and most tourists spend a great deal of time touring or hiking (tramping) round the country or simply sitting back and admiring it over a few drinks. New Zealand is one of the most beautiful and scenic countries in the world with a surprisingly varied landscape. Whether your idea of leisure involves the beach, mountains, forests or the strange thermal areas where forces deep in the centre of the earth make their presence felt, you will never be short of something to see and do. New Zealanders take their leisure time seriously and city dwellers (although many New Zealand cities are little more than country towns by European and North American standards) cannot wait for the weekend to come round so that they can take off to their cabin in the country, known as 'baches' in North Island and 'cribs' in South Island.

In comparison with many other countries, New Zealand doesn't offer a great variety of organised leisure activities, particularly cultural events. However, the situation has improved in recent years and many cities now boast impressive theatres and arts festivals. Nevertheless, if you're a lover of the arts you will need to travel to the major cities to indulge your leisure interests and even then the choice of activities won't be as great as in many other countries. Rural New Zealand has little to offer in the way of culture and even Australians, people not generally known for their cultural awareness, make jokes about the backwardness of small-town New Zealand. The New Zealander's description of themselves as a nation of 'rugby, racing and beer' isn't wholly accurate but there's rarely smoke without fire!

One of the compensations of this reliance on outdoor activities is that there's much to be enjoyed that's inexpensive or even free. The American and European trend for massive Disneyland-style theme parks, where it's possible for a family of four to spend a week's wages in one day, is unlikely to overwhelm New Zealand, although Auckland does have a modest amusement park (situated at the rather intriguingly named Rainbow's End).

Information about local events and entertainment is available from tourist offices or Visitor Information Network (VIN) centres and is also published in local newspapers and magazines. In the main cities there are magazines and newspapers devoted to entertainment, and free weekly or monthly programmes are published by tourist organisations in major cities and tourist centres. Many city newspapers also publish weekly magazines or supplements containing a detailed programme of local events and entertainment.

The main aim of this chapter, and indeed the purpose of the whole book, is to provide information that isn't found in general guide books. General information about New Zealand is available in numerous excellent guide books including *Baedeker's New Zealand*, the *Blue Guide New Zealand*, *Fodor's New Zealand*, *Let's Go New Zealand*, *Lonely Planet New Zealand* and the *Rough Guide New Zealand* (see **Appendix B** for a comprehensive list). There are also a number of guides to the main cities.

TOURIST INFORMATION

All cities, towns and popular tourist spots in New Zealand have a tourist office, usually known as Visitor Information Network (VIN) centre, of which there are over 80 in New Zealand (there are eight in Auckland alone). VIN centres are co-ordinated by the New Zealand Tourism Board (NZTB) but are usually independently owned, although a few (such as Christchurch) are run by the local authority. Tourist offices or VIN centres are usually located in a prominent position, for example in the city hall or another public building. Note that railway stations in New Zealand don't usually have tourist offices, although you will find them at airports. Look for the internationally recognised (green) 'i' symbol. Opening hours vary considerably and during the winter months (April to October) even main city offices are open only for limited hours, such as 10am to 4pm, and in small towns and resorts offices they are usually closed completely (except in winter sports resorts).

Tourist offices provide a wealth of information about local attractions, restaurants, accommodation, sporting events and facilities, package holidays, tours, public transport, car rental and much more. Offices can provide information on a wide range of leisure activities and sports, so you should mention any special interests when making enquiries. They can also book your accommodation, although unless you plan to arrive late or don't have time to look around, it's often better to find accommodation on the spot. If you book through the tourist office you will pay the full rate and probably also a booking fee, while if you book direct you won't only save the booking fee but may also be able to negotiate a lower rate.

Tourist offices use the latest technology and VIN centres can access the NZ Host National Tourism database at the touch of a button and call up and print information. An increasing number of tourist offices in New Zealand are also equipped to deal with enquiries by e-mail (e.g. ✉ visitor@auckland.tourism.co.nz for the Auckland tourist office and ✉ info@wellingtonnz.com). Most cities and regions publish free entertainment magazines and newspapers containing maps and a plethora of information about local attractions and events (distributed by tourist offices, hotels, transport companies and information bureaux).

New Zealand is promoted overseas by the excellent New Zealand Tourism Board (NZTB), which is a mine of information and has offices in many countries including Austria, Belgium, Canada, Denmark, Finland, Germany, Ireland, Italy, Japan, Luxembourg, the Netherlands, Norway, Portugal, Spain, Sweden, Switzerland, the UK and the USA. Among the many publications available from the NZTB is a *Holiday Planner* which is useful reading for anyone travelling to New Zealand for the first time and the first step to the wealth of other literature available from (or via) the NZTB. The *Holiday Planner* provides an information service where you can simply indicate on a card what your interests are (e.g. hotel chains, package tours, car rental or particular cities) and your name and address is sent to the relevant organisations. The NTZB also has an excellent Internet site (💻 www.purenz.com), while other useful sites include 💻 www.tourism.net.nz and www.travelenvoy.com.

HOTELS

In New Zealand the term hotel can be rather confusing for the newcomer. As in Australia, a public house or a bar is usually called a hotel, when in fact it doesn't provide accommodation. Or rather, it may keep a bedroom or two 'for rent' to satisfy a quaint old law that says hotels must offer accommodation, but you aren't expected to ask to stay there! However, you will be pleased to hear that New Zealand has a plethora of 'proper' hotels with accommodation ranging from the most humble to the most luxurious. Standards and service are usually high and an increasing number of hotel staff have completed the nationally-recognised 'Kiwi Host' customer service workshop. Most guide books contain a selection of hotels and other kinds of accommodation and among the best known are the *AA Accommodation New Zealand Guide* and *Friars Guide to Accommodation with Dining*.

Many accommodation properties in New Zealand have adopted the Qualmark Rating system similar to the Michelin star rating or the key rating in the UK. Properties are inspected annually by trained assessors. The Qualmark system awards stars on a scale of one to five whereby one star indicates that the property meets minimum requirements and is clean and comfortable, and five stars indicate that the accommodation is the best available. Properties participating in the system display a sign with the Qualmark system logo (a capital Q in navy and green) together with the number of stars awarded.

Luxury Hotels: Top hotels in New Zealand are comparable with those in any other country, both in terms of facilities and room rates, and can be found in major cities and resort areas. Many leading international names have hotels in New Zealand including Stamford Plaza, Hyatt, Southern Pacific, Sheraton, Carlton and Parkroyal. There are also privately-owned luxury hotels. You should expect to pay between $200 and $1,000 per night for a double room in a luxury hotel.

Sporting Lodges: Sporting lodges are rural country house hotels and are a unique feature of the luxury hotel business in New Zealand. They are invariably set in superb locations in the mountains, by lakes or the sea. Each lodge is individually styled and many are noted for their excellent cuisine. Lodges usually offer fishing (e.g. brown or rainbow trout in a nearby river or lake, or marlin at sea) and golf (New Zealand has over 400 courses), hence the name 'sporting'. Many also offer sports facilities such as diving, snorkelling, water-skiing, sailing, riding, trekking, rafting, jet-boating or skiing. Rates for sporting lodges may be higher than city centre hotels, ranging from between $250 and $1,00 per night and per person for a double room, although tariffs include meals. The New Zealand Lodge Association publishes a catalogue containing details of lodges, *New Zealand Lodges – Luxury Lodges and Sporting Retreats* (🖳 www.lodgesofnz.co.nz).

Mid-range Hotels: For those unable to afford the indulgence of a sporting lodge, there are plenty of mid-range hotels, both in cities and resort areas. These may not be in such prime locations but they usually have good facilities, including a bar and restaurant (usually open to non-residents), and possibly a swimming pool and health club. The main chains include Best Western, Flag Inns, Golden Chain, Manor Motor Inns, Quality Hotels and Pacifica. Room rates in a mid-range hotel are usually between $80 to $250 per night for a double room.

Motels: Motels are found throughout New Zealand, even in quite remote areas, and although they're rarely located in prime positions they are usually easily accessible on or near main roads. In cities they are normally located in the suburbs, but normally offer good access to public transport. One unique feature of a New Zealand motel is that most (although there are a few exceptions) accommodation is more like an apartment than a hotel room, with one or two bedrooms, a living area, kitchenette and a full-sized bathroom. Motels are so well equipped that New Zealanders frequently use motels as holiday bases and not just for the odd one or two night stay. Some motels have restaurants, bars and swimming pools on site, although they aren't generally as well served as hotels. A refreshing change is that chain motels (which can be soulless in other countries) in New Zealand are often family run and while of a consistent standard, also offer genuine, friendly personal service.

Another feature of motels is that they frequently operate 'all in' pricing, which means that you pay a fixed room rate no matter how many people occupy it. You're unlikely to find more than $5 or $10 difference between the rate for a single room and a double or family room, and therefore they are an economical place for families to stay. The main motel chains in New Zealand are Best Western, Flag, Golden Chain and Budget. Expect to pay $70 to $300 per night for a motel room or suite. The Motel 'bible' in New Zealand is Jason's *Motels and Motor Lodges*, and the Motel Association has a comprehensive website (⌨ www.nzmotels.co.nz).

Prices

Hotel prices are quoted inclusive of taxes (GST at 12.5 per cent) and in line with New Zealand's no-tipping policy you won't be charged extra for service. Many hotels in popular resorts have slightly higher room rates during the summer and a minimum stay of three nights, although outside the high season hotels often offer a discount for stays of three nights or longer. Many offer low season discounts, particularly during the winter and early spring months, which may include three nights for the price of two or two nights for the price of one at weekends. Note that many motels don't charge extra in the summer. Hotel prices in New Zealand don't usually include meals, unless otherwise stated, although they frequently have 'special offer' rates which include meals (but you won't be obliged to pay for meals if you require only a room). In smaller hotels and motels without a restaurant, you may be offered breakfast, which is often served in your room so that you can enjoy breakfast in bed.

Facilities

Although facilities vary considerably with the price and category of accommodation, you can usually expect en suite facilities (bath or shower) in a New Zealand hotel. Hotel and motel rooms are usually equipped with a telephone, radio or TV, including satellite TV in top hotels and some motels, plus tea and coffee-making facilities and a small fridge (even in modestly priced hotels) complete with a complimentary bottle of milk (a peculiar New Zealand tradition). More expensive hotels provide room service and a mini-bar, which is always expensive. Power points are usually provided and there's often a razor socket in the bathroom (you will need an adapter to use any appliance without a New Zealand style plug – see **Electricity** on page 96). Most hotels (except those in city centres) have private parking, and where they don't there's usually on-street parking or a secure off-road car park nearby.

In general, New Zealand hotels don't cater well for business travellers, as few business people make a lot of overnight business trips. Business centres with secretarial staff and translation services are usually confined to a few luxury hotels in Auckland, although other main cities do have business hotels. Most hotels have photocopying and fax facilities for their guests' use. Some hotels have swimming pools and health and sports facilities such as gymnasiums, and most top class hotels have a restaurant, coffee shop and bar, although you can often obtain a better and cheaper meal at a local restaurant.

Booking

It isn't usually necessary to book far ahead in New Zealand, except in summer or on public holiday weekends, and during international trade fairs, conventions and festivals in the major cities. In any case, if your chosen hotel or motel isn't available there's usually something similar nearby. The only exception to this is if you're venturing to the more remote southern tip of the South Island, where it's advisable to book, as accommodation is more scarce. You won't usually be shown a room unless you ask and it's usually safe to accept a room without inspecting it. Certainly in the case of a large hotel or a motel, your room will have the same facilities as a similarly priced establishment in Miami or Manchester and may even be decorated in the same 'international' style.

If you're staying in a chain hotel or motel, the receptionist will call ahead and book your next night's accommodation, assuming of course that there's a member in the area where you wish to stay (if not, they may be willing to recommend a hotel in a rival chain). Alternatively there's usually a free courtesy phone in the reception area where you can make your own bookings. If you book ahead within a chain you're usually asked to pay a referral deposit, typically $30. If you change your mind later and wish to cancel, you're expected to notify the hotel by 4pm if you don't want to lose your deposit. Checkout time is usually noon at the latest and if you stay any later you may be charged for an extra day. If you're staying in a small hotel or guest house and wish to leave early in the morning, it's advisable to pay your bill the evening before and tell the proprietor when you plan to leave; otherwise you may find your hosts are still in bed!

BED & BREAKFAST

New Zealand has a long tradition of providing bed and breakfast accommodation (the country's biggest category), usually known as guest houses, which in rural areas are often on working farms. The cost is similar to the cheaper hotels, although guest houses offer a more individual service. The price of a guest house bed usually includes a hearty breakfast, which isn't normally the case in a hotel, therefore the price is actually more reasonable than it looks. Expect to pay around $60 to $100 per night for a room. Not all guest house rooms have en suite facilities, although they will be available nearby and the owners usually allow guests access to most of the facilities of their home, therefore in many ways a guest house is often better served than a hotel. In modest guest houses you may find facilities rather worn or homely to say the least, but if you need anything such as extra blankets or pillows, you need only to mention it to your host and it will appear as if by magic.

You can find guest houses through local tourist offices and VIN centres, from the Federation of Bed and Breakfast Hotels (don't take the term 'hotels' too literally), 52 Armagh Street, Christchurch (☎ 06-358 6928, 💻 www.nzbnbhotels.com from where you can download their brochure) and from books such as *The New Zealand Bed and Breakfast Book* (Moonshine Press) published annually or *The Bed and Breakfast Directory of New Zealand*.

HOMESTAYS

It's possible to stay in private homes in New Zealand as a 'personal guest' of a family. If you're travelling by public transport, your hosts will usually pick you up from the nearest town or village. The difference between this kind of accommodation and a guest house is that you're treated as a member of the family and invited to join them at mealtimes and in other activities around the house (like doing the housework!). Homestay hosts don't usually accept more than one group of guests at a time and most offer homestays as a way of meeting people, rather than simply making money. As many homestays are on farms, you may be able to try your hand at sheep-shearing or roam the wide open spaces on a tractor or horse, while your children help raise new-born lambs. The duration of a stay can be anything from one night to three weeks or more, with the cost between $120 to $400 per night for two people, including all meals (homestays shouldn't be considered as a cheap form of accommodation).

Various organisations arrange homestays including New Zealand Farm Holidays, PO Box 74, Kumeu, Auckland (☎ 09-412 9651, 💻 www.nzfarmholidays.co.nz) and Rural Holidays New Zealand Ltd., PO Box 2155, Christchurch (☎ 03-355 6218, 💻 www.ruralhols.co.nz). A useful publication is *50 Great Farmstays in New Zealand*.

HOSTELS

There's a variety of inexpensive accommodation in New Zealand, including youth and other hostels. These include both privately owned hostels and hostels owned by the Youth Hostel Association of New Zealand (YHANZ) part of the international association, Hostelling International (HI). It's necessary to be a member of HI to use YHA hostels. You can join on a night-by-night basis when you arrive at a hostel, although it's cheaper to take out annual membership, either abroad or in New Zealand costing $30. The YHANZ (💻 www.yha.org.nz) publishes *YHA NZ Hostel Accommodation Guide*, containing hostel addresses.

There are no age restrictions at New Zealand hostels. Hostels fill up early in summer, so you should book in advance if possible, although some hostels don't accept reservations and restrict stays to a maximum of three or four nights. Linen is sometimes provided and where it isn't it can be hired. Hostels vary considerably in size from around 10 to 300 beds, with larger hostels usually having dormitories, although rooms for one to four people are available in many hostels. A dormitory bed costs around $19 per person, per night and a double/twin room in the region of $25 per person.

Hostel hosts are an excellent source of information about the surrounding area and will gladly pass on tips about places to see and things to do (or even temporary employment opportunities often posted on hostel notice boards). They will also usually book your next night's hostel accommodation.

Backpackers: New Zealand is a world pioneer and leader in backpacker accommodation and practically every tourist spot in the country has at least one backpacker hostel. Hostels offer much the same sort of accommodation as youth hostels and some belong to backpacker groups and others are independent. The two main backpacker groups operating in the country are VIP Backpacker Resorts (☎ 09-827 6016, 💻 www.vip.co.nz) and Budget Backpacker Hostels (BBH ☎ freephone

0800-788 336 ⌨ www.backpack.co.nz, generally considered to be *the* backpacker's website in New Zealand). Membership of the group not only qualifies you for accommodation discounts but also for discounts on transport and activities.

CAMPING & CARAVANNING

Camping and caravanning are extremely popular in New Zealand with both New Zealanders and tourists, who flock to the country each year to enjoy holidays in the open air. Campsites in New Zealand are among the best in the world and often in prime beauty spots. Campsites vary considerably from small wilderness sites with fairly basic facilities (or even no facilities) to luxury establishments with a wide range of amenities. Rates range from around $12 per night (usually from noon to noon) at a basic site up to $55 or more at a four-star site for a family of four, a car, and a caravan site or camping space. Some sites charge extra for the use of showers, sports facilities (such as tennis courts) and amenities such as ironing or the use of a freezer. Most sites have different rates for high and low seasons.

Permission is required to park or camp on private property or anywhere outside official campsites. Whether or not it's legal to camp in the countryside depends on the attitude of the local authority (VIN centres can advise you). In rural areas, camping by the roadside is a popular practice, although elsewhere the availability of campsites makes rough camping less popular than in some other countries. Note that areas where there are no campsites may be remote, with even facilities such as clean drinking water difficult to find, and therefore rough camping may be discouraged, particularly if the area is so remote as to make rescue difficult (e.g. in case of a medical emergency). Camping isn't usually permitted alongside walking trails (for which New Zealand is famous), although huts are available in most areas with bunk beds, cooking facilities, toilets and possibly showers, for a fee of from $8 per night.

Holiday and Accommodation Parks of New Zealand (HAPNZ) produces a directory describing the facilities at around 277 member sites, including sites with cabins to rent. It's available from HAPNZ (PO Box 394, Paraparaumu, ☎ 04-298 3283, ⌨ www.holidayparks.co.nz) and from book shops, camping, caravanning and motoring organisations in New Zealand. HAPNZ also provides caravan and travel insurance, travel services, rallies, holidays, reservations and a range of other benefits for members.

The Department of Conservation (DOC) runs around 120 camping grounds in New Zealand, usually in national parks or reserves. These usually offer only basic facilities and there's usually a standard charge (around $5 per adult), although DOC informal camping grounds are free. DOC offices around the country can provide lists of camping grounds.

Motor caravans, known variously as campervans or motorhomes in New Zealand, are much more popular than touring caravans (which are towed behind a car). They vary from luxuriously appointed American-style, Winnebago-type vehicles which can accommodate six people in luxury, to conversions of small Japanese vans with room for just two (who need to be on intimate terms!). Many smaller vehicles have the advantage of being four-wheel-drive, making out of the way places accessible.

You can rent a motor caravan by the day or week from a variety of companies in New Zealand from around $150 per day for the cheapest two berth vehicle up to around $250 per day for the largest. Note that rates are considerably lower in winter and that overseas travel agents can often get good discounts. These rates are for reasonably new vehicles and include basic third party insurance, although there's an extra charge for damage excess waiver (DEW) of around $15 per day, which removes the liability for damage caused to a rented vehicle. If you don't have DEW you must leave a credit card deposit of $800 or more. It's important to note that no matter how comprehensive your insurance cover, you're unlikely to be covered for damage caused by driving on dirt roads (known locally as unsealed roads), even if your rented motor caravan is of the four-wheel-drive type. Rates exclude fuel and personal accident insurance, but include unlimited kilometres. Note that a diesel-powered vehicle is much cheaper to run than one that uses petrol, as they not only offer greater economy but diesel is little over half the price of petrol in New Zealand.

You can book a motor caravan from many companies including Maui, which has offices in Auckland and Christchurch (☎ freephone 0800-651 080), and Britz (part of Budget Rent-a-Car) which has offices in various locations (☎ freephone 0800-831 900). Small local operators offer bargain-priced (i.e. well-worn) campervans from around $40 per day, excluding insurance. You may find the book *New Zealand by Motorhome* by Shore and Campbell (Pelican Publishing Company) useful.

SELF-CATERING

New Zealand offers an abundance of self-catering accommodation and a wide choice of 'mobile' homes, including cabins, serviced motels, tourist flats and condominiums. The most luxurious dwellings have private swimming pools, tennis courts and acres of private grounds, although you may need to take out a second mortgage to pay the bill! Standards vary considerably, from basic, no-frills cabins to luxury flats with every modern convenience.

Cabins: One particular feature of self-catering accommodation in New Zealand is the cabin, which is usually basic, containing only beds and essential furniture, but a step up from a tent. You must provide your own bedding or sleeping bag. In addition to dedicated cabin sites, cabins are also available at many camping and caravanning sites from between $30 to $55 per night. The Holiday and Accommodation Parks of New Zealand (PO Box 394, Paraparaumu, ☎ 04-298 3283, 🖳 www.holiday parks.co.nz) publishes a directory containing details of around 277 member sites.

Tourist Flats: A tourist flat is the New Zealand term for a holiday apartment. Unlike cabins they are usually located in purpose-built buildings and can vary from fairly basic one-room studios to two or three bedroom apartments. They usually contain bedding and linen and a well equipped kitchen, and better quality flats are fully serviced and contain washing machines, dishwashers and TVs (they also provide the use of swimming pools and sporting facilities). A tourist flat typically costs between $50 and $90 per night, depending on the facilities.

Condominiums: An increasingly popular trend in New Zealand are American-style condominiums, which are essentially the same as tourist flats but more luxurious. They are sometimes found in the grounds of luxury hotels and sporting lodges, and boast every modern facility including swimming pools, spas, tennis courts and extensive gardens. The cost ranges from $800 to $2,000 per week, per unit.

It isn't usually necessary to book far in advance for self-catering accommodation, as there's a wide choice and there isn't much of a peak holiday season in New Zealand. However, if you wish to stay in a particular unit for a particular week during the summer, you should certainly book, although if you're flexible you need to book only a week or two in advance or can simply turn up and find somewhere on the spot (if your preferred accommodation isn't available, there's usually somewhere similar nearby).

Various organisations publish guides to self-catering accommodation and an excellent *Where to Stay Guide* is also published by the New Zealand Tourism Board listing the different accommodation options in New Zealand. It's available free from NZTB offices, although a charge is made if you want the guide posted to you. Other good guides include Jasons **Budget Accommodation** and **Motels and Motor Lodges** (the New Zealand equivalents of Michelin guides). Two websites, 💻 www. holidayhomes.co.nz and www.nz-holiday-homes.com, offer excellent guides to renting privately owned holiday homes.

MUSEUMS & GALLERIES

Most exhibits in New Zealand museums and galleries are from recent history, although you can enjoy ancient treasures and old masters at art galleries in some cities. However, there's definitely a preference for more contemporary works and many of the exhibits are by present day Maori and Pakeha (a local term for white, European settlers) artists. The standard of museums and art galleries is generally high (many have living or interactive displays) and even in small towns you're likely to find a local museum where you can learn something of the local history and culture. Admission is usually free except for collections housed in historic buildings, where a small charge is made. The New Zealand Historic Places Trust maintains 45 properties around the country where displays are maintained.

Among the most famous museums and galleries in New Zealand are the Auckland Art Gallery, the New Zealand Maritime Museum also in Auckland, the Te Papa or Museum of New Zealand in Wellington (which has excellent displays of Pacific and Maori cultures as well as exhibits about New Zealand history and European settlement, 💻 www.tepapa.govt.nz), the Canterbury Museum and the Robert McDougall Art Gallery in Christchurch, which is one of the few galleries to exhibit European masters. For information contact Museums Aotearoa, PO Box 10-928, Wellington (☎ 04-499 1313, 💻 www.museums-aotearoa.org.nz).

It's also possible to visit many businesses in New Zealand, particularly those connected with the food and drink industry, including vineyards, distilleries, breweries, mineral water springs, farms and dairies. Technology enthusiasts may prefer to visit a hydroelectric power plant or a mine.

Disabled Access: Like many countries, New Zealand has started to take access for the disabled seriously only within the last decade. The law now requires that new building and redevelopment projects incorporate 'reasonable and adequate' access for disabled people. There are, however, still a lot of old public buildings in New Zealand which cannot be modified for practical or aesthetic reasons. Commercial operators tend to be more forward thinking and most leisure attractions provide disabled access, and hotels and motels are required to provide at least a few units with wheelchair access. Further information can be obtained from the Disability Information Service, 314 Worcester Street, Christchurch (☎ 03-366 6189).

THEATRE, OPERA & BALLET

New Zealand has seven professional theatre companies resident in one or other of the main cities and a number of repertory theatre groups throughout the country, even in smaller towns. Among New Zealand's best known playwrights are Bruce Mason, Joe Musaphia, Greg McGee and Roger Hall, whose play 'Middle Aged Spread' was a major success in London's West End. Wellington is particularly known for its passion for theatre and hosts the renowned International Festival of Arts biennially (in even numbered years). Auckland, Christchurch and Dunedin also have active theatre scenes.

The New Zealand Opera Company dates back to 1954 and the National Opera was established in 1979. New Zealand Opera is more famous outside the country than within, although opera singer Dame Kiri te Kanawa is revered in New Zealand (mainly because she's a New Zealander who has made it on the world stage, rather than because of the average New Zealander's interest in opera). The city of Auckland runs an 'Opera in the Park' season annually in January.

The New Zealand Ballet was founded in 1953 and the National School of Ballet (now part of the New Zealand School of Dance) was established in 1968. Like its counterparts in opera, the New Zealand Ballet has an excellent repertoire of 19th century and more modern works, and performs regularly in New Zealand and abroad.

MUSIC

New Zealand's Symphony Orchestra regularly tours the country and undertakes overseas tours, particularly to Australia and Japan. Most major cities also have their own symphony and concert orchestras. Prominent New Zealand musicians include concert organist Gillian Weir and pianists Michael Houston and Maurice Till. New Zealand is also noted for its metropolitan brass bands (a local tradition), which frequently take part in international competitions and have been world champions on several occasions.

There are few well known New Zealand rock and pop bands, Crowded House being one of the few to attain international fame, and most groups leave for Europe as soon as they achieve some success. Internationally known rock and pop stars do, however, tour New Zealand on a regular basis, mainly in November and December, with tickets for top acts costing at least $50. There are rock, folk and jazz clubs in most cities, although these tend to be quieter and less cosmopolitan than those found in Europe and North America. A weekly gig guide, *The Fis*, is published in Auckland and is available at cafés and bars.

CINEMA

New Zealand produces a number of home-grown feature films which are popular with local cinema-goers and some, such as Roger Donaldson's *Sleeping Dogs* and Jane Campion's *The Piano* (highly acclaimed at Cannes and the Academy Awards) have even received international recognition. Cinema-lovers needn't be concerned, however, as most of the world's big movies are released in New Zealand sooner or later (sometimes before Europe). However, New Zealand's biggest cinema triumph in many a year came in December 2001 with the blockbuster *Lord of the Rings* trilogy, filmed entirely on location in New Zealand and produced by Kiwi Peter Jackson. Extensive marketing campaigns are planned to capitalise on the exposure from the trilogy and NZ Post has even issued some commemorative stamps! There are several successful annual film festivals in New Zealand, including the International Film Festival (now in its 34th year) held in Auckland and the popular 'Incredible Film Festival' showing b-grade and other unusual films.

There are cinemas in the major cities and most towns of any size, including multi-screen centres in the major cities and Auckland now has an Imax screen at its Force Entertainment Centre. Tickets cost an average of around $9 for adults and $6.50 for children (at weekends charges rise to $12 and $7 respectively). Children aged from 3 to 15 must show ID cards when they buy their ticket. There are also concessions for senior citizens and the disabled.

Films are graded by censors according to a unique classification system:

Classification	Audience
G	general viewing
PG (parent guidance)	parents should decide whether the film is suitable for younger viewers
M	only those aged 16 or over
R16	only those aged 16 or over
R18	only those aged 18 or over

Note that only R16 and R18 films are restricted by law to the relevant audience. The censors frequently add a descriptive tag to their rating, such as 'violent content' or 'explicit sexual content', which gives additional guidance and makes it easier for parents to decide which films their children shouldn't see (or conversely, which films children will do anything to try to see!).

SOCIAL CLUBS

There are many social clubs and organisations in New Zealand catering for both foreigners and locals. These include Anglo-New Zealand Clubs, Business Clubs, International Men's and Women's Clubs and Rotary Clubs. Expatriates from many countries have their own clubs in major cities, a list of which is often maintained by embassies and consulates in New Zealand. The Country Women's Institutes of New Zealand and the Women's Division Federation Farmers (WDFF) play an important part in the social life of women in rural areas, where there are few formal social facilities. All towns have a YWCA and YMCA, many of which organise extensive programmes. In keeping with the country's sporting heritage, there are a range of sports clubs in most towns, the most common of which are rugby, soccer, cricket, hockey and netball.

Many local clubs organise activities and pastimes such as chess, bridge, art, music, sports activities, outings, and theatre and cinema trips. Joining a local club is one of the best ways to meet people and make new friends or to integrate into your local community or New Zealand society in general. Ask your local library for information.

EVENING CLASSES

Evening classes are provided by various organisations in cities and large towns in New Zealand. In addition to formal adult and further education, evening classes offer courses and lectures in everything from astrology to zoology. The range and variety of subjects offered is endless and includes foreign languages, handicrafts, hobbies and sports, and business-related courses. Among the most popular classes are cookery (proof that New Zealanders *are* interested in food, contrary to what many people believe) and motor and home maintenance. New Zealanders have a long tradition of do-it-yourself dating back to the days of the early settlers and few people would dream of paying somebody to fix their home or car if they could do it themselves (an old New Zealand saying is 'you can fix it fine with binder twine' – the string used to bind bales of hay!). If you live in a remote area you may find it difficult to find a local tradesman to do odd jobs on your home, therefore classes have a practical as well as a leisure purpose.

NIGHT-LIFE

New Zealand night-life varies considerably depending on the town or region, and in small towns you may be fortunate to find a bar with music, although in contrast, Dunedin with its large student population is the country's live music and pub capital and 'buzzes' with night life. New Zealand pubs are traditionally serious drinking places and shun any trends towards making them more attractive with live music. In cities you will find a wide range of attractions, including jazz clubs, discos, music clubs, karaoke bars, trendy bars, night-clubs and music halls. Although some are fast-paced by New Zealand standards, you're unlikely to find a night-spot that's as dynamic as the top establishments in New York, London or Paris, and the best night life is to be found in Wellington. All such establishments restrict entry to those over 20, which in part accounts for the more mature (i.e. conservative) atmosphere, and strict dress codes are often enforced. The most popular clubs change continually and are listed in newspapers and entertainment magazines. In Auckland the Travel and Information Centre publishes the weekly *Alive & Happening* guide to cultural events and the NZ Herald has a cultural supplement on Thursdays (*7 Days*). In Wellington there are two good weekly guides to cultural events, *City Voice* and *Capital Times*. Although there are a few places in Auckland which keep going until the small hours, you will find that most close early by international standards (many a New Zealand night-club is closed by 1am, simply because the revellers have all gone home!).

GAMBLING

Gambling is a national passion in New Zealand, where gamblers spent more than $1.3 billion in 2000. Gambling is strictly controlled by the state (gambling in some other countries seems completely unfettered in comparison), although compulsive gambling is on the increase. Slot machines and electronic amusement arcade gambling games have been legal only since 1987, but there are now more than 20,000 gaming machines in New Zealand, which are responsible for the problems of the vast majority of compulsive gamblers (estimated to number over 100,000).

The national lottery (Lotto) is the most widespread form of gambling in New Zealand, where over two-thirds of the population buys a ticket each week (the minimum stake is $2). Tickets can be purchased at designated Lotto outlets, including most dairies (corner shops) and postal shops, and the draw is shown live on prime-time TV on Saturday evenings. The New Zealand Lotteries Commission is prepared to go to extraordinary lengths to make sure that as many New Zealanders as possible participate and offers 'multi-draw' entry options for people going on holiday (you can play for up to ten weeks in advance!) and the facility to play Lotto by post if you live in a remote area without a Lotto outlet. Instant-win scratch cards, known as 'scratchies', can also be bought from the same outlets. Some of the proceeds of Lotto are donated to charity, including charities which help compulsive gamblers!

After Lotto, betting on horse racing is the next most popular gambling activity, with over 500 regular race meetings throughout the country each year (an average of ten a week). New Zealanders are even more passionate about horse racing (including harness racing or trotting and flat racing) than Australians and bets are often huge. Bets can be placed at betting offices licensed by the Totalisator Agency Board (TAB), which also accepts bets on Australian races. There's also a Trackside TV Channel, which is often showing in pubs and bars.

Those looking for a more genteel outlet for their gambling passions may like to try their hand at bingo, known locally as housie. Most pubs and clubs have a housie night at least once a week (some every night), where for around $8 you can buy a card entitling you to play some 40 games. Casinos have been legalised within the last few years and there are five in total including the Sky City casino in Auckland with 97 gaming tables, a Keno lounge and over 1,000 slot machines. Sky City is housed in Sky Tower, now one of New Zealand's most famous landmarks after the completion of the 328m (1,000ft) tower topped by a revolving restaurant (which has the added 'attraction' of swaying in high winds!). Opening hours are 11am to 3am from Monday to Thursday) and continuously from 11am Thursday until 3am Monday morning. All advertising for casinos in New Zealand is accompanied by a gambling 'health warning' and the number of an organisation which helps compulsive gamblers (☎ freephone 0800-654 655, ✉ info@gamblingproblem.co.nz).

BARS & PUBS

As a nation in which drinking is virtually an obsession, New Zealand has a vast choice of drinking establishments. Every town of any size has at least one pub or bar, and in many town and city suburbs there's one on every corner. Dunedin is generally considered to have the country's best pub scene. However, despite (or perhaps because of) the popularity of drinking, New Zealand has some of the world's most bizarre licensing laws.

The traditional New Zealand drinking place is the local 'hotel', which is roughly equivalent to a pub in the UK or a bar elsewhere. Despite being called hotels, they rarely offer accommodation. At its most basic the New Zealand hotel can be very rudimentary indeed, with plastic chairs, fluorescent lighting and no music, although the larger establishments offer a choice between public and lounge bars (a lounge bar is more attractively furnished but up to 50 per cent more expensive). Some country hotels even have beer gardens. Most traditional hotels don't serve food and those that do have a rather limited menu. All hotels have a so-called bottle sales counter where you can buy alcohol to take away, which is a consequence of the licensing laws that allow shops and supermarkets to sell wine, but not beer or spirits (although this may change in the next few years).

New Zealand hotels are public houses in the true sense of the word, in that usually all-comers are served. Women drinking in a public bar may attract a few stares in remote places but are unlikely to meet with disapproval. In country areas you may initially feel that you're intruding upon the locals' private territory, but you will usually be warmly welcomed and engaged in conversation. Indeed, you should make an attempt to talk to the regulars, as it may be considered rude not to do so.

Bars are generally more up-market establishments and are usually found in cities and large towns, where you can choose from French-influenced bars, café-bars, brasseries, wine bars and pavement cafés. These places offer none of the traditional New Zealand atmosphere, but as in other countries are fashionable places to see and be seen. Drinks are invariably more expensive than in a hotel, although bars may also serve food.

Licensing Hours: Until 1967 hotels could serve alcohol only until 6pm and, although licensing hours have been liberalised in recent years, the 5 to 6pm 'swill' is still often the busiest time for drinking. The same liberalisation has also resulted in a confusing array of licensing hours applying to different premises in different places. In theory, drinking establishments can apply for a 24-hour licence allowing them to open day and night except on Sundays, when they must close by 3am. In practice, most hotels and bars are open daily from 11am to 10pm and until 10.30pm on Fridays and Saturdays. Even places with a 24-hour licence may be closed by 1am, simply because of a lack of demand for late-night drinking. Establishments that don't serve food aren't usually allowed to sell alcohol on Sundays, although Sunday drinking is permitted in night-clubs, private clubs and places of entertainment, in addition to restaurants.

A few areas of Auckland, Wellington and Christchurch have licensing authorities which don't licence *any* establishments to serve alcohol and are therefore effectively 'dry' (there's still a strong temperance movement in New Zealand). The main effect of this, however, is to encourage drinking and driving, as drinkers are forced to travel to other areas to quench their thirst.

The legal age for drinking in public establishments in New Zealand was reduced in 1999 after much public debate from 20 to 18, although there's much controversy over this measure, as statistics show teenage drinking to be on the increase. On-the-spot fines for under-age drinking have been introduced and are up to $2,000 for the offender and up to $10,000 for the establishment that sold him drink. Identity cards, such as a passport or driving licence, must be shown if requested.

Beer: The most popular drink in New Zealand is beer, which is usually sold in draught form and is similar in taste and strength to British bitter. There are two main breweries in the country, NZ Breweries and Dominion Breweries DB, which together also own the vast majority of drinking establishments and produce a range of beers and lagers. There are also a number of independent breweries and micro (tiny) breweries producing their own draught and bottled brands. Imported and locally brewed versions of foreign beers are available in larger hotels and trendier establishments. Beer is sold in a wide variety of measures which may vary with the city or region. Glasses are designed to hold metric quantities, although beer can also be ordered in imperial quantities, e.g. asking for a pint or half pint will get you around 500ml to 600ml or 250ml to 300ml respectively. The most common measures are a 'seven' (originally 7oz but now 200ml), a 'twelve' (originally 12oz but now 350ml), a 'handle' (500ml) and a jug (containing one or two litres). If in doubt, just ask for a 'small' or 'large' beer (in any case, in most places 'free pouring' is the norm and measures tend to be somewhat academic!).

Wine: New Zealand wine production has boomed in recent years, particularly since 1998, and there are now some 360 vineyards (called wineries) throughout the country, with over 12,000 hectares under vines. In 2000, over 60 million litres of wine were produced with a record export value of almost $170 million. Production and exports are expected to continue to increase over the next few years. The main wine producing area is Gisborne, and most vineyards are open to the public and usually offer free tastings to encourage visitors to buy a few cases. In recent years, vineyards have increased in popularity as places to enjoy a social drink and/or meal with friends. many having cafés and restaurants. Some also hold wine festivals, which are very popular, particularly when free samples are offered! Information about vineyards and wine festivals can be obtained via the Internet (🖳 www.winesofnz.com).

New Zealand wine has gained a first class international reputation for quality in the last decade or so and has even been described by one English wine expert as smelling like 'cat's pee on a gooseberry bush' (also the name of a local wine), which apparently is an accolade when applied to a sauvignon! The best New Zealand wines are white (experts say the country's climate is unsuited to red wine grapes) and made from the sauvignon and Chardonnay grapes, although New Zealand hopes to become a major force in the world production of pinot noir. You'll rarely find a bad New Zealand wine, although the poorer brands tend to be inflicted on the home market rather than be sent overseas to taint the reputation of New Zealand exports! New Zealand also produces (inevitably?) kiwi fruit wine, which supposedly has an acquired taste.

Foreign wines are also available in New Zealand, although they're significantly more expensive because of steep taxes – even those which make the relatively short journey from Australia. You can buy wine by the glass in hotels, although as they're invariably dominated by beer-swilling men, most offer only a poor selection. Domestic wine consumption has increased dramatically over the last five years and stands at 10.3 litres per capita per year, although this is still far behind beer.

Further information about New Zealand's wines can be obtained from the New Zealand Wine Institute (🖳 www.nzwine.com) and from the books *Cuisine Wine Annual* and *Classic Wines of New Zealand*.

Spirits: Spirits are available in most hotels, although the choice is usually limited. New Zealand's only indigenous spirit is kiwi fruit liqueur, which is similar to fruit liqueurs found in other countries. Imported Scotch whisky is expensive (around $30 to $60) and imported gin costs from $27 to $40 per bottle.

RESTAURANTS

New Zealand doesn't rank among the great gastronomic centres of the world as far as restaurant food is concerned, although both choice and quality has improved markedly in recent years. However, the majority of restaurants still follow the British meat-and-two-veg principle, often with a choice of lamb, lamb or lamb. Most towns also have a fish and chip shop, where the quality is usually excellent. Lovers of sponge and custard puddings and ice cream (New Zealand ice cream is excellent) will also be perfectly happy with the fare on offer at their local dining establishments. This isn't to say that foreign cuisine isn't available in New Zealand – most towns have at least one Chinese restaurant, although the food is of the westernised Chinese variety rather than authentic Chinese cuisine, and you can also find French, Italian, Thai, Mexican, Japanese and Indian food in the main cities.

If you're an enthusiastic epicure you will need to head for the main cities, where you will find excellent restaurants comparable with the best London or Paris has to offer. Auckland's Parnell district has a good choice of top restaurants with prices that are much lower than those in similar establishments abroad. However, outside the major cities there's a relative dearth of gastronomic excellence with the notable exception of fish and seafood restaurants, where fresh seafood is prepared and cooked imaginatively, often with a strong Maori influence.

The advantages of eating out in New Zealand include generous portions, friendly service and surprisingly low prices – you can enjoy an excellent three course meal for $50 including drinks.

Bring-Your-Own (BYO) Restaurants: BYO restaurants date back to the days when alcohol licences were hard to come by and restaurants without a licence allowed customers to bring their own wine or other drinks. In return for a small fee (corkage), which is limited by law and shouldn't be more than around 50¢, the waiter uncorked and served you with your own wine. Although licences are easier to come by nowadays, many restaurants choose not to become licensed in order to allow customers to choose their own drinks at the price they want to pay (or can afford). Some licensed restaurants also allow customers to bring their own drinks, although the policy on this is variable and you should make enquiries in advance, particularly if you're inviting guests to dinner. One drawback is that non-BYO restaurants can fix their own corkage fee and you may find yourself paying as much for 'uncorking' as you paid for your bottle of supermarket plonk!

Opening Hours: Restaurant opening hours reflect licensing hours, and as a result many restaurants don't open on Sundays (it's wise to check if you plan to eat in a particular place). Some restaurants that open on Sundays close on Mondays. Booking isn't usually necessary in New Zealand, but is recommended in the more fashionable places, particularly on Fridays and Saturdays.

Tipping: As in other areas of New Zealand life (see page 308), a no-tipping policy usually applies in restaurants (if only other countries would follow suit!). You won't be expected to tip and, should you try to, may be greeted with surprise and even embarrassment by your waiter. Neither is there any service charge. The menu price is the price you pay; no extra charges will be added to your bill and you won't be expected to add anything. However, in some tourist areas in recent years, tipping has become more widespread and not surprisingly, is well-received by the staff, although you should tip only excellent service.

Vegetarianism: New Zealanders used to have an unsympathetic attitude towards vegetarians, who were once thin on the ground. Not eating meat was considered almost unpatriotic in a country which earns millions of dollars from meat exports and where the number of sheep make lamb one of the cheapest and most frequently served dishes. However, this attitude has changed in recent years and at least one vegetarian option is now available at most restaurants. There are a number of vegetarian restaurants in the major cities, and 'fishetarians' can enjoy many excellent seafood restaurants. Consult the NZ Vegetarian website for further information (⌨ www.ivu.org/nzvs).

Smoking: Smoking in a restaurant (or indeed anywhere in public) is much less socially acceptable than in many other countries. All restaurants have a non-smoking area and many have banned it altogether.

Dress: Apart from a few pretentious places in Auckland, Wellington and Christchurch that insist on a jacket and tie, most restaurants don't impose dress restrictions, although you're unlikely to be admitted wearing shorts and a T-shirt. Most New Zealanders don't dress up to eat out, and smart casual dress is usually adequate even for the best restaurants. BYO restaurants (see above) are normally more casual than non-BYO establishments.

At Home: although New Zealanders eat many of the same meals as people in most other western countries, they may have a different emphasis. The traditional cooked 'English' breakfast of bacon and eggs is still eaten in some homes, although many families have adopted the modern fashion for cereal and fruit juices. Cooked lunches are less popular nowadays, many people opting for a quick snack instead. In most homes high tea or tea, eaten between 4 and 7pm, is the main meal of the day rather than dinner. One great 'British' tradition that lives on in New Zealand is that of Sunday lunch, usually consisting of roast lamb and two or three vegetables, which the family eat together. However, even this is gradually dying out, the traditional roast often being replaced by pasta dishes!

LIBRARIES

Almost every town in New Zealand has a local library. Many New Zealanders are avid readers, and the relatively high cost of books (there are few New Zealand publishers and most books are imported from Australia, the UK or the USA) makes the library a popular place to stock up on reading material. Library opening hours and the range of books stocked vary considerably with the size of the town. The larger libraries offer a range of material, including newspapers and periodicals, archives, book reservation services and photocopying. To join your local library you simply need to provide proof of your address, such as a utility bill or bank statement.

16.

SPORTS

New Zealand has the ideal climate and terrain for a wide range of sports, including world class skiing and surfing, both of which you can do on the same day – although why anyone would want to is another matter. Most New Zealanders are passionate about sport, which serves as a symbol of national pride, and New Zealand sportsmen and women are world renowned in a number of sports, notably rugby and sailing. The New Zealand government recently confirmed the country's sport and health-conscious image by appointing a Sports, Leisure and Fitness Minister and making the provision of access to sport for all an official government policy. A recent survey found that over 50 per cent of the adult population belong to a sports or health club, although the New Zealander's love of exercise hasn't had much impact on the rate of heart disease, which kills up to 8,000 people a year. The doctrine that sport is very much for 'the people' is illustrated by the fact that the majority of sports in New Zealand are played at amateur level with little professional sport. The main exception is rugby, which is primarily a professional game at the top level and one of the few sports where professional athletes in New Zealand can earn telephone-number salaries, such as are common in other countries.

While team sports are popular, there's also a large following for many solo sports, particularly those where competitors can pit their wits against the natural elements, such as climbing, rafting and surfing. Despite the dominance of traditional sports such as rugby, New Zealand is by no means old-fashioned in the field of sporting endeavour and many of the latest 'daredevil' sports are practised in New Zealand, including bungee jumping and jet-skiing, both of which are claimed to be New Zealand inventions.

There are two national organisations, both government run, that promote sport in New Zealand. Sport NZ provides a wealth of information regarding sports in general, club information and resources (💻 www.sportnz.co.nz). The Hillary Commission (named after Sir Edmund Hillary, the Kiwis' top national hero) was formed in 1998 and aims to enable New Zealanders of all ability levels and ages to participate in sports activities. The Commission funds sports clubs and associations around the country and is itself funded almost totally by lottery earnings. The Commission can be contacted on PO Box 2251, Wellington (☎ 04-472 8058, 💻 www.hillary sport.org.nz). The websites of both the above organisations are excellent sources of information about sport and sports clubs in New Zealand.

RUGBY

Rugby is New Zealand's national sport (and obsession) and in the past even the prime minister has become embroiled in the selection of the national rugby (union) team, the All Blacks. While many New Zealanders are interested in playing and watching rugby, many more are supporters simply because the success of the national team brings New Zealand such fame and prestige around the world. Interest in rugby in New Zealand fell in the '70s and '80s, when the national team maintained links with apartheid South Africa, but following the demise of apartheid, its popularity and match attendances soared, and New Zealand shuts down to watch a rugby test match. Top players such as Lomu, Mehrtens and Umaga are as revered in New Zealand as top soccer players are in other countries. Rugby professionals have the opportunity to earn more through rugby than almost any other profession and an All Black's annual income can be in the region of $500,000 to $700,000, although this is small-fry compared to what they can earn overseas and several top New Zealand players are now in overseas teams.

The rugby season traditionally lasts from May until September, during which clubs play both rugby union and rugby league at all levels, including international, regional, representative, city and local. While primarily a men's game, New Zealand also has a small but enthusiastically supported women's rugby movement and the national team won the world cup in 1998. New Zealand teams play in a huge variety of league and cup competitions, with the top divisions in both codes (the Super 12 and Super League) including teams from outside New Zealand. The South African national team, the Springboks (or 'Boks') are the All Blacks' traditional arch enemy and the Tri-Nations tournament (consisting of New Zealand, South Africa and the Australian 'Wallabies' team) is regarded as one of the country's major sporting events. The All Blacks are considered by many to be the world's best rugby team and statistically have won most matches. Although rugby largely transcends racial groups, there's also a national Maori side at league level. Tickets to top rugby matches usually cost from $65 to $120.

Anyone with a keen interest in rugby will find they are warmly welcomed by local clubs and even those with absolutely no interest will find that they are unable to escape the country's passion for their national sport. Success for the All Blacks results in almost non-stop coverage of the sport and much merriment and rejoicing, while failure may result in any mention of rugby being unofficially purged from the media as if the sport had been 'disinvented' overnight. Expatriates report that an air of misery descends on the country following an All Blacks defeat, with sulking and moodiness lasting for several days (the country must have been particularly downcast in 1999 when New Zealand lost in the world cup semi-finals!). Information about rugby in New Zealand both at national and international level can be found on the new NZ rugby portal (⌨ www.nzrl.co.nz).

Despite the game's supposedly gentlemanly image, rugby can be a dangerous business in New Zealand. Post-match violence and drunkenness (as is sometimes associated with soccer in other countries) occurs occasionally and being a rugby referee isn't without its risks, with the rate of attacks on referees during and after matches increasing amid demands for greater protection and strike threats from referees.

Touch rugby is a lighter version of 'real' rugby and is extremely popular throughout the country. The game is played on a football pitch and the aim is to score a touchdown by passing the ball backwards and forwards to your team mates. Touch rugby teams must include at least two women or children and the game is supposed to be non-contact. Games are essentially social occasions with 'compulsory' beer and BBQ afterwards. Not only is the game good fun, but it's an excellent way to meet people and you don't have to be a sports fanatic to join in (⌨ www.touchnz.co.nz).

FOOTBALL

Football is played in New Zealand, where it's usually known as soccer (or footie), to differentiate it from rugby football, which most New Zealanders consider 'proper' football. In New Zealand the popularity of soccer lags way behind rugby and its cause hasn't been helped by some schools actually banning it in the past in the fear that pupils would be tempted away from the 'superior' game. Interest in soccer boomed some years ago when the New Zealand national team, the All Whites, qualified for the World Cup. However, in recent times, the New Zealand team has been notably unsuccessful, particularly against the Australian national team, a country not noted for its prowess at soccer. The All Whites' ultimate aim is to reach the World Cup final, although this may not be for a while, as New Zealand failed even to qualify for the 2002 World Cup!

National, northern, central and southern soccer leagues operate in New Zealand, where soccer is played both in summer and winter, although the 'official' soccer season runs from May to September. New Zealand soccer 'stars' are nonentities compared with the cult status of top rugby players and the game is light years away from the standard seen in top European leagues such as the Italian *Serie A* or the English Premiership. Local clubs occasionally sign foreign players and the signing of a British player from a second or third division side makes headline news in New Zealand. Interest is, however, growing at the amateur level and there are local leagues in most areas. A combined New Zealand team has been formed to play in the Australian soccer league and it's hoped this will increase the competitiveness and general standard of soccer in New Zealand.

CRICKET

Cricket is a national passion in New Zealand, as it is in many other countries that derive their national heritage from the UK. There's wide support for the national team and it's popular among participants and spectators at all levels. International one-day series matches between New Zealand and England attract crowds of 25,000 at Christchurch's floodlit Lancaster Park Stadium. Top cricket players are held in as high a regard as rugby stars, although support for cricket has declined in recent years and most young people have a preference for rugby. However, cricket has recently seen a revival mainly thanks to players like Vettori and Martin whose youth and talent (and good looks) appeal greatly to young New Zealanders. The national cricket team, known as the Black Caps, has a good international reputation, although in recent years wins have been few and far between. However, they came close to beating the Australians in the 2001 winter series and experts claim that this is the start of a new winning era! The cricket season runs from November to April and tickets to major international matches cost from $10 to $20. There's also a small but significant women's cricket movement in New Zealand and the national team's matches are followed keenly.

TREKKING

Trekking (or tramping) is New Zealand's name for hiking, which is an institution enjoyed by New Zealanders of all ages, from toddlers to pensioners. Trekking comprises anything from a leisurely afternoon walk to an endurance-testing, near-military route march lasting several days or weeks. The advantage of trekking is that you can make it as easy or as demanding as you wish, and there are plenty of places to trek, even close to major cities. A vast amount of New Zealand is divided into parks (e.g. national, forest and maritime parks) and there's always somewhere new to explore, which in the more remote areas includes many breathtaking spots that are accessible only on foot.

Despite its allusion to wilderness ways, trekking is highly organised in New Zealand and the whole country is criss-crossed with numerous tracks, some of which are internationally famous and attract hikers from around the world. These are known as the Great Walks and can be quite crowded, especially in the summer. The more popular tracks are well signposted (look for 'W' signs) and maintained and often radiate from the city suburbs. The more demanding tracks may not be signposted but are marked on trekking maps. Some of the longer tracks are legendary, including South Island's Routeburn (usually a three day trek through rain forests, mountains and alpine passes), Milford (four days), Kepler (four to five days), Greenstone (two to three days), Hollyford (five to six days), Abel Tasman (three to four days), Heaphy (four to five days) and North Island's Whirinaki Track (three to four days). Some tracks, such as the Abel Tasman, can be walked year round, while others such as the Routeburn are at higher altitudes and may be impassable in winter. October to April is unofficially regarded as the trekking season and some of the most popular routes can be quite congested in January and February.

As well as the well-known tracks there are numerous less-popular tracks, which are just as enjoyable and spectacular in their own right. The Department of Conservation (DOC) can provide the best information and advice about tracks. Each of the 34 national, forest and marine parks has its own DOC headquarters where you can obtain information about local tracks. DOC also runs visitor centres and publishes numerous useful pamphlets (🖳 www.doc.govt.nz).

Although many trekkers (or should they be called trekkies?) take to the tracks independently, it's possible to take a trekking package holiday, which is ideal for the slightly less adventurous. Companies specialising in trekking holidays provide an experienced guide and accommodation in luxury lodges, mountain huts or tent camps, with hot showers and meals. The cost of guided treks ranges from $500 to $950 for a five-day trek (one such operator is Routeburn Walk, PO Box 568, Queenstown, ☎ 03-442 8200, ✉ routeburn@xtra.co.nz). If you don't wish to take a full package tour, you can hire an experienced local guide to show you a route and provide commentary on the flora and fauna.

When trekking independently you need to carry your own food and equipment (take plenty of warm clothing even in summer). Accommodation can be found in Department of Conservation huts (there are nearly 950 of them!) situated along tracks, which may be free or require a modest fee (e.g. between $4 and $35 per night depending on the category) where bunks, cooking facilities and clean water are provided. There's no charge for children under 11. Older children are charged half-price if they have a 'youth ticket'. DOC also sells an annual huts pass, although this isn't valid for huts on the Great Walks. Accommodation in DOC huts is basic and is provided on a first-come, first-served basis. Some independent trekkers prefer to take tents, which can usually be pitched near huts, but cannot usually be pitched alongside tracks in order to protect the unique character of treks.

Note that you must pre-book to walk the Great Routes and obtain a special Great Walks Pass, even when walking independently. The Pass is sold at DOC offices and national park offices. The Milford, Routeburn and Abel Tasman Tracks have a different booking system and passes can be obtained by e-mail from DOC (✉ great walksbooking@doc.govt.nz).

The most popular trekking season is the summer, when many of the Great Walks may be disappointingly crowded, although it's relatively easy to find a quieter, lesser known track. The best time of year to trek as far as the weather goes, is from

November to March/April. You should avoid trekking in the winter particularly in South Island where weather conditions can be severe on the high-altitude walks and some are closed in winter because of avalanche danger. However, whatever the season you should always check the weather forecast and conditions before setting out, as a fine sunny day can turn into a wet and foggy one very quickly. It's worth remembering that although thousands of people trek safely every year in New Zealand, several people die each year in the mountains.

As well as the comprehensive DOC guides and leaflets, there are numerous trekking guides available in New Zealand, including Lonely Planet's *Tramping in New Zealand*, the definitive book on the subject, *New Zealand's Top Ten Tracks* by Mark Pickering, which describes many of the Great Walks and *Wild Walks – North Island* and *Wild Walks – South Island*, both of which describe lesser-known tracks.

General Information

The following notes may help you survive a tramp in the mountains:

- If you're going to take up hiking seriously, then a good pair of walking shoes or boots is mandatory (available from sports and trekking shops). Always wear proper walking shoes or boots where the terrain is rough. Unfortunately, walking boots are usually uncomfortable or hurt your feet after a few hours (if they don't hurt, it isn't doing you any good). Wearing two pairs of socks can help prevent blisters. Break in a new pair of boots on some *gentle* hikes before setting out on a marathon hike around the country.

- Don't over-exert yourself, particularly at high altitudes where the air is thinner. Mountain sickness usually occurs only above 4,000 metres, but can also happen at lower altitudes. A few words of warning for those who aren't particularly fit: **take it easy and set a slow pace.** It's easy to over-exert yourself and underestimate the duration or degree of difficulty of a hike. Start slowly and build up to those weekend marathons. If the most exercise you usually get is walking to the pub and crawling back, you can use chair-lifts and cable-cars to get to high altitudes in some areas.

- **Don't attempt a major hike alone.** Notify someone about your route, destination and estimated time of return. It's a good idea to inform the nearest DOC office of your intentions and ask for their advice before you set out. Check the conditions along your route and the times of any public transport connections (set out early to avoid missing the last bus). Take into account the time required for both ascents and descents. If you're unable to return by the time expected, let somebody know. If you realise that you're unable to reach your destination, for example due to tiredness or bad weather, turn back in good time or take a shorter route. If you get caught in a heavy storm, descend as quickly as possible or seek protection, e.g. in a hut.

- Check the weather forecast, usually available from the local tourist office. Generally, the higher the altitude, the more unpredictable the weather.

- Hiking, even in lowland areas, can be dangerous, so don't take any unnecessary risks. There are enough natural hazards, including bad weather, rock-falls, avalanches, rough terrain, snow and ice, and wet grass, without adding to them.

- Don't walk on closed tracks at any time (they are signposted). This is particularly important in the spring, when there is a danger of avalanches or rock-falls and when tracks may be closed due to forestry work. If you're in doubt about a particular route, ask in advance at the local tourist office.

- Wear loose fitting clothes and not, for example, tight jeans, which can become uncomfortable when you get warmed up. Shorts (short pants to Americans) are excellent in hot weather. Light cotton trousers are comfortable unless it's cold. You can wear your shorts underneath your trousers and remove your trousers when you've warmed up.

- Take a warm pullover, gloves (in winter) and a raincoat or cape. Mountain weather can change suddenly, and even in summer it's sometimes cold at high altitudes. A first-aid kit (for cuts and grazes), compass, identification, maps, small torch and a pocket knife may also come in handy. A pair of binoculars is useful for spotting wildlife. Take a rucksack to carry your survival rations. A 35 to 40-litre capacity rucksack is best for day trips or a 65-litre capacity for longer hikes.

- Take sun protection, e.g. a hat, sunglasses and sun barrier cream, as you will burn more easily at high altitudes (the ozone layer is thin in New Zealand and the sun can be very strong). Use a total sunblock cream on your lips, nose and eyelids, and take a scarf or handkerchief to protect your neck. You may also need to protect yourself against ticks and mosquitoes in some areas.

- Take water to prevent dehydration. This is also much appreciated when you discover that the restaurant or hotel that was 'just around the corner' is still miles away because you took the wrong turning or misread the map.

- Don't take young children on difficult hikes unless you enjoy carrying them. Impress upon children the importance of not wandering off on their own. If you lose anyone, particularly children, seek help as soon as possible and before nightfall. It's wise to equip children with a loud whistle and some warm clothing, in case they get lost.

- Hikers are asked to observe the following general rules:
  - Take care not to damage trees, flowers and bushes.
  - Leave animals in peace (e.g. dogs mustn't be allowed to disturb farm animals).
  - Be careful with fire and never start a fire in a forbidden area.
  - Watch where you walk and keep to paths.
  - Keep streams and lakes pure.
  - Don't litter the countryside.
  - Think of others.
  - Close gates after use.

FISHING

Fishing, whether in the sea, rivers, streams or lakes, is the most popular participation sport in New Zealand and one of the few that doesn't involve a great deal of exertion (unless you're fighting a 100kg marlin). Salmon and trout (weighing up to 5kg) are plentiful in the country's lakes and rivers and are the most popular freshwater catches.

There are two species of salmon in New Zealand: landlocked quinnats (which spawn near the sources of the country's main rivers), that can weigh up to 11kg and sea-run quinnats (which emerge from the sea to spawn in river estuaries), that rarely exceed 1kg. The fishing season varies depending on the area and the catch and usually starts around the 1st October and finishes some time between the 30th April and the 30th June.

Fishing tackle can be imported into New Zealand without restriction (and can be purchased in the USA via the Internet at huge savings over local prices), although it's wise not to import fishing flies, as they must be fumigated before passing through customs (at your expense), which can be frustrating bearing in mind their relatively small value. All anglers require a fishing licence which can be purchased from tackle and sports shops, although Maoris claim they have the right (enshrined in the Treaty of Waitangi) to fish without a licence and this has occasionally been upheld by the courts. Note that you must carry the licence with you at all times when fishing and obey the rules and regulations (there are huge fines for not doing so!). The cost of a fishing licence is $12 per day, $26 per week, $36 per month or $55 for a whole season. The country is officially divided into 26 fishing regions, where it's supervised by conservation officers or countryside rangers. It's possible to hire a local guide (ask for a quotation first) to find the best local fishing spots. The New Zealand Professional Fishing Guides Association, PO Box 16, Motu, Gisborne (⌨ www.flyfishing.net.nz) can also provide information and assistance. There are several good books about fishing in New Zealand including the *North Island Fishing Guide* and the *South Island Fishing Guide* by John Kent.

New Zealand's clear coastal waters are ideal for sea fishing; deep-sea fishing is also popular, although it's naturally more expensive, as it requires the purchase or hire of a boat and special equipment (for information contact the Game Fishing Charter Association, PO Box 263, Paihia). The best location for deep sea fishing is the north-east of the North Island, while other good spots include the Bay of Islands around Russel, Mercury Bay, Tutukaka near Whangari, Tauranga and Whakatane. Some keen fishermen even venture as far as the Chatham Islands, 850km (528mi) east of New Zealand. Boats and tackle can be hired throughout New Zealand and no licence is needed for game or deep sea fishing. Popular catches include mako, thresher and hammerhead shark, blue, black and striped marlin, kingfish, and tuna (which is also the Maori word for eel).

WATER-SPORTS

New Zealand is a mecca for water-sports, the most popular of which are outlined below. All instructors and operators of organised water-sports in New Zealand must comply with Ministry of Transport safety codes, but it's wise to check that they do before booking.

Jet-skiing: New Zealand invented jet-skiing (jet-boating) and it's enjoyed by people of all ages. A jet-ski (or jet-boat) is a propeller-less, LPG-powered craft which can reach up to 70kph (43mph), turn through 360 degrees within its own length and plane over just a few inches of water. Jet-skiing is usually done in coastal waters and on lakes, although they can also negotiate shallow river gorges that are inaccessible to most other craft. The most popular areas for jet-skiing pleasure rides are Waimakariri near Christchurch, the Buller and Makaroa regions, the Rangitaiki River gorges, and the Wanganui and Waikato River below the Huka Falls. Jet-skis can be hired in many beach resorts and on some inland lakes. There are restrictions on the use of jet-skis in most resorts. **However, unless you're an experienced rider, it's wise to steer well clear of jet-skis, which are deadly in the wrong hands (both to riders and to anyone who comes into contact with them).**

Kayaking: Kayaking is broadly similar to canoeing and is a popular New Zealand water-sport, particularly among the less well-off water-sports' enthusiasts. Kayaking is enjoyed in coastal waters and on lakes and rivers, and can range from a sedate paddle along a lakeside to negotiating the torrents of a raging river gorge. Kayaks and safety equipment (a helmet should always be worn) can be bought or hired in most popular kayaking areas. Further information can be obtained from the New Zealand Canoeing Association (NZCA), PO Box 284, Wellington (☎ 04-560 3590, 🖳 www.rivers.org.nz).

Rafting: Rafting is a slightly more challenging alternative to kayaking, entailing the navigation of often hostile white-water in a large inflatable raft accommodating four to eight people, and is an extremely popular sport in New Zealand. The most popular (and safe) way to raft is to take part in an organised trip, which includes a qualified guide and tuition. Trips usually last from two to five days and food and camping equipment is included. Trips cost between $75 and $130 per person per day. Rafting is also a popular winter sport, when a wetsuit is considered essential. Rivers are graded on a scale I (gentle) to VI (unraftable); the best rivers for rafting are generally considered to be the Shotover, Kawarau and Rangitata, all in South Island. Bear in mind that rafting is a high risk sport.

Rowing: New Zealanders are enthusiastic rowers, and there are plenty of lakes and rivers on which to practise this sport in all its guises, including both leisure and competitive rowing. The country also fields a team in dragon boat racing, which is particularly popular in south-east Asia.

Sailing: Sailing is one of New Zealand's favourite sports (the country boasts the world's highest per capital boat ownership) and Auckland has even gone so far as to dub itself the 'City of Sails' (like Wellington it has a reputation for being windy). New Zealand secured an impressive and unexpected victory in the 1995 America's Cup and successfully defended the title in the Hauraki Gulf in 2000. Yacht harbours are found throughout the country, the most popular of which include the Bay of Islands, Hauraki Gulf and the Marlborough Sounds. More adventurous yachtsmen venture to the Pacific islands, which, with their idyllic climate and unspoilt beauty, make ideal yachting destinations (provided you discount nuclear testing by the French, which has understandably made France unpopular with New Zealanders).

Sailing isn't necessarily a pursuit just for the wealthy (unless you yearn to own an ocean-going yacht), as there are numerous opportunities to hire a boat and spend some time on the ocean wave or pottering around the coastline. A variety of boats are available for 'bare-boating', where a hire company provides the yacht and sailing equipment and you provide the crew and provisions. For less intrepid sailors, it's possible to hire a professionally crewed yacht, where the crew also wait on you. There are sailing clubs in most areas, details of which can be obtained from Yachting NZ, PO Box 33-789, Takapuna, Auckland (☎ 09-488 9325).

Scuba Diving & Snorkelling: New Zealand is a mecca for scuba divers and snorkellers, and the country's waters are full of exotic fish and plant life. Jacques Cousteau rated New Zealand's waters as one of the top ten diving destinations in the world. Popular diving spots include the Poor Knights Islands near Whangerei (where the waters are particularly clear), the South Island fjords (famous for their unusual red and black coral) and the kelp forests off Stewart Island (with their huge paua shell fish). The main diving season is from February to June, although in the warmer, more sheltered waters off the Bay of Islands near Auckland it's possible to dive year round. The former Greenpeace flagship 'Rainbow Warrior' (sunk by French secret service agents in an operation against anti-nuclear protestors) has been scuttled in this area to provide a haven for sea life.

Along the coast there are numerous dive stores offering tuition, equipment rental, the filling of air bottles, and information on dive locations and organised trips. Divers need a Professional Association of Diving Instructors (PADI) certificate, and tuition is offered in most diving areas in New Zealand. Always learn with a qualified and reputable outfit and avoid 'cowboy' operators. Further information can be obtained from the New Zealand Underwater Association (NZUA), PO Box 875, Auckland (☎ 09-623 3252, ⌨ www.nzunderwater.org.nz). The NZUA publishes a bi-monthly magazine, *Dive NZ*.

Swimming: Most New Zealanders are taught to swim at an early age, and swimming is a popular leisure and competitive sport. Despite the country's abundance of sea, rivers and lakes, it isn't necessary to head for the great outdoors if you're a keen swimmer. Most towns have at least one public indoor swimming pool, some of which are equipped with waterchutes, wave machines and a range of other facilities, such as saunas and gymnasia. In several places in New Zealand it's possible to swim with dolphins, which, apart from the thrill, is claimed to have valuable therapeutic powers. 'Dolphin swimming' is possible (subject to the dolphins being able to fit you into their schedule) in the Bay of Islands, Whakatane and Kaikoura in South Island.

On surfing beaches, swimmers must stay within the swimming area defined by flags, which may be hoisted from around 6am until 6 or 7pm in summer. They're placed to indicate the safest swimming area in the prevailing conditions and also indicate the area under closest scrutiny by lifesavers. **Swimmers are urged by lifesaving associations never to swim outside patrolled areas (most beach drownings are on unpatrolled beaches).** If you get into trouble while swimming off a beach manned with lifesavers, you should raise one arm in the air, which will alert the lifesavers. Take care not to venture too far out, as it isn't uncommon for swimmers to be swept out to sea. Note that there's a danger of stinging jellyfish and sharks in some waters, although your chance of encountering either of these on patrolled beaches is small.

Surfing: New Zealanders don't quite share the passion for surfing that their Australian neighbours have, although it's a popular pursuit. Many coastal areas have a surf lifesaving club (SLSC) for children and adults, where surfing, swimming and surf rescue combine as a sport, leisure pursuit and public service (i.e. lifesavers on beaches and at swimming pools). The best surfing areas are those around Auckland and Dunedin. Windsurfing and river surfing are also popular in New Zealand. Information can be obtained from Surfing NZ, PO Box 13-289, Johnsonville (☎ 04-479 0468, ✉ surfingnz@xtra.co.nz).

SKIING

Few people associate New Zealand with snow, but the first commercial ski slopes opened in 1947 and the country is internationally recognised as a top skiing destination. The New Zealand ski season extends throughout the European and North

American summer, beginning in June and ending in November, and professional skiers and ski bums from the northern hemisphere often ski and train in New Zealand out of season.

There are 12 commercial skiing areas, in both North and South Islands, all of which can be reached by road. All skiing areas have ski lifts, ski schools and equipment rental facilities, and offer a choice of accommodation from guest houses to good quality hotels. Few skiing areas have accommodation virtually on-piste, as is common in Europe, and a short journey is usually necessary to reach the slopes. A number of package tour operators offer skiing package holidays. If you're travelling independently, lift passes cost from $30 to $60 per day, the rental of skis, boots and poles from $30 per day, and lessons from $30 for a half-day group class. Nordic (cross-country) skiing is also possible in New Zealand, where there's one Nordic skiing area and 12 club fields (open to the public) with more basic facilities.

Helicopter and glacier-skiing are increasing in popularity in South Island, although both are only for the experienced and are expensive sports. Several operators offer off-piste heli-skiing in the southern Alps and you can glacier-ski the Tasman Glacier, although this will cost you around $700! An unusual feature of New Zealand skiing is that a range of facilities not usually associated with skiing are also offered in (or near) ski resorts, including jet-skiing, rafting, canoeing, trekking and bungee-jumping. These are often available in the valleys, which are usually free of snow.

North Island: Whakapapa and Turoa are North Island's main skiing areas, situated on Mount Ruapehu (an active volcano) around four hours by road from Auckland. They attract over 400,000 visitors a year and the high altitude (2,800m) means that skiing is possible well into November.

South Island: One of the most popular ski resorts in South Island is Mount Hutt, which is around an hour by road from Christchurch. Its location and advanced snow-making system means that it's often the first resort to open and the last to close. It's popular with all-round sports fans, as its proximity to Christchurch makes it possible to surf in the morning and ski in the afternoon. Other resorts include Wanaka, located in New Zealand's 'Alpine' zone five hours from Christchurch. It features slopes suitable for beginners and for experts, plus facilities for hell-skiing. The powder snow and demanding terrain has also made the area popular with snowboarders in the last few years. Wanaka is the only ski resort in New Zealand where it's possible to find accommodation on the mountain. Queenstown has the best all-round facilities in addition to two world class ski areas, the Remarkables and Coronet Peak, both within 30 minutes' drive from the town. Queenstown boasts over 100 restaurants, night-clubs, cafes and bars, several big hotels and good shopping. It's also possible to enjoy trout fishing or go wine tasting in the nearby vineyards.

Information: The free *NZ Ski and Snowboard Guide* published annually by Brown Bear offers a wealth of useful information and there's also a Snow Phone operating during the skiing season (☎ 0900-344 444) offering recorded messages on conditions. Two useful websites are 🖳 www.snow.co.nz and 🖳 www.nzski.com.

Skier's Highway Code

As ski slopes become more crowded, the possibility of colliding with a fellow skier has increased dramatically. Happily, the result of most clashes is just a few bruises and dented pride; nevertheless, the danger of serious injury is ever present. You cannot always protect yourself from the lunatic fringe, e.g. the crazy novice who skis way beyond his limits and the equally loony 'expert' who skis at reckless speeds with a total disregard for others. The following guidelines from the International Ski Federation's (FIS) Code of Conduct for skiers may, however, help you avoid an accident:

- **Respect for others:** A skier must behave in such a way that he neither endangers nor prejudices others.
- **Control of speed and skiing:** A skier must adapt his speed and way of skiing to his ability and to the prevailing conditions of terrain and weather.
- **Control of direction:** A skier coming from above, whose dominant position allows him a choice of paths, must take a direction which assures the safety of a skier below.
- **Overtaking:** A skier should always leave a wide enough margin for the overtaken skier to make his turn. (As when motoring, the most dangerous skiing manoeuvre is overtaking.)
- **Crossing the piste:** A skier entering or crossing a piste must look up and down to make sure that he can do so without danger to himself or to others. The same applies after stopping.
- **Stopping on the piste:** Unless absolutely necessary, a skier must avoid making a stop on the piste, particularly in narrow passages or where visibility is restricted. If a skier falls, he must clear the piste as soon as possible.
- **Climbing:** A climbing skier must keep to the side of the piste or, in bad visibility, keep off the piste altogether. The same goes for a skier descending on foot.

There's no foolproof way to avoid an accident (apart from avoiding skiing altogether). Obey the FIS code and make sure that you're well insured for both accidents and private liability (see **Chapter 13**).

CYCLING

Cycle touring is a popular sport and pastime in New Zealand, although it's some way behind countries such as France. While it's true that much of the terrain is mountainous or hilly, roads are generally well surfaced and largely traffic free. The hilly terrain is a boon for mountain biking, which is also popular. Mountain bikes may not be ridden in New Zealand's national parks, although their growing popularity has led the authorities to reconsider and they may be permitted in some parks in the future. Helmets must always be worn when cycling in New Zealand.

It's hardly worth taking your own bicycle to New Zealand, where a wide range of new and used bikes are available at reasonable prices. It's also possible to hire touring cycles, mountain bikes and even tandems in many places. Organised cycling package holidays are popular, and in some areas (such as Mount Ruapehu on the Otago Peninsula) there are shuttle bus services which take you to the top of the mountains or extinct volcanoes, thus allowing you to experience the pleasure of the downhill descent without the pain of the uphill journey.

One contradiction to New Zealand's otherwise cyclist-friendly culture is that cycles cannot be taken on most buses or trains. Long-distance coaches accept bikes (for a fee of $10), but usually only if you remove the pedals and wrap the chain (e.g.

in newspaper) – see **Chapter 10**. Note also that, despite New Zealand's relatively low crime rate, the theft of bicycles is high and care should be taken to secure your bike when it isn't in use, particularly if it's an expensive model.

Useful books on cycling include the **Pedallers' Paradise** series and Lonely Planet's guide **Cycling NZ**. Further information can be obtained from Cycling NZ, PO Box 1057, Wellington (☎ 04-471 1100, ▣ www.cycling.org.nz) and from the NZ Mountain Bike Association, PO Box 371, Taupo (☎ 07-378 952).

GOLF

New Zealand is a relatively new player in the golf world, although several of its courses have obtained international recognition. There are, in fact, over 400 golf courses in the country, of which around 70 have opened in the last ten years (it's said that nowhere in New Zealand is more than 50km/31mi from a course). Courses are relatively uncrowded, which makes them increasingly popular with Japanese golfers who, coming from such a densely populated land, are unaccustomed to the choice and space of New Zealand's golf courses. An added attraction for most golfers (certainly those of more modest means) is the relatively liberal attitude of most golf clubs, which, with the exception of a few top clubs, don't have long waiting lists or high membership fees. The vast majority of clubs also welcome non-members, a round costing from $25 to $30. The bigger clubs have resident professionals, clubs, trolleys (known as trundlers) and motorised buggies for hire, while smaller clubs offer few facilities – you may even be expected to leave your green fees in an honesty box.

The New Zealand Tourism Board can provide information about golf in New Zealand or you can contact the NZ Golf Association, PO Box 11-842, Wellington (☎ 04-385 4330, ▣ ww.nzga.co.nz). An interesting book is **50 Top New Zealand Golf Courses** by Rex Gould.

CLIMBING & MOUNTAINEERING

New Zealand's greatest sporting hero is Sir Edmund Hillary, one of the first two people to conquer Everest, and the country is home to some of the highest peaks in the southern hemisphere, offering challenges for even the most experienced mountaineers. Most mountaineers head for the Southern Alps, where it's usual to hire a guide or take advice from a local Alpine club, of which there are several. Rock climbing is also popular in New Zealand. In North Island, popular climbing areas include the Mount Eden Quarry near Auckland, Whanganui Bay and Motuoapa near Lake Taupo. The Wharepape rock climbing field near Te Awamutu offers over 40 different climbs suitable for advanced climbers and beginners. In the South Island, Port Hills near Christchurch and Castle Hill are popular climbing spots. Tuition and equipment (for sale and hire) is available in climbing areas.

Note that a number of climbers are killed annually in New Zealand, many of whom are inexperienced and reckless, and others owe their survival to rescuers who risk their own lives to rescue them. **It's extremely foolish, not to mention highly dangerous, to venture into the hills without an experienced guide, proper preparation, excellent physical condition, sufficient training, and the appropriate equipment and supplies.**

Useful addresses for mountaineers and climbers include the Federated Mountain Clubs of New Zealand Inc., PO Box 1604, Wellington (☎ 04-233 8244, ▄ www.fmc. org.nz), the New Zealand Alpine Club, PO Box 786, Christchurch (☎ 03-377 7595, ▄ www.alpineclub.org.nz) and the NZ Mountain Guides Association Inc., PO Box 10, Mount Cook (☎ 03-435 1814, ▄ www.nzmga.co.nz). Other useful websites for climbers and mountaineers are ▄ www.climb.co.nz, which includes information about equipment, mountain safety and weather conditions, and ▄ nzalpine.org.nz.

ADVENTURE SPORTS

Although New Zealand may have a rather staid reputation (undeservedly) in certain areas, this certainly isn't true when it comes to adventure sports. The New Zealanders' passion for dangerous sports, which often involve throwing yourself from great heights or challenging the forces of nature, is virtually unparalleled. Sporting daredevils certainly need never be short of challenges in New Zealand, where ever more risky adventure sports are continually being invented by thrill-seeking (or should it be suicidal?) New Zealanders. The book *Extreme* NZ by Alison Dench advertises itself as a 'thrill seekers' guide' and a useful website is ▄ www. adventurenet.co.nz which includes an online adventure magazine.

Bungee Jumping: Bungee (or bungy) jumping (entrusting your life to an elasticated rope) can be experienced at a number of locations throughout the country, and New Zealanders claim to be responsible for inventing the 'sport'. The home of bungee jumping is Queenstown, where you can jump from the Kawarau River Bridge (43m) or the Skippers Bridge (71m). If those aren't high enough, you can try jumping from the 102m Pipeline or from a helicopter (but preferably not when coming in to land!).

Caving & Cave Rafting: Caving is a popular sport and there are numerous clubs. However, New Zealanders have also invented cave rafting, whereby intrepid cavers float through underground cave systems on large inner tubes. Cave rafting is available at Waitomo (North Island) and Wesport and Greymouth (South Island).

Flightseeing: When New Zealanders aren't scrambling over their country's terrain or wading through its water, they enjoy nothing more than taking to the air and admiring it from afar, a pursuit which has been dubbed flightseeing. You can take a trip (or learn to fly) in a skiplane or floatplane, a helicopter, a vintage aircraft or even a hot air balloon (which is popular in Auckland, Christchurch, Hamilton and Rotorua).

Glacier Walking: A walk along a glacier is one way to appreciate one of the most incredible feats of nature. The Fox, Franz Josef and Tasman Glaciers in the Southern Alps are open to walkers, although it's best to join a guided tour if you aren't an experienced mountaineer.

Parachuting & Sky-Diving: Both solo and tandem parachuting and sky-diving are available in New Zealand, where there are centres near Auckland, Greymouth, Mount Hutt, Napier, Nelson, Queenstown and Taup.

Paragliding: Paragliding (or parapenting) is a combination of hang-gliding and parachuting. It's available in Queenstown and Wanaka, where it's also possible to try tandem paragliding (paragliding attached to an instructor) if you don't have the time or inclination to undergo training.

Rap Jumping: Rap jumping is another New Zealand invention and much like abseiling, which is common in most countries, except that it involves descending a cliff face head first rather than feet first. The Bay of Islands, Wanaka and Queenstown are popular rap jumping areas, where instructors are available to initiate newcomers into the sport.

OTHER SPORTS

The following is a selection of other popular sports in New Zealand:

Baseball: Baseball has been popular for many years in New Zealand, where it's mostly played at amateur level.

Basketball: Basketball is growing in popularity in New Zealand, where it's played enthusiastically in schools. There's also a national basketball league, the season commencing in April and finishing around October. The national basketball team is named the Tall Blacks, a tongue-in-cheek pun on the name of the national rugby team.

Bowls: Bowls is a sport enjoyed mainly, but not exclusively, by older people in New Zealand. There are outdoor bowling greens in most towns and also indoor bowling greens in some areas which can be used year round. Bowling clubs often serve tea and cucumber sandwiches in the British tradition, which tells you something about the kind of members they tend to attract.

Hockey: Hockey is played to a high standard in New Zealand by both men and women, although it loses out to more popular sports in terms of media coverage. There are both club and national teams, and the New Zealand women's team has been particularly successful in recent years.

Horse Riding: New Zealand has a world-wide reputation for breeding high quality bloodstock, and horses still have a working role on many farms, where they remain the best means of crossing the often rough terrain. Although competitive riding is common in New Zealand, the most popular form of riding is 'horse trekking', which involves spending anything from a day to a week or more riding across the country's farmland, forests, hills and beaches. Stables are found in all areas, where it's possible to hire a horse and tack (or stable your own horse) and join an organised trip. A hard hat must always be worn when riding. New Zealand has produced a number of world class riders and achieved notable success in international competitions (although the nearest most New Zealanders ever get to a horse is betting on them).

Hunting: Despite New Zealand's conservation-minded image, hunting has a large following, and there are few inhibitions about bagging the local wildlife. Sika stags are hunted in North Island and red stags in both North and South Islands, while in the more mountainous areas hunters take pot-shots at wily tahr and chamois. Most hunters hire a local guide to lead them to their prey on account of the difficult terrain and unpredictable weather in the main hunting areas. On a more modest level, ducks, swans, pheasant, quail and geese are the main game birds in New Zealand. The only drawback for the keen hunter (or good news for the quarry) is that a short season is enforced, commencing the first weekend in May and extending for a maximum of eight weeks. A permit is required to own a gun in New Zealand. Further information can be obtained from The NZ Shooting Federation, PO Box 701, Manurewa, Auckland (☎ 09-296 1813, ✉ nzshootingfed@xtra.co.nz).

Marching: Marching is a traditional New Zealand female sport which dates back to the 1930s and is still popular today. It's taken seriously, and participants are divided into four grades: adults (16+), junior (12 to 16 years), midget (7 to 12 years) and introductory.

Netball: Although most New Zealand sports have a predominantly masculine image (not surprising given the dominance of rugby and adventure sports), women participate in most sporting activities and also have their own sports. One of the most popular women's sports in New Zealand is (English) netball, which is generally taken much more seriously here than in the 'mother' country. New Zealand netball is known for its precision and strict adherence to the rules and traditions, which makes it much more than just a casual pastime. The national netball team (the Silver Ferns) has enjoyed considerable success in international competition.

Tennis & Squash: Tennis is played throughout New Zealand and is particularly popular in the more fashionable suburbs of Auckland and Wellington. Most places aren't far from public courts or a private club. If you wish to join a private club, you should find it neither particularly expensive nor conservative, although most have strict dress codes. Squash is also a popular sport, in which New Zealand has produced a number of world-class players, including world champions Ross Norman, Susan Devoy and Leilani Joyce. Details are available from New Zealand Squash (☎ 09-836 0309, ✉ nzsquash@nzsquash.co.nz).

Triathlon: Triathlon (a gruelling combination of swimming, running and cycling, which are carried out consecutively on the same day) is as popular in New Zealand as in Australia. Many New Zealanders participate in triathlon events simply as a way of keeping (super) fit, although there are also many highly regarded competitive triathlons for athletes of all abilities and both sexes.

17.

SHOPPING

New Zealand isn't noted for offering a very interesting or exciting shopping experience. Traditionally, many New Zealanders were almost self-sufficient and shopped only for the basic necessities that they couldn't grow or make themselves (they still have a strong preference for making or growing things themselves wherever possible, particularly in rural areas). Fortunately, the situation has improved considerably in recent years, with an influx of international chain stores and designer shops in towns and cities. Naturally, you won't find the same choice of shops or merchandise on offer in New Zealand that you will in the USA, the UK or even Australia, because the market is so much smaller than in those countries. However, a shopping trip in New Zealand is now a much more rewarding experience than was previously the case.

Although New Zealand shoppers complain endlessly about increasing prices, they now receive a better deal than they did in the past. The removal or reduction of punitive taxes on imported goods (such as electrical equipment) has made many goods better value, although they've risen in price in dollar terms, and increased competition has also helped reduce prices. Competition has additionally forced retailers to take more care in the quality of goods and services they offer and how they present their wares, which in the past was at best uninspired and at worst poor. People from the UK will recognise several names on the New Zealand high street, although it's important to note that they don't usually sell the same goods as their British equivalents. For example, Woolworths is a major supermarket chain and Boots is purely a chemist, so you shouldn't expect to buy music and household wares there as you can in the UK. Australians will also find many of their favourite stores in New Zealand, many of which are operated on a franchise basis. As in most other western countries, many modern shopping centres have been built outside towns, with the effect that shops have moved out of town centres and left them run-down and neglected.

Credit cards (e.g. Visa and Mastercard) are widely accepted in shops in New Zealand, even in out of the way places and Kiwis love store charge cards. Cheques are also accepted, although shops are reluctant to accept them, as there are no cheque guarantee cards in New Zealand. When paying by cheque, you should have some form of identification – many shops ask for a credit card. Debit or EFTPOS cards (see page 227) are the preferred method of payment in most shops (New Zealanders can even pay court fines with a debit card in many areas!). The Mondex system, a kind of debit card where a card is 'topped up' with a sum of money, which is used to purchase goods and services, has recently been introduced in New Zealand, although it's by no means in widespread use.

Goods and services tax (GST) at 12.5 per cent is levied on almost everything you buy in New Zealand. You can assume that tax is included in the price unless there's an indication to the contrary. Usually, tax-exclusive prices are displayed only in outlets that attract mainly traders, e.g. a hardware store which serves local farmers.

SHOPPING HOURS

The standard shopping hours in New Zealand are 8.30 or 9am until 5pm Mondays to Fridays and 8.30 or 9am to noon on Saturdays. Shops don't usually stay open on Saturday afternoons, although shops in tourist areas may stay open on Saturday afternoons in summer. Most shops have late night opening one day a week (usually Thursday or Friday), when they stay open until 8.30 or 9pm. A limited amount of

Sunday shopping is permitted in New Zealand, but as some shops stay closed while others open, planning a Sunday shopping trip can be an uncertain business. As in other countries, supermarkets tend to buck the trend and in cities many stay open late every day. You'll also find that the traditional New Zealand 'dairy' (see below) operates an open-all-hours policy, remaining open from when the proprietor gets up until he's too tired to continue (usually until 9 or 10pm). All shops are closed on Christmas Day, Good Friday and Easter Sunday.

LOCAL SHOPS & SERVICES

Despite the proliferation of out-of-town shopping centres, there are still plenty of small local shops in most towns and city suburbs in New Zealand, although fewer than in the past. Shops tend to follow the British pattern with a grocer (general provisions), butcher, baker, greengrocer (fruit and vegetables) and chemist (pharmacy). Most suburban shopping streets have a Pacific Island shop selling housewares, toys and assorted other household essentials and bric-a-brac. A curiosity left over from New Zealand's British heritage, although becoming less common, is that fresh milk is delivered to homes each morning in many areas. In smart suburbs in major cities many shops that used to sell everyday goods (such as food) have been taken over by outlets selling gifts, stationery, arts and crafts, and Maori and Polynesian artefacts and reproductions. Although interesting for visitors, these are of little use to residents, who often need to visit shopping centres and supermarkets for the essentials. This is particularly true in many shopping arcades in Auckland and Wellington. In common with other countries, petrol (gas) stations in New Zealand carry a selection of basic grocery items and are particularly handy in the evenings and on Saturday afternoons and Sundays, when other shops are closed.

Dairies: The dairy is a great New Zealand tradition. It isn't just a dairy – in fact in most cases it isn't a dairy at all (there appear to be few New Zealanders who can remember when dairies made butter and cheese) – and a more accurate description of a dairy nowadays is a corner shop, convenience store or mini-market. The dairy was once the mainstay of New Zealand shopping where everyone did most of their daily shopping, although nowadays (with the proliferation of supermarkets) most tend to be patronised only for odds and ends that have been forgotten at the supermarket or in emergencies and some are suffering from declining trade and look rather neglected. However, the traditional dairy soldiers on and is the one place where you can be sure of buying essentials on Sundays, when everything else is closed. (Dairies are also focal points for the local community and an excellent source of help, information, advice and local gossip.)

Dairies sell a 'little bit of everything', particularly tinned and packet foods, and in some you can also buy fresh fruit, vegetables and meat, perhaps locally produced. There's usually a display of confectionery (lollies), a variety of soft drinks (but generally no alcohol) and an impressive range of ice cream, which is of excellent quality and consumed enthusiastically in New Zealand. A dairy is also often the best place to buy snacks (at any time of day) and usually offers a choice of sandwiches and pies, although they may be limited to meat (lamb mince) or bacon and egg. In country areas you may also find hardware and clothing (although you shouldn't expect much choice). Dairies are noted for their personal service (they're usually owner-operated) and if there's anything you particularly want, the friendly proprietor will usually obtain it for you. Prices in dairies are inevitably higher than in supermarkets.

SUPERMARKETS

Most people do their food shopping at supermarkets, many of which are located out of town, so you may need a car to get there (a few supermarkets in cities offer free shuttle buses for car-less customers). The Australian retail giant Woolworths operates some 96 stores throughout New Zealand under three brand names: Price Chopper, Big Fresh and Woolworths at Gull. Woolworths also offers an Internet shopping service (🖳 www.woolworths.co.nz) in Auckland, where orders can be placed by computer and delivered to your home. There's a huge variety of supermarkets in New Zealand and it's wise to do some local research when moving into a new area. Some supermarkets, such as Pak 'N' Save and Shop Rite, operate on a pile-'em-high-and-sell-'em-cheap basis, which means you can expect warehouse-style decor (i.e. none), little choice, budget brands and minimal service, but rock-bottom prices. New World is a slightly more upmarket supermarket and has recently refurbished its stores, whose emphasis on fresh food and delicatessen counters has been hugely popular with New Zealanders.

If you want attractive surroundings, a wide choice of household brands, separate bakery and delicatessen counters, attentive service, and a pack-and-take-to-your-car service, you will find that several supermarkets offer this, but their prices are correspondingly higher. The better quality supermarkets offer some popular brands from the USA and Europe, although shipping costs make these expensive and there's usually a local New Zealand equivalent that's just as good. Note that supermarkets sell wine, but don't sell any other alcohol, which you must buy from hotel (pub) bottle shops (see page 285), although this is expected to change in the near future.

FOOD

One of the pleasures of New Zealand is the wide range of fresh food that's available at reasonable prices. However, shopping for many foods, particularly fruit and vegetables, tends to be seasonal, as most shops sell only what's available from local farmers. Unlike in Europe and North America, you cannot usually buy most produce out of season (e.g. strawberries in mid-winter) – it may be available but will be expensive. The authorities are also careful about the foreign produce they allow into the country as a protection against importing pests and diseases. However, New Zealand is a major food producer (and exporter) particularly in meat, dairy produce and fruit, and although the choice may not be as great as in some other countries, quality is excellent and prices competitive. In recent years New Zealanders have become more cosmopolitan in their approach to food and cooking, and as a consequence there are numerous specialist food stores and counters at supermarkets.

Meat: Meat is usually good value in New Zealand, as it's one of the country's major industries, and most families can afford to dish up a meat dish at each meal. There are over 48 million sheep in New Zealand and the country exports around $1,770 million worth of lamb annually. Not surprisingly, lamb is good value and all joints are inexpensive and readily available, plus a range of lamb products such as pies, burgers, sausages (known as snarlers) and paté. Hogget is one-year-old lamb, i.e. it actually is a lamb and not mutton sold as lamb, as in many other countries. If you have the freezer space, you may wish to consider buying a whole lamb (bought either whole or jointed as preferred), which, with prices starting as low as $100, represents good value. Poultry, pork and beef are also common, but less popular than lamb, although New Zealanders do like their steak, which is of top quality (it's often served garnished with oysters in a dish known as a 'carpet bagger'). Venison is also an increasingly popular meat in New Zealand and is available from many butchers and supermarkets (New Zealand has become a major exporter of venison in recent years). You can buy meat from a supermarket or a local butcher, where it may be fresher and locally produced – the grazing lamb you passed on your way to work in the morning may well be riding home in your car boot in the evening!

Dairy Products: Dairy products are plentiful and cheap in New Zealand, so much so that hotels and motels often leave a free bottle of milk in rooms. They're one of the country's major exports, and New Zealand even exports to Caribbean countries. However, although the quality of dairy produce is excellent, the variety often isn't, and many dairies offer a choice of cheddar, cheddar or cheddar. It's possible to buy New Zealand versions of soft cheeses such as Brie and Camembert and even imported cheeses, although you must usually buy them from a delicatessen rather than a dairy or supermarket. If you eat a lot of cheese, you may find a trip to a cheese factory (mostly found in South Island) worthwhile, many of which open their doors to the public and sell huge portions of cheese at factory prices.

Fruit & Vegetables: New Zealand greengrocers (and supermarket fruit and vegetable sections) offer a relatively wide choice of fruit and vegetables, which is midway between what you would find in Western Europe and a street market in the Pacific islands. Among the commonplace Gala apples, pears, strawberries, tomatoes and potatoes, you will find a variety of exotic fruits and vegetables. Pumpkin and asparagus are popular accompaniments to a main meal, particularly in areas with large Maori communities. Unusual produce includes the feijoa (a lemon-like fruit with a much sweeter flavour), tamarillos (with a subtle, slightly tart flavour), kumara (a sweet potato and a staple of the Maori diet), boysenberries, kiwano and the ubiquitous kiwi fruit. In many areas of New Zealand you will find roadside stalls selling freshly picked fruit and vegetables, and you can also pick your own produce. Stalls often operate on the honour system – when they're unattended you leave the money for what you take in a box. This is a good way to buy kiwi fruit, which can be bought for just a few cents each when the crop has been larger than expected.

Seafood: A wide range of seafood is available in New Zealand, appealing to all tastes. If you want 'international' species such as cod and haddock, you can find them, but there's also a huge variety of local fish available. More exotic seafood includes green-lipped mussels, Pacific oysters, smoked eel, pipis, paua, toheroas (local clams) and shark (sometimes known as lemon fish). Note that New Zealand whitebait isn't the same fish as whitebait in other countries but is a tiny, thread-like, transparent fish with a subtle flavour. Generally, seafood isn't such good value as meat, as much of New Zealand's catch goes for export and the country's fish wholesalers must buy fish from South America to satisfy local demand. It's illegal to deal in trout commercially, so if you enjoy trout you will usually need to catch it yourself. This isn't difficult, as the country's rivers, lakes and streams are teeming with both rainbow and European trout. The same applies to oysters, which are frequently found in New Zealand's clear waters, but which you aren't permitted to harvest.

Bakery & Confectionery: New Zealand bakers and supermarkets sell a fairly predictable range of bread and confectionery. You can buy white and brown loaves (sliced or unsliced) together with a variety of rolls in different shapes and sizes and pink iced buns, which are a national tradition. As anywhere, shop bread varies between delicious and tasteless, and it's usually a matter of shopping around until you find a baker you like. In some of the more adventurous bakeries and supermarkets you can also find French-style baguettes, croissants and even Italian-style ciabatta bread. The New Zealand 'national dessert' is pavlova (or 'pav'), named after the famous Russian ballerina and introduced from Australia, where it was invented. It consists of meringue, cream and fruit (usually kiwi fruit) and is available in all shapes and sizes, both baked in-store and 'factory' made.

Those from the UK and USA should note that foodstuffs in New Zealand shops are sold in metric quantities, although it's still common for older people to ask for half a pound of butter or two pounds of potatoes. This is a foreign language to the ears of young shop assistants, who have never heard of Imperial weights and measures. Conversion tables are shown in **Appendix D**. A price guide for the most popular foods is published by Statistics New Zealand (🖳 www.stats.govt.nz) and available from New Zealand missions.

MARKETS

Most towns have markets on one or two days a week, and in major cities there may be a market (or a number) on most days of the week. Markets are cheap, colourful and interesting, although you need to be careful what you buy. Items commonly for sale in markets include fruit and vegetables, meat, fish, clothes, art and craft items, household goods, jewellery and books. Food markets are often the best place to buy fresh food. In areas with a large Maori community, there are Polynesian markets selling ethnic foodstuffs, seafood and textiles. Art and craft markets are also common in major cities and resort towns, where artisans can often be seen at work, although prices may be substantially higher than at local shops.

Flea markets are popular in the major cities and sell second-hand goods, including clothes, books, records, antiques and miscellaneous bric-a-brac. In some places you may find that what are advertised as markets are actually indoor mini-shopping centres, where the area is divided into small shop units operated on a permanent basis. Note that haggling isn't usually done in New Zealand markets, where prices are as displayed. Check with your local council or tourist office for information about local markets.

DEPARTMENT & CHAIN STORES

New Zealand has a variety of department and chain stores with branches in most major towns and cities. For the uninitiated, a department store is a large store, usually with several floors, which sells almost everything and may also include a food hall. In a large department store, each floor may be dedicated to a particular kind of goods, such as ladies' or men's fashions, or furniture and furnishings. Chain stores are simply stores with a number of branches, usually in different towns and cities.

One of the major New Zealand department stores is Farmers (nothing to do with farming), which sells almost everything and offers medium quality goods at modest prices. K-Mart is also a cheap-and-cheerful, sell-anything store. Warehouse, with its slogan 'where everyone gets a bargain', is New Zealand's biggest chain store, and its huge, red barn-like stores are found throughout the country (Warehouse is blamed for the closure of many small stores in towns). Bond & Bond and Noel Leeming are chain stores with a wide variety of products and a good selection of household goods and electrical appliances, including computers. Smith and Caughey is a famous Auckland department store, while Wellington has Kirkcaldies and Stains. See also **Clothing** on page 286.

Recent years have seen a trend towards huge shopping centres, known as 'mega-centres', found in major suburban areas, which include all New Zealand's major chain stores as well as numerous restaurants and cafés, and cinema complexes. The Australian company, Westfield, has recently bought and refurbished nine centres in key locations. As in other countries, these shopping centres are tremendously popular, and visiting them constitutes a major 'leisure' activity.

ALCOHOL

New Zealand has some of the world's most bizarre licensing laws, which date back to the UK's oppressive licensing laws during the First World War, when workers were kept as far away from alcohol as possible lest their performance in the munitions factories was affected (or they caused an explosion!). New Zealand's laws have been reformed at a much slower pace even than in the UK, although further changes are planned over the next few years (plans for liberalisation seem to slip back further each time there's an outbreak of drunken behaviour at a cricket or rugby match). All in all, buying a bottle of your favourite tipple can prove rather frustrating in New Zealand, where you cannot buy alcohol anywhere on Sundays and may even have difficulty finding somewhere to get a drink.

Pubs (known as hotels) usually have a 'bottle sales counter' or a separate 'bottle shop' (equivalent to a US liquor store or a UK off-licence) on the premises, although these have limited opening hours, high prices and a poor selection compared with similar establishments in other countries. Bottle shops usually have a good choice of beer, but the selection of wines and spirits is usually limited. Supermarkets have entered the alcohol market in recent years but are currently permitted to sell only wine and beer (of which they stock a wide variety at competitive prices), although they aren't permitted to sell spirits. They're easily the cheapest place to buy wine unless you buy direct from vineyards (known as a wineries), which are allowed to sell their produce direct to the public and have become a good source of inexpensive (depending on where you go) wine in bulk. Dairies and grocery shops can also obtain a licence to sell wine, although few do.

The majority of New Zealand wine is white and made from the sauvignon blanc grape, although chardonnay is becoming increasingly popular. You can also choose from a wide selection of Australian wines. Wine is sold in 75cl bottles, wine boxes and barrels (casks) of varying capacities. Imported wines (other than from Australia) are also available, but aren't popular, as they're simply too expensive for most people. Beer is sold in cans of 440ml, usually in trays of 24 known as a 'two dozen lot' (New Zealanders have a way with words), although bottled beer is much more popular. You can also buy a flagon containing 2.25 litres, which is sometimes still known as a 'half g' (half gallon) as it's equivalent to four pints. New Zealanders aren't generally great spirit drinkers partly because spirits aren't widely available and are expensive. However, if you miss your favourite tipple, most major brands are available, including whisky (e.g. American, Canadian and Scotch) and local gin, which is relatively good value for money.

TOBACCO

New Zealanders aren't generally heavy smokers, which is just as well, as it's fast becoming socially unacceptable (see page 197) and has been banned in public buildings and some restaurants. As in most other countries, tobacco is becoming ever more expensive. The government grabs over 80 per cent of the cost of a packet of cigarettes in duty, ostensibly to promote good health and encourage people to give up smoking. Both international and local brands are available, the price of a pack of 20 starting at around $8.80, although a recent test declared that New Zealand brands contained twice as much nicotine as American and Canadian brands. Rolling tobacco is even more expensive (the government believes it's more damaging to your health), costing around $24.50 for 50g.

CLOTHING

New Zealanders aren't noted for their fashion-consciousness, although a wide range of clothing (both locally made and imported) is available. As in any country, prices vary considerably according to the quality and where you shop, although clothes in New Zealand are generally more expensive than in Europe and North America. The cheapest clothing is available from chain stores, such as K-Mart or Farmers, where you will find uninspiring designs but plenty of choice. Mid-range shoppers may favour department stores, which stock better quality clothes at higher prices. Millers Fashion Club is a leading chain of women's clothing stores which has done much to make women's clothing more competitive (like many New Zealand retailers, it originated in Australia). Glassons, Max Fashions, Principals and Jean Jones are also popular nationwide chains.

Factory outlet shops are a growing influence in the clothing industry and include Dressmart in Auckland, which offers good value and unparalleled choice. Main cities, including Auckland and Wellington, have an increasing number of trendy boutiques and designer stores, where you will find brands (e.g. Barbour, Driza-Bone and Timberland) from leading American, Australian and European designers with correspondingly high prices. There are also several up-and-coming local designers in New Zealand, including Chrissie Potter and Amanda Nicolle, and New Zealand fashion has achieved record sales since it first participated in the London Fashion Week in 1999. In 2001, for the first time, the country held its own Fashion Week in Auckland, which received international acclaim. Unless you're a fashion 'victim' or move in the trendiest circles, it isn't usually worthwhile buying designer clothing in New Zealand, where most people aren't prone to label snobbery. Casual clothing is acceptable for most situations, and country or farm clothing is considered fashionable even by those who never go near a farm, let alone work on one.

Despite the ready availability of wool, woollen garments can be expensive, although anything in sheepskin is a bargain (you never know, it might come back into fashion one day!). Hand-knitted garments are popular. Cotton clothes are the cheapest and most popular in New Zealand, as they're cool in summer and warm in winter, particularly when worn in layers. Canterbury is famous for its rugby shirts, which can be worn for any occasion. Swanndri is a well known brand of woollen shirts and jackets, which have become something of a classic and are affectionately known as 'swannis' in New Zealand. Shoes tend to be expensive, even though the country manufactures over 1 million pairs a year.

FURNITURE & FURNISHINGS

The average New Zealand home is furnished much as it would be in Europe or North America. The staple items of furniture are the three-piece suite (usually called a lounge suite), and the dining table with four or six chairs. All kinds of furniture are available, from antique or reproduction to modern, and quality ranges from bargain-priced flat-pack or second-hand furniture to exclusive handmade and designer items. Most properties in New Zealand have large fitted wardrobes in the American style, which are often walk-in rooms fitted with shelves and rails, thus rendering bedroom furniture other than a bed and a dressing table unnecessary. Fitted kitchens are also standard in new properties, and basic appliances (oven, hob and refrigerator, and possibly also a washing machine and dishwasher) are included in the price.

HOUSEHOLD GOODS

New Zealand used to be notorious for the high cost of domestic appliances as a result of swingeing import taxes designed to protect local industries. In the '80s, however, the government decided to allow imports on more favourable terms and as a result New Zealanders have been able to replace their ageing home appliances with modern equipment at more reasonable prices. A huge choice of home appliances is available in New Zealand, and smaller appliances such as vacuum cleaners, grills, toasters and electric irons aren't expensive and are usually of good quality. All electrical goods sold in New Zealand must conform to local safety standards. It pays to shop around, as quality, reliability and prices vary considerably (the more expensive imported brands are usually the most reliable). Before buying household appliances, whether large or small, it may pay you to check the test reports in consumer magazines.

It isn't usually worthwhile shipping bulky domestic appliances to New Zealand, such as a refrigerator, washing machine or dishwasher, which irrespective the shipping expense may not meet local safety regulations or fit into a New Zealand kitchen. However, if you own good quality small household appliances it's worth bringing them to New Zealand, as all that's usually required is a change of plug, provided you're coming from a country with a 220/240V electricity supply (see page 96). Don't bring a TV to New Zealand (other than from Australia), as it won't work (see page 127).

SECOND-HAND BARGAINS

There's a lively second-hand market in New Zealand for almost everything, from antiques to cars, computers to photographic equipment. You name it and somebody will be selling it second-hand. With such a large second-hand market there are often bargains to be found, particularly if you're quick off the mark. Many towns have a local second-hand or junk store and charity shops (e.g. Salvation Army) selling new and second-hand articles (where most of your money goes to help those in need). In some places (e.g. Wellington) you can even buy goods which have been rescued from the city dump and which are displayed in a special warehouse at the site!

If you're looking for a particular item, such as a camera, boat, or motorcycle, you may be better off looking through the small ads in specialist magazines than in more general newspapers or magazines. The classified ads in local newspapers are also a good source of bargains, particularly for items such as furniture and large household appliances. Shopping centre and newsagent bulletin boards and company notice boards may also prove fruitful. Another place to pick up a bargain is at an auction, although it helps to have specialist knowledge about what you're buying (you will probably be competing with experts). Auctions are held in New Zealand throughout the year for everything from antiques and paintings to cars and property.

There are antique shops and centres in most towns, and antique street markets and fairs are common in the major cities (where you can pick up interesting early New Zealand artefacts – but you must get there early to beat the dealers to the best buys). For information about local markets, inquire at your local tourist or information office. Car boot (trunk) and garage (yard) sales, where people sell their surplus belongings at bargain prices, are gaining popularity in New Zealand. Sales may be advertised in local newspapers and signposted on local roads (they're usually held at weekends).

NEWSPAPERS, MAGAZINES & BOOKS

New Zealand doesn't offer a particularly wide choice of daily newspapers, a situation that has been exacerbated by the closure of a number of long-established newspapers in recent years. There are no national newspapers in New Zealand, where newspapers are regional (centred on the major cities) and aren't distributed throughout the country. As a result, most New Zealand newspapers tend to have a provincial feel, although they do contain national and international news. The major newspapers include the *New Zealand Herald* (Auckland), the *Dominion Times* (Wellington), the *Evening Post* (Wellington), the *Waikato Times* (Hamilton), the *Christchurch Press* and the *Otago Daily Times* (Dunedin). Most daily newspapers are published from Mondays to Saturdays and separate titles are published on Sundays, e.g. the *Sunday Star* in Auckland. Other popular publications include the weekly *National Business Review*, New Zealand's main business magazine, and *The Truth*, a weekly 'shock-horror' tabloid.

Politically, most newspapers take an even-handed approach, as they're mainly independently owned. The content of most newspapers, which are usually broadsheets, is fairly standard and includes news, business, sport, and TV programmes, while the Thursday, Friday and Saturday editions are the best for advertisements such as situations vacant (jobs), property and cars. Friday editions of most newspapers include a substantial 'what's on' entertainment section.

Newspapers are sold by newsagents and from street stands (where you leave the money in an honesty box) and vending machines, where depositing your money opens the door giving you access to the newspapers inside. A daily newspaper costs around $1 and Sunday papers around $1.50. You can also have newspapers delivered to your home. Free local newspapers are distributed to homes in most cities and are useful for finding local services, jobs, property and cars for sale.

Expatriates will be pleased to hear that you can buy Australian, American and British newspapers (e.g. the *Observer* and *Sunday Times*) in major cities a day or two after publication. There are also eight Chinese newspapers in New Zealand serving the local Chinese community of more than 90,000.

A wide range of magazines is available for sale in New Zealand catering for most tastes, including sports, hobbies, and home and business topics. However, on account of the relatively small population, many are imported from abroad, particularly from

Australia and the USA, and there are only some 70 indigenous titles, of which the *New Zealand Women's Weekly* has the largest circulation.

Most book shops in New Zealand stock a good selection of books, including a wide choice of titles published in Australia, the UK and the USA. However, on account of the relatively small print runs of New Zealand publishers and the cost of shipping books from other countries, they're relatively expensive (Americans will be horrified). Note that it's possible to buy books at reasonable prices via the Internet from a number of Internet 'book shops', the largest of which is the American company Amazon (⌨ www.amazon.com). Second-hand bookshops thrive in the major towns, many allowing you to part-exchange old books for others. See also **Libraries** on page 258.

DUTY-FREE & SHOPPING ABROAD

Apart from their personal effects, those entering New Zealand aged over 17 (whether as visitors or residents) are permitted to import a limited amount of goods duty-free (i.e. free of goods and services tax at 12.5 per cent). These include:

- 200 cigarettes or 250g tobacco or 50 cigars (or a mixture of all three provided they don't weigh more than 250g);

- one 1,125ml bottle of spirit or liqueur;

- up to 4.5 litres of wine or beer (six 75cl bottles);

- other goods up to a value of $700.

When leaving New Zealand, you may purchase duty-free goods at duty-free shops in central Auckland, Wellington or Christchurch and at airports. If you buy duty-free goods from a city duty-free shop, they're delivered free to the airport in time for your departure and it isn't possible to take them with you when you leave the store. If you prefer, you can have your purchases shipped to an address abroad, which duty-free shops are happy to arrange. Although buying goods duty-free saves you 12.5 per cent on New Zealand prices, if you're travelling via the Far East or the USA you may be able to obtain a better deal there, depending on what you wish to buy.

Many New Zealanders take advantage of trips to locations such as Hong Kong and Singapore to buy luxury items, e.g. cameras, watches, jewellery, small electronic goods and computer software, which are substantially cheaper in these places than in New Zealand. The savings are, however, limited by the high cost of air travel, even to the nearest Far Eastern city. Considerable savings can also be made by buying goods via the Internet, and although you will need to pay duty and GST on imports (check in advance), substantial savings can still be made on many goods, particularly CDs, books and sports equipment purchased in the USA. **Note that when buying expensive goods overseas, you should insure them in transit for their full value.**

RECEIPTS & GUARANTEES

When shopping, you should always insist on a receipt and keep it until you've left the shop or reached home. This isn't just in case you need to return or exchange goods, which may be impossible without the receipt, but also to verify that you've paid if an automatic alarm goes off as you're leaving the shop or any other questions arise. If you're paying in cash, you should check receipts immediately (particularly in supermarkets), because if you're overcharged it's often impossible to obtain redress later. You need your receipt to return an item for repair or replacement (usually to the place of purchase) during the warranty period. It's wise to keep receipts and records of major purchases made while you're resident in New Zealand, particularly if your stay is for a short period. This may save you both time and money when you finally leave the country and are required to declare your belongings in your new country of residence.

If you buy something which is faulty, damaged or doesn't work or measure up to the manufacturer's or vendor's claims, you can return it and obtain a replacement or your money back (unless you bought it at auction). Note that extended warranties or money-back guarantees don't affect your statutory rights as a purchaser, although the legal status of a warranty may be unclear. Some stores offer an exchange of goods or a money-back guarantee for any reason, which isn't required by law, although this guarantee is usually for a limited period only and goods must be returned unused and as new. Some stores attempt to restrict your rights to a credit note or to replacement goods when an item is faulty or unfit for use, which is illegal. Signs such as 'no refunds given', 'no responsibility for loss or damage', 'goods left for repair at your own risk' and 'all care but no responsibility taken' are meaningless and unlawful. All goods must be of 'merchantable' (reasonable) quality and fit for the purpose for which they were sold, and it's illegal for sellers to include a clause in the conditions of sale that exempts them from liability for defects, product faults and lack of care. Most traders will back down once you show that you know the law and are determined to obtain your legal rights.

Consumer protection laws are monitored and enforced in New Zealand by the Ministry of Consumer Affairs (PO Box 1473, Wellington, ☎ 04-474 2750, 🖳 www. consumer-ministry.govt.nz), which has local offices throughout the country. You can also obtain advice and assistance from a local Citizens' Advice Bureau (☎ freephone 0800-367 222, 🖳 www.consumer.org.nz).

18.

ODDS & ENDS

T his chapter contains miscellaneous information. Although all topics aren't of vital importance, most are of general interest to anyone planning to live or work in New Zealand, including everything you ever wanted to know (but were afraid to ask) about subjects as diverse as tipping, toilets and the tuatara.

NEW ZEALAND CITIZENSHIP

After three years' residence in New Zealand you can apply for New Zealand citizenship, which carries the right to vote in New Zealand elections and hold a New Zealand passport, making it no longer necessary to apply for a returning resident's visa (see page 60) when leaving the country. In order for your application to be successful, you must provide proof of good character, show your knowledge of the responsibilities and privileges of New Zealand citizenship and speak and understand English. You will have to attend a citizenship ceremony and take an oath or affirmation of allegiance. Children born of New Zealand residents automatically become New Zealand citizens and can hold dual nationality where permitted under the law of their parents' countries of birth or nationality. Foreign nationals who marry New Zealanders can apply for citizenship immediately they take up residence in New Zealand and those who live with a New Zealand partner in a genuine de facto relationship can apply for citizenship after two years. Enquiries regarding citizenship should be made to the Citizenship Office, PO Box 10-526, Wellington (☎ freephone 0800-225 151, ▣ www.citizenship.govt.nz).

CLIMATE

Being an island nation, New Zealand's climate tends to be dominated by its ocean setting, although it experiences a variety of climatic patterns due to its mountainous terrain. Climatic conditions vary considerably and include sub-tropical, sub-Antarctic, semi-arid (mainly in the Northland region), super-humid, frost-free, and sub-Alpine with permanent snow and ice in the mountainous areas. The eastern regions experience a drier climate than the west, on account of prevailing westerly winds, the wettest area being the south-west (west of the Southern Alps). Being in the southern hemisphere, New Zealand's seasons are the opposite of those in the northern latitudes, i.e. summer (December to February), autumn (March to May), winter (June to August) and Spring (September to November). Unseasonal weather is rare.

The most important characteristic of New Zealand weather is its changeability. North Island tends to be warmer and drier than South Island, although the highest mountain peaks often have snow year round. The average rainfall on North Island is around 1,300mm. Daytime temperatures in Auckland average 23°C (73°F) in summer and 14°C (57°F) in winter, while in Wellington they range from 26°C (79°F) in summer to as low as 2°C (35°F) in winter. Wellington is renowned for its extremely windy weather, which can also make the sea crossing between the two islands rough. Variations in weather and temperature in South Island are more pronounced, and the Southern Alps have 'wet' (west) and 'dry' (east) sides. On the east side of the Southern Alps rainfall can be as low as 300mm (droughts are fairly common) and temperatures a lot warmer than on the west side. Snow is a permanent feature on the highest peaks. Christchurch averages temperatures of around 22°C (71°F) in summer and 12°C (54°F) in winter, while Dunedin averages 19°C (66°F) in summer and 10°C (50°F) in winter.

Average temperatures, rainfall levels and sunshine hours for the main towns and cities are shown below. Bear in mind that the temperatures are averages and it can be much warmer or colder on individual days:

Town/City	Average Temp (°C) Summer	Winter	Average Annual Rainfall (mm)	Annual Hours Sunshine
NORTH ISLAND:				
Bay of Islands	25	15	1,648	2,020
Auckland	23	14	1,268	2,140
Rotorua	23	12	1,511	1,940
Napier	24	13	780	2,270
Wellington	20	11	1,271	2,020
SOUTH ISLAND:				
Nelson	22	12	999	2,410
Christchurch	22	12	658	1,990
Queenstown	22	8	849	1,940
Dunedin	19	10	772	1,700
Invercargill	18	9	1,042	1,630

CRIME

New Zealand has a reputation as a low-crime country and is a safe country by international standards, although both serious crime (such as murder) and petty crime (such as burglary) have risen considerably in the last few decades. The only real 'no-go' areas are certain parts of Auckland, where residents of the more affluent parts of the city dare not venture. (The North Shore area of Auckland has recently experimented with New York-style 'zero tolerance' policing.) In reality, although strangers wandering into high-crime areas are at risk of being mugged, knifed or even murdered, the risk is much, much lower than, for example, in most US cities. A worrying trend, however, is that an increasing number of violent attacks and rapes are racially inspired, particularly against Asians and Pacific Islanders. However, it should be noted that, overall, race relations in New Zealand are excellent and the envy of many other countries.

There's a huge difference between crime levels in the major cities and in rural areas, where it's still common to find communities where people never lock their homes or their cars when leaving them unoccupied, a practice which used to be common throughout New Zealand. In urban areas, however, good door and window locks and an alarm system are considered essential. Car theft (see page 180) is also a problem in cities and it's wise to have an immobiliser and alarm system fitted to your car (although little notice may be taken of it when it's triggered).

The last Crime and Safety Survey (1996) carried out among the New Zealand population revealed that 1 in 14 houses had been burgled in the previous year and one in five people had been victim of some kind of assault. In the light of these worrying findings and the general rise in crime, the coalition government elected in 1999 has introduced a series of measures designed to reduce the rate of crime (such as the DNA testing of criminals, including burglars, and greater police funding) and to provide greater support for the victims of crime. For example, a Sentencing and Parole Bill passed in 2001 sets out sentencing guidelines for judges and juries. Future initiatives include a task force on youth offending, which is a particular problem in some cities. Crime statistics published in mid-2001 show that these measures have been at least partially successful: burglary and car theft rates are both down by nearly 15 per cent and the resolution of crime is the highest for a decade. Violent crime is still, however, on the increase, and convictions for domestic violence have risen significantly, although it's believed that this may be due to greater public awareness of the problem and the fact that more domestic violence is reported to the police. It's hoped that the next Crime and Safety Survey, due out in mid-2002, will confirm the decrease in crime. Further information and statistics on crime can be obtained from the Minister of Justice, PO Box 180, Wellington (☎ 04-494 4700, 🖳 www.justice.govt.nz).

Despite the statistics, you can safely walk almost anywhere at any time of the day or night in most parts of the country. However, it's important to take the same precautions as you would in any country. Beware of pickpockets and bag-snatchers in cities and keep a close eye on your belongings in shops and when using public transport, particularly trains and the Interislander ferry. If your luggage is stolen on public transport, you should make a claim to the relevant authority, as they may make an ex-gratia payment for lost, stolen or damaged baggage.

Most New Zealanders are law-abiding and their 'criminal' activities amount to little more than speeding, 'pulling a sickie' (i.e. taking a day off work to go to the beach), or exaggerating a road or workplace accident in order to secure a more generous payout from the ACC. (Insurance companies recently reported that genuine insurance claims were believed to be inflated by $50 million annually by otherwise law-abiding citizens.) White collar fraud and corruption has become a more serious problem in recent years and a number of respected companies have been rocked by financial scandals, which were previously unknown in New Zealand.

Gangs: Gangs are a problem in New Zealand, particularly in the poor inner-city areas of Auckland and Wellington, although there's some gang activity in most large towns. As gangs' main activity tends to be inter-gang warfare, most people rarely come into contact with them, except when a gang organises a 'convention' in a public place or at a major rock concert or sporting event, although gang 'meets' are usually well publicised and characterised by a much larger than usual police presence. The best advice is never to consider buying or renting a home in an area known for gang activity and to stay well away from events or areas where gangs are likely to congregate.

Prisons: Tougher sentencing in recent years has created something of a prison crisis in New Zealand, where the prison population at the end of 1999 was around 5,500, a substantially higher figure than a few years ago. Three new prisons were due to be completed in 2002 and the authorities are experimenting with more liberal punishments, such as home detention, electronic tagging and community work.

Drugs: New Zealand has been described as having the perfect climate for the cultivation of cannabis, and plantations are tucked away in most parts of the country, particularly in Northland, which is dubbed New Zealand's 'cannabis capital'. Police regularly trace and destroy plantations, but many more are believed to remain undiscovered and this doesn't allow for plants that are grown literally on the window sills and balconies of homes throughout the country.

Recreational smoking of cannabis or marijuana ('electric puha' as it's known in some places) is commonplace, although it's illegal and its possession is punishable by a $1,000 fine and/or 12 months' imprisonment. As in many other countries, there's pressure on the government to legalise cannabis, headed by the National Organisation For The Reform of Marijuana Laws (NORML). While most people feel this is unlikely to happen, plans to punish possession by on-the-spot fines, similar to parking tickets, have been seriously proposed in recent years. The police tend to concentrate on tracing and prosecuting growers (using helicopter patrols in rural areas) and dealers rather than casual users, and they rarely raid homes in search of small quantities. However, vehicles driven by 'likely looking' drug users (those with glazed eyes and flowers in their hair?) that are stopped for traffic offences may be searched for drugs.

Ecstasy is a popular alternative to cannabis, particularly among teenagers, and the use of hard drugs such as heroin and cocaine is increasing. (New Zealand's official 'Just Say No' anti-drugs campaign is often criticised for its lack of impact.) However, this is much less of a problem than in the USA or Western Europe, as New Zealand maintains relatively effective border controls aimed at keeping 'nasties' (including illicit fruit and vegetables) out of the country.

ECONOMY & TRADE

New Zealand is a prosperous country with a successful economy and a gross domestic product (GDP) in 1999 of some US$72 billion (the GDP per head is around US$14,600). Approximately 60 per cent of GDP derives from services, a third from manufacturing and 10 per cent from agriculture. The national economy is, however, highly reliant on agriculture, particularly the export of dairy products, meat and wool. Any slump in world prices of these commodities badly affects the economy. The economy is also highly dependent on Far Eastern markets, and the economic crisis that befell that region in 1997–98 caused a recession in New Zealand. Since then, however, the economy has recovered.

Agriculture: Modern methods and machinery are used extensively on New Zealand farms, where productivity is among the highest in the world. The land is ideally suited for dairy farming, and grass grows almost year round in the north of the country. The main cereal crops include wheat (around 320,000 tonnes per year), barley (200,000 tonnes), maize (160,000 tonnes) and oats (60,000 tonnes). Other important crops are kiwi fruit (inevitably!), apples, pears, tobacco, potatoes and peas. The livestock population of New Zealand includes nearly 46 million sheep (more than 12 times as many as the human population), some 4.3 million cattle, over 1 million goats and 450,000 pigs. New Zealand is the world's fifth largest exporter of wool with an annual 'clip' worth $980 million.

Forestry: Timber production is an important industry in New Zealand, which produces some 14 million cubic metres annually. Over half (85 per cent of it pine) is used for lumber and around 40 per cent for pulp. Most native forests were cut down by the early European settlers in the late 1800s and an extensive reforestation programme in recent decades has seen the planting of imported varieties of fast-growing trees such as Douglas fir instead of native New Zealand trees such as rimu and miro, most of which are slow-growing. A plantation of a North American species of pine in the Kaingaroa State Forest, said to be the largest planted forest in the world, is commercially exploited by a consortium of government and private industry.

Fishing: Fishing is a small but important industry in New Zealand, where the annual catch is some 600,000 tonnes, much of which is exported. The most common freshwater and marine species are blue grenadier, orange roughy, mackerel, barracuda, blue whiting, crayfish, lobster and squid.

Mining: In the '70s, New Zealand mineral output increased substantially as new deposits of oil and natural gas were exploited. Annual output is around 2 million tonnes of coal, 9.3 million barrels of oil and 3.4 billion cubic metres of natural gas. Other minerals produced in large quantities are gold, silver, limestone, iron ore, bentonite, silica sand and pumice; pearlite, sand, gravel, limestone, clay, dolomite and magnesite are also found in New Zealand, where deposits of uranium and thorium are also believed to be present.

Manufacturing: In 1992, around a quarter of a million people were employed in manufacturing (mostly in Auckland), although this has since declined to around 140,000. The principal products are paper and paper products, chemicals, metal goods, machinery, clothing, timber, electrical machinery, refined petroleum and printed materials. All car manufacturing and assembly plants have been closed down over the last few years. Manufacturing is modern and automated, although New Zealand has insufficient workers and raw materials to support much heavy industry.

Energy: In keeping with its environmentally-friendly image, around 75 per cent of New Zealand's electricity is produced by hydroelectric power and most of the rest from coal and oil-fired plants. In addition, underground steam is used to produce a substantial amount of electricity in North Island. Major hydroelectric facilities are located on the Waikato river in North Island and on the Clutha and Waitaki rivers in South Island. New Zealand has an electricity generating capacity of around 7.4 megawatts, with an annual output of around 27 billion kilowatt-hours (figures which are merely academic to the residents of Auckland, who suffered a catastrophic power cut lasting several months in early 1998!).

Foreign Trade: The value of exports from New Zealand totals more than $24 million annually. The UK, the USA, Japan and Australia are among the country's major trading partners. New Zealand is the largest exporter of dairy products in the world (dairy products are exported chilled to many regions, including the Middle East and the Caribbean) and the world's fifth largest exporter of wool. Other important exports include meat, wood and fish. In total, agricultural products account for over half of all exports. Imports have risen significantly in recent years and in 2000 totalled nearly $32 million and primarily include manufactured goods, heavy machinery, petroleum, chemicals, iron, steel, plastic materials and textiles. New Zealand import tariffs are generally low (many having been reduced or abolished in recent years) and around half of manufactured goods are imported free of duty. Further information is available from the Ministry of Foreign Affairs and Trade, Private Bag 18-901, Wellington (☎ 04-494 8500, 🖳 www.mft.govt.nz).

GEOGRAPHY

New Zealand lies in the South Pacific Ocean south-east of Australia and comprises two main islands, called North Island and South Island (they were named in the 19th century by the British, who obviously exercised a great deal of imagination in christening them), plus numerous smaller islands (of which Stewart and Chatham are the most important). Associated with New Zealand are Ross Dependency (in Antarctica) and Niue, Tokelau and the Cook Islands (in the Pacific Ocean). The capital of the country is Wellington, although Auckland is the largest city. Contrary to popular belief (and much to the relief of most New Zealanders) New Zealand isn't just off the coast of Australia, but some 2,000km (1,250mi) away across the Tasman Sea. New Zealand covers an area of 270,534km² (104,461mi²), which makes it comparable in size to the UK.

New Zealand is a mountainous country, some 60 per cent of which is between around 200m (655ft) and 1,070m (3,500ft) above sea level, including over 220 mountains above 2,000m (6,550ft). The principal mountain ranges in North Island extend along the eastern side, where the north central region has three active volcanic peaks: Mount Ruapehu (2,797m/9,176ft), the highest point on the island, Mount Ngauruhoe (2,291m/7,516ft) and Tongariro (1,968m/6,456ft). Mount Taranaki (2,518m/8,261ft), a solitary extinct volcanic cone, is situated near the western extremity of the island. North Island has numerous rivers, most of which rise in the eastern and central mountains, including the Waikato River (435km/270mi), the longest river in New Zealand. It flows north out of Lake Taupo (606km²/233mi²), the country's largest lake (where mineral springs are also found), into the Tasman Sea in the west. North Island has an irregular coastline, particularly on its northern extremity, the Auckland Peninsula, where it's just 10km/6mi wide.

South Island has a more regular coastline than North Island and in the south-west is characterised by deep fjords. The chief mountain range of South Island is the Southern Alps, a massive range extending from the south-west to the north-east for almost the entire length of the island (17 peaks in the range are over 3,000m/9,842ft high). Mount Cook (3,754m/12,316ft) is the highest point in New Zealand and rises from the centre of the range, which also contains a number of glaciers. Most of the rivers of South Island, including the Clutha River (338km/210mi long), the longest river on the island, rise in the Southern Alps. The largest lake is Lake Te Anau (342km²/132mi²) in the southern part of the Southern Alps. The Canterbury plains in the east and the Southland plains in the extreme south are the only extensive flat areas on the South Island.

The islands of New Zealand emerged in the Tertiary period and contain a complete series of marine sedimentary rocks, some of which date from the early Paleozoic era. Much of the topography of New Zealand has resulted from warping and block faulting, although volcanic action has also played a part in its formation, particularly that of North Island, where it continues to this day. Geysers and mineral hot springs occur in the volcanic area, particularly around Rotorua. New Zealand is within an earthquake zone and minor (usually unnoticeable) tremors occur almost monthly, although records show that serious earthquakes occur, on average, only once every 210 years.

Much New Zealand plant life is unique, and of the 2,000 indigenous species some 1,500 are found only here, including the golden kowhai and the scarlet pohutukawa. North Island is home to predominantly subtropical vegetation, including mangrove swamps in the north. The forest, or so-called bush, of North Island is mainly evergreen with a dense undergrowth of mosses and ferns. Evergreen trees include the kauri (the traditional wood used for house building in New Zealand), rimu, kahikatea and totara, all of which are excellent timber trees. The only extensive area of native grassland in North Island is the central volcanic plain. The eastern part of South Island is, for the most part, grassland up to an elevation of around 1,500m, while most forests are situated in the west (consisting mainly of native beech and Alpine vegetation at high altitudes).

With the exception of two species of bat, New Zealand has no indigenous mammals. The first white settlers (who arrived early in the 19th century) found a kind of dog and a black rat, both of which had been introduced by the Maoris around 500 years earlier and are now almost extinct. All other wild mammals are descended from deer, rabbits, goats, pigs, weasels, ferrets, and opossums, all of which were imported by early western settlers. No snakes and few unusual species of insects inhabit New Zealand (unlike Australia which is infested with them), although it does boast the tuatara, a lizard-like reptile with a third eye believed to be a distant relative of the dinosaurs. New Zealand has a large population of wild birds, including 23 native species which include the songbirds bellbird and tui and flightless species such as the kiwi (from which New Zealanders take their colloquial name), kakapo, takahe and weka. The survival of flightless birds is attributed to the absence of predatory animals (with the exception of domestic cats). The sparrow, blackbird, thrush, skylark, magpie and myna are among the most prevalent imported species.

New Zealand's rivers and lakes contain a variety of native edible fish, including whitebait, eel, lamprey and freshwater crustaceans, particularly crayfish. Trout and salmon have been introduced and are found in waters throughout the country. The surrounding ocean waters are the habitat of snapper, flounder, blue cod, hapuku, tarakihi, swordfish, flying fish, shark, and whales, in addition to a variety of shellfish including oysters, mussels and toheroas.

GOVERNMENT

New Zealand is a parliamentary democracy modelled on the British system. It is, however, unicameral, that is with one legislative body only, the House of Representatives, and no upper house (it was abolished in 1951 and is unlikely to be reinstated). The House of Representatives or parliament consists of Members of Parliament (MPs) who sit in the Parliament Building in Wellington and is regarded by most New Zealanders as the country's largest source of hot air, easily outperforming any of New Zealand's impressive geothermal geysers (not that it's any different from most other seats of government in this respect).

The executive branch of the government consists of the Prime Minister and her cabinet (New Zealand had a female Prime Minister, Jenny Shipley, for the first time in 1997, a trend continued by Helen Clark, the present Prime Minister). New Zealand has a Governor-General (G-G), who's appointed by the British Crown, although it's largely an honorary position and he rarely participates in government and usually intervenes only in constitutional matters. The G-G is appointed by the sovereign every five years on the recommendation of the government of the day and his most important (ceremonial) role is to dissolve the outgoing parliament and invite the leaders of the parties elected to power to form a new government.

Political Parties: Politics in New Zealand has traditionally been dominated by two parties: the National Party, which favours right-wing social policies and a market-orientated approach to the economy, and the Labour Party. The Labour Party traditionally favoured left of centre policies, including comprehensive social welfare spending, but during the '80s 'converted' to what were previously thought to be National Party policies, including economic reform and financial market deregulation. Other parties which currently have a voice include New Zealand First (a National Party splinter group), ACT, the Greens and the Alliance Party, a coalition of left-wing parties. In late 1999 the elections were won by a coalition of the Labour

Party, the Alliance Party and the Greens. Most elections attract a string of independents and minority parties, together with what can best be described as 'loony' parties (such as Legalise Cannabis and Natural Law).

Voting & Elections: New Zealand recently changed to a system of proportional representation (PR) from the first-past-the-post (FPP) system previously used. The kind of PR used in New Zealand is known as Mixed Member Proportional (MMP) system, which is designed to ensure that each political party's share of seats in parliament corresponds to its share of the vote. Voters have two votes: a 'party vote' is cast for the party of their choice and the other vote is for their preferred candidate. Parties are allocated seats in proportion to the number of party votes they receive and then candidates are allocated to those seats according to the votes they polled individually. The House of Representatives consists of 120 MPs, one representing each of the 60 electoral districts and 55 who are allocated according to the number of votes each party receives. The final five seats are reserved for candidates from Maori electoral districts. Some politicians have recently proposed that the number of MPs be reduced to save money (a sensible idea, which would no doubt prove popular in many countries!).

New Zealand's new system of MMP, while generally being recognised as an improvement over FPP, has caused something of an upheaval in the political system and has allowed smaller parties to obtain a presence in parliament for the first time, although no party can obtain a seat in parliament unless it obtains at least 5 per cent of the total vote. It has also created a situation where it's impossible for a single party to obtain an overall majority and thus two or more parties are forced to co-operate in a coalition to form a government. Some politicians have argued for a return to FPP, although this is unlikely to happen.

Parliamentary elections are held every three years, although the government can call an early election (which it rarely does, preferring to allow each parliament to run its course). Although many New Zealanders are apathetic about politics on a daily basis, they're usually keen to exercise their right to vote and the turnout in elections is rarely less than 80 per cent. Additionally, the New Zealand government doesn't hesitate to call referenda on subjects considered of great importance to the country. Recent referenda have included proportional representation (which was accepted by a small majority) and changes to the national superannuation system (which was rejected by a small percentage).

Legislative Process: New laws in New Zealand begin life as 'bills', which are 'read' to parliament. Bills undergo first and second readings before being passed to a select committee for discussion and consideration of submissions by interested parties. The select committee must report back to parliament within six months. A bill is then debated, and the House of Representatives considers it on a clause-by-clause basis. After a third reading, it's passed to the Governor-General (G-G) for assent and then becomes law. In theory, the G-G can reject laws using reserve power, particularly if he feels that the government is acting unconstitutionally. However, in practice, he's bound by convention to follow the advice of the government and give his assent to bills. Under the Constitution Act 1986, the British parliament is unable to make laws affecting New Zealand, although some British laws (the Imperial Acts, such as the Magna Carta and Habeas Corpus) are enshrined in New Zealand law.

Judiciary: New Zealand has a fiercely independent judiciary which, as with many other aspects of law and government, is modelled on the British system with some antipodean modifications. Judges are nominated from the ranks of the legal profession (barristers or solicitors with a minimum of seven years' service) and appointed by the G-G (not by the government or the electorate). Judges must retire on reaching the age of 68, although they may be re-appointed for up to two years. The Judicial Committee of the Privy Council is New Zealand's highest legal authority. The highest court is the Court of Appeal, whose decisions are final unless leave is granted to appeal to the Privy Council. The principal trial courts are the high court, staffed by the chief justice and 32 high court judges, and the district courts. Justices of the peace may, in some cases, try minor criminal cases. Special courts and tribunals determine matters relating to labour disputes, workers' compensation, land rights and family law.

All registered electors between the ages of 20 and 65 may be summoned to serve on a jury, although those in certain occupations, e.g. police officers, and those with criminal convictions which resulted in more than three years' imprisonment are excluded. Anyone called for jury service may apply to be excused on religious grounds or when service would cause unnecessary hardship.

Local Government: New Zealand is divided into 14 local government regions, an arrangement which was instituted in 1989. The regions are: Auckland, Bay of Plenty, Hawke's Bay, Northland, Taranaki, Gisborne, Waikato, Manawatu, Wanganui, and Wellington in North Island; and Canterbury, Otago, Nelson-Marlborough, Southland, and West Coast in South Island. These 14 regions are subdivided into 20 cities and 59 districts, with local government elections held every three years.

LEGAL & GENERAL ADVICE

As in other developed countries, fees charged by solicitors and barristers are sky-high and legal fees for even a simple case, e.g. a breach of contract, can run into tens of thousands of dollars. Junior lawyers charge at least $125 per hour and advice from a senior lawyer is likely to cost at least $175 an hour. Most New Zealand lawyers are qualified both as solicitors and barristers, i.e. they can work as advocates in court and don't need to appoint a separate barrister to perform this task. New Zealand has a system of legal aid which provides assistance to those who cannot afford to pay a solicitor, although the budget is tight and changes are continually being made to the system in order to streamline it and make it more cost effective. Those requiring legal aid for civil cases may find it difficult to obtain free legal assistance.

The Legal Services Board also operates a 'duty solicitor' scheme, which provides free and immediate legal aid to anyone who's arrested by the police. If you're arrested, you're entitled to a consultation with a solicitor and to have him present during an interview. In most towns and cities, usually in the poorer areas, there are community law centres (there are around 20 nationally) financed by public funds and other means (such as fund-raising). They provide free legal advice and representation to those unable to afford it, within the limits of their resources. Most towns also have a Citizens' Advice Bureau (☎ freephone 0800-367 222, 🖥 www.consumer.org.nz), where you can obtain free and confidential advice on a wide range of matters.

MARRIAGE & DIVORCE

Like many countries, New Zealand has declining marriage and rising divorce rates, although the divorce rate has remained stable at around 10,000 annually since 1996 and the average length of a marriage is around 15 years (longer than in most other western countries). An increasing number of New Zealanders are choosing to marry later in life or to remain single, although there was a slight increase in the number of marriages performed in 2000, which was around 20,000. New Zealand also has many single mothers, many of whom are in this position by choice and happily juggle career and family. While more women are choosing to wait to have families until later in life (the average childbearing age rose from 25.5 to 28 between 1999 and 2002), New Zealand also has one of the world's highest rates of unmarried teenager pregnancies. An increasing number of New Zealanders choose a simple civil ceremony rather than a church service, mainly because of the informality it provides and the much reduced cost. It's possible to marry anywhere in New Zealand, not just in a church or at a registry office, assuming that you can find a clergyman or registrar willing to perform the ceremony (a Dunedin couple recently married in the city's municipal swimming pool!).

New Zealand recognises de facto relationships, i.e. unmarried couples (both heterosexual and homosexual) living together, who have many of the rights and responsibilities of married couples, including the same rights regarding the inheritance of property (from 1st February 2002). Under new legislation, de facto couples are entitled to an equal share of the family home and other 'chattels', irrespective of who owns them. However, the new law applies only to de facto relationships of three years or longer. Note that under the new law, you can also make alternative arrangements for the division of your property, which is known as 'contracting out'. Advice regarding the new legislation should be sought from a lawyer or your local community law centre (see **Legal & General Advice** above).

MILITARY SERVICE

There's no conscription (draft) in New Zealand, where members of the armed forces are volunteers. The minimum age for enlistment has recently been raised to 17 in line with United Nations guidelines on the enlistment of minors. The New Zealand Army, Royal New Zealand Air Force (RNZAF) and Royal New Zealand Navy (RNZN) are separate services under the control of the Ministry of Defence. The army numbers around 4,400 regular personnel, the air force around 2,900 and the navy around 2,000. In addition there's a part-time reserve force called the Territorial Army (or 'Terries'), which trains in the evenings and at weekends and can be called up to assist the regular forces in an emergency. Members of the armed forces can expect to be posted to a new base every two to three years, a practice which may be changed, as it's believed to be largely responsible for the high number of service personnel who resign after their initial term. In a bid to make military life more attractive, the navy has recently (among other steps) introduced maternity uniform, which allows women to continue military service during a pregnancy!

New Zealand spends around 1 per cent of its GDP on defence. Budget cuts of 30 per cent since 1989 have recently been reversed by an increase of almost $750 million to provide new equipment such as armoured personnel carriers and transport aircraft and to recruit 500 personnel. In line with the New Zealand government's 'e-solutions' policy, the defence ministry has introduced an 'e-recruiting' strategy, thought to be in the world's first in the armed forces. Prospective recruits can now sign up online and it's hoped that this method may encourage more people to enlist. The size of New Zealand's military forces reflects the small size of the country, and there has been discussion about whether the navy and some other elements of the armed forces are viable on such a small scale, and whether they should be merged with the Australian armed services. For its part, Australia periodically takes its smaller neighbour to task for spending what it considers to be too little on defence. Australia spends around 2 per cent of its GDP on defending not only Australia but also the surrounding region.

New Zealand is a signatory to a number of defence treaties, including the Five Power Defence Agreement with Malaysia, Singapore, Australia and the UK, and the ANZUS alliance with Australia and the United States. New Zealand contributed forces to the western alliance during the Gulf War and contributes to peacekeeping duties around the world and has a particularly strong presence in East Timor, Mozambique and Sierra Leone, where New Zealand troops are in charge of de-mining operations. New Zealand operates a strict anti-nuclear defence policy and doesn't allow visits by foreign military forces carrying nuclear weapons, e.g. warships, which has caused friction between New Zealand and the USA.

PETS

New Zealanders are enthusiastic animal lovers and many people keep dogs and cats. However, cats have received a 'bad press' in recent years, as they're believed to be responsible for the decimation of New Zealand's wildlife. Cats aren't indigenous to New Zealand, and flightless birds such as the kiwi had few natural predators until the first European settlers landed their pets on the country's shores. If you plan to take a pet to New Zealand, it's important to check the latest regulations, which are complex. Given the distance (unless you're travelling from Australia) and container regulations, it's best to entrust the transportation of pets to a specialist shipping company.

New Zealand has strict regulations regarding the import of animals in order to prevent animal diseases entering the country, and pets and other animals cannot be imported without authorisation from customs. You must obtain an import permit, which is available from the Director of Animal Biosecurity, Ministry of Agriculture and Forestry (MAF), PO Box 2526, Wellington (☎ 04-498 9625, 🖳 www.quarantine.co.nz). Note that if your pet needs to undergo a period of quarantine, the import permit will be approved only if accompanied by a letter from an MAF-approved quarantine establishment (there are only three) confirming that your cat or dog has a reserved place. You require a 'zoo-sanitary certificate' and a health certificate from a veterinary surgeon in your home country, and your pet will need to undergo a period of quarantine after its arrival in New Zealand. All animals must be vaccinated against rabies and must have had a Rabies Neutralising Antibody Tritation test no less than six months before they enter quarantine. A repeat test must be done within 30 days of the start of quarantine. Cats and dogs imported from Australia, Hawaii, Sweden, Norway or the UK need not be quarantined, provided they're microchipped, are older than 16 weeks and have been resident in the exporting country for a minimum of six months previous to travel. The cost of transporting a cat or small dog from Europe or the USA, including all necessary paperwork, is likely to be at least $600, with quarantine accommodation costing from around $40 per day.

For further information contact the Ministry of Agriculture and Forestry, PO Box 2526, Wellington (☎ 04-498 9625, 🖳 www.quarantine.co.nz), a New Zealand diplomatic mission or NZ Customs (☎ freephone 0800-428 786 or 09-300 5399 from abroad). Customs also have a comprehensive website (🖳 www.customs.govt.nz) or you can contact one of the following offices: Auckland International Airport, PO Box

73-003 (☎ 09-275 9059), Christchurch, PO Box 14-086 (☎ 03-358 0600) or Wellington, PO Box 2218 (☎ 04-473 6099).

POLICE

New Zealand has a single national police force, which is controlled by a commissioner appointed by the Minister of Police and is divided into six operational regions, each headed by an assistant commissioner. Over 500,000 crimes are reported annually in New Zealand (estimated to be less than half the number actually committed), of which less than half are solved by the police (although this is much better than the record of police forces in many other countries and the crime resolution rate is currently the highest for a decade). Police officers (known as constables) can be identified by their dark blue (almost black) uniforms and peaked caps with a chequered band.

Police morale is low as a consequence of poor pay and insufficient resources, and the force has undergone something of a manpower crisis in recent years, as several Australian state forces have 'poached' New Zealand police officers, who can earn 10 to 20 per cent more in Australia. The fact that policing is similar in both countries and police exams are standardised has contributed to the problem. Police officers are forbidden to strike, although several hundred recently took part in a silent protest march (against poor pay and conditions) in Wellington during their off-duty hours.

New Zealand police officers are generally approachable, although some people consider them tyrannical. They don't usually carry guns, although they do carry handcuffs, batons and controversial pepper sprays. When guns are necessary (usually only when confronting armed criminals), members of the Armed Offenders Squad (AOS) are called in to deal with the incident. AOS members serve only part-time and many have more mundane duties between armed call-outs. The police force doesn't routinely deal with motorists in New Zealand, which is the responsibility of the Traffic Safety Service that patrols highways, sets speed traps (their favourite pastime) and handles motoring offences.

POPULATION

The population of New Zealand in mid-1999 was estimated at around 3.8 million (it's difficult to keep track, as at any given time 'half' the population is overseas, mostly in Australia) and is forecast to reach some 5 million by 2025. New Zealand is a sparsely populated country, with only some 14 inhabitants per square kilometre or around 31 per square mile (there are actually more New Zealanders per square mile in London!). Around three-quarters of the population lives in North Island and 85 per cent in urban areas (half in cities). The populations of New Zealand's major cities are roughly as follows: Auckland 1,090,000, Wellington 347,000, Christchurch 341,000, Hamilton 169,000, Dunedin 112,000 and Napier/Hastings area 115,000.

New Zealand is less ethnically diverse than most other developed nations, including Australia. Approximately 80 per cent of New Zealanders are of European (mainly British) descent and are known as *pakehas* by Maori (meaning 'white man' and not a derogatory term). The majority of the remaining inhabitants are Maori and other Polynesian Islanders. At the last census there were around 320,000 Maoris, 45,000 West Samoans, 24,000 Cook Islanders, 9,000 Niue Islanders and 7,500 Tonga

Islanders. There are around 90,000 people of Chinese extraction and around 40,000 of Indian origin. In recent years the population balance has been slowly changing in favour of non-Europeans. Two factors are responsible for this: first, the Maori and Polynesian population have an increasing birth rate and a decreasing death rate compared with those of European descent (which have remained static), as standards of health and welfare in these communities have improved; and second, the proportion of new immigrants of European descent is falling in favour of immigrants from other regions, particularly Asia.

RELIGION

New Zealand has a tradition of religious tolerance, and residents have total freedom of religion without hindrance by the state or community. New Zealand is a secular society and has no official state religion, although the majority of people are Christians, the main denominations being Anglican (25 per cent), Presbyterian (18 per cent) and Roman Catholic (16 per cent). Methodist and other Protestant denominations are also represented and there are also considerable numbers of Jews, Hindus, and Confucians. Most Maoris are members of the Ratana and Ringatu Christian sects. Only some 15 per cent of New Zealanders regularly attend religious services and the number is declining, even among those who claim to be followers of a particular religion.

SOCIAL CUSTOMS

All countries have peculiar (sometimes in both senses of the word) social customs and New Zealand is no exception. As a country substantially populated by people of British ancestry, it's inevitable that many New Zealand social customs are modelled on those of Britain with local influences, which have become more pronounced over the years. In general, New Zealanders tend to think that the British are prudish and snobbish. On the other hand, they tend to think that Australians and Americans are crass, although they share their pioneering spirit, common in all countries with a strong European heritage. Most New Zealanders try to strike a balance between these two extremes, while also doing things differently, just to prove that they really are different from their neighbours and ancestors. It's also important to note that although New Zealand's Maori community is a minority in terms of numbers, its cultural influence extends across racial barriers. The following are a few New Zealand social customs it may be helpful for you to be familiar with:

- New Zealanders tend to prefer first name terms except when it clearly isn't appropriate (for example, when addressing your prospective boss during an interview). When in doubt take your cue from your host or colleagues. It's usual for people at work to call each other by their first names, even when they're much higher or lower in the pecking order, and those who work together often also socialise together. It's common for friends to shorten names or use nicknames.

- It's considered socially acceptable to drop in on friends and acquaintances uninvited (and they will almost certainly do the same to you). You can also expect your neighbours to drop in uninvited, which is usually out of genuine friendliness rather than nosiness (or a desire to pass judgement on your interior decor). Indeed, if your new neighbours don't pop round, it's considered polite to call on them and introduce yourself.

- Direct questions about, for example, your likes and dislikes or your family shouldn't be considered as rudeness, as it usually indicates genuine interest and friendship (New Zealanders generally prefer not to 'beat about the bush').

- Don't be surprised to receive invitations to social gatherings, such as parties or barbecues, from people you hardly know. This is particularly common when moving into a new area or starting a new job. It's done out of genuine warmth rather than any sense of duty and should be accepted in the spirit in which it's intended. Indeed, it would be considered rude to turn down such an invitation out of hand. It's usual to 'bring a bottle' if you're invited to a party or to a BYO (Bring Your Own) restaurant, i.e. a restaurant which doesn't have a licence to sell alcohol.

- Casual dress is normal in most situations, e.g. shorts are often worn to work in the summer and jeans are acceptable in most restaurants and night-clubs. New Zealanders rarely wear formal dress such as evening dresses and dinner jackets. If you're invited to an event where formal attire is required, it will be clearly stated on the invitation.

- New Zealanders generally respect other people's customs, cultures, tastes, traditions and orientations, whether social, political or sexual. In fact, they usually have a particular regard for independent thinkers and those who dare to be different. This dates back to the pioneering days, and tolerance towards other ideas and cultures, provided they don't involve physical or emotional harm, is enshrined in New Zealand law. Nevertheless, if you have any bizarre tastes or habits, it's wise to keep them under wraps until you've ascertained whether or not your colleagues or acquaintances share them. Some New Zealanders, particularly older people, can be prudish and may even consider it a virtue.

TIME DIFFERENCE

New Zealand lies within a single time zone. Summer daylight saving time, an advance of one hour, is observed between the first Sunday in October and the third Sunday in March. New Zealand hasn't taken to the 24-hour clock system, and times in most timetables are shown according to the 12-hour clock system. Therefore, times are marked either 'am' or 'pm', or are printed in light type to indicate before noon and heavy type to indicate after noon. If in doubt, it's better to ask than to arrive 12 hours late (or early) for your flight or bus!

Bear in mind that there's a substantial time difference between New Zealand and Europe (and to a lesser extent the USA) and you should check the local time abroad before making international telephone calls. For example, when calling western Europe, you'll need to phone either first thing in the morning or last thing at night. The time difference between Wellington at noon in January and some major international cities is shown below:

SYDNEY	LONDON	CAPE TOWN	TOKYO	LOS ANGELES	NEW YORK
10am	midnight	2am	9am	4pm	7pm
					(the previous day)

TIPPING

Tipping isn't a general custom in New Zealand (Americans please note!), although you may wish to leave a tip when you've had exceptional service or have received good value. New Zealanders almost never tip and, in fact, some people regard it as patronising or even insulting. Neither is it customary to round up amounts (e.g. taxi fares) to the nearest dollar or so, although most people won't complain if you do. Service charges aren't added to bills in hotels and restaurants and you won't be expected to add your own.

TOILETS

Public toilets in New Zealand are generally clean and are commonly found in parks, council and tourist offices, shopping centres, department stores, and bus and railway stations. The most sanitary (sometimes even quite luxurious) toilets are found in hotels, restaurants, public and private offices, large stores, museums, galleries, airports, car parks, petrol stations and near popular beaches. Hotel (i.e. pub) and bar toilets vary from no-go areas to spotless. New Zealanders don't use euphemisms like powder room, restroom or bathroom as Americans do, and the toilet is more likely to be referred to as the 'loo', which is considered quite a polite term, or the 'dunny'. Public toilets are usually free (when they aren't, you may be required to pay a few cents to gain access to a cubicle) and don't normally have an attendant.

Some toilets have nappy (diaper) changing facilities and facilities for nursing mothers, and an increasing number also have special facilities for the disabled. Toilets are usually marked with the familiar male and female symbols, whereas disabled toilets are generally used by both sexes and indicated by the international wheelchair sign. Toilets for the disabled may be locked to keep out 'unauthorised' users, in which case there will be a notice nearby explaining where the key can be obtained.

19.

THE KIWIS

Who are the New Zealanders? What are they like? Let's take a candid (and totally prejudiced) look at the New Zealand people (Kiwis), tongue firmly in cheek, and hope they forgive the flippancy or that they don't read this bit (which is why it's hidden away at the back of the book). The typical Kiwi is friendly, generous, outspoken, hard working, honest, inquisitive, patriotic, adventurous, bold, chauvinistic, modest, lethargic, down-to-earth, optimistic, relaxed, parochial, a compulsive gambler, self-reliant, practical, sartorially challenged, emotionless, hospitable, polite, decent, a beer drinker, open, conservative, prudish, garrulous, a suicidal driver, old-fashioned, casual, understated, cosmopolitan, a conservationist, good-humoured, a conformist, classless, a rugby and cricket fan, self-deprecating, generous, sincere, naïve, nationalistic, a carnivore, open, insular, a philistine, competitive, proud, a habitual traveller, informal, sociable, idealistic and a foreigner.

You may have noticed that the above list contains 'a few' contradictions (as does life in New Zealand), which is hardly surprising, as there's no such thing as a typical Kiwi and few people conform to the popular stereotype. People from the North and South Islands are also supposed to have different characters, although foreigners will hardly notice the difference. New Zealand is a multicultural country (though not nearly as much as Australia) and a nation of foreigners – even the Polynesians, the country's oldest inhabitants, came from somewhere else – many of whom have little in common. However, despite its racial mix, New Zealand isn't a universal melting pot, and different ethnic groups such as Maoris, Chinese, British and assorted other Europeans often live separate lives with their own customs, neighbourhoods, shops, clubs, restaurants, newspapers and sports.

New Zealanders pride themselves on their lack of class-consciousness and don't have the same class distinctions and pretensions common in the 'mother' country (England), and consider the British to be snobbish (although descended from the British, the Kiwis have been trying to live it down for over a century). However, New Zealand isn't exactly a classless society, and status is as important there as it is anywhere else, although it's usually based on education or money rather than birthright. New Zealand generally has no class or 'old school tie' barriers to success and almost anyone, however humble his origins, can fight his way to the top of the heap (although colour 'barriers' aren't always so easy to overcome). Kiwis don't much like Asians or any 'exotic' foreigners, although you will generally be accepted provided you can blend into the background (green aliens will have no problems). Economic necessity has led to closer ties with Far Eastern and the Pacific countries and increased immigration from Asia (much to the horror of New Zealand's xenophobes).

Ties between New Zealand and the UK remain strong, although they've loosened somewhat in recent years and there's even talk of changing the New Zealand flag (a silver fern on a black background has been suggested – which would certainly be different) and of becoming a republic, although there isn't much of a republican movement in New Zealand (unlike, for example, Australia). Despite that fact that most Kiwis are of British stock, few still have close connections with the UK and many have no attachment to the Union Jack (which is incorporated in their flag). However, there remain many similarities between Kiwis and the British, and New Zealand still copies many of the old country's habits (and new ideas) – in some ways Kiwis are considered to be more British than the British. The country even shares the UK's obsession with the weather, which is a popular topic of conversation. Not surprisingly, all New Zealand's bad weather, which usually consists of torrential rain in the South Island and howling gales in the North Island, comes from Australia.

Most rancour is reserved for the Aussies, who spend much of their time making jokes about Kiwis (e.g. 'The Kiwis have found a new use for sheep – wool' and 'What do you call a Kiwi in a suit? The defendant.'). New Zealanders feel culturally threatened by 'loud-mouthed' Aussies (in the same way that Canadians do by Americans) and New Zealand is often referred to disparagingly as the eighth state of Australia (tens of thousands of Kiwis live in Australia, and Sydney has a larger population of Kiwis than most New Zealand cities). Kiwis have much in common with their closest neighbours (who thankfully aren't *too* close) and they've even been known to marry them. Although they don't much like comparisons being made, Kiwis are actually quite similar to (but much quieter than) Aussies, with whom they share their colourful language (with local idioms and Maori words thrown in for good measure), drinking habits, 'tucker' (food) , sports, sheep, lack of 'culture' and isolation from the rest of the world (among other things).

Most immigrants get on well with their Polynesian cousins (they officially stopped fighting each other in the 19th century), who sensibly mostly live in the warmer North Island (only one in 16 lives in South Island). The main cause of (mild) friction is the competition for top dog between the inhabitants of the country's two major cities, Auckland (New Zealand's largest city and the world's largest Polynesian city) and Wellington (the nation's capital). The Maoris arrived in 'the land of the long white cloud' (*Aotearoa*) by canoe around 925 AD from other Pacific islands (they're superb sailors and have been called the 'Vikings of the South Seas'). The white man (*pakeha*) didn't arrive in any great numbers until the 19th century, although it didn't take him long to assert his 'authority' and rob the Maoris of their land, which was done 'legally' under the infamous Treaty of Waitingi (which cleverly has never been ratified – otherwise the Maoris would own a lot more land than they do at present).

In recent years there has been an upsurge in Maori cultural awareness, and *Maoritanga* (the Maori way of life) is now taught in schools along with the Maori language. This has inevitably resulted in the question of land ownership and fishing rights being raised by Maori activists (perhaps influenced by the Aborigines' example in Australia) and has led to a number of clashes in recent years. Although many Maoris are second-class citizens, their plight is much less than that of Australia's Aborigines. Despite their differences of opinion, intermarriage between Maoris and whites is common and there are fewer and fewer full-bloodied Maoris left in New Zealand (it's estimated that 1 in 12 New Zealanders are half Maori and many more are part Maori). This may have something to do with the traditional Maori greeting (*hongi*) which consists of pressing noses together with the eyes closed and making a low 'mm-mm' sound.

Kiwis are passionate about sport and, when not debating the price of lamb, are discussing the latest rugby or cricket results. The All Blacks rugby team is internationally acclaimed and star players are feted in the same way as soccer stars in many other other countries. The All Blacks perform their famous *haka* war dance before matches to intimidate their opponents (although having Jonah Lomu on your side is enough to scare anyone), but unfortunately this didn't seem to work in 1998, when they lost an unprecedented five matches in a row. Apart from rugby, New Zealand's other important sport is cricket and, although they haven't had much of an international team since Richard Hadlee retired in the '80s, they would *never* resort to such things as bowling underarm to win a test match (unlike their neighbours,

Australia). The Aussies are the old sporting enemy, with whom the Kiwis compete passionately at all sports (the Kiwis also enjoy beating the Poms). Apart from rugby, cricket and a few other sports, most New Zealand 'sports' involve trying to commit suicide by hurling yourself off bridges, out of planes or into boiling rapids (you cannot accuse Kiwis of being wimps!).

New Zealanders aren't noted for their cuisine (something else they inherited from the British), which largely consists of numerous ways of serving lamb, fish and chips, meat pies and the obligatory tomato sauce (which goes with everything), ice cream, kiwi fruit and pavlova (New Zealand's national dish, although invented in Australia). Kiwis are voracious carnivores and among the biggest meat-eaters in the world – in fact things haven't changed a lot since the first Polynesian settlers ate each other. Kiwis generally have an unhealthy diet of biscuits, cakes, fast food and take-aways, despite the country's abundance of fresh fruit and vegetables (in New Zealand, a salad is *haute cuisine*). To compensate for their lack of culinary skills New Zealanders have been making some passable wines in recent years with 'catchy' names such as 'cat's pee on a gooseberry bush', although most Kiwis are beer drinkers. One of the secrets of enjoying a meal in New Zealand is to drink a lot (which the Kiwis do with gusto); when you're drunk, most food tastes good.

The Kiwis are famous for their relaxed pace of life (except when motoring, when they're hell bent on reaching the next life as fast as possible), particularly in rural areas where a rush consists of a brisk walk to the nearest pub (or a ride on a tractor). Outside Auckland and Wellington, night-life usually consists of watching TV or getting drunk (or both) and most Kiwis are tucked up in bed by 9pm (you would also be if you had to get up at 5am to milk the ewes). Kiwis go to extraordinary lengths to 'amuse' themselves (which is why they partake in all those death-defying sports), and a popular pastime in a pub in Napier (called 'bar-fly hopping') involves bouncing on a trampoline and trying to attach yourself to a wall with Velcro! New Zealand is notorious as a cultural backwater (even *Australians* make fun of it), although it isn't as (all) black as it's painted (at least in the major cities) and the Maoris have a thousand years of culture and history in New Zealand.

The Kiwis are slow to make changes, both individually and as a nation, and the country is often reckoned to be around 20 years behind the rest of the world (which isn't surprising, as it used to take that long to get there from Europe or North America – assuming you could find it at all!). Not so long ago, Kiwis were still wearing '60s fashions and driving around in Morris Minors and Ford Anglias. However, it isn't true that they don't have electricity, although it may sometimes appear that way when visiting Auckland. The country is so far from anywhere that it was one of the last places on earth to be inhabited by man (if you went any further south you'd fall off the edge of the world) and although most people have heard of New Zealand, few actually know where it is. Sometimes you don't just feel as if you're in the most isolated country in the world, but on a different planet altogether (the end of the world will probably be a few weeks late reaching New Zealand). Not surprisingly, New Zealand can appear a little detached from the rest of the world, and newspapers and news bulletins rarely mention anything happening overseas unless it's something particularly dramatic (such as the world price of lamb going through the floor).

New Zealand politics are deadly boring, even to Kiwis, although things have livened up in recent years with the introduction of proportional representation. Nowadays, you never know which politicians will jump into bed with whom (metaphorically speaking) and how long they will remain bedfellows, which makes for a lively parliament but hardly adds to the stability of government. New Zealand has (surprisingly) always been at the forefront of social change and is something of an economic laboratory. It was the first self-governing country to give women the vote in 1893 (25 years before the UK) and in 1998 New Zealand's women were rated fourth in the world by the United Nations at gaining access to power. New Zealand was also one of the first countries (in 1938) to establish a system of social security (including a national health service), the first to introduce an old-age pension and the first to institute an eight-hour working day. Both sexes have equal rights and opportunities in law, and New Zealand is one of the few countries in the world to have had a woman prime minister (and possibly the *only* one to have had two!). Nevertheless, as in most democracies, Kiwis have a healthy disrespect (contempt) for their politicians.

Immigration has undeniably made New Zealand a culturally richer, more diverse and interesting country, although it's now closed to many of the sort of people who made it was it is today. However, if you're rejected, try to look on the bright side; the New Zealand Dream isn't always the paradise it's cracked up to be. Despite its isolation from the real world, the country isn't completely detached from the problems that beset other countries. These include a spiralling crime rate (particularly youth crime and delinquency), high unemployment, homelessness, a worsening drug problem, welfare dependency, a rising divorce rate, a horrific road accident-rate (aided by widespread drunken driving), many single-parent families (which make up almost a quarter of Kiwis), racial tensions and an economy that's too dependent on crumbling Asian markets. These problems are by no means unique to New Zealand in today's turbulent world and many are shared by other western countries.

Now for the good news! New Zealand is one of the most open, liberal, stable and tolerant societies in the world. It has a strong economy, political stability, an excellent education system, a skilled workforce, a high standard of living, some of the most desirable cities to be found anywhere and one of the cleanest environments in the world (the country declared itself the world's first nuclear-free zone in 1985). New Zealand is also renowned for its wealth of natural beauty, outdoor lifestyle, wholesome food, friendly people, sports prowess, freedom, public healthcare system and excellent local government. Although immigrants may occasionally criticise some aspects of New Zealand life, relatively few consider leaving (permanently) and most are proud to call themselves Kiwis. In fact, immigrants from a vast range of backgrounds firmly believe that New Zealand (God's Own Country or 'godzone') is one of the best countries in the world. Put simply, New Zealand is a great place in which to live, work and raise a family.

A final word of caution for newcomers – whatever you do don't make jokes about Kiwis and sheep, which are in bad taste and to be avoided at all costs.

Up the All Blacks! Long live New Zealand!

20.

MOVING HOUSE OR LEAVING NEW ZEALAND

When moving house or leaving New Zealand there are many things to be considered and a 'million' people to be informed. The checklists contained in this chapter are designed to make the task easier and with luck help prevent an ulcer or a nervous breakdown, provided of course you don't leave everything to the last minute (only divorce or a bereavement causes more stress than moving house). See also **Moving House** on page 95 and **Relocation Consultants** on page 83.

MOVING HOUSE

When moving house within New Zealand the following items should be considered:

- If you live in rented accommodation, you must give your landlord notice (the period will depend on your contract). If you don't give sufficient notice, you will be required to pay the rent until the end of your contract or for the full notice period. This will also apply if you have a separate contract for a garage or other rented property, e.g. a holiday home.
- Inform the following:
  - your employer;
  - your present and new council if you're a homeowner and are moving to a new area. When moving to a new area, you may be entitled to a refund of a portion of your property taxes (rates).
  - your electricity, gas and water companies;
  - your telephone company (or companies);
  - your insurance companies (for example health, car and home), banks, post office, stockbroker and other financial institutions, credit and charge card companies, hire purchase companies, solicitor and accountant, and local businesses where you have accounts;
  - your family doctor, dentist and other health practitioners. Health records should be transferred to your new doctor and dentist, if applicable.
  - your children's and your own schools. If applicable, arrange for schooling in your new area. Try to give a term's notice and obtain a copy of any relevant school reports or records from current schools.
  - all regular correspondents, subscriptions, social and sports clubs, professional and trade journals, and friends and relatives. Give or send them your new address and telephone number. Arrange to have your mail redirected by NZ Post.
  - your local consulate or embassy, if you're registered with them (see page 77).
- If you have a New Zealand driving licence or a New Zealand registered car, give the authorities your new address as soon as possible after moving.
- Return library books and anything else borrowed.
- Arrange removal of your furniture and belongings by booking a removal company (see page 95) well in advance. If you have only a few items of furniture to move, you may prefer to do your own move, in which case you could need to hire a van.
- If you're renting, make sure that you get your bond returned.

- Arrange for a cleaning and/or decorating company for rented accommodation, if required.
- Cancel milk and newspaper deliveries.
- **Ask yourself (again): 'Is it really worth all this trouble?'**

LEAVING NEW ZEALAND

Before leaving New Zealand permanently or for an indefinite period, the following items should be considered *in addition* to those listed above under **Moving House**:

- Give notice to your employer(s), if applicable.
- Check that your family's passports aren't out of date.
- Check whether any special requirements (e.g. visas, permits or inoculations) are necessary for entry into your country of destination by contacting the local embassy or consulate in New Zealand. An exit permit or visa isn't required to leave New Zealand.
- Book a shipping company (see page 95) well in advance. International shipping companies usually provide a wealth of information and may also be able to advise you on various matters concerning your relocation. Find out the exact procedure for shipping your belongings to your country of destination from the embassy in New Zealand of the country to which you're moving (don't rely entirely on your shipping company). Special forms may need to be completed before arrival. If you've been living in New Zealand for less than a year, you're required to export personal effects, including furniture and vehicles, that were imported tax and duty-free. Arrange to sell anything that you won't be taking with you, e.g. car and furniture.
- Sell your house, apartment or other property, or arrange to let it through a friend or a letting agency (see **Chapter 5**).
- You may qualify for a rebate on your tax payments (see page 234). If you're leaving New Zealand permanently and have been a member of a company superannuation scheme, you may be entitled to a refund or may be able to have your fund transferred to a new employer's fund. Contact your company personnel office or superannuation company for information.
- If you have a New Zealand-registered car which you're permanently exporting, you should ask the New Zealand authorities to de-register the vehicle and register it in your new country of residence on arrival.
- Depending on your destination, your pets may require special inoculations or may need to go into quarantine for a period (contact the embassy of your country of destination for information).
- Contact your telephone and other utility companies well in advance, particularly if you need to have deposits refunded.
- Arrange health, travel and other insurance as necessary (see **Chapter 13**).
- Depending on your destination, arrange health and dental check-ups for your family before leaving New Zealand. Obtain a copy of your health and dental

records and a statement from your health insurance company noting your present level of cover.

- Terminate any outstanding loan, lease or hire purchase contracts and pay outstanding bills (allow plenty of time, as some companies may be slow to respond).

- Check whether you're entitled to a rebate on your car and other insurance. Obtain a letter from your New Zealand car insurance company stating your number of years of no-claims discount.

- Check whether you need an international driving permit or a translation of your New Zealand or foreign driving licence for your country of destination.

- Give friends and business associates in New Zealand a temporary address and telephone number where you can be contacted overseas.

- If you're travelling by air, allow plenty of time to get to the airport, register your luggage, and clear security and immigration.

- Buy a copy of *Living and Working in* ******** before leaving New Zealand. If we haven't written it yet, drop us a line and we'll get started on it right away!

Have a safe journey!

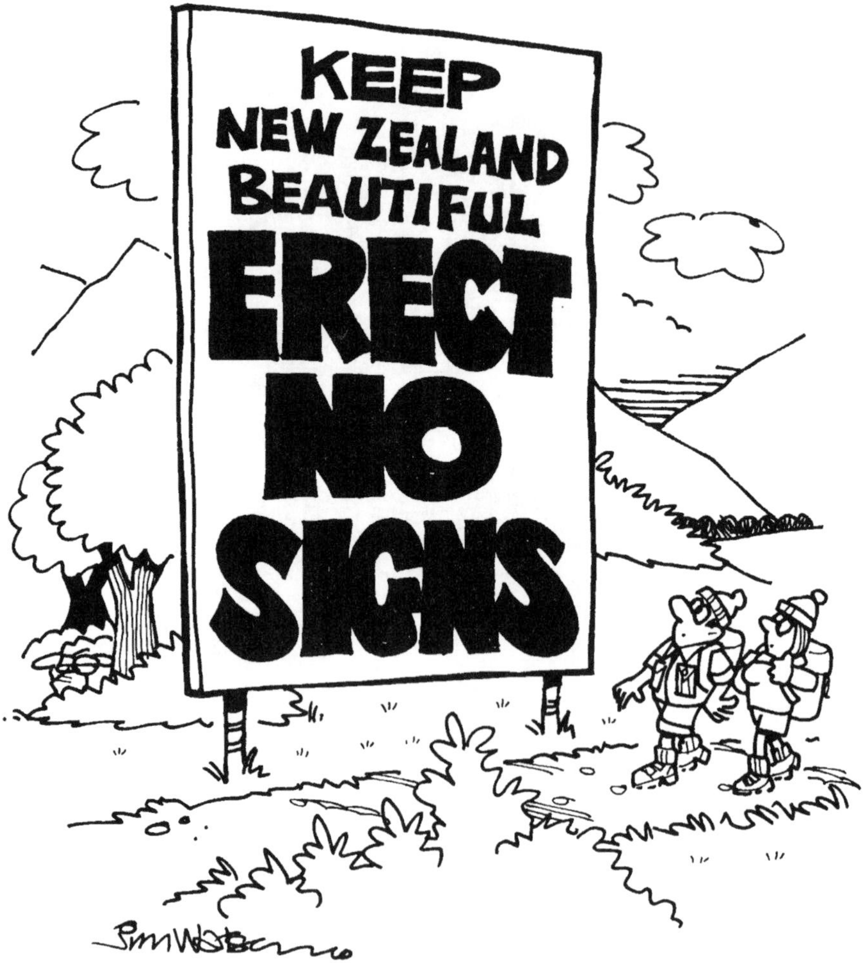
KEEP
NEW ZEALAND
BEAUTIFUL
ERECT
NO
SIGNS

APPENDICES

APPENDIX A: USEFUL ADDRESSES

Embassies & Consulates

Most foreign embassies in New Zealand are located in the capital Wellington (as you would expect), although some countries have their missions in Auckland. Note that business hours vary considerably and embassies close on their national holidays as well as New Zealand's public holidays. Always telephone to check the business hours before visiting.

Argentina: Level 14, 142 Lambton Quay, Wellington (☎ 04-472 8330).

Australia: 72–78 Hobson Street, Thorndon, PO Box 4036, Wellington (☎ 04-473 6411).

Austria: 57 Willis Street, Wellington (☎ 04-499 6393).

Belgium: 12th Floor, 1–3 Willeston Street, Box 3841, Wellington (☎ 04-917 0237).

Brazil: 10 Brandon Street, Wellington (☎ 04-473 3516).

Canada: 3rd Floor, 61 Molesworth Street, Box 12049, Wellington (☎ 04-473 9577).

Chile: 19 Bolton Street, Box 3861. Wellington (☎ 04-471 6270).

China: 2–6 Glenmore Street, Kelburn, Wellington (☎ 04-472 1382).

Czech Republic: 48 Hair Street, Wainuiomata, PO Box 43-035, Wellington (☎ 04-939 1610).

Finland: 6th Floor, Simpson Grierson Building, 44–52 The Terrace, PO Box 2402, Wellington (☎ 04-499 4599).

France: 34–42 Manners Street, Wellington (☎ 04-384 2555).

Germany: 90–92 Hobson Street, Thorndon, Box 1687, Wellington (☎ 04-473 6063).

Greece: 5–7 Willeston Street, Box 27157, Wellington (☎ 04-473 7775).

India: 180 Molesworth Street, Box 4045, Wellington (☎ 04-473 6390).

Indonesia: 70 Glen Road, Kelburn, Box 3543, Wellington (☎ 04-475 8699).

Iran: 151 Te Anau Road, Roseneath, Wellington (☎ 04-386 2976).

Ireland: 6th Floor, 18 Shortland Street, PO Box 279, Auckland (☎ 09-302 2867).

Israel: 13th Floor, Equinox House, 111 The Terrace, PO Box 2171, Wellington (☎ 04-472 2362).

Italy: 34 Grant Road, Thorndon, PO Box 463, Wellington (☎ 04-473 5339).

Japan: Level 18–19, Majestic Centre, 100 Willis Street, Wellington (☎ 04-473 1540).

Korea: Level 11, ASB Bank Tower, 2 Hunter Street, PO Box 11-143, Wellington (☎ 04-473 9073).

Malaysia: 10 Washington Avenue, Brooklyn, Box 9422, Wellington (☎ 04-385 2439).

Mexico: Level 8, Perpetual Trust House, 111–115 Customhouse Quay, PO Box 11-510, Wellington (☎ 04-472 0555).

Netherlands: Investment House, Corner Ballance & Featherstone Streets, Box 840, Wellington (☎ 04-471 6390).

Norway: 61 Molesworth Street, Wellington (☎ 04-471 2503).

Papua New Guinea: 279 Willis Street, PO Box 197, Wellington (☎ 04-385 2474).

Peru: Level 8, Cigna House, 40 Mercer Street, Wellington (☎ 04-499 8087).

Philippines: 50 Hobson Street, Thorndon, Box 12042. Wellington (☎ 04-472 9848).

Poland: 17 Upland Road, Kelburn, PO Box 10-211, Wellington (☎ 04-475 9453).

Portugal: 33 Garfield Street, Parnell, PO Box 305, Auckland (☎ 09-309 1454).

Russia: 57 Messines Road, Karori, Wellington (☎ 04-476 6113).

Singapore: 17 Kabul Street, Khandallah, PO Box 13-140, Wellington (☎ 04-479 2076).

Spain: PO Box 72-071, Papakura, Auckland (☎ 09-299 6019).

Sweden: 13th Floor, Vogel Building, Aitken Street, Thorndon, Wellington (☎ 04-499 9895).

Switzerland: Panama House, 22 Panama Street, Wellington (☎ 04-472 1593).

Thailand: 2 Cook Street, Karori, Box 17226, Wellington (☎ 04-476 8618).

Turkey: 8/15 Murphy Street, Thorndon, Wellington (☎ 04-472 1292).

United Kingdom: 44 Hill Street, Wellington (☎ 04-924 2888, 🖳 www.britain. org.nz).

USA: 29 Fitzherbert Terrace, Box 1190, Wellington (☎ 04-462 6000, 🖳 http:// usembassy.state.gov/wellington).

Government Departments

Births, Deaths & Marriages, PO Box 10-526, Wellington (☎ freephone 0800-225 252, 🖳 www.bdm.govt.nz).

Citizenship Office, PO Box 10-526, Wellington (☎ freephone 0800-225 151, 🖳 www.citizenship.govt.nz).

Department for Courts, PO Box 2750, Wellington (☎ 04-494 8800, 🖳 www.courts. govt.nz).

Department of Child, Youth and Family Services, PO Box 2620, Wellington (☎ 04-918 9100, 🖳 www.cyf.govt.nz).

Department of Conservation, PO Box 10-420, Wellington (☎ 04-471 0726, 🖳 www.doc.govt.nz).

Department of Corrections, PO Box 1206, Wellington (☎ 04-499 5620, 🖳 www.corrections.govt.nz).

Department of Inland Revenue (IRD), PO Box 39-050, Wellington (☎ freephone 0800-377 774, 🖳 www.ird.govt.nz).

Department of Internal Affairs, PO Box 805, Wellington (☎ 04-495 7200, 🖳 www.dia.govt.nz).

Department of Labour, PO Box 3705, Wellington (☎ 04-915 4000, 💻 www.dol. govt.nz).

Department of Prime Minister & Cabinet, Parliament Building, Wellington (☎ 04-471 9074, 💻 www.dpmc.govt.nz).

Department of Social Development, Private Bag 39-993, Wellington (☎ 04-916 3860, 💻 www.msd.govt.nz).

Department of Survey and Land Information, Private Bag 5501, Wellington (☎ 04-460 0110, 💻 www.linz.govt.nz).

Land Information New Zealand (LINZ), Private Bag 5501, Wellington (☎ 04-460 0110, 💻 www.linz.govt.nz).

Ministry for the Environment, PO Box 10-362, Wellington (☎ 04-917 7400, 💻 www.mfe.govt.nz).

Ministry of Agriculture & Forestry, PO Box 2526, Wellington (☎ 04-474 4100, 💻 www.maf.govt.nz).

Ministry of Agriculture & Forestry, Quarantine Services, Private Bag 966, Hamilton (☎ 07-838 5384, 💻 www.quarantine.co.nz).

Ministry of Civil Defence, PO Box 5010, Wellington (☎ 04-473 7363, 💻 www.civil defence.govt.nz).

Ministry of Consumer Affairs, PO Box 1473, Wellington (☎ 04-474 2750, 💻 www.consumer-ministry.govt.nz).

Ministry of Culture and Heritage, PO Box 5364, Wellington (☎ 04-499 4229, 💻 www.mch.govt.nz).

Ministry of Defence, PO Box 5347, Wellington (☎ 04-496 0270, 💻 www.defence. govt.nz).

Ministry of Education, PO Box 1666, Wellington (☎ 04-463 8000, 💻 www.min edu.govt.nz).

Ministry of Fisheries, PO Box 1020, Wellington (☎ 04-470 2600, 💻 www.fish. govt.nz).

Ministry of Foreign Affairs & Trade, Private Bag 18-901, Wellington (☎ 04-494 8500, 💻 www.mft.govt.nz).

Ministry of Health, PO Box 5013, Wellington (☎ 04-496 2000, 💻 www.moh. govt.nz).

Ministry of Housing, PO Box 10 729, Wellington (☎ 04-472 2753, 💻 www.min housing.govt.nz).

Ministry of Justice, PO Box 180, Wellington (☎ 04-494 4700, 💻 www.justice. govt.nz).

Ministry of Maori Development (*Te Puni Kokiri*), PO Box 3943, Wellington (☎ 04-922 6000, 💻 www.tpk.govt.nz).

Ministry of Pacific Island Affairs, PO Box 833, Wellington (☎ 04-473 4493, 💻 www.minpac.govt.nz).

Ministry of Research, Science & Technology, PO Box 5336, Wellington (☎ 04-472 6400, 💻 www.morst.govt.nz).

Ministry of Transport, PO Box 3175, Wellington (☎ 04-472 1253, 💻 www. transport.govt.nz).

Ministry of Women's Affairs, PO Box 10 049, Wellington (☎ 04-473 4112, 💻 www.mwa.govt.nz).

Ministry of Youth Affairs, PO Box 10 300, Wellington (☎ 04-471 2158, 💻 www. youthaffairs.govt.nz).

New Zealand Customs, PO Box 29, Wellington (☎ freephone 0800-428 786, 💻 www.customs.govt.nz).

New Zealand Immigration Service, PO Box 27 149, Wellington (☎ 04-384 7929, 💻 www.immigration.govt.nz).

The Treasury, PO Box 3724, Wellington (☎ 04-472 2733, 💻 www.treasury. govt.nz).

Magazines & Newspapers

Destination New Zealand, Outbound Newspapers, 1 Commercial Road, Eastbourne, East Sussex BN21 3XQ, UK (☎ 01323-726040, 💻 www.outbound-news papers.com).

New Zealand News UK, Commonwealth Publishing, 3rd Floor, New Zealand House, Haymarket, London SW1Y 4TE, UK (☎ 020-7747 9200, 💻 www.nznewsuk.co.uk).

New Zealand Outlook, Consyl Publishing, 3 Buckhurst Road, Bexhill-on-Sea, East Sussex TN40 1QF, UK (☎ 01424-223111, 💻 www.consylpublishing.co.uk).

TNT Magazine New Zealand, 14–15 Child's Place, London SW5 9RX, UK (☎ 020-7373 3377, 💻 www.tntmag.co.uk).

Miscellaneous

Archives New Zealand, PO Box 12-050, Wellington (☎ 04-499 5595, 💻 www. archives.govt.nz).

National Library of New Zealand, PO Box 1467, Wellington (☎ 04-474 3000, 💻 www.natlib.govt.nz).

Statistics New Zealand, PO Box 2922, Wellington (☎ 04-495 4600, 💻 www. stats.govt.nz).

TeachNZ, PO Box 1666, Wellington (☎ freephone 0800-832 246, 💻 www.teach nz.govt.nz).

APPENDIX B: FURTHER READING

There are many useful reference books for those seeking general information about Australia including the *New Zealand Official Year Book* published annually by Statistics New Zealand. A selection of books about New Zealand are listed below (the publication title is followed by the name of the author and the publisher's name in brackets). Books prefixed with an asterisk (*) are recommended by the author. Some of the books listed are out of print, but you may still be able to find a copy in a book shop or library.

Living & Working

Emigrate with Caution, Nicola Butler (Livingwords)

Finding a Job in New Zealand, Joy Muirhead (How To Books)

***The New Zealand Immigration Guide**, Adam Starchild

The Small Business Book: A New Zealand Guide, Robert Hamlin & John English (Bridgit Williams)

Your Successful Small Business: A New Zealand Guide to Starting Out and Staying in Business, Judith Ashton (Viking Pacific)

Tourist Guides

***AA/Baedeker's New Zealand** (AA Publishing)

***Australia & New Zealand Travel Planner** (TNT Magazine)

Berlitz Pocket Guide to New Zealand (Berlitz)

***Berlitz Travellers Guide New Zealand** (Berlitz)

***Blue Guide New Zealand** (A & C Black)

Destination New Zealand, Hildesuse Gaertner & Sue Bollans (Windsor)

Essential New Zealand (Automobile Association)

Fielding's New Zealand, Zeke & Joan Wigglesworth (Fielding)

***Fodor's Gold Guides: New Zealand** (Fodor)

***Frommers New Zealand from $50 a Day**, Elizabeth Hanson & Richard Adams (Macmillan)

Insider's New Zealand Guide, Harry Blutstein (MPC)

***Landmark Visitor's Guide: New Zealand**, Korner-Bourne (Landmark Publishing)

***Let's Go New Zealand** (Macmillan)

***Lonely Planet New Zealand** (Lonely Planet)

***Maverick Guide to New Zealand**, Robert W. Bone (Pelican)

Nelles Guide: New Zealand (Verlag Nelles)

New Zealand 2001: Budget Travel Guide, V. Jacquemont (Thomas Cook Publications)

New Zealand at Cost, Fay Smith

New Zealand Handbook, Jane King (Moon)

*New Zealand Insight Guide, J. Hollis (Insight Guides)

*New Zealand: A Travel Survival Kit, Tony Wheeler & Nancy Keller (Lonely Planet)

*New Zealand: The Rough Guide, Laura Harper (The Rough Guides)

Travellers Survival Kit: Australia and New Zealand, Susan Griffith (Vacation Work)

Visitor's Guide to New Zealand, Grant Bourne & Sabine Korner-Bourne (Moorland)

Food & Wine

Fine Wines of New Zealand, Keith Stewart (Grub Street)

James Halliday's Australian and New Zealand Wine Companion, James Halliday

New Taste in New Zealand, Lauraine Jacobs & Stephen Robinson (Ten Speed Press)

Pocket Guide to the Wines of New Zealand, Michael Cooper (Mitchell Beazley)

Rough Guide to Auckland Restaurants, Mark Graham (Rough Guides)

Weekends for Food Lovers, Kerry Tyack (Charles Letts Publishing)

Weekends for Wine Lovers in North Island (New Holland Publishers)

Weekends for Wine Lovers in South Island (New Holland Publishers)

Wines of New Zealand, Michael Cooper (Millers)

The Wines of New Zealand, Rosemary M. George (Faber & Faber)

Miscellaneous

Australia and New Zealand Contact Directory, Sheile Hare (Expat Network)

*Australia & New Zealand by Rail, Colin Taylor (Bradt)

Back Country New Zealand (Hodder)

Beautiful New Zealand, Peter Morath (Hale)

Culture Questions: New Zealand Identity in a Transitional Age, Ruth Brown (Kapako)

Dictionary of New Zealand English, H.W. Oarsman (Oxford University Press)

National Parks & Other Wild Places of New Zealand, K. Ombler (New Holland Publishers)

New Zealand –A Visual Celebration, Graeme Lay & Gareth Eyres (New Holland Publishers)

New Zealand in Pictures (Paperboards)

New Zealand Ways of Speaking English, Allan Bell & Janet Holmes (Multilingual Matters)

Oxford Illustrated History of New Zealand, Keith Sinclair (Oxford University Press)

A Personal Kiwi-Yankee Dictionary, Louis S. Leland Jr

Politics in New Zealand, Richard Mulgan (Auckland UP)

*Smooth Ride Guide to Australia & New Zealand (FT Publishing)

Truth About New Zealand, A. N. Field (Veritas)

Wild New Zealand, B. Coffey (New Holland)

Wild New Zealand: Reader's Digest (Reader's Digest)

APPENDIX C: USEFUL WEBSITES

There are dozens of expatriate websites and as the Internet increases in popularity the number grows by the day. Most information is useful, and websites generally offer free access, although some require a subscription or payment for services. Relocation and other companies specialising in expatriate services often have websites, although these may only provide information that a company is prepared to offer free of charge, which may be rather biased. However, there are plenty of volunteer sites run by expatriates providing practical information and tips. A particularly useful section found on most expatriate websites is the 'message board' or 'forum', where expatriates answer questions based on their experience and knowledge and offer an insight into what living and working in America (or in a particular state or town) is *really* like.

Below is a list of websites not otherwise mentioned in the text. Note that websites are listed under headings in alphabetical order and the list is by no means definitive.

General Websites

British Expatriates (💻 www.britishexpat.com and www.ukworldwide.com). Two sites designed to keep British expatriates in touch with events in and information about the UK.

Direct Moving (💻 www.directmoving.com). General expatriate information, tips and advice, and numerous links.

Escape Artist (💻 www.escapeartist.com). One of the most comprehensive expatriate sites, including resources, links and directories covering most expatriate destinations. You can also subscribe to the free monthly online expatriate magazine, *Escape from America*.

ExpatAccess (💻 www.expataccess.com). Aimed at those planning to move abroad, with free moving guides.

ExpatBoards (💻 www.expatboards.com). A comprehensive site for expatriates, with popular discussion boards and special areas for Britons and Americans.

Expat Exchange (💻 www.expatexchange.com). Reportedly the largest online 'community' for English-speaking expatriates, including articles on relocation and a question and answer facility.

Expat Forum (💻 www.expatforum.com). Provides cost of living comparisons as well as over 20 country-specific forums.

Expat Network (💻 www.expatnetwork.com). The UK's leading expatriate website, which is essentially an employment network for expatriates, although it also includes numerous support services and a monthly online magazine, *Nexus*.

Expat World (💻 www.expatworld.net). Information for American and British expatriates, including a subscription newsletter.

Expatriate Experts (💻 www.expatexpert.com). Run by expatriate expert Robin Pascoe, providing advice and support.

Global People (💻 www.peoplegoingglobal.com). Includes country-specific information with particular emphasis on social and political issues.

Living Abroad (💻 www.livingabroad.com). Includes an extensive list of country profiles, which are available only on payment.

Outpost Information Centre (⌨ www.outpostexpat.nl). Contains extensive country-specific information and links operated by the Shell Petroleum Company for its expatriate workers, but available to everyone.

Real Post Reports (⌨ www.realpostreports.com). Includes relocation services, recommended reading lists and 'real-life' stories written by expatriates in cities throughout the world.

SaveWealth Travel (⌨ www.savewealth.com/travel/warnings). Travel information and warnings.

Trade Partners (⌨ www.tradepartners.gov.uk). A UK government-sponsored site providing trade and investment (and general) information about most countries, including the USA.

The Travel Doctor (⌨ www.tmvc.com.au/info10.html). Includes a country by country vaccination guide.

Travelfinder (⌨ www.travelfinder.com/twarn/travel_warnings.html). Travel information with warnings about danger areas.

World Health Organization (⌨ www.who.int). Health information.

World Travel Guide (⌨ www.wtgonline.com). A general website for world travellers and expatriates.

Websites for British Expatriates

British Expatriates (⌨ www.britishexpat.com and www.ukworldwide.com). These websites keep British expatriates in touch with events and information in the United Kingdom.

Trade Partners (⌨ www.tradepartners.gov.uk). A government-sponsored website whose main aim is to provide trade and investment information for most countries. Even if you aren't intending to do business, the information is comprehensive and up to date.

Websites for American Expatriates

Americans Abroad (⌨ www.aca.ch). This website offers advice, information and services to American expatriates.

American Teachers Abroad (⌨ www.overseasdigest.com). A comprehensive website with numerous relocation services and advice as well as teaching opportunities.

US Government Trade (⌨ www.usatrade.gov). Provides a wealth of information aimed principally at Americans intending to trade and invest abroad but useful for anyone intending to move abroad.

Websites for Women

Career Women (⌨ www.womenconnect.com). Contains career opportunities for women abroad plus a wealth of other useful information.

Expatriate Mothers (⌨ http://expatmoms.tripod.com). Help and advice on how to survive as a mother on relocation.

Spouse Abroad (💻 www.expatspouse.com). Information about careers and working abroad. You need to register and subscribe.

Third Culture Kids (💻 www.tckworld.com). Designed for expatriate children.

Women Abroad (💻 www.womanabroad.com). Advice on careers, expatriate skills and the family abroad. Opportunity to subscribe to a monthly magazine of the same name.

Worldwise Directory (💻 www.suzylamplugh.org/worldwise). Run by the Suzy Lamplugh charity for personal safety, the site provides practical information about a number of countries with special emphasis on safety, particularly for women.

APPENDIX D: WEIGHTS & MEASURES

New Zealand uses the metric system of measurement. Nationals of a few countries (including the Americans and British) who are more familiar with the imperial system of measurement will find the tables on the following pages useful. Some comparisons shown are only approximate, but are close enough for most everyday uses. In addition to the variety of measurement systems used, clothes sizes often vary considerably with the manufacturer (as we all know only too well). Try all clothes on before buying and don't be afraid to return something if, when you try it on at home, you decide it doesn't fit (most shops will exchange goods or give a refund).

Women's Clothes

Continental	34	36	38	40	42	44	46	48	50	52
UK	8	10	12	14	16	18	20	22	24	26
USA	6	8	10	12	14	16	18	20	22	24

Pullovers   Women's   Men's

Continental	40	42	44	46	48	50	44	46	48	50	52	54
UK	34	36	38	40	42	44	34	36	38	40	42	44
USA	34	36	38	40	42	44	sm	medium		large		xl

Note: sm = small, xl = extra large

Men's Shirts

Continental	36	37	38	39	40	41	42	43	44	46
UK/USA	14	14	15	15	16	16	17	17	18	-

Men's Underwear

Continental	5	6	7	8	9	10
UK	34	36	38	40	42	44
USA	small	medium		large	extra large	

Children's Clothes

Continental	92	104	116	128	140	152
UK	16/18	20/22	24/26	28/30	32/34	36/38
USA	2	4	6	8	10	12

Children's Shoes

Continental	18	19	20	21	22	23	24	25	26	27	28	29	30	31	32
UK/USA	2	3	4	4	5	6	7	7	8	9	10	11	11	12	13

Continental	33	34	35	36	37	38
UK/USA	1	2	2	3	4	5

Shoes (Women's and Men's)

Continental	35	35	36	37	37	38	39	39	40	40	41	42	42	43	44	44
UK	2	3	3	4	4	5	5	6	6	7	7	8	8	9	9	10
USA	4	4	5	5	6	6	7	7	8	8	9	9	10	10	11	11

Weight

Avoirdupois	Metric	Metric	Avoirdupois
1 oz	28.35 g	1 g	0.035 oz
1 pound*	454 g	100 g	3.5 oz
1 cwt	50.8 kg	250 g	9 oz
1 ton	1,016 kg	500 g	18 oz
1 tonne	2,205 pounds	1 kg	2.2 pounds

* A metric 'pound' is 500g, g = gramme, kg = kilogramme

Length

British/US	Metric	Metric	British/US
1 inch	2.54 cm	1 cm	0.39 inch
1 foot	30.48 cm	1 m	3 feet 3.25 inches
1 yard	91.44 cm	1 km	0.62 mile
1 mile	1.6 km	8 km	5 miles

Note: cm = centimetre, m = metre, km = kilometre

Capacity

Imperial	Metric	Metric	Imperial
1 pint (USA)	0.47 litre	1 litre	1.76 UK pints
1 pint (UK)	0.57 litre	1 litre	0.26 US gallons
1 gallon (USA)	3.78 litre	1 litre	0.22 UK gallon
1 gallon (UK)	4.54 litre	1 litre	35.21 fluid oz

Square Measure

British/US	Metric	Metric	British/US
1 square inch	0.45 sq. cm	1 sq. cm	0.15 sq. inches
1 square foot	0.09 sq. m	1 sq. m	10.76 sq. feet
1 square yard	0.84 sq. m	1 sq. m	1. 2 sq. yards
1 acre	0.4 hectares	1 hectare	2.47 acres
1 square mile	259 hectares	1 sq. km	0.39 sq. mile

Temperature

° Celsius	° Fahrenheit	
0	32	freezing point of water
5	41	
10	50	
15	59	
20	68	
25	77	
30	86	
35	95	
40	104	

Note: The boiling point of water is 100°C / 212°F.

Oven Temperature

Gas	Electric	
	°F	°C
-	225–250	110–120
1	275	140
2	300	150
3	325	160
4	350	180
5	375	190
6	400	200
7	425	220
8	450	230
9	475	240

For a quick conversion, the Celsius temperature is approximately half the Fahrenheit temperature.

Temperature Conversion

Celsius to Fahrenheit: multiply by 9, divide by 5 and add 32.
Fahrenheit to Celsius: subtract 32, multiply by 5 and divide by 9.

Body Temperature

Normal body temperature (if you're alive and well) is 98.4° Fahrenheit, which equals 37° Celsius.

APPENDIX E: MAP OF NEW ZEALAND

The map below shows the major towns and cities and the principal geographical features of New Zealand.

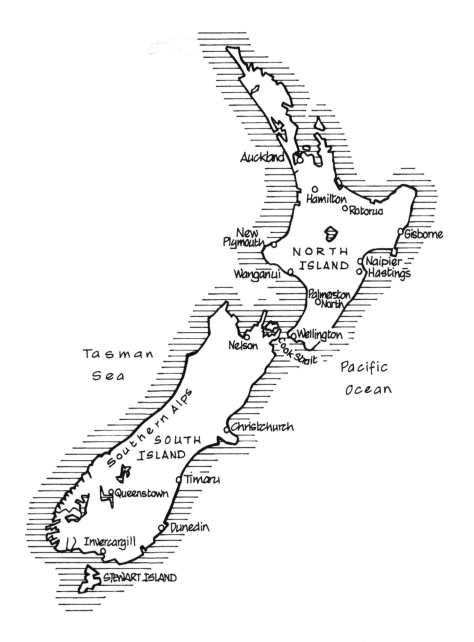

SUGGESTIONS

Please write to us with any comments or suggestions you have regarding the content of this book (preferably complimentary!). We are particularly interested in proposals for improvements that can be included in future editions. For example, did you find any important subjects were omitted or weren't covered in sufficient detail? What difficulties or obstacles have you encountered which aren't covered here? What other subjects would you like to see included?

If your suggestions are used in the next edition of *Living and Working in New Zealand*, you will receive a free copy of the Survival Book of your choice as a token of our appreciation.

NAME: _____

ADDRESS: _____

_____

_____

Send to: Survival Books, PO Box 146, Wetherby, West Yorks. LS23 6XZ, United Kingdom.

My suggestions are as follows (please use additional pages if necessary):

INDEX

BUYING A HOME ABROAD

Buying a Home Abroad is essential reading for anyone planning to purchase property abroad and is designed to guide you through the jungle and make it a pleasant and enjoyable experience. Most importantly, it's packed with vital information to help you avoid the sort of disasters that can turn your dream home into a nightmare! Topics covered include:

- Avoiding problems
- Choosing the region
- Finding the right home & location
- Estate agents
- Finance, mortgages & taxes
- Home security
- Utilities, heating & air-conditioning
- Moving house & settling in
- Renting & letting
- Permits & visas
- Travelling & communications
- Health & insurance
- Renting a car & driving
- Retirement & starting a business
- And much, much more!

Buying a Home Abroad is the most comprehensive and up-to-date source of information available about buying property abroad. Whether you want a detached house, townhouse or apartment, a holiday or a permanent home, this book will help make your dreams come true.

Buy this book and save yourself time, trouble and money!

Order your copies today by phone, fax, mail or e-mail from: Survival Books, PO Box 146, Wetherby, West Yorks. LS23 6XZ, United Kingdom (☎/📠 +44 (0)1937-843523, ✉ orders@ survivalbooks.net, 💻 www.survivalbooks.net).

ORDER FORM
ALIEN'S GUIDES / BEST PLACES / BUYING A HOME / WINES

Qty.	Title	Price (incl. p&p)*			Total
		UK	Europe	World	
	The Alien's Guide to America	Autumn 2002			
	The Alien's Guide to Britain	£5.95	£6.95	£8.45	
	The Alien's Guide to France	£5.95	£6.95	£8.45	
	The Best Places to Buy a Home in France	Autumn 2002			
	The Best Places to Buy a Home in Spain	Summer 2002			
	Buying a Home Abroad	£13.45	£14.95	£16.95	
	Buying a Home in Britain	£11.45	£12.95	£14.95	
	Buying a Home in Florida	£13.45	£14.95	£16.95	
	Buying a Home in France	£13.45	£14.95	£16.95	
	Buying a Home in Greece & Cyprus	£13.45	£14.95	£16.95	
	Buying a Home in Ireland	£11.45	£12.95	£14.95	
	Buying a Home in Italy	£13.45	£14.95	£16.95	
	Buying a Home in Portugal	£11.45	£12.95	£14.95	
	Buying a Home in South Africa	Summer 2002			
	Buying a Home in Spain	£13.45	£14.95	£16.95	
	How to Avoid Holiday & Travel Disasters	Summer 2002			
	Rioja and its Wines	£11.45	£12.95	£14.95	
	The Wines of Spain	£15.95	£18.45	£21.95	
				Total	

Order your copies today by phone, fax, mail or e-mail from: Survival Books, PO Box 146, Wetherby, West Yorks. LS23 6XZ, UUK (☎/▤ +44 (0)1937-843523, ✉ orders@survivalbooks.net, ▄ www.survivalbooks.net). If you aren't entirely satisfied, simply return them to us within 14 days for a full and unconditional refund.

Cheque enclosed/please charge my Delta/Mastercard/Switch/Visa* card

Card No.   _ _ _ _   _ _ _ _   _ _ _ _   _ _ _ _

Expiry date_____   **Issue number (Switch only)** _____

Signature _____   **Tel. No.** _____

NAME _____

ADDRESS _____

_____

_____

* Delete as applicable (price includes postage – airmail for Europe/world).

LIVING AND WORKING IN AUSTRALIA

Living and Working in Australia is essential reading for anyone planning to spend some time in Australia, including holiday-home owners, retirees, visitors, business people, migrants, students and even extraterrestrials! It's packed with over 500 pages of important and useful information designed to help you **avoid costly mistakes and save both time and money.** Topics covered include how to:

- Find a job with a good salary & conditions
- Obtain a residence permit
- Avoid and overcome problems
- Find your dream home
- Get the best education for your family
- Make the best use of public transport
- Endure motoring in Australia
- Obtain the best health treatment
- Stretch your dollars further
- Make the most of your leisure time
- Enjoy the Australian sporting life
- Find the best shopping bargains
- Insure yourself against most eventualities
- Use post office and telephone services
- Do numerous other things not listed above

Living and Working in Australia is the most comprehensive and up-to-date source of practical information available about everyday life in Australia It isn't, however, a boring text book, but an interesting and entertaining guide written in a highly readable style.

Buy this book and discover what it's *really* like to live and work in Australia.

Order your copies today by phone, fax, mail or e-mail from: Survival Books, PO Box 146, Wetherby, West Yorks. LS23 6XZ, United Kingdom (☎/▤ +44 (0)1937-843523, ✉ orders@ survivalbooks.net, ⌨ www.survivalbooks.net).

ORDER FORM

LIVING & WORKING SERIES / RETIRING ABROAD

Qty.	Title	Price (incl. p&p)*			Total
		UK	Europe	World	
	Living & Working Abroad	£14.95	£16.95	£20.45	
	Living & Working in America	£14.95	£16.95	£20.45	
	Living & Working in Australia	£14.95	£16.95	£20.45	
	Living & Working in Britain	£14.95	£16.95	£20.45	
	Living & Working in Canada	£14.95	£16.95	£20.45	
	Living & Working in France	£14.95	£16.95	£20.45	
	Living & Working in Germany	£14.95	£16.95	£20.45	
	Living & Working in the Gulf States & Saudi Arabia	Autumn 2002			
	Living & Working in Holland, Belgium & Luxembourg	£14.95	£16.95	£20.45	
	Living & Working in Ireland	£14.95	£16.95	£20.45	
	Living & Working in Italy	£14.95	£16.95	£20.45	
	Living & Working in London	£11.45	£12.95	£14.95	
	Living & Working in New Zealand	£14.95	£16.95	£20.45	
	Living & Working in Spain	£14.95	£16.95	£20.45	
	Living & Working in Switzerland	£14.95	£16.95	£20.45	
	Retiring Abroad	£14.95	£16.95	£20.45	
				Total	

Order your copies today by phone, fax, mail or e-mail from: Survival Books, PO Box 146, Wetherby, West Yorks. LS23 6XZ, UK (☎/▤ +44 (0)1937-843523, ✉ orders@survivalbooks.net, ▭ www.survivalbooks.net). If you aren't entirely satisfied, simply return them to us within 14 days for a full and unconditional refund.

Cheque enclosed/please charge my Delta/Mastercard/Switch/Visa* card

Card No. _ _ _ _   _ _ _ _   _ _ _ _   _ _ _ _

Expiry date_____ **Issue number (Switch only)** _____

Signature _____ **Tel. No.** _____

NAME _____

ADDRESS _____

' _____

* Delete as applicable (price includes postage – airmail for Europe/world).